From Bedroom to Courtroom:
Law and Justice in the Greek Novel

ANCIENT NARRATIVE

Supplementum 21

Website
www.ancientnarrative.com

Subscriptions and ordering
Barkhuis
Kooiweg 38 9761 GL Eelde the Netherlands
info@barkhuis.nl www.barkhuis.nl

From Bedroom to Courtroom

Law and Justice in the Greek Novel

by

Saundra Schwartz

BARKHUIS &
GRONINGEN UNIVERSITY LIBRARY
GRONINGEN 2016

γηράσκω δ᾽ αἰεὶ πολλὰ διδασκομένη

to

P, E, L, J

Book design: Barkhuis

Cover design: Nynke Tiekstra, Rotterdam

Image on cover: "Phryne Revealed before the Areopagus", oil on canvas, by Jean-Léon Gérôme, 1861

ISBN 9789492444080

Contents

List of Tables

Preface

This book has had a long gestation. It originated as a doctoral dissertation under the guidance of Prof. Suzanne Saïd at Columbia University. Parts of that dissertation became articles published in journals and other collections. The present book is a thorough overhaul of the original dissertation, enriched (I hope) by years of more or less autodidactic study of ancient Greek and Roman law. In a sense, it attempts to bridge the fields of Greek literature, Roman imperial history, and legal history. Each has its own jargon and ongoing controversies; I have endeavored to make this book intelligible to an audience with diverse interests. I am grateful to Gareth Schmeling and the editors of the *Ancient Narrative Supplementa* for their support of a book that, like the heroine of Heliodorus' novel, works hard to prove that hybridity is a virtue.

There are many to thank. In addition to Suzanne Saïd, the other members of the committee, William Harris, Dirk Obbink, Roger Bagnall, Alan Cameron, and James Rives, probably do not realize how the challenging questions they asked reshaped the book. A summer fellowship at the Center for Hellenic Studies supported research on imperial Greek trials that has borne fruit for many years. Judith Perkins, Steve Nimis, and Rhoda Feinberg provided moral support and encouragement along the way. I am grateful to Tom Bingham and the History department of the University of Hawai`i, for allowing me the opportunity to complete this book. I am grateful to Robert Littman, Daniel Harris-McCoy, and the anonymous reviewers of the manuscript for their engagement my manuscript. Finally, I was saved by a trio of copy-editors along the way: Betty Hoffenberg, Maureen Schwartz, and Libby Hoffenberg, grammar maven *extraordinaire*. I take full responsibility for any remaining infelicities of style or fact. Finally, I cannot even begin to fathom the amount of patience and support I have received from my family near and far. I dedicate this book to Peter, Elena, Libby, and Judah Hoffenberg.

A Note about Transliteration

Because this study encompasses both Athenian and Roman sets of legal vocabulary, I have chosen to italicize Latin terms and phrases and to leave specialized Greek terms in the original language, while translating where relevant. I trust that the reader will be able to differentiate between the two languages. To prevent confusion and to enhance ease of readings, commonly used Greek words are transliterated but not italicized: agon (contest), apologia (defense), boukoloi (herdsmen), daimon (spirit), demos (people), dikē (justice), ephebe (young man), erastes (lover), eros (love), hamartia (error), hetaera (courtesan), oikoumene (civilized world), paideia (culture), pathos (emotional appeal), pepaideumenos (educated man), phratry (brotherhood), polis (city-state), rhetor (speaker), sophrosyne (self-control), strategos (general), telos (goal), topos (commonplace).

Introduction

In ancient Greek and Roman culture, marriage was traditionally an institution for the propagation of patrilineal bloodlines, particularly when property was at stake. This was true at least among the elites whose perspectives are so disproportionately represented in the surviving literature from antiquity. At some point, however, there arose the concept that mutual love and fidelity ought to be the foundation of marriage. This ideal is espoused in a genre known as the Greek ideal romance, or novel. The five extant novels that have survived in full present a model of normative sexuality. They typically begin when boy and girl fall in love, undergo a series of adventures that test their love for each other, and end with their blissful union (or reunion) in marriage.

This study, however, is not about love. It instead focuses on the dark side of the romantic ideal: adultery, the inversion of the emblematic value of conjugality. The concept of fidelity is inseparable from that of infidelity. Michel Foucault observed that the Greek novels reflect a 'new erotics, [which] organizes itself around the symmetrical and reciprocal relationship of a man and a woman.'[1] The portrayal of 'sexual symmetry' in the novels was a radical ideal during the first centuries C.E.[2] The concept is illustrated not only through the depiction of couple's mutual commitment to chastity, but also through the important juxtaposition with the adulterous love triangle. It represents the purest recipe for dramatic conflict, using the basic ingredients of desire, sex, betrayal, jealousy, and violence. As a scholar of the modern novel has observed, 'It is the unstable triangularity of adultery, rather than the static symmetry of marriage, that is the generative form of Western literature as we know it'.[3] It is certainly true for the Greek novels as well.

To delay the formulaic happy ending, the authors of the novels introduce a string of threats to the lives and chastity of the protagonists. One of the most prominent of these intervening obstacles is the courtroom trial. Almost all trials originate from an act or suspicion of adultery, the paramount crime in the world

---

[1] Foucault 1988, 232. Responses to Foucault: Konstan 1994a; Goldhill 1995; Whitmarsh 2011; Montiglio 2013. A succinct overview of sexuality in the novels can be found in Morales 2008.

[2] Konstan 1994a.

[3] Tanner 1979, 12.

of the Greek novels. Each of the five surviving complete Greek novels has at least one trial scene; some trials take up a considerable portion of the narrative.[4] Fragments of lost novels corroborate that trial scenes were an expected element of ancient Greek fiction.[5]

Adultery loomed over ancient Greek and Roman imagination. It tapped anxieties that a stranger might seduce a woman and thus corrupt marriages and destabilize peaceful relations between men. The scenario finds its earliest written expression in the epics of Homer and extending to the literature and legislation promoted by the Roman emperor, Augustus, who subjected marriage and adultery (at least among the senatorial elite) to regulation by the state. In the ancient imagination, the husband's discovery of his wife and her lover in flagrante delicto was a stock episode, immediately recognizable in the exaggerated form it often takes in comedy:

> The tale generally (but not invariably) follows a predictable pattern: an account of the marriage (generally between a frisky young wife and an older, rather dim-witted husband), followed by a description of the initial meeting between the wife and the young adulterer, their bamboozling of the husband, and (often, but not always) a final confrontation in which the guilty pair are caught in the act and either punished or, just as often, afforded the opportunity for a final triumph over the all-too gullible spouse.[6]

The adultery scenario is a paradigmatic moment of crisis that demands some form of redress. From the perspective of the courtroom, the conjugal bedroom remained a 'black box', a space beyond public purview. In lived experience, the only witnesses to the comings and goings into the interior space of the bedroom were members of the household; however, in literary narrative the distinction between private and public spaces is flattened as the internal operations and mysterious logic of the bedroom are laid open to inspection.[7] As readers, we become eyewitnesses to crime in intimate spaces. Bodies are displayed for all to see in the courtroom, while lovers plead behind closed doors in high rhetorical style. Private concerns are elevated to the status of public interest and the bedroom is transformed into a kind of stage itself where, as in the public trial scenes, the drama plays out

[4] See the Babylonian trial in Chariton, book 5 (of 8 books); the trials in Ephesus in Achilles Tatius, books 7-8 (of 8 books); Heliodorus, trials in Athens in book 1 and in Meroe in book 10 (of 10 books).

[5] For example, Iamblichos *Babyloniaka* fr. 35 in Stephens and Winkler 1995, 228-233; and a fragment of *Panionis* in Parsons 2007.

[6] Porter 1997, 428.

[7] Perkins 2002.

the politics of chastity, as it were, and the impossibility of ascertaining the truth of sexual relations. Through narrative, readers are able to peer into the darkened bedroom and gain a sense of certainty about the events inside this private space, a certainty that eluded judges in a courtroom setting.

Greek literature had a long and vibrant tradition of staged debates going back to the Homeric epics and continuing throughout antiquity. Indeed, the motif of the trial is ubiquitous in world literature. Virtually all societies have mechanisms for mediating between claims that might otherwise lead to violence, and stories of trials are a way to reflect on social crises and individual choice. The interconnection between the law and literature is the subject of a thriving interdisciplinary 'movement', as it styled itself at its beginning in the 1980's.[8] The relationship between law and literature is, in a certain respect, self-evident. Lawyers craft stories in court to help them win cases; judges interpret and rewrite those stories in rulings; witnesses give depositions; and reporters cover cases for the public. The courtroom is a space consecrated to narratives that carry with them momentous consequences for individuals and for society.

Many great literary works reflect moments of crisis that challenge the relationship between law and society.[9] Both law and literature create narratives about justice and reflect upon the place of law in society. Literary fiction is often driven by characters that cross boundaries and challenge social norms. Some judges and lawyers produce legal texts that have a very literary quality, and authors of fictional narratives can exhibit a highly specialized knowledge of the law.[10] Yet, there is a significant distinction between the two modes of telling stories about law. Practitioners (and scholars) of the law tend to begin with a literal and precise approach to codes, statutes, and rulings, whereas readers of literary representations of law are conditioned to construe the narrative metaphorically. In this study, I attempt to bring these modes into dialogue, while acknowledging the particularities of how legal texts and literary texts reflect lived experience and are thus construed differently according to context and genre.

In literature, trial scenes engage the reader in forming a verdict along with the judge, in essence, a process of educating the citizens' faculty of judgment.[11] Aeschylus' *Eumenides,* the final tragedy of his trilogy, *The Oresteia*, illustrates how a fictional trial scene may perform the important civic function of inviting reflection upon the means of justice. Similarly, the defense speech of Socrates, as memorialized by Plato's *Apologia*, inspired a genre in which a wise man declares his

[8] Overviews of the field can be found in Weisberg 1992; Posner 1998; Dolin 2007.
[9] Ziolkowski 1997.
[10] Weisberg 2002.
[11] Nussbaum 1995.

fidelity to his ideals before an audience of judges. The trial of Jesus, as it circulated in the gospel narratives, inspired a genre of stories of Christians tried under the auspices of Roman authorities.[12] Such *causes célèbres* have left a mark on the historical record; we can only imagine how many other locally notorious trials provided fodder for gossip throughout the towns of the Roman Empire.[13] Trials in the public spaces of the cities drew crowds of onlookers and entertainment-seekers.[14] These were the ancient analogues to present-day narratives about trials, in print and on screen. 'Procedural drama' is a robust formula for the generation of new television episodes, week after week.[15] The genre provides the satisfaction of closure at the end of the show, while at the same time auguring infinite material for the next week's episode. The very repetitiveness and openness of the genre lends such stories about the law a quasi-mythic function: the trial scene is a resilient formula for the exploration of dramatic conflict within a framework that presumes justice is a stable and transcendent force in the world. Robert Cover has eloquently argued that the trial is not only an event in which the law is applied, but is also an arena for competing narratives of justice:

> A legal tradition is part and parcel of a complex normative world. The tradition includes not only a *corpus juris*, but also a language and a mythos—narratives in which the *corpus juris* is located by those whose wills act upon it. These myths establish the paradigms for behavior. They build relations between the normative and the material universe, between the constraints of reality and the demands of an ethic. These myths establish a repertoire of moves—a lexicon of normative action—that may be combined into meaningful patterns culled from the meaningful patterns of the past.[16]

Along the same lines, Mary Beard has made a case for understanding the outrageously far-fetched scenarios of the declamations as products of 'mythic thinking' in that they present traditional themes 'without concern for origin or authorship, but are focused instead on reception, re-telling, re-elaboration.'[17] She makes the important point that in the culture of the declamations, the law replaces the gods

---

12 On narratives of the trial of Jesus see Lincoln 2000, Skinner 2010; on the legal and historical context, see Giovannini and Gryzbek 2008.

13 Kadri 2005.

14 On crowds in the Roman forum, see Bablitz 2007.

15 Denvir 1996; Bergman and Asinow 1996; Harriss 2008.

16 Cover 1983, 9.

17 Beard 1993, 58. On declamation's role in creating role models of Roman masculinity, see Gunderson 2000.

as the superhuman authority that governs the cosmos, and 'legalism itself' rather than actual, everyday law validates the fictive debates in the declamations.[18]

Unlike the Roman declamations, the Greek novels embrace the divine realm, especially the deified form of *Fortuna*, or Τύχη, as the transcendent force that guides the protagonists toward their happy ending. The power of the gods subverts legalism, as in the trial of Melite in Achilles Tatius' novel, where a hyper-legalistic oath is subverted in an ordeal of the water of the River Styx. As the following chapters will illustrate, the fictional courtrooms of the Greek novels shed light upon deeply embedded cognitive structures—the *mentalité*—of the readers who originally consumed the novels in which trial scenes play a prominent role.[19]

The Greek novels are but one part of what G. W. Bowersock describes as 'a larger context of fabrication and rewriting' that reached its peak circulation in the second century.[20] My contention is that courtroom scenes reflect aspects of the dynamic and fluid process whereby Roman law was understood, subverted, and received by the Greek-speaking inhabitants of the Roman Empire. Of course, fiction is not fact. By its very nature, the characters, actions, and settings in the novel do not claim to correspond to specific referents in the contemporary world of the novels' original audiences. It would be mistaken to take the trials in the novels, which dance on the line of verisimilitude, as conclusive evidence of any 'real world'. They tend to be moments of outsized drama, an opportunity to introduce weeping defendants, vengeful accusers, grandiose speakers, and cheering mobs to amplify pathos on the legal stage.

At best, the novels reflect the tastes and expectations of their readers. Sets of opposing speeches are embedded within a larger narrative and thus create an ironic distance from which the readers can observe the vagaries of the legal arena and the inherent uncertainty of verdicts. Courtrooms, as imagined in literary works, function as spaces for the competitive assertion of important cultural values. Aeschylus' *Eumenides,* which dramatized the mythic foundation of the Areopagus court, was first performed when Ephialtes' reforms were transferring most of the powers of the traditional high court of Athens to the democratic courts, thus precipitating a political crisis.[21] Likewise, over the course of the three or so centuries when the novels were written and received by Greek-speaking audiences,

---

[18] Beard 1993, 60.

[19] The term *mentalité* was pioneered by historians of the *Annales* school in the 1960's to refer to habitual patterns of thought that are discernible over long periods of social history; see Boureau 1989.

[20] Bowersock 1994, 13. Stephens and Winkler include forty-two fragments on papyri in their collection, twenty-four of which they date to the latter half of the second century; see Stephens and Winkler 1995, 480-481.

[21] Ziolkowski 1997, 32.

Roman legal culture—its institutions, procedures, personnel, and jargon—was spreading into communities throughout the empire. The appearance of Roman law was not a single moment of crisis but rather a geographically varied process of adaptation at the local level, driven by pragmatic concerns involving jurisdiction when Greeks began to have dealings with increasing numbers of Roman citizens. The shift from Greek courts to Roman legal venues entailed using a different language, the formulating of grievances in terms that were coherent with Roman procedure, and working with magistrates and bureaucrats who operated with a set of laws that were an outgrowth of the structure of Roman society and reflected a distinctly different culture from that of the Greek polis. Although the translation of Latin legal terminology into Greek was not uniform, inscriptions and papyri attest to the tenacity of Greek speakers to have Roman legal records translated into their own language.[22]

One of the peculiarities of Roman law was the state's involvement in the regulation of marriage and criminalization of adultery, an abiding concern throughout Augustus' reign to rebuild Roman society after the devastation of civil war. There was no reason for Greeks to have been particularly concerned with this raft of legislation; as far as we know, the Augustan laws targeted only Roman society, in particular the senatorial class. In 19 B.C.E., the *lex Julia de maritandis ordinibus* restricted the right of legal marriage, *matrimonium iustum*, to particular classes and imposed various sanctions on the unmarried or childless. After a year or so, Augustus introduced another piece of legislation, the *lex Julia de adulteriis coercendis*, which made adultery liable to public prosecution. A full generation later, in 9 C.E., the *lex Papia Poppaea* limited the ability of unmarried and childless persons to claim inheritances. The causes and effects of this legislation have been the subject of much specialized scholarship, the particulars of which have limited bearing on the trials in the Greek novels. Nevertheless, it is clear that these laws established an ideal of marriage that emphasized procreation and the preservation of the Roman elite.[23]

It is worth noting that the marriages of provincials were not within the ambit of the Augustan legislation. Augustus' *Res Gestae* (6.1) only mentions that he was given (but refused) the *cura legum et morum*, the 'care of laws and morals,' but there is no mention of laws on marriage and adultery. This suggests that Augustus'

[22] Laffi 2013. A recent assessment of the percentage of Roman citizens estimates that no more than one third of the free population had Roman citizenship before 212 C.E.; see Laval 2016.

[23] For an overview of the complex history of the legislation and a summary of the scholarship, see Raditsa 1980.

regulations on marriage and adultery were not intended for implementation outside of the Roman elite. In the early Principate, there was not yet a critical mass of Roman citizens outside of Rome who would have been theoretically subject to the laws of Augustus. Provincials, many of whom aspired to be like the imperial elites, were more likely to assimilate to the new ideology of marriage through communication channels other than the law.[24] For example, senators who were married and had families had an advantage when the emperor assigned provinces. Those men had earned their governorship by conforming to the expectations enshrined in the Augustan laws. When a governor arrived in the province, his behavior, his *habitus*, conveyed the Augustan ideals of marriage and family to provincials aspiring to positions of influence. Members of local elites wishing to collaborate with imperial rule might have expected to gain some advantage by imitating the representatives of Rome.[25] Thus the ideals, if not the literal laws, of Rome shaped provincial attitudes about marriage and, more importantly, adultery. Whereas matrimonial customs were deeply rooted in local societies throughout the empire, the rupture of marriage—adultery—posed a challenge to established communal modes of private redress. What happened, then, when an alternative avenue for pursuing a grievance was made available in the form of a public prosecution for adultery? Did high profile trials of sexual misbehavior—such as the affair of Julia, the emperor's own daughter, in 2 B.C.E.— communicate to local elites that their own sexual affairs, too, were subject to official punishment?

These are difficult questions to answer definitively. Given the private nature of adultery and the risk of personal embarrassment, it is hard to imagine that prosecutions of adulterers were routine; yet, Cassius Dio noted that there were thousands of cases of adultery on the docket when he came to Rome at the beginning of the third century to serve as prefect in Rome under the Severans.[26] This suggests people did in fact use the court system to prosecute cases of adultery. It is virtually impossible to track the frequency of such trials from the first to the fourth centuries C.E. throughout the empire; nevertheless, Dio's anecdote suggests that, at least at Rome, adultery trials were not uncommon. This may provide a context for the novelists' choice to structure trial scenes around acts of adultery.

Trial scenes were an expected element of the ancient novel, as attested by Photius, the ninth-century commentator who was familiar with more examples of fictional works than we are today. In his *Bibliotheca,* he describes a novel, now lost, called *The Wonders Beyond Thule,* written by Antonius Diogenes, in the following terms:

---

[24] Ando 2000, particularly chapter 1.

[25] Bourdieu 1977.

[26] Cassius Dio 76,16,4.

> Ἔστι δὲ ἐν αὐτοῖς καὶ μάλιστα, ὡς ἐν τηλικούτοις πλάσμασί τε μυθεύμασι, δύο τινὰ θηράσαι χρησιμώτατα· ἓν μὲν ὅτι τὸν ἀδικήσαντά τι, κἂν μυριάκις ἐκφυγεῖν δόξῃ, εἰσάγει πάντως δίκην δεδωκέναι, καὶ δεύτερον ὅτι πολλοὺς ἀναιτίους ἐγγὺς μεγάλου γεγονότας κινδύνου, παρ' ἐλπίδας δείκνυσι πολλάκις διασωθέντας.
>
> In this story in particular, as in fictional works of its kind, there are two especially useful things to observe: first, that he presents a wrongdoer, even if he appears to escape countless times, paying the penalty just the same; second, that he shows many innocent people, though on the brink of great danger, being saved many times in defiance of expectations.[27]

Photius clearly recognizes the episodic quality of the plots—that villains escape 'countless times' (μυριάκις) and heroes survive danger 'many times' (πολλάκις). More importantly, he categorizes the genre's characters into two basic types: 'the wrongdoer' (τὸν ἀδικήσαντά τι) and 'innocents' (ἀναιτίους). In doing so, he conceptualizes the plot as essentially motivated by the pursuit of justice; love is strangely absent. The fact that the ending comes when the villain 'pays the penalty' (δίκην δεδωκέναι) underscores a plot structure built upon the concept of just deserts, a formula Aristotle noted was so appealing to audiences because it meshed with conventional ideas of justice.[28] The trial scenes thus mirror expectations of how justice works, whether within the formal system of law or outside of it.

The fictional trial scenes in the novels reflect Greek readers' understanding (and misunderstanding) of the distinctively Roman customs and laws that governed imperial courts and increasingly influenced the operation and use of local courts in the Roman Empire over the course of the first four centuries C.E. The main corpus of this study consists of three of the five Greek extant Greek novels: *Callirhoe* by Chariton (henceforth abbreviated C); *Leucippe and Clitophon* by Achilles Tatius (AT); and the *Aethiopica* by Heliodorus (H).[29] The sole trial scene in *Daphnis and Chloe* by Longus (L) proves the rule that a trial scene was *de rigueur*: instead of adultery, it revolves around a pedestrian case of property damage caused by goats.[30] *Anthia and Habrocomes* by Xenophon of Ephesus (XE)

---

[27] Photius *Bibliotheca* Cod. 166 [112a]; trans. Sandy 1989, 782 (adapted).

[28] Aristotle *Poetics* 1453a2-35.

[29] On the titles of the novels, see Whitmarsh 2005; Goold 1995, 3-4; Tilg 2010, 214-230.

[30] The rustic trial of Daphnis in L 2.12-19 is discussed extensively in S. Schwartz 2005.

contains trial-like scenes that lack legal detail, possibly due to the novel's epitomized style.[31] Legal motifs are present in abundance in the Latin novels of Petronius and Apuleius.[32] In early Christian narratives, scenes of trial, punishment, and execution assume an unmatched centrality; these provide another point of comparison for the novel's depiction of trials.[33] Although these other fictional and semi-fictional works have much to contribute to the project of exploring how Roman law was understood in the empire, I have chosen to focus on the Greek novels in order to focus on the evolution of the trial scene through three novelists of the first centuries of the empire.

The portrayal of law in the novels of Chariton, Achilles Tatius, and Heliodorus is a bricolage. It draws from a range of sources: the declamations, the Attic orators, the revival of the culture of the classical polis, and the experience of living under Roman rule while grappling with distinctly Roman (i.e., foreign) ways of conceptualizing legal disputes. Did imperial Greeks understand the procedures and laws in the Attic orations, at least a half a millennium in the past? How did Greeks make sense of Roman law, with its many edicts, rescripts, law, and rulings?[34] The surviving laws of classical Athens and Rome serve as landmarks for assessing whether the authors actually understood—or cared about—the nuances and technicalities of the law.

It is important to underscore that the Greek novelists were not jurists. Their representation of laws and legal procedures is irrelevant to the history of Roman jurisprudence. Yet, the storyworlds they create in their novels theoretically correspond to the 'horizons of expectations' that ancient readers brought to these narratives.[35] The realism of the novels is a literary style, a convention derived from rhetorical traditions that were actively revived in the imperial period. Their vision of the classical past was mediated by books, particularly those deemed to be canons of Atticism.[36] Verisimilitude was a matter of the author's narrative ringing a bell of familiarity in the reader's mind, of reminding the reader of something he

---

[31] Hägg 1966, O'Sullivan 1994.

[32] Petronius *Satyrica* 107-8; Apuleius *Metamorphoses* 3,1, 10,6-12; see Bodel 2010.

[33] This argument is developed further in S. Schwartz 2003b, 2007. See also Haight 1945, 48-80; Musurillo 1954, 253-254; Lincoln 2000; Aubert 2010; Skinner 2010. On the relationship between Greco-Roman, Jewish, and Christian fictional and semi-fictional literature see Pervo 1987, 1994; Edwards 1987, 1991; Bowersock 1994, 1-28, 121-160; Wills 1994, 223-238; 1995; C. M. Thomas 2003; Kensky 2010.

[34] Schiavone 2012.

[35] A. Billault 1991, 24; Fusillo 1991, 56-57; Egger 1994b, 271. For an analysis of how the Attic orators used this strategy, see Schmitz 2000. On 'horizons of expectations', a critical concept in reception studies, see Jauss 1982, 28. The cognitive process of building storyworlds is discussed at length in Herman 2009, 105-136.

[36] Morgan 1978, 1982; Kloft 1989; Arnott 1994; Swain 1996, 28-29.

or she has seen, heard, experienced, or read.[37] For example, Chariton's narrative of the daughter of Hermocrates of Syracuse explicitly incorporates well-known incidents and figures from the historical past.[38] On the other hand, Achilles Tatius' story of lovers traveling through Alexandria and other major cities of the eastern Mediterranean is vaguely contemporary but curiously avoids overt reference to Rome.[39] Although Heliodorus does not allude to historical figures, his portrayals of Athens and Delphi suggest an elaborately classical setting.[40]

What seems on the surface to be a chaotic jumble of historically useless detail in the trial scenes may be due to the experience of living in between two unequal legal regimes, the local and the imperial.[41] The challenge of untangling the legal references in the novels is compounded by the multiplicity of sources available to imperial era Greeks: literary and rhetorical texts, experiences with local legal cultures of various Greek cities, contact with Roman institutions and personnel, and the reinvention of classical Greece in the Roman Empire. A similar interpretive hurdle exists for the analysis of the legal disputes in the comedies of Plautus and Terence, where legal references bring to light a complex textual stratigraphy deposited through the translation of Athenian New Comedy, replete with Attic legal customs and jargon, into terms comprehensible to Latin-speaking audiences in Italy two centuries later.[42] During the Roman Empire, the diffusion of Roman law necessitated adjustment of local legal traditions and procedures in the provinces. I shall argue that trial scenes in the Greek novels shed an indirect light on this process of acculturation to the Roman administration of justice in the Greek-speaking provinces.

The historical study of Greek reception of Roman law relies principally on evidence of papyri, inscriptions, and other documents; literary evidence is sometimes adduced to corroborate a shaky argument.[43] The legal procedures and scenarios in the novels present other insights into the Greek conceptualization of Roman law. To be sure, the fact that these are works of fiction limits their evidentiary value for actual law; instead, they offer a rare view into how a judicial process proceeded from beginning to end. My analysis consists of a quasi-ethnographic,

---

[37] S. Bartsch 1989; Morgan 1993.

[38] Chariton's historiographical pose has been much discussed; see W. Bartsch 1934; Reardon 1996; De Temmerman 2002.

[39] Swain 1996, 111-113.

[40] Bowie 1977; Pouilloux 1983; Rougemont 1992; Oudot 1992; S. D. Smith 2007.

[41] Gabba 1982.

[42] Scafuro 1997, 193-231.

[43] For recent analyses of Roman law as a force of acculturation, see Fournier 2010, Ando 2011a, and Bryen 2012.

Geertzian 'thick description' of the trial scenes in the novel.[44] I treat the three novels as artifacts that originated at different moments in the history of Roman Empire. Chariton's novel is widely believed to be one of the earliest of the extant complete novels, perhaps as early as 41 C.E. and Heliodorus' the latest, perhaps composed in the third or fourth century. Achilles Tatius falls between the two, around 160 C.E.[45] Because of the intractable difficulties of establishing precise dates for the Greek novels, I have chosen to use the novels as general indicators—snapshots—of the aftermath of major legal developments. Accordingly, Chariton's novel falls after the Julio-Claudian era in the generations that inherited the Augustan legislation on marriage and the family. Achilles Tatius created his novel at the height of the Second Sophistic in the Antonine era when Hadrian cemented the partnership between Greeks and Romans in governing the empire. Although Heliodorus' date is contested, there is little doubt that it was written after the Severan project of rationalizing Roman law and finally extending it to all the empire's inhabitants in 212 C.E. Collectively, the eleven trial scenes in these three texts reflect the impact of the spread of Roman law on the way Greek-speakers thought about rights, liabilities, differences in legal status, due process—and, in general, the transformation of law from a communal project specific to a particular polity to a professionalized system that dealt in abstractions that could in turn be applied to cases across a vast, multicultural empire. By having characters navigate through exotic and treacherous legal waters, the texts reveal an acute perception of the opportunities—and pitfalls—created during a period of tremendous development across the multiple legal milieux of the eastern provinces of the Roman Empire.

---

[44] 'Doing ethnography is like trying to read (in the sense of 'construct a reading of') a manuscript—foreign, faded, full of ellipses, incoherencies, suspicious emendations, and tendentious commentaries, but written not in conventionalized graphs of sound but in transient example of shaped behavior'; Geertz 1973, 10.

[45] For the most recent estimates of the dates of Chariton and Achilles Tatius, see Bowie 2002. The case for placing Chariton in the middle of the first century C.E. is laid out in full in Tilg 2010, 36-78. There is a possibility that Heliodorus wrote his novel in the middle of the third century; however, the *testimonia* place him around the third quarter of the fourth century. I discuss the complex question of Heliodorus' historical context at greater length in the introduction to Part III.

Rhetoric and Realia

Details of everyday life in the ancient fiction supplement the picture of imperial culture and society.[46] Because the Latin novels are set in a more or less contemporary context, the correspondence between representation and reality is relatively more straightforward than it is in the Greek novels.[47] Direct verbal allusions to Roman law are easier to detect in Latin than in Greek. For example Apuleius' *Apologia,* the text of his defense to a charge of magic, proves that he was familiar with the law and serves as a solid point of comparison for the legal elements in his *Metamorphoses*.[48] In contrast, in the Greek novels, the allusion to Roman law is partially obscured by the interference of translation.[49] Rome is for the most part absent from the world of the Greek novels. Swain has attributed this curious feature of the novels to Hellenocentrism, as expressed in Greek readers' desire to have 'their social and ethical concerns to be played out in a world entirely their own'.[50] Sometimes Latin legal concepts are transposed into Greek terms, whereas in other instances traditional Greek legal customs, especially surrounding the practices of betrothal (ἐγγύησις) and wedding (γάμος), are emphasized in the narrative.[51] Nevertheless, Rome is an absent presence that exerts a gravitational pull on the representation of verisimilar storyworlds.

Many studies have profitably identified aspects of legal realia, nuggets of historical reality in Greek fiction; to ask whether or not discrete details of the law in the novels are 'accurate' or 'true' seems inadequate. This study aims to examine not only the legal details, but also the Gestalt of justice. Does anything about the way fictional characters interact with the law indicate whether the novelists and their readers were cognizant of a shifting relationship between local Greek law and the law of the Roman Empire?

A useful model for understanding of the social reception of law is to be found in *The Common Place of the Law,* a sociological study of attitudes toward the law in contemporary American society by Patricia Ewick and Susan C. Silbey. Rather than ask their interviewees about 'the law', Ewick and Silbey instead invited them

46 Bowie and Harrison 1993, 166; Scarcella 1970, 1977; Futre Pinheiro 1989; Alvares 1993.

47 Colin 1965a; Duncan-Jones 1974; Millar 1981; Shaw 1984; Hopkins 1993.

48 On the law in Apuleius' *Metamorphoses*, see Norden 1912; Colin 1965a; Summers 1967, 1970, 1971; Elster 1991; Gebhardt 2009; Bodel 2010; Baker 2012. On the influence of declamations on the Latin novels, see van Mal-Maeder 2003, 2007.

49 Zimmermann 1957; Karabélias 1990; De Temmerman 2002; Papathomas 2010. References to νόμος and θεσμός (and their derivatives) in the Greek novels are gathered in Scarcella 1990.

50 Swain 1996, 113.

51 Calderini 1959, 29; Scarcella 1976; Liviabella Furiani 1988; Egger 1994a.

to describe situations when they faced conflicts and how they resolved them. The researchers were thus able to elicit narratives that reflect a picture of the law as a living presence in the lives of real people who use and misuse, understand and misunderstand, and engage and avoid the law and its institutions. To describe the totality of the law's effects upon the general social consciousness, they use the term 'legality' to describe

> an emergent structure of social life that manifests itself in diverse places, including but not limiting itself to formal institutional settings. Legality operates, then, as both an interpretive framework and a set of resources with which and through which the social world (including that part known as the law) is constituted.[52]

Ewick and Silbey distinguish three types of 'legal consciousness'. In the first type, which the authors label 'Before the Law', law is conceived of as 'an objective realm of disinterested action'. In this view, law consists of impartial and authoritative rules, procedures, and hierarchies. Reliance upon documents leads to the reification of the law as separate and above normal social relations. The second type, 'With the Law', regards legality as a competitive game to be played out in a bounded arena by self-interested players. Resourceful individuals approach the law tactically and use the law as an instrument to get what they want. Finally, the third type of legal consciousness, 'Against the Law', emphasizes resistance, subversion, and sometimes evasion of law, particularly when it is perceived as arbitrary. This view is informed by awareness that power defines rules and norms, that 'might makes right'. This attitude seems cynical, but in fact is informed by a deeply held sense of justice.[53]

The methodological shift from a focus on the law proper to the Gestalt of legality is a useful model to understand how people in the ancient world envisioned the law. For example, Serena Connolly's study of petitions submitted by individuals living in the late third century C.E. reveals a lively and variegated picture of the strategies real people used in approaching the Roman judicial system for help in resolving conflict.[54] As an element of daily life in Greco-Roman cities, trials and other legal hearings provided material for the imagined universes of ancient fiction. The trial scenes of the novels of Chariton, Achilles Tatius, and Heliodorus show people—fictional characters— navigating and experiencing legal institutions and procedures. The novels reflect not a unitary ideal of the law,

---

[52] Ewick and Silbey 1998, 23.
[53] Ewick and Silbey 1998, 45-49.
[54] Connolly 2010, 98-136.

but rather multiple and overlapping forms of legal consciousness suggesting that the assimilation of Roman law into Greek culture was a dynamic process, theoretically subject to continual negotiation.

The influence of rhetorical training is ubiquitous in the literature of the Roman Empire.[55] The Greek novels were part of this trend. It is generally accepted that the readers were drawn from the same general segment of Greek society that filled the rhetorical schools.[56] In the opening of the Latin novel, *Satyrica*, Petronius ridicules the far-fetched situations of the declamations, the exercises that were the basis of rhetorical education, for creating a 'cancer of cases' (*rerum tumore*) that made the students feel 'transported to an alien planet' (*in alienum orbem terrarum delatos*). Quintilian criticized such exercises for being hollow; Tacitus resigned himself to the reality that speakers had to resort to colorful tricks of the trade in order to get the attention of busy judges and noisy onlookers.[57] To train young, Greek-speaking men in the skills they would need for public life in assemblies, law courts, and before magistrates of various types, teachers utilized declamations (μελέται) based upon fictional court cases and historical speeches drawn from an imaginary world D. A. Russell has dubbed 'Sophistopolis'.[58] Though easy to dismiss for their absurd premises, such exercises were a serious method for inculcating social values for the class that managed the civic and imperial administration.[59]

Inferences derived from the novels themselves suggest that their authors assumed at least some of their readers would appreciate the play of legal jargon and argumentation in the trial scenes.[60] Written primarily from the perspective of elite city-dwellers, the novels envision a world where the Greek city stands at the center of life. The novels present norms of behavior for the educated elite (πεπαιδευμένοι). They espouse a conservative social ideology that reinforced the values of a patriarchal, Greek-speaking, civic elite and the traditional, polytheistic religious practices of the Greco-Roman world.[61] The length of the works suggests

---

[55] Much has been written on rhetoric the Greek novels; see Barwick 1928; Kestner 1973-1974; Billault 1979 and 1990; S. Bartsch 1989; Ferrini 1991; Laplace 1994; Birchall 1996; Doulamis 2001 and 2011. On debates in the novels see chapters by Bost-Pouderon, Jouanno, Daude, Brethes, De Temmerman, Morgan, and Berranger-Auserve in Pouderon and Peigney 2006. Finally, for the construction of character in accordance with rhetorical precepts, see De Temmerman 2014, 26-45.

[56] Stephens 1994; Bowie 1994.

[57] Quintilian *Institutio Oratoria* 10,2,11 and Tacitus *Dialogus de Oratoribus* 20.

[58] Russell 1983, 21-39.

[59] Webb 2001.

[60] For an overview of scholarship on the readership of the novels, see Hunter 2008; Paschalis, Panayotakis, and Schmeling 2009.

[61] Swain 1996, 101-103; Saïd 1999; Morgan 1989b; Dowden 1996.

that they would have been read silently, or perhaps aloud in intimate settings.[62] Perhaps a father might have purchased a copy of a novel, which would have been quite expensive, to bring home and have read aloud as entertainment for the entire family.[63] Stories of young people falling in love, remaining loyal in the face of danger, marrying, and then returning to the city was a genre of wholesome entertainment that would communicate to their children their anxious parents' expectations of suitable marriages. In this vein, Sophie Lalanne argues that the plots of the novels mirror *rites de passage* for the teenagers who must separate from their families, undergo various tests, and then return home to assume their adult roles in the community of the polis.[64] Similarly, Tim Whitmarsh has argued that the narratives of journeys from center to periphery and back (sometimes) illustrate the relationship between the self and society and the development of a specifically Greek identity during the Roman imperial era.[65]

The relative expansion of Roman citizenship formalized relationships between self and society. As more people were granted the right to access Roman modes of dispute resolution, a new cadre of functionaries—clerks, advocates, jurists, and secretaries to the emperor—arose to meet the demands placed on the courts. Students from land-owning families with the means to pay for education were prepared to serve as members of city councils, and perhaps functionaries in the imperial administration.[66] Literacy was essential but, more importantly, the ability to speak in a stylized manner communicated membership in the elite and hence access to channels of influence.[67] Even apparently silly declamatory themes challenged students to hone their skills of persuasive argumentation, to systematize complex sets of facts, and to grapple with contradictory rules—skills that were vital to the work of the courts.[68] Ambitious students might advance to law schools in Beirut or Rome, an arduous path that involved learning Latin and mastering the technical vocabulary and conceptual framework of Roman law. Those who took this route must have believed they had much to gain by learning Latin and assimilating into the culture of the imperial administration. Inscriptions documenting the deeds of a third-century jurist, M. Cn. Licinius Rufinus of Thyatira in Lydia, sketch a picture of how one such 'unambiguously Greek' descendant of

[62] Starr 1990/1; Konstan 2009.
[63] Konstan 1994b, 220.
[64] Lalanne 2006.
[65] Whitmarsh 2011.
[66] Beard 1993; Richlin 1996; Bloomer 1997; Gunderson 2003. On schools, see Marrou 1956; Cribiore 2001; Watts 2006.
[67] Hägg 1983, 90-100; W. V. Harris 1989, 248.
[68] On the serious legal issues in the declamations, see Bornecque 1902; Lanfranchi 1938; Parks 1945; Bonner 1949; Winterbottom 1982.

an Italian family became a prominent figure in his city and made a career in the imperial administration through his expertise in Roman law; a client of his commemorated him as 'most experienced in the law'.[69] He attained the consular rank, became an *amicus Caesaris,* and under the Severan dynasty held the post of *a libellis* in which he was responsible for managing rescripts to petitions, both in Greek and in Latin, the more prestigious language. Others less inclined to pursue formal training would have likely acquired a practical knowledge of Roman law simply through the experience of handling legal affairs of various sorts in a population where there were growing numbers of people who had acquired Roman citizenship.[70] At all levels of proficiency, the beneficiaries of a good, rhetorical education were positioned to be brokers between the differing legal cultures of the Greek cities and the Roman Empire. The values of rhetorical education radiated beyond the circle of students and teachers to influence the broader culture.

The author of an early and well-known romance came from a distinctly legal milieu, albeit on a more humble level than the third-century Rufinus. In the proem to his novel, *Callirhoe*, Chariton presents himself as a clerk of the rhetor Athenagoras. As such, he is representative of the personnel who staffed civic and legal institutions in the Greek cities of the Roman Empire.[71] This is the only *testimonium* we have for Chariton, but it opens a window onto his social context. In Roman law, the functions that we might associate with the practice of the law were split between jurists and orators. In Latin, jurists (*iuris prudentes*) provided technical legal advice not only to pleaders but also to judges and advocates (*rhetores,* ῥήτορες) such as Chariton's employer, Athenagoras, whose expertise lay primarily in speaking before magistrates, judges, and jurors. People from the uppermost stratum of society usually did not do this for their living; however, there were some from 'a less exalted social level' who made advocacy their career.[72]Advocates gathered around the court of a magistrate and made themselves available to

---

[69] *IG* X,2(1), no. 142: Λικίννιον Ῥουφεῖνον τὸν κράτιστον καὶ λαμπρότατον καὶ ἐνπειρότατον νόμων ὑπατικόν; see Millar 1999.

[70] C. P. Jones 2007.

[71] C 1,1,1: Χαρίτων Ἀφροδισιεύς, Ἀθηναγόρου τοῦ ῥήτορος ὑπογραφεύς, πάθος ἐρωτικὸν ἐν Συρακούσιας γενόμενον διηγήσομαι; see Schmeling 1974, 19; Karabélias 1990, 369-396; Alvares 1993; Edwards 1994. Rohde (1914, 520 in reprint edition) originally believed 'Chariton of Aphrodisias' was a pseudonym, meaning literally 'Man of the Graces' from the City of Aphrodite, an appropriate hometown for a writer of erotic fiction. Inscriptions attest to the presence in Aphrodisias of an Athenagoras and a Chariton, though there is no way of positively identifying these two with the novelist and the rhetor for whom he worked; see Ruiz-Montero 1994, 1007. The relevant inscriptions are in Calder and Cormack 1962. For 'Chariton', see no. 552 (= CIG 2846); for 'Athenagoras', see nos. 437, 438 (= CIG 2748), 462, 475, 517, 519, 532, 565.

[72] Crook 1995, 37-46.

be 'Vicarious Voices' for litigants in a wide variety of cases.[73] While their chief job was not the interpretation or creation of law, they knew enough about the practical aspects of the law to be able to sort through the facts of a case and arrange them in the most persuasive fashion.

For more technical legal matters, the services of other professionals were needed. Cicero refers to the practice among the Greeks of hiring assistants, whom he calls *pragmatikoi*, to give professional speakers legal advice.[74] During the Principate, freedmen and other private individuals served as secretaries (*notarii*) who took the minutes of the proceedings; the many reports of proceedings in the papyri confirm that there was incentive to retain a record of what had been said in court.[75] This may well have been one of the functions that Chariton performed in his duty as a clerk (ὑπογραφεύς). Many details throughout the novel suggest that Chariton was conversant with the administrative aspects of legal transactions. This is illustrated by series of transactions revolving around the sale of Callirhoe between the pirate/slave-trader, Theron, and Leonas, the manager of a larger estate.[76] However, ὑπογραφεῖς were not scribes who simply took dictation; more than that, they acted as moral agents and took responsibility for what they wrote. In documentary papyri they always identified themselves at the end of the documents they helped write.[77] They scanned agreements to ensure that they accurately reflected the intentions of their illiterate clients. If the rhetor acted as a 'Vicarious Voice', his clerk, the ὑπογραφεύς, acted as a 'Vicarious Hand'. We might expect they had a similar proficiency with the practical application of the law. It is quite plausible that Chariton's ability to parse complex legal dilemmas was honed at his day job. Achilles Tatius is likewise associated with the world of rhetoric. The sophistic style of *Leucippe and Clitophon*—particularly in the trial speeches— reflects the influence of rhetorical training and suggests that he, like Chariton, was familiar with the practice of law.[78] Though he does not identify his occupation or name, biographical *testimonia* unanimously point to Alexandria, the setting for a major portion of the novel, as the author's hometown. Both Eustathius, the twelfth-cen-

---

[73] Crook 1995, 58-118.

[74] Cicero *de Oratore* 1,198.

[75] Crook 1995, 61. For reports of proceedings, see Coles 1966. On *notarii*, see Teitler 1985, 38-44.

[76] Zimmermann 1957, 72-81. Chariton's interest in law has also been noted by Calderini 1913, 223-224; Scarcella 1990, 250-252; Karabélias 1990; Ferrini 1991, 34-37.

[77] Youtie 1975.

[78] Russell 1983, 38 n.100.

tury archbishop of Thessalonica, as well as Thomas Magister, a fourteenth-century Byzantine scholiast, refer to him as 'Achilles Tatius the Rhetor'.[79] This may be an inference based on the stylistic qualities of the novel, yet there is no compelling reason to rule out this attribution: like Chariton, Achilles Tatius' interest in trials is difficult to mistake.

As people experienced in the business of the law courts, novelists and readers must have been keenly aware of the hierarchies of authority. Above them were imperial officials of various types as well as the ruler himself; below were free lower-class citizens, peasants, freedmen, and slaves. As Roman citizenship was granted to more inhabitants of the Roman Empire, its value waned and social class became a more significant factor in determining the odds of achieving success in a courtroom. Members of the local civic councils, the *decuriones*, were recognized for the positions of honor they customarily held in their cities. Status symbols such as distinctive dress, special seats in the theater, and public perquisites made their social superiority unmistakable.[80] The ability to speak in the Attic style of Demosthenes, a skill that required years of arduous practice to learn, effectively raised an insurmountable barrier between the wealthy, leisured class and the masses.[81] The pervasive consciousness of status is reflected in the novelists' interest in the effects of the protagonists' change in social status. The novelists and their readers seem to have taken a perverse pleasure in identifying with protagonists who are subjected to disabilities of status. The reader could vicariously experience the situation of a free person who is treated as a slave, a social inferior, an exile, and a foreigner—at least temporarily. In the end, the freeborn heroes are restored to their innate, elite status. The fundamentally conservative nature of the ancient novels' outlook is clear: rarely is the justice of the social order called into question—unless it happens to be the protagonist who suffers degradation.

Roman Law in the Greek World

In order to understand the representation of the law in fiction, we need to know something of the world of law as it might have been experienced and understood by inhabitants of the eastern provinces of the Roman Empire. Papyri, inscriptions, juridical texts, and law codes document the laws of Rome as they were used in

[79] Eustathius, *Comm. in Odysseam* 14,350: ὁ τὰ ἐρωτικὰ παίξας Ἀλεξανδρεὺς ῥήτωρ and Thomas Magister, *Ἐκλογὴ ὀνομάτων καὶ ῥημάτων Ἀττικῶν,* s.v. ἀναβαίνω: Ἀχιλλεὺς ὁ ῥήτωρ ἐν Λευκίππῃ. Both references come from Vilborg 1955, 167-168. Biographical details are summarized by Vilborg 1962, 8; see also Whitmarsh 2011, 83-84.

[80] Garnsey 1970, 234-245.

[81] Schmitz 1997.

the Greek-speaking parts of the empire and so establish a general context for the expectations contemporary readers might have brought to their reading of trial scenes in the Greek novels.

The accommodation of Roman law by already established legal cultures in the Roman Empire is a topic that, until recently, has been under-explored. Traditionally, Roman law has been seen as an edifice of rationality that inexorably supplanted local legal customs as the empire spread. This illusion is due in part to the fact that so much of what is known about Roman law comes from the *Digest,* the monumental codification of the law in the sixth century under the Byzantine emperor Justinian.[82] Before the discovery and publication of papyri from Roman Egypt in the late nineteenth and early twentieth centuries, the relative paucity of evidence rendered the study of the laws of the Greek cities in the imperial period a moot point. In 1891, Ludwig Mitteis, papyrologist and student of Theodor Mommsen, established the framework for the history of Roman law in the Greek East in his monumental *Reichsrecht und Volksrecht in den östlichen Provinzen des römischen Kaiserreichs*, which revealed a complex process of local adjustment to imperial law. His analysis rests on a wide range of sources: epigraphic, juristic, historiographical, and literary evidence, as well as documentary papyri that were beginning to come to light, such as the Syro-Roman law book, a collection of Roman and indigenous laws compiled and used by Syrian Orthodox Christian communities in Late Antiquity. Mitteis coined the term *Volksrecht* to refer to the laws of peoples before contact with Rome, as distinct from the bastardized version of Roman law that resulted from the fusion of local and Roman practices.[83] His collection of material from the Hellenistic period to Late Antiquity is organized into three parts: the foundation of Hellenistic law, the reception of Greek law in the eastern Roman Empire, and a thematic overview of particular aspects of private law. As a jurist, Mitteis focused on how peoples of the eastern provinces conceived of rights and duties before and after the introduction of Roman law, and how the implementation of Roman law in turn was shaped by local practices.[84]

The general understanding is that Rome demanded that Greek cities cede control over foreign affairs (sovereignty), but allowed them retain their own local legal processes (autonomy), unless there was a particular interest at stake for Rome. The result was a mosaic of legal cultures that differed from city to city,

[82] Schiavone 2012.

[83] Mitteis 1891, 5-6.

[84] A concise summary of the response to Mitteis' theory can be found in Oudshoorn 2007, 25-31.

inhibiting any sort of anti-Roman solidarity.[85] Comparing Hadrian's establishment of the council of the Panhellenion to the British Raj's encouragement of the Brahmin administration of traditional Indian law, Simon Swain argues that Hadrian's purpose in promoting traditional Greek culture was not simple philhellenism, but a calculated measure to co-opt the local elite:

> [In India], as in the case of the Greeks, an ancient written culture with a prestige language commanded respect from the ruling power which was consequently keen to further the position of those already in control by referencing the impulses of their traditions.[86]

By the time the Romans first absorbed Greek regions into their growing empire in the early second century B.C.E., most city-dwelling Greeks had already experienced political life under foreign—i.e., Macedonian—rule. Nominally the constitution of many Greek cities was democracy, albeit in a defanged form, with a general tendency towards empowerment of the council over the assembly.[87] By the time Chariton wrote his novel, another three centuries under foreign rule—now Roman—had solidified the position of propertied elites throughout the cities of the Greek world.[88] The resulting political identity of Greek city-dwellers was dual: they were both subjects of an empire and citizens of autonomous poleis. Accordingly, they lived under at least two sets of rules: the imperial edict and the traditional laws of their cities.

The phenomenon of multiple concurrent jurisdictions—legal pluralism—is illuminated by anthropological studies of societies undergoing the process of decolonization in the middle of the twentieth century.[89] In a survey of scholarship on this topic, Sally Engle Merry defines legal pluralism as 'a situation in which two or more legal systems coexist in the same social field', specifically where 'the sovereign commands different bodies of law for different groups of the population varying by ethnicity, religion, nationality, or geography, and when the parallel legal regimes are all dependent on the state legal system'.[90] The model emphasizes the way legal systems interact dialectically over time. Plural legal systems are

---

[85] A succinct overview of this process may be found in Ando 2012, 76-85.
[86] Swain 1996, 72-73.
[87] A. H. M. Jones 1940, 157-169.
[88] Millar 1993, 118; Habicht 1997, 287-289.
[89] Pospíšil 1958; Moore 1973, 1978; Nader and Todd 1978; Nader 1997.
[90] Merry 1988, 870-871.

often 'stacked' or 'nested', though in practice there is 'rampant boundary crossing' by legal actors and 'fragmentation' of imperial authorities'.[91] Studies of modern empires provide a useful comparative model for exploring the dynamics of legal transformation that, for the legal history of the Roman Empire, are obfuscated in the codifications of Roman law by Theodosius II and Justinian the Great, made long after local laws and legal institutions were eclipsed by Roman law. The model of legal pluralism makes intuitive sense for the Roman Empire; ancient documentary evidence illustrates a legally pluralistic society in which disputes often crossed jurisdictional boundaries.[92]

The foundations for this legal pluralism began well before the Roman period. Various types of treaties created mechanisms for mediating between citizens of different poleis. In the Hellenistic and Roman periods, cities granted citizenship to outsiders, usually in order to honor celebrities and large landowners. Epigraphic evidence attests to the significance of holding citizenship in multiple poleis, principally with regard to council membership, liturgies, and the holding of magistracies. Citizenship was principally a marker of social identity, but in theory it also granted access to legal venues in other cities.[93] Hellenistic and imperial Greek laws are reflected in the epigraphic and papyrological record. Documentary papyri of Roman Egypt indicate that Roman law was superimposed to an extent upon the Hellenistic law, which had coexisted with, and in parts supplanted, the native Egyptian law before it.[94] Unfortunately, the papyri do not offer direct parallels to the sensationalistic crimes of Greek novels. Adultery, murder, and seduction rarely surface among the private papers of an average Roman citizen living in an Egyptian village; nevertheless, important legal issues such as inheritance, taxation, leases, sales, and other everyday transactions are well-represented in the papyri. The evidence for Roman law is more systematically organized thanks to the *Digest*; however, the impact of laws emanating from Rome on the legal customs in the communities of Greek provinces can be difficult to assess, particularly in matters that were not of interest to the ruling power. The general policy of the Roman imperial administration seems to have been to allow local laws to stand, unless they came into conflict with Roman interests. The historical evidence, fragmentary as it is, provides a sketch of the Romanization of Greek law and the Hellenization of the imperial administration during the first three or four centuries

---

[91] Benton 2002, 8-9.

[92] Ando 2011b, 22-28; Bryen 2012.

[93] On the phenomenon of multiple citizenship, see the articles collected in Heller and Pont 2012.

[94] Modrzejewski 1986.

C.E. As we shall see, the novels also provide an indirect perspective into this process.

The spread of Roman law is not merely a legal question, but one with cultural implications.[95] Since the publication of Mitteis' work, the view of the unifying power of Roman law has been modified. One view holds that the Romans were less interested in the supposed 'compulsory elimination' of local laws than in the more pragmatic project of keeping the peace in the provinces.[96] The work of the Roman jurists, professional consultants to emperors and magistrates who were unfamiliar with local laws and who had to make authoritative rulings that would be accepted by the provincials, was instrumental in the adaptation of the traditional law of the city of Rome to the diversity of populations living outside Italy throughout the Roman Empire.[97] On the other hand, provincials would not necessarily know from year to year what kind of policies a particular Roman magistrate would decree in his edict.[98] The evidence of inscriptions, especially from Asia Minor, shows the interaction between the laws of Greek cities and Roman law. For example, Julien Fournier examines changing conceptions of citizenship and the administration of justice through the lens of the epigraphic records of four representative Greek cities: Athens, Sparta, Rhodes, and Mylasa, from 129 B.C.E. to 235 C.E.[99] His study shows that Greek civic governments adapted to Roman practices while still retaining their own institutions and legal customs. The process was not systematic but was tailored to the needs and customs of each city.[100] Papyrological studies of the Roman administration of justice among the Greek-speaking inhabitants of Egypt paint a picture of a society in which documentation played an important role in negotiating layers of legal authority. Benjamin Kelly's study of petitions concerning everyday conflicts illustrates a consciousness that legal complaints could be pursued along more than one channel.[101] Judicial claims were frequently delegated, deferred, and dropped.

Litigants who understood how to work the system were better able to achieve their goals. Occasionally, legal documents were taken out of context and used for political purposes. Andrew Harker untangles the complex history of the transmission and reception of the *Acta Alexandrinorum,* a group of papyri that purport to

---

[95] Ando 2011a.

[96] Galsterer 1986, 24.

[97] Frier 1985; Honoré 1994.

[98] Bryen 2012, 776-777.

[99] Fournier 2010.

[100] Other epigraphic studies of the civic administration in the Greek East, can be found in van Bremen 1996; Ando 2000; Dmitriev 2005; Zuiderhoek 2009.

[101] Kelly 2011.

be documents arising from the acrimonious disputes between the Greek and Jewish communities of Alexandria that were played out in the court of the Roman emperors.[102] The reports took on a life of their own after the events and, with the acts of Christian martyrs, formed a new genre of popular literature. The resulting impression suggests that Greek readers in the Roman Empire were vitally interested in knowing what took place before the tribunals of Roman authorities.

The ancient Greek novels reflect an awareness of changing the boundary between public and private under Roman rule. The use of punishment as a public spectacle grew while legal proceedings receded to the magistrate's tribunal or the governor's *praetorium*. Trials by juries of hundreds or thousands of citizens were a memory that could only be imagined through texts. The Greek novels present an overview of all aspects of the trial, both public and private, encompassing crime, arrest, speeches, deliberations, verdict, and punishment. This may seem self-evident; however, it is important to underscore that all literary representations of trials are shaped by the power dynamics of society and its cultural discourses.[103] For example, during the period of the Athenian democracy in the fifth and fourth centuries B.C.E, the literary spotlight was on the trial phase, during which common citizens addressed their pleas directly to juries comprised of hundreds of citizens. In contrast, during the Roman Empire, trials by large citizen juries became less frequent as legal cases were presented to magistrates and their councilors instead of to citizen audiences. The procedure of the *cognitio* (or *cognitio extra ordinem,* as it is often called in modern scholarship) became the most common procedure for trials in the Empire because magistrates were not required to apply the Roman formulary procedure to people who were not Roman citizens.[104] Eventually, provincials who held Roman citizenship did not even bother with local justice, but appealed directly to the Roman ruler.[105] Under the *cognitio*, the magistrate had authority to determine how to handle matters presented to him at the provincial level.[106] Litigants who could afford it employed the service of professional speakers to present their cases.[107]

A trend toward moving trials from open and publicly accessible places, such as the forum, to more restricted interior spaces, such as a magistrate's *cubiculum,* is detectable from the beginning of the Empire in Rome, Italy, and the provinces.[108] Roman governors of larger provinces traveled on a circuit through the

---

[102] Harker 2008; Musurillo 1954.
[103] Foucault 1979.
[104] Peachin 1996, 7-9.
[105] Millar 1977, 465-477; Ando 2000, 362-373.
[106] Sherwin-White 1963, 1-23.
[107] Crook 1995.
[108] de Angelis 2010; Capponi 2010; Aubert 2010.

territory in order to administer justice. The governor's visit, known as the *conventus,* was a major event in the life of a town. Dio Chrysostom (35,15) describes a mob scene of 'litigants, judges, public speakers, governors, attendants, slaves, pimps, muleteers, hawkers, panderers, companions, and torturers: as a result, those having the goods sell for the highest price, and there is nothing idle in the city, neither animals nor houses nor women'.[109] Much of the real business of the law—that is, the hearing of competing litigants, the assessing of claims, and the rendering of verdicts—took place in controlled spaces that could be more easily closed to the public. It became necessary to keep written records because the trial did not take place before a large group of witnesses who could testify to what had occurred. [110] With the increasing reliance on paperwork, the issuance of rescripts, or responses to appeals, came to occupy a greater portion of the emperor's duties.[111] In the third century, Septimius Severus delegated to appointed judges the responsibility for handling the mounting volume of petitions.[112] A class of professional legal consultants arose to help keep track of the emperor's edicts and his numerous replies.[113] The bureaucracy connected to the administration of the law grew. The effect was a minimization of opportunities for the masses to directly observe and therefore learn about the process of Roman adjudication and sentencing.

Despite this trend—or perhaps because of it—the public expected legal spectacle.[114] As trials moved out of the public eye, into the magistrate's audience halls and onto the page, the punishment phase became more public. Assemblies could be so large that they typically needed to gather in the theaters.[115] Shrewd rulers (whether Roman administrators or *decuriones*) understood the necessity of vetting the issues presented to large body of spectators: it was more expeditious to present a defendant to the crowd after he had already been condemned. Executions of criminals became a regular feature of entertainment.[116] By the time the criminals were presented to the spectators in the arena, their guilt had already been decided. This was a win-win situation for the rulers: if the crowd demanded the execution of the criminal, then they could feel as if they shared in the dispensing of justice. If the spectators thought that the criminal deserved to live, then the ruler could

[109] On the scale of the *conventus,* see Boatwright 2000, 98; Ando 2000, 376.

[110] Coles 1966; Musurillo 1954.

[111] Millar 1977, 203-272.

[112] Peachin 1996.

[113] Frier 1985; Honoré 1994.

[114] Slater 1995; Peachin 1996, 1-3.

[115] McDonald 1943.

[116] Colin 1965b; Callu 1984; MacMullen 1990; Hinard 1987; Coleman 1990; Potter 1993; Vismara 1994.

display mercy (*clementia*) to the criminal while simultaneously gratifying the people.[117] In the later second century C.E., the distinction in Roman penal law between *honestiores* and *humiliores* assumed a place in this dynamic. The courtroom was not a level playing field; high social status conferred a distinct advantage.[118] Magistrates who tried cases *extra ordinem* had a degree leeway to assess penalties. During the first centuries of the empire, a growing demand for games, coupled with a decrease in the acquisition of captives through war and the spread of citizen rights, meant that victims for the arena were increasingly difficult to find. Ramsay MacMullen has argued that during this period, criminal penalties became increasingly harsh. Roman citizens were no longer necessarily immune from crueler forms of punishment. Citizens of higher status, or *honestiores*, were exempt from harsher penalties; *humiliores*, on the other hand, found that they were subject to the death penalty in an increasing number of capital offenses. This dichotomy in penal law reinforced existing class distinctions. Citizenship mattered less than the person's *habitus*, the persona he projected.[119] In the provinces, there were many Roman citizens who could not even speak Latin; the magistrate was less likely to show sympathy with such a person than with someone of his own social class.[120]

During the imperial period, Greeks negotiated their place in a fluctuating system where the layer of Roman rule floated above local systems of power. The mesh was not perfect; the overlaps and gaps created ambiguity and confusion. Some cities were free and lived under their own constitutions, whereas others were part of an imperial province.[121] In the New Testament, the *Acts of the Apostles* shows how an individual might navigate the layers of varying jurisdictions.[122] Erwin Rohde, a 19th-century pioneer of modern studies of the ancient Greek novel, saw its readers as alienated, fatalistic, disillusioned, urbane, and individualistic.[123] The view persisted well into the middle of the twentieth century; for example, B. E. Perry envisioned readers who felt a deep sense of loss and fatalism in 'the new order of things, which had deprived them of the normal functions and aspirations of citizenship by making them subjects of a big empire on a par with

[117] Potter 1996; Dowling 2006.

[118] Garnsey 1970, 99-100. Vertical relations of patronage mitigated to a degree the horizontal class distinctions; see Rilinger 1988, 274-279.

[119] Bourdieu 1977. Bourdieu's model has been influential in studies of the Second Sophistic, particularly well illustrated in Gleason 1995.

[120] MacMullen 1990, 216.

[121] Colin 1965b; A. H. M. Jones 1940.

[122] S. Schwartz 2003b.

[123] Rohde 1914.

vast numbers of foreigners and expatriates'.[124] And yet, despite this hypothetical alienation and disenchantment with politics, the Greek novels present characters who experience not anomie but a surfeit of laws, privileges, and social ranks—which they navigate with aplomb. Greeks of the imperial period were well aware of the privileges and honors conferred by identification as citizens of a Greek city, as members of the upper classes, and as possessors of Roman *ius*. That knowledge, along with a demanding rhetorical education steeped in the images of past grandeur, created an urban elite that was articulate and adept at using the complexities of the legal system to its advantage.

The Form of the Trial Scene

A trial is an event governed by ritualized actions that are performed in a space consecrated for the purpose of hearing narratives about the past in order to render justice and, if required, determine punishment. The boundedness of the trial lends itself to being represented in a formulaic manner, as can be seen in samples of court reports preserved on papyrus.[125] In Roman law, a lawsuit consisted of a prescribed series of actions, narratives, and speech-acts by participants playing predetermined roles. Likewise, the literary representations of trials exhibit features of formulaic sequences, analogous to Homeric 'type-scenes'. In her study, *Homer and the Resources of Memory*, Elizabeth Minchin argues that type-scenes are more than mnemonic devices for bards; they are expressions of culturally determined, but deeply embedded, cognitive frameworks for interpreting experience.[126] Drawing upon the insights of the cognitive psychology—the study of how the brain processes, organizes, and retrieves memories—Minchin suggests that type-scenes are templates for organizing sensory input with maximum efficiency. Influenced by the science of artificial intelligence, the field of cognitive narratology begins from the premise that readers use stored memories of patterns of events in order to make sense of narrative structures.[127] These templates for complex sequences of events (usually social), referred to as 'scripts', reflect deep-seated cultural assumptions about how the world operates. This type of 'scripted knowledge' facilitates the communication of information about the world:

---

[124] Perry 1967, 6-7.
[125] Coles 1966.
[126] Minchin 2001.
[127] Schank and Abelson 1977; Herman 1997, 1047-1049.

> Because we all have a wide range of experiences in common, we have a large number of scripts in common. It is possible, therefore, that one person can communicate with another simply by making a brief reference to a script. It is not necessary to express all its details since both parties, it is assumed, already share this information. A speaker need only mention one key action from the scripted sequence and this so-called script-pointer activates the whole script in the mind of his or her listener.[128]

In employing type-scenes, storytellers tap into cultural patterns of understanding experience. Because these scripts seem so 'natural' to the members of the community in which they circulate, they serve as ready-made patterns for writers of fiction—that is, narratives whose purpose is, to varying extents, to make the reader believe in the plausibility of the world imaginatively constructed in the narrative. Type scenes thus reveal the shared cognitive blueprints of a universe that would seem realistic to readers and authors who share expectations about how the world is supposed to work. In order for the authors to successfully sustain the illusion that these invented stories are true, they must in fact adhere closely to their audience's assumptions of how the world works, since their narratives do not rest on independent facts.

A few general observations about the typical pattern of trials in the Greek novels are in order. Essentially, a trial scene consists of a verbal dispute between two parties, initiated by an accusation, judged by a third party who functions in an official capacity, witnessed by an audience, and entailing punishment or reward. The centerpiece of the trial scene is the contest of speeches, the ἀγὼν λόγων, a concept with deep roots in Greek thought that conditioned the readers' expectations of a trial scene.[129] The courtroom scene, like the ἀγὼν λόγων, highlights a clash of values and dramatizes social ideology. The expectation is that a trial is a zero-sum game, consistent with the imagery of athletic competition used in rhetorical treatises to classify types of arguments.[130] Regardless of the political setting, a prominent theme in the Greek novels is the public interest in private matters. The trial scene is a formula not only for the exposition of competing ideas, but also for the valorization of the moral position implicitly supported by the text.

---

[128] Minchin 2001, 37.

[129] Lloyd 1992; Dubischar 2001; Barker 2009. Disputes and stories about competing claims to justice are nearly universal in human culture; see Nader 1997.

[130] Russell 1983, 136-141.

Trials are rhetorical moments *par excellence*; representations of trial scenes reflect an interest in dissecting the relationship between persuasion and truth.[131] Because the speeches are embedded in a broader narrative, the reader is given a context against which to gauge their truthfulness—i.e., the speeches' factual consistency with the facts of the narrative. This detailed, circumstantial framework renders the appreciation of speeches in fictional narrative as fundamentally different from the experience of reading the text of speeches alone and detached from any broader context. Both the Attic orations and the declamations were commonly included in the corpora of rhetorical education. In fiction, the novelist has the power to create in the reader's mind the illusion of objective truth. When there is a gap between the facts as laid out in the narrative and the accounts presented by the various parties to the trial, a space opens for detached observation of the use and misuse of rhetoric, such as the hollowness of an adversary's claims or the naïveté of an inexperienced speaker. The reader thus participates in the imaginative construction of a literary space of justice.

This study concentrates on those trials that are described in extensive detail and excludes a small number of legal actions only briefly alluded to in the narratives.[132] Because the focus of this book is on scenes that show the complete process of the law, summaries of trials mentioned only indirectly or in passing have been omitted.[133] Although there is some overlap between trials and other scenes of deliberation, the criterion of an accusation eliminates most of these.[134] Given these considerations, eleven full trial scenes are identified in the three novels that form the corpus of this study. A summary is shown in Table 1:

---

131 Ferrini 1991, 34, 42.

132 A crude approximation of the relative prominence of trials in the five extant Greek novels is revealed in the frequency of justice-related words. A search using the string ΔΙΚ in the *Thesaurus Linguae Graecae* yielded a total of 373 separate passages (excluding false hits). Thirty-nine percent of all instances were found in the novel of Chariton, with Heliodorus (28 percent) and Achilles Tatius (24 percent) trailing close behind. Xenophon of Ephesus (3 percent) and Longus (14 percent) had fewer hits, not surprising given their relative brevity.

133 Hägg 1971, 87-88. For a formal narratological definition of scene and summary, see Bal 1985, 104-106. Examples of summaries of trials are the trial imagined by the pirates in their debate concerning what to do about the kidnapped Callirhoe (C 1,10), and the trial briefly narrated to Clitophon by Menelaus, his traveling companion (AT 2,33).

134 On debates in general, see the collection of articles in Pouderon and Peigney 2006.

Table 1. Overview of the Trial Scenes in Chariton, Achilles Tatius, and Heliodorus

	PARTIES	CRIME	VENUE	JUDGE	AUDIENCE	VERDICT
1	Hermocrates v. Chaereas (C 1,4-6)	Uxoricide	Agora of Syracuse	Jury court empaneled by magistrates	Demos	Not guilty
2	Chaereas v. Theron (C 3,4)	Tomb Robbery and Kidnapping	Theater of Syracuse	Magistrates?	Demos meeting as an assembly including women	Guilty; crucifixion.
3	Dionysius v. Mithridates (C 5,4-9)	Malfeasance	Special hall in royal palace in Babylon	Persian king	All of Babylon	Not guilty
4	Dionysius v. Chaereas (C 5,1-6,2)	Bigamy	Same as above	Same as above	Same as above	Dionysius is awarded Callirhoe.
5	Thersander v. Melite and Clitophon (AT 7,7,1-6)	Murder of Leucippe	Ephesus, a courtroom near temple of Artemis	Member of royal clan presiding over a council	Unspecified public	Clitophon is guilty; torture and execution.
6	Thersander v. Priest, Melite, Leucippe, Sostratus (AT 8,7-15)	Sacrilege	Same as above; grove on the temple precinct	Same as above; the gods	Same as above; Clitophon	Not guilty
7	Aristippus v. Cnemon (H 1,9-14)	Patricide	Athens	Demos	'Everyone'	Guilty; sentenced to exile
8	Kinsmen of Demaenete v. Aristippus (H 1,14-17; 2,8-9)	Entrapment of Demaenete	Same as above	Same as above	Unspecified	Guilty; exile and property confiscation
9	Arsace v. Charicleia (H 8,8-15)	Poisoning of Cybele	Memphis, palace and outside the city walls	Persian nobles	Demos	Guilty; burning at the stake
10	Charicleia v. Hydaspes (H 10,9-17)	Infanticide, sacrilege	Meroe, pavilion on the plain, near altar	Gymno-sophists	Ethiopians	Not guilty; law abrogated by popular acclamation
11	Charicles v. Theagenes (H 4,17-21; 10,34-38)	Abduction	Same as above	Hydaspes	People and army of Meroe	Not guilty

The analyses that form the body of this study show that each trial scene is a rich and varied nexus of topoi. The representation of a trial in narrative is bounded by two events: a crime and a verdict. Although crime, arrest, and punishment are, strictly speaking, external to the courtroom proceeding, they are inseparable from it, as will become clear. In the Greek novels, the crime that sets a trial in motion is usually melodramatic: adultery, murder, kidnapping, or corruption. A description of the crime, usually committed in private, always precedes the account of the trial. This may seem self-evident; however, one only has to compare with the contemporary popular genre of 'procedural dramas', which present the audience with the hermeneutic challenge of solving a mystery along with professional detectives or attorneys.[135] In the Greek novels, by the time the trial begins, the reader already knows what happened. The effect of constructing the narrative of a trial in this way is to shift the focus to embedded narratives that retell the same story from different perspectives. The venue of the courtroom and the threat of punishment raise the stakes in the competition. The text is created for a culture that valued rhetorical inventiveness. The reader's pleasure comes not from solving a mystery but, as Photius observed, from seeing wrongdoers punished and the innocent vindicated—that is, in reinforcing the genre's moral position.[136]

Courtrooms are portrayed as bounded spaces where highly technical rules govern all action. Typically, an introductory phrase about the convening of the court serves to demarcate the trial scene from the rest of the narrative. Breaking the rules can lead to surprising reversals and challenge the efficacy of the judicial process. Variations across jurisdictions are a subject of interest to the novelists. Trials are set in Greek cities, as well as in the tribunals of kings and of imperial officials beyond the frontiers of the Greek world.[137] Intermediary officials also take part in trials: for example, Persian satraps are involved in trials, either as parties or facilitators. Crowds of spectators are omnipresent in the novels; they serve as the emotional wallpaper, an internal audience that, like a chorus in Greek drama, channels the response of the ideal reader to the events in the court. Eruptions of the crowd's joy, anger, astonishment, and pity punctuate the trial scenes. References to details of the spaces of courts, their personnel, and their procedures lend a realistic aura to the trial. It is not unexpected to find historical anachronisms and imprecise terminology in the escapist fantasies of the Greek novels, whose

[135] Harriss 2008.

[136] Photius *Bibliotheca* Cod. 166 [112a]; trans. Sandy 1989, 782.

[137] Mapping of the limits of the civilized world occupied Greek intellectuals of the Second Sophistic, see Richter 2011, 114-134.

purpose was not to document actual events, but to entertain and to propound a certain worldview.[138]

In the majority of scenes, the defendant is the male protagonist. Although there are instances of female protagonists on trial, they are more likely to be involved in trials insofar as their safety or marital status gives rise to legal actions. Villains, on the other hand, tend to be cast as accusers; less frequently does a protagonist initiate a lawsuit. Accusers are more likely to run away, or to kill themselves out of the view of the reader. Characters who are otherwise portrayed in a neutral or positive light assume the role of villain by virtue of their opposition to the hero in a trial scene. Sometimes the innocent protagonist is unjustly captured, enslaved, beaten, berated, or imprisoned. The level of violence during the arrest reflects the villain's animosity to the hero, and signals the moral polarity in the coming trial. A prison scene might serve as a hiatus in the narrative to allow the defendant to articulate his or her plan of action, a function that resembles the prison scenes in the acts of early Christian apostles and martyrs.[139] Generally, however, the narrative time between arrest and trial is minimal: typically, the imprisonment lasts only until the court opens the next morning.

The moral universe of the novels has little ambiguity. Seldom is there any doubt as to the guilt or innocence of the parties; therefore, chance and paradox destabilize the reader's expectations for the final outcome of the trial. Evidence and witnesses appear by chance at the last moment. A bereaved lover tries to commit suicide by falsely confessing to a capital crime. Parties to the trial lie, withhold information, and manipulate their opponents. Often the outcome of the trial is paradoxical. The novelists do their best to maximize the shock value of such upsets by placing them at critical moments and exaggerating the spectators' shock. Magic, amulets, and ordeals contribute to the atmosphere of uncertainty. Despite the expectation that the verdict will be a moment of truth, trials often confound or subvert justice, and thereby perpetuate the dramatic conflict.

Trials are rarely simple affairs; most are episodes in extended litigation. Their very complexity is the key to their entertainment value. Trials fail because certain dilemmas—particularly involving bigamy and adultery—are so difficult to untangle cleanly. Hence trials-by-ordeal, which function as a deus ex machina, are a convenient device to bring closure to extremely messy cases. If the defendant is convicted, the punishment becomes a moment of high drama. Modes of punishment are always painful and spectacular: torture, crucifixion, burning at the stake, and being hurled from a high place (*praecipitatio*). Sometimes the punishment is carried out; more usually it is interrupted at the last moment. The more spectacular

[138] On the use of entertaining narratives as a tool for edification of Christians, see Pervo 1987.
[139] Perkins 2002.

the punishment, the greater the pathos of the wrongly punished defendant. Justice is instead accomplished through other means such as miracles, religious tests, or trials by combat. Justice lies outside the parameters of the law and occurs on the level of 'Providence' or 'Fortune', terms that serve as code for plot.

The study of fictional trial scenes straddles the disciplines of history and literature. Beginning with a formal analysis of the trial scenes, I consider how each trial functions within the broader narrative. Next, I consider possible literary influences.[140] The interest in justice is in no way particular to the novels; there was a vast literature during the Second Sophistic that concern matters of the law. Tragedy and New Comedy also lend many motifs to the novels; this is apparent in the context of trial scenes that explore legally ambiguous situations that resonated with post-classical Greeks. Parallels from the rhetorical tradition, in the form of speeches delivered in actual cases as well as fictitious ones, are taken into account.[141] Once the generic conventions and possible literary influences have been noted, I assess whether or not the legal procedures and disputes portrayed in fiction are consistent with evidence of substantive and procedural law, mostly Roman but not excluding Greek legal customs and institutions. Details drawn from the contemporary world, when they do occur, seem to slip in unconsciously, taken for granted as presumably timeless features of everyday life that need no special explanation.[142] Because of the inherent elusiveness of interpreting fiction as a form of historical evidence, the structure of the present book reflects a conscious decision to focus upon an in-depth analysis of three novels, rather than a broader survey of Greek authors of the first four centuries C.E. Needless to say, the standard disclaimer in studies of the ancient world applies: because evidence is fragmentary the conclusions will be qualified rather than absolute. As I hope to show, trial scenes in the three novels that form the corpus of this study suggest the contours, sometimes distorted through the filter of cultural nostalgia, of the impact of legal reforms that occurred decades prior to the time of the texts' composition, upon the imagined community of the literate elite of the Greek East.

---

[140] Perry 1967, 29. For a concise overview of the novels' literary parallels, see Fusillo 1991, 17-120; Ruiz-Montero 1996, 29-85.

[141] On ἀγῶνες in drama, see Duchemin 1968; Lloyd 1992; Scafuro 1997; Dubischar 2001.

[142] For example, the *eirenarch* in Xenophon of Ephesus; see Rife 2002.

I

Chariton, *Callirhoe*

In the Shadow of the *Lex Julia de adulteriis coercendis*?

At the beginning of the last book of Chariton's novel, *Callirhoe*, there appears a brief plot recapitulation, which reads like a laundry list of obstacles to a happy ending:

> οὐκέτι λῃστεία καὶ δουλεία καὶ δίκη καὶ μάχη καὶ ἀποκαρτέρησις καὶ πόλεμος καὶ ἅλωσις, ἀλλὰ ἔρωτες δίκαιοι ἐν τούτῳ <καὶ> νόμιμοι γάμοι.
>
> There will be no more piracy or slavery or litigation or fighting or suicide or war or captivity; now there will be rightful love and lawful marriage. (C 8,1,5)

The last two terms, 'rightful love and lawful marriage', underscore the interconnected nature of the two motifs that structure this 'juridical romance novel': love and law.[1] Two pairs of trials are set in contrasting political settings: the first pair unfolds in the well-governed polis of Syracuse, the second in the court of the Persian king. In Syracuse, Callirhoe's first husband is acquitted for killing the heroine because he thought she was having an affair. In Persia, Callirhoe's second husband suspects a powerful satrap of attempting to seduce Callirhoe. Adultery is presented as a men's issue: Callirhoe's sexual behavior is never subject to scrutiny in the course of the trials; rather, the focus is on the men's actions in response to threats, imagined or real. Callirhoe emblematizes the paradox of the 'virtuous bigamist', a woman of prudence (σωφροσύνη) simultaneously married to two different men.[2]

Adultery underlies the representation of trial scenes in *Callirhoe.* They reflect—and distort—a world transformed by Augustus' attempt to implement moral and social reform by means of legislation. Augustus initiated a series of legislative acts between 18 B.C.E. and 9 C.E. that, among many other measures, altered the nature of adultery by granting any citizen legal standing to prosecute a

---

[1] Karabélias 1990, 373.

[2] G. Anderson 1984, 108. On Callirhoe's pregnancy, the plot device whereby Chariton sets up the paradox, see S. Schwartz 1999, Trzaskoma 2010, Kanavou 2015.

husband who condoned his wife's adultery.[3] In effect, he opened the most private space of the home—the bedroom—to public scrutiny. Chariton's elaboration of trials instigated by allegations of adultery playfully dramatizes the futility of addressing adultery through prosecution in a court of law. Although the precise date of Chariton's novel is not secure, a date in middle of the first century C.E. would place it, if not at the actual moment of the reforms, then in their penumbra. Scholars have identified a general Augustan feel to the novel. Stefan Tilg, for example, has collected passages that seem to echo Augustan literature, particularly Virgil's *Aeneid.*[4] Persius' reference 'Callirhoe', a piece of light reading, points to a first-century date.[5] Catherine Connors has made a case that the choice of Syracuse as the setting for the novel is a nod to its symbolism within the narrative of Augustus' empire, as the site of Octavian's defeat of Sextus Pompey and the pirates.[6] In my analysis of Chariton's trial scenes, I consider the possibility that Chariton's novel illuminates the reception of the Augustan legislation and, more generally, the promotion of a new ideology that valorized 'correct' marriage as the moral bedrock of the governing classes throughout the empire.

The social and legal customs concerning adultery changed over the course of antiquity. Traditionally, adultery was treated primarily an affront to the honor of the husband. It almost goes without saying that the double standard was the norm: adultery applied to sexual relations between a married woman and a man other than her husband. In 17 B.C.E. the *lex Julia de adulteriis coercendis* marked a turning point in the history of adultery in the Greco-Roman world. Through measures enacted at different times during Augustus' reign, the state declared a vital interest in the sexuality of married persons by making adultery a crime subject to prosecution, by any citizen, in a *quaestio,* a standing court in Rome.[7] The entanglements generated by extramarital affairs thus became the subject of specialists of jurisprudence and rhetoric. A spike in interest in the topic is suggested in the contrast between the late Republican *Rhetorica ad Herennium,* which did not deal with adultery, and the rhetorical works of Seneca the Elder and Quintilian in the first century C.E., in which adultery is a recurrent theme.[8] In the Augustan period, historians and antiquarians wrote about archaic adultery laws. For exam-

---

[3] A lively overview of the Augustan legislation can be found in Raditsa 1980.

[4] Tilg 2010.

[5] Persius *Satire* 1,134; Weinreich 1962, 13; Barr 1987, 87.

[6] Connors 2002. On the positive reception of Augustan reforms in the Greek world, see Spawforth 2012.

[7] McGinn 1998, 140-215.

[8] On the *Rhetorica ad Herennium,* see Bonner 1949, 25. A survey of the Latin declamations set on the theme of adultery is to be found in Lanfranchi 1938, 439-462.

ple, Dionysius of Halicarnassus (2,25) and Livy (1,58) both described the punishment of adulterers during the period of the Roman monarchy. Plutarch also shows an antiquarian interest in adultery when he attributed to Solon a law prohibiting the killing of an adulterer (Plutarch *Solon* 23) and relates an anecdote about the absence of adultery in Sparta (*Lycurgus* 15).[9]

Stories of trials involving adultery would have been available to the novel's original audience from various sources, such as the Attic orators, whose speeches were read as models of rhetoric rather than as legal precedents. The early laws of Athens and other poleis did not necessarily define adultery as a crime as much as they limited the scope of the husband's (or guardian's) power to seek redress against an adulterer. There has been much debate about whether adultery was itself a crime, or whether it was subsumed under the Athenian law of justifiable homicide.[10] The pseudo-Aristotelian *Constitution of the Athenians* refers to a public indictment against adultery, a γραφὴ μοιχείας, but no orations survive from a particular trial on that charge.[11] Few of the extant Attic orations openly address adultery, suggesting perhaps that it was customarily dealt with outside of the courts. In *Against Neaira*, Apollodorus quotes an Athenian law that forbade a woman who was found with an adulterer (μοιχός) from attending public religious rites and granted any man the right to punish her in any way he wished (short of death) if she violated the law.[12] The same oration includes a law requiring a husband to divorce a wife caught committing adultery.[13] The securest conclusion about the Athenian adultery law is that there was 'a range of different procedures to be followed in cases of adultery'.[14]

---

[9] The evidence for the punishment of adulterers in early Rome is, like the laws of Draco and Solon, inconclusive and possibly influenced by debates about adultery legislation around the time of Augustus. Gagarin (1986, 52) observes that evidence for the earliest laws in Athens is 'late, relatively meager, sometimes inconsistent, and selective'. Treggiari (1991, 265) notes that Dionysius of Halicarnassus is more valuable as evidence for attitudes in Augustan era than for archaic practice. For an invaluable comparative survey of classical Athenian and Middle Republican Roman laws of adultery, see Scafuro 1997, 193-231.

[10] Ogden (1997, 26-27) notes that Draco's law of homicide, which allowed a man to kill an adulterer caught 'in the act', functioned as the law of adultery by default. Kapparis (1995, 110), however, assumes that there had to have been a law to address what happened when a husband did not kill the adulterer in the act.

[11] [Aristotle] *Athēnaiōn Politeia* 59,3; see Harrison 1968, 34 n.31.

[12] [Demosthenes] 59,85-86; cf. Aeschines 1,183-184.

[13] [Demosthenes] 59,87. The statute is generally accepted as authentic; see Kapparis 1999, 354-360.

[14] S. C. Todd (1993, 278) argues against Cohen's 'substantivist' hypothesis that there was a single statute dealing with adultery; Cohen 1991. The term, μοιχεία, covered a number of different types of illicit sexual intercourse and is inclined to the view that the provisions

By contrast, in Roman law a *paterfamilias* theoretically had *ius vitae necisque*, a 'semi-mythical' right of life and death over his dependents.[15] As with Athenian law, early Roman law debarred adulteresses from participation in public religious rites. Husbands were expected to divorce their adulterous wives. Eventually, the law allowed a husband to prosecute a wife for adultery, but only after he divorced her.[16] Roman sources discuss who had the right to punish an adulteress. For example, Aulus Gellius preserves a 'highly tendentious' quote by Cato the Elder that a husband could do so only if he caught her in the act.[17] Roman custom demanded that a father consult with a *consilium* of relatives before disciplining a son or daughter still under his authority.[18] The Augustan laws reaffirmed this principle by allowing a father to kill a daughter who was still under his power (*in potestatem*), but only on condition that he caught the adulterer in the act in his own house, and killed both lovers in a single blow without delay.[19] In contrast, the husband's rights were more restricted: he did not have the right to kill his wife and could only kill an adulterer who was of a lower social status.[20]

Despite the law's efforts to define adultery, uncertainly lingered. Although the immediate effect of the Augustan redefinition of the private act of illicit sexual intercourse as a public crime is unclear, the evidence of the *Digest* attests that a multitude of legal complications ensued.[21] Based upon a limited number of high profile trials for adultery, it has been argued that the Augustan laws gave a pretext to politically motivated accusations.[22] The Greek novels present fictional scenarios in which the natural consequence of adultery is a courtroom trial. Details such as venue, time, official personnel, rules of order are relatively straightforward to compare with both Greek and Roman legal procedure. Legal jargon and the conceptualization of crime in the novels require attention; as we shall see, Chariton avoids trials on adultery per se. Instead, suspicions of adultery give rise to other charges. He refrains from directly tackling adultery lest it detract from the novel's

---

on adultery were subordinate to a more general law that limited self-help in certain situations and required adjudication before the aggrieved party could inflict punishment; see Cantarella 1991b.

[15] The power persisted until the fourth century C.E. mainly to legitimize child exposure; see W. V. Harris 1986.

[16] Treggiari 1991, 263-319.

[17] Gellius 10,23,5; Treggiari 1991, 269.

[18] Treggiari 1991, 269. Scafuro (1997, 390) notes that the family council has 'no counterpart in Athenian sources'.

[19] *Digest* 48,24.

[20] Treggiari 1991, 282-285.

[21] On the effects of the Augustan legislation, see Treggiari 1991, 294-298; McGinn 2002, 46-47; Pomeroy 2007, 3-8.

[22] Garnsey 1967, 58; Treggiari 1991, 509-511.

paramount value, prudence (σωφροσύνη)—in spite of the paradoxical situation that the heroine of the novel is technically a bigamist.

Trial 1.
A Crime of Passion: Uxoricide
Syracuse v. Chaereas (Chariton, *Callirhoe* 1,4-6)

The Story

Callirhoe's rejected suitors conspire to undermine her marriage to Chaereas by convincing him that she is unfaithful. They plant evidence of a party at his house, but when Chaereas goes into his house, he finds Callirhoe oblivious to the commotion outside and the happy couple reconciles. The rival suitors then hire an actor to convince Chaereas to spy on his own house. Upon seeing a strange man (in fact the housemaid's lover) enter his house, he angrily rushes to confront Callirhoe, who awaits him in the darkness of her bedroom. When she recognizes his breathing, she runs to embrace him; however, he kicks her in the abdomen and she loses consciousness. Presuming that she is dead, Chaereas shuts himself in his house all night in order to torture the maids, and thereby learns the truth of his wife's innocence and of his mistake.

Out of respect for Callirhoe's father, the famous general, Hermocrates, the next morning the council hastens to a convene panel of judges. The entire city gathers to watch the trial while Chaereas' rivals stir up the crowd. After the speech for the prosecution, which is only referred to indirectly in the narrative, Chaereas unexpectedly uses his allotted time to accuse himself bitterly, pleading to be punished mercilessly for 'stripping the people of its crown'. Hermocrates vouches for his son-in-law, asserting that he knows the accidental death was due to the actions of conspirators, whom he will not gratify with a second corpse. The general then moves to adjourn the trial in order to perform the burial. The jury acquits Chaereas, and the narrative immediately shifts to the scene of Callirhoe's funeral.

Analysis

In the Greek novels, it is taken for granted that the public has a vested interest in the protagonists' marriage. The wooing of Callirhoe and her marriage to Chaereas unfolds against a backdrop of political rivalry. A man from Acragas, the only city in Sicily that did not come to the aid of Syracuse against the invading Athenians during the Peloponnesian Wars, marshalls Callirhoe's rejected suitors in a military campaign to trick Chaereas into believing his wife is unfaithful.[1] They successfully rouse Chaereas' sexual jealousy, which affects not only his marriage but also the entire polis of Syracuse. The hero's emotional instability is a leitmotif throughout the novel, and causes him to lose his beloved wife, his standing in his hometown, and his freedom. He eventually redeems his masculinity, his *virtus*, by winning *gloria* in a military victory over the Persians.[2]

The incident that precipitates Chaereas' fall is built upon a segment in the archetypal adultery scenario that I shall call the 'bedroom showdown', the critical moment when a cuckold's directly confronts the adulterous couple inside the conjugal home. It is worth a brief digression to focus on an early expression of this archetype, a benchmark for the history of the portrayal of adultery. The elements of this scenario appear in trial scenes elsewhere in the Greek novels. It appears in the song of Demodocus in *Odyssey* 8,266-366, where the bard tells the story of how Hephaestus entrapped his wife Aphrodite and her lover Ares. The scenario is focalized through the husband and consists of three phases: discovery, entrapment, and exposure. It begins when Hephaestus is told of his wife's adulterous affair by the sun-god Helios, who serves as messenger and watchman (ἄγγελός, 8,270; σκοπιήν, 8,302). Hephaestus' anger (κεχολωμένος, 8,270; θυμαλγέα μῦθον, 8,273; χόλος ἄγριος, 8,304) motivates him to lay a trap for the lovers, a golden net unnoticed by Ares, who waits for Aphrodite's arrival home. Once he joins her in bed, the net falls on the lovers, who are literally caught in the act of sexual intercourse.

The cuckold then opens his bedroom to the public view and exposes the adulterous pair to the community of the gods. Hephaestus summons Zeus and the other gods to gather around the doorway and delivers a speech of righteous indignation (8,306-327), the centerpiece of the scene. He invites them look into the bedroom and witness the truth. Demodocus specifies that only the male Olympians gathered, whereas the goddesses stayed away out of shame (αἰδώς, 8,324). The space

---

[1] C 1,2,5: ἐφοπλιῶ γὰρ αὐτῷ Ζηλοτυπίαν, ἥτις σύμμαχον λαβοῦσα τὸν Ἔρωτα. On the significance of Acragas (or Agrigentum), see Thucydides 7,33,2. Chariton makes use of Thucydides elsewhere in the novel; see Luginbill 2000.

[2] Balot 1998, 151. See also Scourfield 2003; De Temmerman 2009; Guez 2009.

for judgment is clearly masculine; respectable women shun it. The onlookers' gaze devolves into ridicule, which rebounds on both Hephaestus' stratagem and Ares' opportunism. Observing the scene, Apollo and Hermes guffaw that the chance to sleep with Aphrodite would be worth it at twice the price (8,333-42), insinuating that she is a prostitute. Poseidon, on the other hand, takes the matter more seriously and attempts to arbitrate. He asks Hephaestus to accept compensatory damages and agrees to stand surety for Ares, who is then released from the trap. The adulteress, on the other hand, is both objectified and demonized. At the level of narrative, the only two verbs of which Aphrodite is the grammatical subject are 'sat down' and 'arrived' (ἕζεθ', 8,290 and ἵκανε, 8,362). It is only through Hephaestus' denunciation that a degree of agency is ascribed to her. He asserts, 'Aphrodite insults me but loves Ares' (8,308-9), in effect placing the blame upon the adulteress for provoking a contest between two men. Her lack of self-control causes the conflict: Hephaestus calls her 'pretty but unable to control her passion' (8,320). By referring to her as 'the daughter of Zeus' (Διὸς θυγάτηρ) and insisting that his father-in-law must reimburse the brideprice he paid for her, Hephaestus emphasizes her status as an object of exchange.

This brief episode illustrates the underlying cognitive script for narrating adultery. The public exposure of the lovers in the bedroom is an integral component of the paradigm. Public and private are inverted as the judging community is drawn into the bedroom, the innermost space of the home. Ancient readers would have recognized that this was a typical adultery scenario from descriptive elements such as darkness, an informant, the husband's absence from the home, entrances and exits from the bedroom, surveillance, the husband's fury, and a weapon. In subsequent literary iterations of the 'bedroom showdown', the judges and spectators in the courtroom replace the gods standing at the bedroom door, a shift apparent in Aeschylus' *Oresteia*. The trilogy begins with the absent husband's return to a home that has been infiltrated by another man. The motif is tragically reversed when the lovers ensnare the cuckold and murder him, leading to anarchy within the household and the entire community. Ultimately, the crisis is resolved by the establishment of a forum for communal judgment. The function of the courtroom is to contain the potential for impassioned violence inherent in the love triangle. The trial scene delimits a narrative space where the community articulates and reaffirms the proper relations between husband and wife, and between male rivals.

The suspected adultery of Callirhoe triggers not one, but two 'bedroom showdowns'. The narratives follow the archetypal adultery scenario, as focalized though the eyes of a callow husband. Chaereas reads the signs of adultery (garlands, wine, and perfume planted outside his home by his rivals) but his judgment fails and he is tricked into assuming that Callirhoe has a lover. Once inside the bedroom, Chaereas' ability to assert authority collapses: he stands speechless, indecisive, and powerless (C 1,3,4). The reader peers directly into the intimate space of the bedroom where Callirhoe is oblivious to the commotion outside her house. He rushes into the bedroom to confront the (non-existent) adulterer, and the accusations fly. In the end, expected outcome of the type scene is subverted: husband and wife peacefully reconcile behind closed doors. An aphorism in iambs, perhaps from New Comedy, marks the resolution: 'Differences between lovers are easily placated and they gladly accept any excuse (πᾶσαν ἀπολογίαν)'. Most English editions translate ἀπολογίαν in this way, but I suggest that the legal sense of term as a 'speech of defense', is also relevant, an adumbration of the trial to come.[3]

The second iteration of the bedroom showdown is more elaborate. An actor, hired by Chaereas' foes, claims that he saw an adulterer enter his house, but Chaereas' trust in Callirhoe stands firm and declares that he would spare Callirhoe regardless of whether or not she harms him (ἀδικούσης, C 1,4,7). The implication here is that the husband stands as judge over the wife, a role Chaereas seems to abdicate.[4] It is only after he sees with his own eyes a strange man groomed for a midnight tryst entering his house, that Chaereas takes action. As did the defendant in Lysias' famous oration, *Against Eratosthenes*, Chaereas tries to catch the man 'red-handed' (ἐπ' αὐτοφώρῳ, C 1,4,10), a specific phrase that was an important precondition leading to arrest and summary execution in Athenian law.[5]

Once again, Chariton subverts the expected outcome of the bedroom showdown: the wife's fidelity is exposed. The bedroom is dark and silent except for the sound of Chaereas' breathing. Callirhoe had been waiting for her husband to return: happy to see him she runs to him but after he violently kicks her, she appears as the 'image of death'.[6] When the truth of Callirhoe's innocence comes to light, Chaereas, 'seething with anger', stays up all night to torture the maids (C 1,5,1), which is presented as a routine measure for addressing infractions

---

[3] C 1,3,7: εὔκολοι δὲ τοῖς ἐρῶσιν αἱ διαλλαγαὶ καὶ πᾶσαν ἀπολογίαν ἡδέως ἀλλήλων προσδέχονται. The first English translation (1764) reads 'mutual excuses'; see *Chariton: The Loves of Chaereas and Callirrhoe* 1764, I.14. Reardon (1989, 25) translates it as 'any justification'; Goold (1995, 4), 'any apology'; and Trzaskoma (2010, 8), 'any excuse'.

[4] An echo of this appears in *Anthia and Habrocomes,* where the hero says that he would never be persuaded to wrong his beloved willingly. See XE 2,4,4: οὐ γὰρ ἄν ποτε πεισθείην ἑκὼν Ἀνθίαν ἀδικῆσαι.

[5] On Chariton's use of Lysias, *Against Eratosthenes,* see Kapparis 2000 and Porter 2003. For a discussion of meaning of ἐπ' αὐτοφώρῳ as 'red-handed' or 'in the act' in Athenian law and oratory, see E. M. Harris 1994.

[6] C 1,5,1: νεκρᾶς εἰκόνα. For parallels in Menander's *Perikeiromene* and *Rhapizomene* see Borgogno 1971. The topos of the battered pregnant wife is discussed by Guez 2009, 27-28.

within the household.[7] This may reflect that Roman law and custom granted a master the power of life and death over his slaves; during the time of Augustus, the *senatus consultum Silianum* (10 C.E.) dealt with murder of a master, the punishment of the household slaves, and its impact upon inheritance.[8] Even though Chaereas is aware that he is the cause of her death, his rage drives him to torture his servants. Like Oedipus of Sophocles' *Oedipus Tyrannus*, Chaereas is the chief suspect, the lead interrogator and, as we shall see in the trial, a zealous prosecutor. Unlike Sophocles, however, Chariton 'makes no attempt to surprise the reader, or to keep him in ignorance of the true state of affairs'.[9]

The point of the trial is not the detection of truth, but the display of a man overpowered by emotion.[10] The death of the Syracusan general's daughter is a tragedy for the entire city. She represents the celebrity status of the civic leader's family. Out of respect for Hermocrates, the magistrates immediately allot a jury to hear a charge of murder.[11] The entire demos of Syracuse, including a claque of Callirhoe's rejected suitors, rushes to watch the trial in the agora, the famous forum of Syracuse where the Roman governor's *conventus* was held.[12] The image of people shouting back and forth evokes the atmosphere of the forum where magistrates held tribunals in venues where crowds of observers could mill around and watch proceedings.[13]

The prosecutor's speech is alluded to only in passing. The first speech to be presented in *oratio recta* is Chaereas' (C 1,5,4); in effect, it takes the place of the prosecution in the narrative. Instead of defending himself, Chaereas 'casts the first

---

[7] On the novel's conventional, upper-class view of the social gulf between free and slave see Saïd 1994. Torture is often threatened in the Greek novels, but rarely carried out; cf.the torture of Habrocomes by his master Apsyrtus in XE 2,6,2-3 and the near torture of Clitophon in AT 7,12,1.

[8] Ulpian in *Digest* 29,5,15 discusses the torture of slaves belonging to one spouse when the other spouse has been killed; the *senatus consultum Silianum* discussed in A. Watson 1987, 134-138.

[9] Perry 1930, 113.

[10] On Chaereas' emotionality as evidence of his incomplete paideia, see M. Jones 2012, 79-89.

[11] C 1,5,2: οἱ ἄρχοντες ἐκλήρουν δικαστήριον τῷ φονεῖ, διὰ τὴν πρὸς Ἑρμοκράτην τιμὴν ἐπισπεύδοντες τὴν κρίσιν. The term used to describe the action of empaneling the jury, ἐκλήρουν, connotes the drawing of lots, a procedure attested both in the classical period in Athens as well as in Rome; see Hansen 1991, 197-199; Allen 2000, 309-312; Sherwin-White 1963, 16. In an edict from Cyrene dates 5/4 B.C.E., Augustus orders that the magistrate supervise the drawing of lots for judges (V,87, 120); see Anderson 1927.

[12] Cicero *In Verrem* 4,67. Mason 1974, 1; McDonald 1943, 40, 152. On claques, hecklers, and agitators in the courts in Athens and Rome respectively see Bers 1985, 2, 9; Slater 1995.

[13] Bablitz 2007.

vote for condemnation'. Although the reader is alerted that Chaereas did 'something strange and never before done in a courtroom' (πρᾶγμα καινὸν καὶ ἐν δικαστηρίῳ μηδεπώποτε πραχθέν, C 1,5,4), in fact this was a cliché in Greek declamatory exercises. Known as προσαγγελία or self-denunciation, it was a ploy of characters desperate to persuade a jury to condemn them to death; D. A. Russell dubs it a form of 'ostentatious euthanasia'.[14]

In Chaereas' case, the critical issue—or στάσις, the technical term in the rhetorical treatises—is not one of fact: it is indisputable that Chaereas dealt the fatal blow to Callirhoe, but the reader knows it was accidental. Antiphon's *Second Tetralogy* was commonly used as a model for making a case to prove lack of intention. It concerns a story of a boy who threw a javelin and accidentally killed another boy, and was the *locus classicus* for describing the nature of intentionality and responsibility. Logically, Chaereas' action is analogous to the boy's, but with the important difference that Chaereas' accident occurs not in the public space of the gymnasium but in the privacy of the bedroom where there are no witnesses. Reflecting the habits of thought ingrained by rhetorical education, the narrator supplies for the reader what would be the proper rhetorical tactic in this type of defense; namely, to emphasize the effects of slander, jealousy, and the unintentional nature of the act (οὐ τὴν διαβολήν, οὐ τὴν ζηλοτυπίαν, οὐ τὸ ἀκούσιον, C 1,5,4). The conspiracy against Chaereas explains the slander and the jealousy. In the preceding narrative, Chaereas is 'overpowered by anger' (κρατούμενος δὲ ὑπὸ τῆς ὀργῆς, C 1,4,12), thus laying the foundation for what the declamations allow as valid grounds for a defense. Feelings such as love, filial piety, numbness, or fainting were held to be exonerating circumstances.[15] In modern terms, we might call it a case dependent upon circumstantial evidence; however, to prove that the action was unintentional nature requires the most rhetorical skill to prove. If Chaereas had made a genuine defense, his theoretical speech would have rested upon the quality of the action. Rhetorical handbooks identify a strategy, known as *colores* or χρώματα, whereby subtle details and insinuations cast the action in a different light.[16] A defendant claiming on lack of intentionality typically appealed to the judges' sense of pity. The Greek term usually translated as 'unintentional' (ἄκων or ἀκούσιον), subsumes a wide range of meanings, such as 'accidental' due to external force (βία) or necessity (ἀνάγκη), including misfortunes such as love (ἔρωτες) and disease (νόσος).[17] Error or ignorance could also prove that an injury

---

[14] C 1,5,4: πρῶτος τὴν καταδικάζουσαν ψῆφον ἤνεγκεν. Russell 1983, 35-36.

[15] Seneca *Controversiae*: love, 9,5,12; filial piety: 1,1,15; numbness: 1,1,16; 1,4,7, 7,1,6, 7,1,17, 7,1,20; fainting: 7,1,1, 7,8,11.

[16] Bonner 1949, 55-56.

[17] Rickert 1989, 30.

was accidental, and therefore excusable. In the declamatory courtroom, external circumstances and internal attitudes were functionally equivalent.[18]

Chaereas' actual speech is brief, only six sentences long. It consists of a crescendo of imperatives to the jurors: stone me, examine me, do not bury me, do not pollute the land, throw my body into the sea (καταλεύσατε, ζητήσατε, μὴ θάψητε, μὴ μιάνητε, καταποντώσατε). Public stoning was a traditional form of punishment usually reserved for especially egregious infractions against the state or its most fundamental religious morals, crimes such as treason or patricide.[19] It was the punishment that Oedipus begged the Thebans to inflict on him (Sophocles, *Oedipus at Colonus* 435). Chaereas justifies his plea by claiming that he 'stripped the people of its crown' (C 1,5,4). The killing of the general's daughter is equivalent to an act of treason; the fate of Callirhoe is promoted to an affair of state. Chaereas begs to be handed over to the public executioner on the grounds that it is 'humane' (φιλάνθρωπον C 1,5,5)—an expression associated with rhetorical appeals to mercy.

To justify his plea for the death penalty, Chaereas uses an *a fortiori* argument that this would have been appropriate if he had killed a mere handmaid belonging to Hermocrates (C 1,5,5). It is a strange assertion, clearly hyperbolic in light of what we know about penalties for the murder of slaves in Greek and Roman law. It is worth noting that Chariton makes no distinction between civil and criminal law. In the extant novels, trials are predominantly criminal, with the salient exception of the trial of Daphnis in Longus' *Daphnis and Chloe*, in which the sole trial scene concerns a civil suit for property damage.[20] Although the penalties for the murder of a slave, either by a master or someone else, changed over time, execution as a penalty was virtually unknown.[21]

In comparison with real laws, we can see that Chaereas' plea is imaginary, belonging to the world of rhetoric rather than that of the law. In fact, there was an actual procedure for handling the murder of slaves in Roman law, the *lex Aquilia*, which went into effect at some time in the third or second centuries B.C.E. It

---

[18] Rickert 1989, 90 n. 21.

[19] Traditionally, death and the stoning of the corpse was the punishment for the voluntary killing of a parent; see Saunders 1991, 255; Pease 1907, 13; Hirzel 1909; Parker 1983, 294-295; Gras 1984.

[20] Schwartz 2005.

[21] The scholarly opinion regarding the right of Athenian masters to kill their own slaves is canvassed by Gagarin 1988, 74 n. 44. Likewise, the traditional power (*ius vitae necisque*) of the Roman *paterfamilias* over the lives of his dependents, including and slaves, became limited during the imperial period, and a ruling of Constantine in the (*Code of Theodosius* 9,12,1) criminalized the use of excessive force in the killing of a slave by his master; see Wiedemann 1981, 10, 174.

declared that the killing of a slave by someone other than a master was tried as a civil suit for property damage; this provision of the law was concerned with the slave only as an object owned by someone else.[22] Later in the first century B.C.E., the intentional murder of another person's slave became defined as a criminal act under a provision of the *lex Cornelia de sicariis et veneficis*, which was passed during the dictatorship of Sulla and stated that whoever killed any person should be punished (not necessarily executed) without regard to the status of his victim.[23] The type of execution Chaereas envisions for himself is clearly a fantasy. To magnify the gravity of Callirhoe's death, Chaereas equates his crime to treason. Here we enter the realm of tragedy: he begs the jury to find some 'unspeakable punishment', calling his deed 'worse than patricide or temple robbery', two proverbially reprehensible crimes. He begs the jury, 'Do not bury me, do not pollute the earth, but throw my unholy body into the sea'. His request evokes Creon's decree against the traitor Polyneices, (Sophocles *Antigone* 203-6). The tenor of his plea also evokes another 'unspeakable' punishment, that of the *poena cullei*, the archaic Roman punishment for parricide that ordered the convict be sewn into a bag and thrown into the sea with a cock, snake and monkey (*Digest* 48,9,9).[24] Burial at sea (καταποντισμός) is historically attested in the Greek world as the punishment of traitors and other enemies, because it completely eliminated any possibility of marking the burial place.[25] Of course none of these punishments are to be taken literally; Chariton conjures the most gruesome punishments of an imaginary past, when justice was more visceral, in order to magnify the implications of the death of the novel's title character.

Chaereas' self-subverting defense is itself subverted when Hermocrates, the father of the victim, intervenes by advocating for Chaereas (συνηγόρησε, C 1,5,6). As appropriate for the character of a general, the style of his speech is deliberative rather than forensic. Only seven sentences long, it features repeated use of the first-person singular verbs related to perception (ἐπίσταμαι, βλέπω,

---

[22] *Digest* 9,2,2: *Lege Aquilia capite primo cavetur: 'ut qui servum servamque alienum alienaque quadrupedem vel pecudem iniuria occiderit, quanti id in eo anno plurimi fuit, tantum aes dare domino damnas esto'*. On the treatment of the slave in cases of injury, see A. Watson 1987, 54-58. On the date of the *lex Aquilia*, see Jolowicz 1952, 287.

[23] *Digest* 48,8,1,2: *Et qui hominem occiderit, punitur non habita differentia, cuius condicionis hominem interemit*. On damage to slaves, including death, under Roman law, see Buckland 1908, 29-31 (page citations are to reprint edition). On the master's liability in the death of his slave, see A. Watson 1987, 123-127.

[24] On denial of burial in Classical Athens as a form of social erasure, see Allen 2000, 216-219.

[25] Demosthenes 23,169 Lysias 14,27, Isocrates 1,12,122, Polybius 2,60,8; see Cantarella 1991a, 99. In XE 4,2,6, Habrocomes is thrown into the Nile, which seems to be the Egyptian version of this punishment, at least as imagined by a Greek author. Parker 1983, 47.

λυπήσω, ἤκουσα), followed by a series of hortatory subjunctives of verbs of action (ἀπίωμεν, μὴ παραδῶμεν, ποιήσωμεν, θάψωμεν). By asserting, 'I know that what happened was an accident', Hermocrates proclaims the de facto verdict. Further argument is moot because the reader already knows that Hermocrates' version is consistent with the earlier narrative, and therefore is constructed as true. The internal audience—the jurors, the populace gathered in the agora, and the victim's father—are congruent with the reader's perspective.

Character is the key to persuasion in the courtroom in Syracuse. Hermocrates senses a conspiracy, a reflexive response by a tyrant (e.g. Creon in Sophocles, *Antigone* 289-93), but here the reader knows Hermocrates' suspicions are true. The rejected suitors' plot against Chaereas is tantamount to a plot against the city of Syracuse. He testifies that he heard Callirhoe say that she would prefer Chaereas to live rather than herself. The resolution of the trial exemplifies the Roman value of *concordia* (ὁμόνοια), harmony between the oligarchical and democratic segments of the city.[26] In comparison with the overwhelming necessity of the burial, everything else—even the court itself—is irrelevant. After Hermocrates intervenes, the trial scene quickly dissolves. Hermocrates closes his speech by urging the audience—presumably the entire population of Syracuse—'not to surrender the body to time nor to let the corpse become unlovely by prolonging the trial' (C 1,5,7). The judges instantaneously affirm Hermocrates' proposal with a vote for acquittal (C 1,6,1).

The narrative immediately turns to the funeral scene. Fear that the heroine's beautiful corpse will decompose precludes all other legal matters. The trial scene is indeed irrelevant (τὸ περισσὸν δικαστήριον, C 1,5,7) as Hermocrates claims: it is a foregone conclusion. The trial is but an intermission in the sequence from death to burial; it functions to slow the narrative in order to highlight the extreme pathos of the hero's loss of Callirhoe, the good wife who is the emblem for Syracuse under the wise leadership of her father.

The first trial of Chariton's novel clearly establishes that adultery is a fundamental concern of the ideal romance. The author has created a chaste version of the bedroom showdown. There is no adultery, only the mutual love of husband and wife. Alone in the bedroom, they affirm their fidelity. Outside the bedroom they are subject to the community's gaze; in the public spaces of Syracuse, appearances are manipulated. The callow husband is contrasted with the wise and experienced civic leader. Hermocrates' active involvement in his daughter's marriage is consistent with the late republican Roman aristocratic form of marriage *sine manu*, whereby the bride remained under her father's authority. Callirhoe embodies her father's prestige. Chaereas' histrionic self-denunciation seems to be

[26] On ὁμόνοια between mass and elite, see Zuiderhoek 2008, 431-435.

inspired by patriotic responsibility as much as by love for his beautiful wife. He is a young man beholden to his father-in-law, the victorious leader who rules, like Augustus, by his personal *auctoritas*. Finally, although the husband's suspicion of his wife's infidelity sets in motion a grand civic trial, the character of Callirhoe is deprived of agency. Controversy swirls around her, but she remains securely inside her house and, ultimately, her tomb.

Trial 2.
Pirates of the Mediterranean:
Tomb Robbery and Kidnapping
Chaereas v. Theron (Chariton, *Callirhoe* 3,4)

The Story

Unbeknownst to the city of Syracuse, a pirate named Theron plunders Callirhoe's tomb and finds her alive among the grave goods. After much debate among the crew, Theron decides to sell her into slavery in Ionia. When the tomb robbery is discovered, Chaereas leads a naval expedition to find Callirhoe. By a stroke of fortune, he encounters the pirate skiff adrift on the high seas and recognizes Callirhoe's grave goods among the dead bodies on board. Theron plays dead until thirst betrays him. He fabricates a story about being a Cretan who recently boarded the ship. Chaereas tows boat to Syracuse, where the people greet it with wonder. Callirhoe's mother recognizes the funeral offerings and all the women of Syracuse wail. Hermocrates then convenes a public inquiry.

The entire population— including women—immediately assembles in the theater. Chaereas, dressed in mourning, rises to the platform and briefly retells how he found the stolen grave goods. Public slaves escort Theron in chains into the theater, along with equipment for torture. One of the magistrates interrogates him, but he holds to his pretense and appeals to the Syracusans for mercy. The crowd is moved to pity, when a fisherman in the audience suddenly recognizes the pirate. The spectators begin to shout that Theron is lying. The magistrates summon the fisherman to testify. Theron's repeated denials only reinforce the crowd's credence in the fisherman's story. Torturers are summoned to whip Theron until he confesses.

Theron is condemned to death, but Chaereas appeals for a stay of execution so that Theron can help him find Callirhoe. Hermocrates decrees that the laws must not be broken, even if it makes the search for Callirhoe more difficult. Another expedition to find Callirhoe is formed. Accompanied by a crowd of onlookers, Theron is led off to the site of his impalement in front of Callirhoe's tomb overlooking the sea. The scene then shifts to the preparation of the expedition.

Analysis

The outlaw is a prominent figure in ancient fiction. He animates the ambiguities at the edges of the law. The criminal underworld is an inversion of the world of law, and thus is 'good to think with'.[1] In Plato's *Republic* (351c), Socrates asks Thrasymachus whether it is conceivable that any group of people—a city, an army, bandits, thieves—can function in concert without justice. The paradoxical conclusion that even criminals require a system of justice seems to inform the novel's representation of outlaws as both anarchical and organized. They mock the laws of the state while simultaneously mimicking its institutions. As in the polis, bandits in the novels have leaders who debate in assemblies. The novelists can imagine no better way to represent what outlaws think than by presenting their positions in opposed speeches.

From the outset, there is no doubt that Theron is a villain. B. E. Perry describes him as having 'a bad man's soul as conceived by a pious and middle class mind, and the author outdoes himself in describing it'.[2] As a person without citizenship, Theron operates as a law unto himself: he is introduced into the narrative as 'man ready to do anything, who sails the seas for the sake of crime' (C 1,7,1). He is actually guilty of the sort of egregious crimes to which Chaereas confesses in the first trial. Both force Callirhoe away from her first marriage and into a second; however, whereas Chaereas had acted unintentionally, Theron is deliberate and clever. The arc of his crime and punishment is the counterpart to Chaereas' trial; together, the two trials form a diptych that reinforces the conventional expectation that the judicial institutions of Syracuse will reward the good and punish the bad—particularly when the bad happens to be without social standing or citizenship.

The specific details of Callirhoe's abduction and subsequent sale reveal an awareness of the slipperiness of law in the interstices between jurisdictions. The narrative of the crime is relatively lengthy (C 1,7-14). Theron recruits accomplices who are eager for 'banditry, breaking into a tomb, or temple robbery'. After they sail away with the stolen contents of Callirhoe's tomb—including Callirhoe

---

1 Bertrand 1988; Hopwood 1998.

2 Perry 1930, 118.

herself—they hold a quasi-assembly. Their speeches echo conventional discourses on justice (C 1,10). The first pirate urges doing the 'right and holy thing' by returning the funeral offerings and ransoming Callirhoe to her husband and father. A second pirate scoffs at him for expecting them to 'act like philosophers' (νῦν ἡμᾶς κελεύεις φιλοσοφεῖν, C 1,10,4). He is pragmatic: if her relatives are lenient, the magistrates and the assembly will prosecute them because they brought back the evidence of their tomb robbery. Furthermore, Callirhoe is a problematic type of stolen goods: her capacity for speech and her unmistakable upper-class beauty will broadcast their crime. And so he proposes that they kill her 'so as not to carry around our own prosectuor' (καθ' αὑτῶν τὸν κατήγορον, C 1,10,7). Dissatisfied with either plan, Theron makes an executive decision to sell Callirhoe in some faraway place and leave before she can gather the courage to accuse them.

The sale of Callirhoe establishes the fundamental flaw that threatens to undermine the status of Callirhoe's second marriage and consequently the legitimacy of the child to whom she will eventually give birth. Theron rules out Athens because of its proverbial litigiousness, where people love gossip and lawsuits. For outlaws, Athens is the city to avoid.[3] The worst sort of legal trouble is to be found in Athens where, Theron says, 'the Areopagus and magistrates are more oppressive than tyrants' (C 1,11,7). The emphasis on the Areopagus reflects its revival in the imperial period as the principal governing council of Athens.[4] In the historical period in which the novel is set, the democratic courts were busier than the Areopagus, whose function in classical period was largely symbolic. In Chariton's time, readers must have been aware that the popular courts were sovereign in Athens, through their familiarity with Attic orations and Plato's *Apology*. In the Roman period, however, the Areopagus was considered by the Romans to be the most venerable governmental body, analogous to the Senate in that it was comprised of *ex officio* magistrates drawn primarily from the city's elite. The Areopagus of the Roman period held a wide range of powers: in addition to its traditional function as a homicide court, it also heard trials for impiety, oversaw weights and measures, and ruled on matters of citizenship and public finances.[5] Between the gossipy demos and the tyrannical Areopagus and magistrates, Athens was a criminal's worst nightmare.

Ionia, a Greek province of the Persian Empire, is a place where the people are used to 'living in the lap of luxury and minding their own business' (τρυφῶντες

[3] Oudot 1992, 102. For an exhaustive analysis of all twenty-two references to Athens in the novel of Chariton, see S. D. Smith 2007.

[4] Oliver 1980, 1-33; see also trial 7, below.

[5] Fournier 2010, 137-157.

καὶ ἀπράγμονες, C 1,11,7), and thus proves to be the ideal place to conduct shady business deals. Chariton takes great care in delineating all the steps of Theron's sale of Callirhoe to Leonas, the manager of a large estate owned by Dionysius, 'the first among the Milesians'.[6] Once the pirate notices the conspicuously moneyed—and bereaved—Dionysius, he finds his mark. He furtively rushes to finalize the sale with a cash payment, lest Callirhoe's extraordinary beauty betray the fact that she is a kidnapped aristocrat.[7] Like a slick salesman, he pretends to take Leonas, Dionysius' estate manager, into his confidence and builds up his anticipation for this once-in-a-lifetime offer of a 'maid of a wealthy woman from Sybaris', a place associated with luxury. Leonas eagerly offers to pay Theron in cash on the spot, before the sale has been duly registered (πρὸ τῆς καταγραφῆς, C 1,14,4). When Leonas informs his master of the purchase, Dionysius sends him to town to see a lawyer, ominously named 'Adrastus' ('not to be done') to conclude the deal (C 2,1,6). Leonas goes to the agora, only to discover that his 'friend' has taken the money and run. The sale seems legitimate enough—money was exchanged, hands were shaken—but it is not properly registered with the civic authorities. It is a plot device straight from the imagination of a bureaucrat who appreciated the consequences of neglecting to file the proper paperwork. Meanwhile, Theron disappears on the open sea, where his ship is blown off course.

In a clumsy but necessary intrusion, the narrator interjects that 'Providence' spared Theron from dying of thirst with the rest of the pirates in order to save him for torture and crucifixion (C 3,3,12). In a space of less than two chapters, Theron's ultimate punishment is foreshadowed no fewer than four times.[8] Chariton tips his hand: we know what will happen, but we do not yet know how it will happen. By another stroke of fortune (i.e., authorial engineering), Chaereas' trireme happens to meet with Theron's trading skiff. After duly calling out to the crew of the other ship and boarding it, the Syracusan crew discovers gold and begins to behave as pirates themselves, eager take the treasure. The high seas are inherently anarchical. In this case, as soon as Chaereas comes out of the hold where he had been in mourning and recognizes the booty as Callirhoe's funeral offerings, the rowers obediently return to their proper stations.

At this point, Chaereas reasserts his authority. In contrast to his earlier frenzied investigation of his household slaves, here he begins with a measured interrogation. He asks Theron four simple questions: Who are you? Where are you

---

6 Zimmermann 1957, 72-81; Karabélias 1990, 382-386.

7 C 1,12,1: κρύφα δὲ καὶ διὰ χειρὸς ἔσπευδε τὴν πρᾶσιν. The term διὰ χειρὸς, refers an immediate cash payment, in contrast to a mere promise; see Pringsheim 1950, 74-77; Zimmermann 1957, 73-74.

8 C 3,3,12; 3,4,7; 3,4,10, twice.

sailing? Where did these things come from? and What have you done with their owner? (C 3,3,17). Theron identifies himself as a Cretan, (C 3,3,17), a typical opening for a speech of deception.[9] He invents a story about a brother in the army, a band of pirates, a missed boat, a storm, and various detours. Chaereas then orders his crew to tow the skiff to Syracuse, an action that may reflect actual ancient maritime law. Demosthenes' *Against Timocrates* records a lawsuit that arose when the captains of a trireme conveying an official Athenian embassy seized a small ship from Naucratis carrying a cargo of nine talents. Because at the time (355 B.C.E.) Athens was allied with Persia, against whom Egypt had revolted, the Athenian authorities claimed that the money on board the ship was seized legally and therefore belonged to the state; the captains, however, refused to turn the money over.[10] Demosthenes' speech shows that the state claimed to have jurisdiction over its ships even when they were far away from the city. In this light, it becomes clear that Chaereas assumes the role of a dutiful captain by remanding the matter to the Syracusans.

The first trial in Syracuse ended with the funeral of Callirhoe; the second begins with the return of Callirhoe's burial goods. The populace gathers at the harbor, where it was when Chaereas set sail, and Hermocrates again demonstrates his leadership. Chariton once again raises the bar for novelty: 'Rumor ran in front, and hastened to reveal many paradoxical and novel things' (C 3,4,1). Everything about this trial is grander and more urgent than the first. In contrast to Chaereas' trial, with its classicizing features (the archons and the selection or jurors by lot), the trial of Theron is convened at Hermocrates' command.

The Syracusans instantaneously assemble for Theron's trial in the theater, a permanent space specifically designed to accommodate a large mass of spectators. The use of theaters as meeting places for assemblies is not unusual: there is evidence that this was done as early as the fourth century B.C.E. and became common practice in the Roman period.[11] Archaeological remains of the theater at Syracuse show that it was the largest in Sicily.[12] In the world of the Greek novels, the theater takes on the functions of the classical agora.[13] The reference to women at this assembly confirms this point (C 3,4,4): it was unusual for women to be included in citizen assemblies throughout the ancient period, though it was less

---

[9] Crete was a stereotypical haven for pirates and liars; see Homer *Odyssey* 13,256, 14,199, 19,172. In the Homeric *Hymn to Demeter* 2,123, Demeter, disguised as an old woman, introduces herself to the daughters of Celeus as a Cretan woman who had been kidnapped by pirates. On Crete as a historical haven for piracy, see Brulé 1978.

[10] Demosthenes 24,11-12.

[11] McDonald 1943, 37-96; Csapo and Slater 1995, 286, 291, 300-301.

[12] Holloway 2000, 151.

[13] Saïd 1994, 224-225.

unusual for them to attend theatrical performances.[14] Theron is objectified in the theater and distanced from the audience, thus opening possibility for misinterpretation and deception on a mass scale.

Theron is subjected to a preliminary hearing (ἀνάκρισις), which Hermocrates announces as 'a more lawful procedure' (νομιμωτέραν, C 3,4,3). The nature of the ἀνάκρισις in classical Athens is not entirely clear, since most of our evidence for the procedure comes not from the hearing itself, but from references to it in orations delivered at the trial stage. Legal historians conjecture that it was a preliminary hearing before a magistrate to decide whether a case could be tried.[15] In certain respects, the ἀνάκρισις served to ensure that there were grounds for moving ahead to trial. In Theron's case, what purports to be an ἀνάκρισις ends not with the magistrate's ruling on the necessity of a jury trial, but with a vote by the assembly of the Syracusans. In effect, the proceeding is a trial with Hermocrates and the magistrates acting as the presiding officials while the assembly renders the final verdict for execution.

The procedural technicalities are subordinated to the narrative's contrast between Chaereas' trial and Theron's interrogation. In a reprise of the opening scenario of the first trial, Chaereas speaks first as prosecutor, but this time his accusation is directed at someone other than himself. He again appears pale, unwashed, and dressed in black.[16] Overwhelmed by grief, he is unable to speak, but the Syracusan crowd cries out words of encouragement. He recapitulates the events of the previous third-person omniscient narrative.[17] His narration begins, 'This is the time not for speaking, but for grieving', an echo of Hermocrates' declaration in the first trial scene. A string of studied antitheses follows: the expedition that was lucky but unlucky; the ship found 'wandering in fair weather, but suffering under its own private storm'; it contained 'everything of hers except for her', including the 'half-dead' Theron among a mass of corpses.

In contrast, Theron's defense is a series responses to questions posed under threat of torture by the interrogating magistrates. Public slaves escort him into the theater along with the implements of torture.[18] The interrogation unfolds in the theater before the collective gaze of spectators. In Greek and Roman practice,

---

[14] On women in the audience in the theater, see Csapo and Slater 1995, 286-293, 306-217.

[15] Harrison argues that the point of the hearing was to define the case in such a way that the jury could vote simply between acquittal and condemnation; see Harrison 1971, 95. Todd, on the other hand, suggests that it may have been an inquisitorial procedure whereby the archon ensured there were grounds for a case to go to trial; see Todd 1993, 126-127.

[16] Cf. Apuleius *Metamorphoses* 10,6, where the poisoned boy's father goes directly from the funeral to the trial.

[17] On the narrative uniformity of Chariton's novel, see Fusillo 1991, 123-128.

[18] Cf. H 1,13,1, where Cnemon is led in chains to the popular assembly.

torture typically took place in public, but outside of the courtroom proceedings; we see that Chariton has condensed torture and trial in order to augment the gravity of the crime.[19] As Theron stands at center stage, one of the magistrates poses questions that repeat Chaereas' investigation aboard the ship (C 3,4,8, cf. C 3,3,17).[20] Surrounded by torture equipment, handcuffed, and flanked by executioners, Theron spins the event to suit his rhetorical aims. For example, he repeats the invented story he told Chaereas (C 3,4,8-9, cf. C 3,3,18), but adds that he had presumed that his fellow-sailors were merchants, not tomb-robbers (C 3,4,8), creating the illusion of plausibility with a detail drawn from a literary topos that played on the ambiguity between merchants and pirates (e.g., Homer *Odyssey* 3,73-4). His claim that he survived because he had never done anything violent in his life echoes his earlier answer to Chaereas when he attributed his survival to his piety (εὐσέβεια, C 3,4,9; cf. C 3,3,18). The audience remains susceptible to pathos and loses sight of the main issue, as in the first trial in Syracuse, when it forgot the murder victim and instead pitied the alleged murderer (C 1,5,6). In an echo of Chaereas' first trial, Theron appeals to the Syracusans' mercy (φιλανθρωπία).[21] There is an intimation that the tapestry of half-truths will win over the listeners. An authorial interjection reminds the reader that although the Syracusans believed Theron had been saved by his piety, he had really been saved by his impiety in order that he could be punished even more, thereby pointing simultaneously forward to Theron's punishment and backward to a moment prior to the crime. Once again, as in Chaereas' trial, the rhetorical move works: the spectators are ready to acquit him and send him home. The audience fails to distinguish between rhetoric and reality.

In Theron's trial, persuasion is inherently unjust (τῆς ἀδίκου πειθοῦς, C 3,4,10). So Chariton introduces the supernatural agency of Callirhoe's avenging spirit (δαίμων τις τιμωρὸς Καλλιρόης, C 3,4,10) to stop the proliferation of falsehoods in the courtroom. The audience is alienated from the defendant, an inversion of its empathy for Chaereas in the first trial. Torture, alluded to briefly as an unofficial and private matter, is here moved to the foreground. The torture of Theron in effect becomes the telos of this trial scene. Everything leading up to it reinforces the differential treatment of defendants based upon their social class.

---

[19] V. J. Hunter 1994, 91-93.

[20] C 3,4,8: ἐπεὶ δὲ ἐν μέσῳ ἔστη, τῶν ἀρχόντων εἷς ἀνέκρινεν αὐτόν. Blake places the comma after τῶν ἀρχόντων, construing the sentence as 'he stood in the middle of the magistrates, one asked etc.'; see Blake 1938, 44. Goold places it before τῶν ἀρχόντων, 'He stood in the middle, one of the magistrates asked etc.' (see Goold 1995, 156), which seems more consonant with the theatrical setting.

[21] C 3,4,9: δῆμος ἐπὶ φιλανθρωπίᾳ περιβόητος; cf. C 1,5,5 φιλάνθρωπόν ἐστιν ἂν παραδῶτέ με δημίῳ.

In a surprising turn, the crowd takes an active role in the proceedings. When an anonymous fisherman in the crowd recognizes Theron and shouts, 'He is lying', (C 3,4,11), the audience's attention shifts to the speaker while the magistrates order the informant to take the stand.[22] Just as Chaereas' prior self-incrimination led the jury to disbelieve him, Theron's denial renders the fisherman's assertion more believable. The crowd, here serving as an extension of the reading audience, is able to see through the rhetoric and know the truth.

Theron's lie, discovered only by chance, precipitates a crisis in the courtroom. The next step is to torture Theron in full view of the spectators in the theater.[23] In Attic oratory, the procedure for torturing slaves (βάσανος) happened outside the courtroom. It was a means to distinguish truth from fiction:

> [T]ruth in the lawcourt can only provisionally and polemically be distinguished from falsehood. The two issues are linked in the body of the tortured, who on the rack, on the wheel, under the whip assumes a relationship to truth. Truth is constituted as residing in the body of the slave; because he can apprehend reason, without possessing reason, under coercion he is assumed to speak the truth. The free man, the citizen, because he possesses reason, can lie freely, recognizing that he may lose his rights, but choosing to gamble that his authority will authorize his speech.[24]

Elsewhere in the novel, torture of slaves takes place in the house or a less public setting.[25] Theron, not a slave, possesses the kind of rationality that DuBois ascribes to the free man: the power to gamble and lie. Now called 'the impious one' (τῷ δυσσεβεῖ, C 3,4,12), Theron is whipped. As he had earlier shown stamina aboard the ship, so too, as if he holds out under torture. The trial is a wrestling match, a contest of endurance where the 'prizes of Providence' (τῆς Προνοίας τὰ ἔπαθλα τῶν ἀγώνων, C 3,4,7) hang in the balance. He ultimately loses the gamble and finally confesses under the 'overpowering truth' (παγκρατὴς ἡ ἀλήθεια, C 3,4,13).

Theron's torture and execution would have resonated with imperial age Greeks. In Athenian law, judicial torture and execution were applied mostly to

---

22 The recognition of a defendant in the middle of an assembly also appears in the *Euboicus* of Dio Chrysostom; see Highet 1973.

23 An overview of the question of the practical meaning of βάσανος in Attic oratory is presented in Thür 1996. Mirhady reconsiders Headlam's argument that the challenge to torture was 'the relic of some other form of ordeal' Headlam 1893; Mirhady 1996.

24 DuBois 1991, 68.

25 C 1,5,1; see also the interrogation of Phocas by Dionysius, C 3,9,7.

slaves; however, there is evidence that it was applied to free non-citizens, particularly in crimes against the state.[26] Under the laws of Rome bandits and pirates categorically received the cruelest punishments.[27] The scene of Theron's exemplary punishment affords the reader a private sadistic pleasure that can be enjoyed in the imagination, without the horror of blood or pain. The passive construction, 'a vote of death was cast' (θανάτου ψῆφος ἠνέχθη, C 3,4,15), makes it appear that the city acts in unison, thus validating the reader's sympathies. There is little subtlety to the verdict: the city's antipathy toward the villain is an expression of its identification with the protagonists.

Any semblance of an actual judicial proceeding dissolves as Hermocrates once again intervenes to propose an official expedition to find Callirhoe. Acting now as a deliberative assembly, the spectators swiftly ratify his plan. Chaereas requests that the execution be delayed so that Theron can help him find Callirhoe. In a repetition of the first trial, the prosecutor becomes the defendant's advocate (συνηγορῶ τῷ πωλήσαντί μου τὴν γυναῖκα, C 3,4,15): Chaereas makes an argument based upon necessity and asks for a stay of execution so that Theron can help him find his wife.[28] Hermocrates rejects the appeal summarily, standing upon strict adherence to the law; he says, 'It is better to take more trouble in finding Callirhoe than to break the laws'.[29]

After the trial is adjourned, a large portion of the crowd follows Theron to the site of his crucifixion (ἀνεσκολοπίσθη, C 3,4,18) in front of Callirhoe's tomb, overlooking the sea. The symbolism of this space reflects the Roman practice of hanging famous brigands in their old haunts, so as to deter others as well as to appease the victim's relatives.[30] The final glimpse in this sequence belongs to the criminal: 'From his stake, he gazed out over the sea where he took Hermocrates' daughter captive, whom not even the Athenians could take' (C 3,4,18). In an allusion to the famous, historical Athenian expedition against Syracuse, Theron is cast as an enemy worse than the Athenians because of his injury to the novel's heroine.

---

[26] Bushala 1968, 62-63; Cantarella 1991a, 41-46; Todd 1993, 141.

[27] MacMullen 1990, 205, 209. Eventually, tomb robbery and kidnapping were made capital crimes under the third-century C.E. legislation of Severus, a likely formalization of a practice that had long affected non-citizens who did not have immunity from capital punishment; see *Digest* 47,12,7 (tomb robbery) and 48,15,1 (kidnapping).

[28] Cf. Hermocrates' call for the 'necessary funeral' in C 3,4,15: λογίσασθέ μου τὴν ἀνάγκην, cf. C 1,5,7: ἐπὶ τὸν ἀναγκαῖον ἀπίωμεν τάφον.

[29] C 3,4,16: βέλτιον, εἰπὼν, ποιήσασθαι τὴν ζήτησιν ἐπιπονωτέραν ἢ λυθῆναι τοὺς νόμους. Cf. C 3,4,3.

[30] *Digest* 48,19,28,15. On the practice of punishing the criminal where the crime was committed, see MacMullen 1990, 358 n. 312.

Trial 3.
A Hellene in the King's Court: Malfeasance
Dionysius v. Mithridates (Chariton, *Callirhoe* 5,4-9)

The Story

On his expedition to find Callirhoe, Chaereas is shipwrecked on the shore of Ionia. He is sold as a slave to the vast estate of Mithridates, the satrap of neighboring Caria, who makes him his freedman after he learns that he is the husband of the famous Callirhoe, now married to Dionysius, an aristocrat of Miletus. Mithridates offers Chaereas the opportunity to send a letter to Callirhoe; meanwhile, she has found the wreckage of Chaereas' ship and assumes he is dead. Chaereas' letter falls into the wrong hands and is ultimately forwarded to Dionysius, who becomes very upset when he reads this letter from the man whose cenotaph he had dedicated. He suspects the satrap of plotting to seduce Callirhoe, and Dionysius asks Pharnaces, the satrap of Ionia, to help him bring the case to the attention of the king of Persia. The multi-party correspondence only piques everyone's interest in seeing the beautiful heroine—including the Persian king himself, who summons both parties to his court in Babylon. Mithridates uses his personal connections to prepare for his trial and brings Chaereas along as a surprise witness. Meanwhile, rumors of Callirhoe's beauty spread through the Persian Empire. Along the Royal Road to Babylon, gawkers hoping to catch a glimpse of Callirhoe delay Dionysius' arrival at the Persian capital.

The trial is postponed due to a thirty-day religious festival. Both sides prepare as if for war and the populace of Babylon, men and women alike, is divided in two factions: the satrapial, pro-Mithridates party, and the popular, pro-Dionysius party. Dionysius puts his faith in the evidence of the letter while Mithridates, confident that the opportune revelation of the still-living Chaereas before the court will vindicate him, feigns anxiety by ostentatiously consulting his lawyers.

The venue for the trial is a majestic audience hall in the royal palace, where the king sits on a throne flanked by his entourage. The letters are read aloud and the audience applauds the king's sense of justice. Dionysius is ready to deliver his accusation, but Mithridates interrupts to request the presence of Callirhoe. Dionysius protests but no one pays attention to him; everyone is titillated at the prospect of seeing the beautiful Callirhoe. The court is then recessed until Callirhoe can appear. When Dionysius informs her that she is summoned to court, she laments the indignity of having to appear in public and become the talk of Asia and Europe.

On the next day, a crowd of spectators gathers outside the palace. Everyone is stunned once Callirhoe enters the courtroom. Dionysius accuses Mithridates of flouting the king's laws and exploiting his hospitality by trying to insinuate himself into his wife's affections. The crowd is incensed and the king glares angrily at the satrap, but he coolly refutes the charges. He defends his reputation and then cleverly attacks the legitimacy of Dionysius' marriage. His speech culminates in the revelation of Chaereas. The courtroom breaks out in pandemonium, as a rapid-fire exchange of accusations breaks out between the two men. The king adjourns the proceedings in order to consult his advisors. Mithridates' brilliant defense wins an acquittal and he is sent away with gifts; however, the issue of Callirhoe's marital status remains unsettled. The king then deliberates over whether he should arbitrate between Dionysius and Chaereas. The king gives Dionysius and Chaereas five days to prepare their cases and takes custody of Callirhoe while the case is pending.

Analysis

As we have seen in Chariton's first two trials, the politics of Syracuse are congruent with the sentimental concerns of its ruling elite. The novel's third trial in the novel begins as a complaint of a provincial against a governor. As soon as the plot moves into the Persian Empire, the political dynamic changes. In Ionia, at the westernmost edge of empire, the networks of provincial patronage shape the way justice is administered. Chariton models the Persia, which assumed a mythic status in the imagination of imperial Greeks, on the politics and procedures of the Roman imperial administration of which he had firsthand knowledge.[1] The maintenance of good relations with the local satraps preoccupies Dionysius, the 'foremost' man of Miletus. He hosts them when they travel through Miletus and invites them to attend the dedication of a monument on his estate. This plays out against the rivalry between the powerful satraps of Ionia and Caria. Chaereas and

[1] S. Schwartz 2003a.

Callirhoe, on the other hand, both arrive in Ionia as slaves, without social standing in this strange territory.

Once again, a suspicion of adultery brings the protagonists to the seat of imperial power. The complex sequence of events leading up to the trial is constructed upon a legal ambiguity that will come back to haunt Dionysius, the party who initiates the lawsuit. After Callirhoe is sold by Theron as a slave to the estate of Dionysius, she discovers that she is pregnant and consents to marry her master 'for the purpose of begetting children, according to Greek laws' (C 3,2,2), with the expectation that it will confer legitimacy on her unborn child, who otherwise would be born into slavery.[2] Callirhoe's status as a freedwoman has a direct bearing on the legality of Dionysius' marriage to her.

Chaereas experiences a parallel demotion of status and consequent reinstatement within the framework of provincial society in the Persian Empire. Chaereas and his friend Polycharmus are shipwrecked, captured by slave-traders, and sold as slaves to Mithridates' large *latifundium*. One of the overseers on the estate is murdered by slaves (C 4,2,8), a very serious offense in Roman law.[3] In the course of interrogating the rebels, Mithridates asks Polycharmus who is responsible for the trouble. Misconstruing the question, Polycharmus answers, 'Callirhoe' (C 4,2,8). Mithridates recognizes the name from the dedication of Chaereas' cenotaph in Miletus and hastens to the site of the rebels' crucifixion; the satrap rescues Chaereas in order to use him as a pawn in a scheme to win the beautiful Callirhoe.

As the characters cross over into Persian territory, the plot illustrates the operation of patronage in an empire. At the highest social strata, it was a business of competing, self-interested governors or satraps seeking to win prominent clients and undermine the power of their rivals. Superimposed upon the relations of hospitality is a fully articulated view of society as a system of duties and obligations that serve the interests of the powerful. Mithridates' new client is instrumental in his play for power.[4] He coaxes Chaereas to write Callirhoe a letter, to be delivered by his servants. Mithridates adds his own cover letter and sends gifts of gold and jewelry. The letters are intercepted in transit when the servants, sent to deliver the letters, get drunk and are arrested at a tavern in Priene. The local magistrate (στρατηγός) then confiscates the letters and takes the initiative to deliver them to Dionysius.[5] The magistrate appends his own letter, in which he addresses Dionysius as his 'benefactor' (εὐεργέτῃ C 4,5,8). Over the course of this episode, the

[2] The rationale for her choice is discussed more fully in S. Schwartz 1999.

[3] Bradley 1994, 113-137.

[4] Elsom 1992.

[5] The scenario is plausible; see A. H. M. Jones 1940, 212.

letter is read and misread six times; the only one who is ignorant of the letter is its intended recipient, Callirhoe.[6]

Dionysius suspects foul play and surmises that the letter is a forgery perpetrated by the satrap in order to seduce Callirhoe. Dionysius makes a preemptive strike against the would-be adulterer by lodging a formal complaint against the satrap to the Persian king, casting it as a matter of malfeasance rather than seduction. This tactic ultimately brings all the main characters to Babylon, the capital of the Persian Empire, where the Persian king himself adjudicates the case. The journey to the seat of Persian power is informed by the rich tradition of romantic historiography of the *Anabasis*.[7]

The exchange of letters seems to be modeled on the legend of the last days of Themistocles, the great Athenian general and Panhellenic leader who ended his career in the Persian court.[8] The story is related by a number of historians and was also the premise for a series of fictional letters attributed to Themistocles. In elements of his story include a letter to the king, a friend who acts as intermediary, and a secret transport. Most pertinent is the episode in which the Greek protagonist initiates contact with the Persian king. Thucydides presents a letter written by Themistocles after his exile from Greece in which he asks the king to do him a favor by receiving him. In Diodorus' account, Themistocles first flees to a personal guest-friend in Asia Minor by the name of Lysitheides, who was a friend (φίλος) of the Persian king. He asks his friend to introduce him to the king; his friend demurs at first, then agrees, and transports him through Persia by hiding him in a wagon decorated as the carriage of a royal concubine so as not to be waylaid en route.

Preparation of the Charges

In his quest for justice, Dionysius follows in the footsteps of Themistocles. The power relations on the estates of wealthy landlords in Asia Minor prefigure the court at the imperial capital, where all the king's subjects are slaves (C 4,6,4, 6,1,1). The dynamic of political rivalry escalates over the journey eastward: just as the grandiose private estate of Dionysius dwarfs the city of Syracuse, it is in

[6] Létoublon 2003, 283-288.

[7] For example, in Herodotus and Xenophon of Athens. Specific echoes of Xenophon's journey to Persia in Chariton's novel as discussed in Trzaskoma 2011.

[8] On the identification of Athenocentrism and Panhellenism, see Hall 1989, 16-17. Plutarch's account basically follows Diodorus'. See Thucydides 1,137,3, Diodorus *Historical Library* 11,54–59, Plutarch *Themistocles* 22–32; discussed in Lenardon 1978, 139–153. On the fictional letters, see Penwill 1978.

turn overshadowed by Mithridates' estate in Asia Minor. The city of Babylon is much grander than anything yet encountered in the novel. The power differentials among Dionysius, the two satraps, and the emperor are analogous to those among the local elites, governors, and Roman emperor. Dionysius' status as a member of the elite of a provincial city gives him personal connections with the local satraps; he hosts the visiting representatives of the imperial regime (C 4,1,7–8). This depiction conforms to the traditional socio-political relationships between members of the upper classes in the cities of the Roman provinces and the imperial administration.[9] In reality, this kind of accusation would have put the plaintiff in great peril: he would have had to be very confident he could win, and win fast; otherwise, not unlike a modern-day whistle-blower, he ran the risk of retaliation by a governor who had the protection of the emperor who assigned him to the province.[10]

Despite his prestige in Miletus, Dionysius is powerless at the imperial level and so turns to one imperial official in order to lodge a complaint against another. He appeals to the highest-ranking imperial magistrate who is capable of advancing his case against the satrap in an audience with the king.[11] Written documents assume a crucial role in the plot of the lawsuit. Chariton delineates a formal business of petition and response in the context of the relations between patrons and clients within an empire. When Dionysius wishes to accuse one satrap of trying to seduce his wife, he naturally appeals to another satrap for help. In a private interview, he presents his complaint to Pharnaces, the satrap of Lydia and Ionia, whom he addresses as his 'master' or *dominus* (ὦ δέσποτα, C 4,6,1). Pharnaces agrees to sponsor Dionysius' petition because his province shares a long border with Mithridates' (C 4,6,2)—but his interest is erotically motivated: he, too, now desires Callirhoe.

Pharnaces sends a confidential letter to the king on Dionysius' behalf (C 4,6,3). Chariton's acquaintance with forms of legal correspondence is clear; the structure and content of this letter generally conform to documentary evidence for the procedure used in official petitions to the Roman emperor and to other officials.[12] Pharnaces' letter establishes the terms of the coming lawsuit: he frames the issue as a case of an arrogant governor abusing his power in order to injure an important provincial. Pharnaces reports to the king that Mithridates corrupted Dionysius' wife while he was his guest in Dionysius' home.[13] More relevant to the

[9] Edwards 1994, 703–712.
[10] Brunt 1961, 206-207.
[11] Ando 2000, 336-385.
[12] For a detailed analysis of the petition process, see S. Schwartz 2003a.
[13] Chariton repeatedly invokes the archetypal triangle of Menelaus, Helen, and Paris in C 2,6,1, 5,2,8, 5,5,9, and 8,1,3. On the Homeric resonances equating Callirhoe with Helen,

trial, however, Pharnaces casts the problem as one of diplomacy rather than mere seduction. Desire in and of itself was not necessarily a prosecutable crime; it was only until one of the parties took action that it could be addressed through the judicial system. Such a charge required evidence of adulterous intent.[14]

Accordingly, Pharnaces' letter (C 4,6,4) characterizes Mithridates' actions not in terms of adultery, but in terms that directly impact the king's political interests. He writes that the satrap 'corrupts' (διαφθείρει), brings 'great ill repute and disorder' to the king's affairs (μεγάλην ἀδοξίαν, ταραχήν) and 'blameworthy illegality' (παρανομία, μεμπτή), and his insolence (ὕβριν) cannot be overlooked. This is the type of petition to which the ruler of a vast empire was likely to pay attention, one in which the king's authority could be invoked as a check upon the excesses of provincial governors, particularly in a diverse place such as Asia Minor, with its patchwork of jurisdictions among hundreds of communities.[15] A provincial who brought a lawsuit against a governor needed support from the community, from other imperial officials, or from friends who had influence in the emperor's court.[16] Pharnaces closes the petition with a formulaic call for remedy: do not ignore Mithridates' arrogance (τὴν ὕβριν μὴ δύνασθαι λαθεῖν, C 4,6,4).[17]

Literarily, the scene brings to life the implicit ideology underlying petitions to the Roman emperor. In the eyes of Greeks, this system distinguished Rome from all preceding world empires; as Aelius Aristides noted, 'It is very easy for [the emperor] to stay where he is and manage the entire civilized world by letters, which arrive almost as soon as they are written, as if they were carried by winged messengers'.[18] The letter serves as a pivot between the scene of Dionysius's consultation with Pharnaces and the king's consultation with his advisers and can be imagined in cinematic terms: the narrative first focuses upon Pharnaces writing the letter, then zooms in on the letter itself and pans back out and to show the king reading the letter. The scene thus animates the ideology underpinning the system of imperial subscriptions in the Roman Empire; namely that there was a direct connection between the petitioner and the Great King. Legal sources provide

---

see Laplace 1980 and Manuwald 2000, 144 n. 48. Reardon (1982, 9) notes that 'Mithridates and the King are simply doublets of Dionysius'; however, if patronage relationships are factored in, the triangles multiply: not only Chaereas-Callirhoe-rival (i.e., Dionysius or the king), but also Dionysius-Callirhoe-rival (i.e., Mithridates or the king).

[14] Roman jurists were concerned with the logistics of adultery and recognized that abetting adultery was punishable under the *lex Julia de adulteriis coercendis*. See, for example, *Digest* 4,5,10. For a fuller discussion, see Daube 1972; Treggiari 1991, 278-279.

[15] A. H. M. Jones 1937, 59-95; Millar 1996; Fournier 2010, 62-87.

[16] Brunt 1961; Millar 1977, 434-447.

[17] On formulae in the request period of official petitions, see White 1972, 41-61.

[18] Aelius Aristides *Roman Oration* 33; trans. Oliver 1953, 899.

thousands of examples of subscriptions to petitions that purport to be written by the emperor.[19] The addressing of appeals was integral to the Roman emperor's public image. The reality of the process was much more complex: the emperor could not write each and every subscription to which his name was attached, and so relied on the support of various legal advisers and secretaries. The fiction that each judgment came personally from the emperor was essential for maintaining the emperor's aura of authority.[20] Details drawn from the activities of the Roman emperor flesh out the image of the Persian king as the dispenser of justice, a typical aspect of imperial power in Greek, Achaemenid, and Roman sources.[21]

The king reads the letter and consults his friends (φίλοι, C 4,6,5). This is reminiscent of Hellenistic and Roman rulers consulting advisers, here projected onto the Persian custom of royal banquets, so vivid in the imaginations of classical Greek authors.[22] The Persian king's council deliberates along the lines suggested by Pharnaces' letter (C 4,6,5) and so sets the parameters for the upcoming trial scene. In a faint echo of the account of the debate after the conspiracy against the Magi in Herodotus (3,80-82), opinion is split: some councilors envy Mithridates and others support him; on that basis, some favor defending the reputation of Dionysius, while others are disposed to protect Mithridates from scandal. Herodotus' debate between isonomia and oligarchy is transformed into a debate over the reputations of important men. In Herodotus' account, Darius weighs the two positions and decides that monarchy is best because in an oligarchy, competition for honor turns private rivalries become public affairs (Herodotus 3,82,3).

Dionysius' complaint about incitement to adultery is recast as an issue of *maiestas,* the diminution of the state's majesty—here, the authority of the Persian king. He is an absolute monarch with a sense of justice and mercy, positive royal qualities, such as those attributed to the Roman emperor, as well as negative qualities normally attributed to 'Oriental' despots and tyrants, particularly a susceptibility to passion.[23] The king makes the final decision to hear the case while he is

---

[19] Honoré (1994) includes 2,609 rescripts dating from the third century alone in his study.

[20] Millar 1977, 203-252; Turpin 1991; Honoré 1994, 1-48.

[21] The association between Persian kingship and justice is made explicitly in the story of Deioces the Mede in Herodotus 1,96-100. On the representation of Darius as the 'King of Justice', see the analysis of the royal inscriptions on the Darius' tomb at Naqš-i Rustam in Briant 2002, 210-213.

[22] See Briant 2002, 307-315. On the φίλοι of Hellenistic monarchs, see Walbank 1984, 68-71. On Roman emperors' consultation with *amici* in matters of correspondence, see Millar 1977, 223.

[23] On Chariton's depiction of Persia as part barbarian, part Roman, see Alvares 1993, 180-186. The story of Gyges and Candaules in Herodotus 1,8-13 is the paradigm for the conjunction of eros and power under barbarian monarchies. On the representation of the despot as erastes in Herodotus, see Hartog 1988, 330-331. The motif of the bedroom as a site of

alone at night with 'wine and darkness acting as his advisers' (σύμβουλοι, C 4,6,7). His feelings are presented as a μέν-δέ clause: righteous indignation with what he perceives as an attack on his majesty (μισοπονηρία μὲν διὰ τὸ τῆς βασιλείας εὐπρεπές, C 4,6,6) and worries about Mithridates' contemptuousness. In the end, simple self-interest drives his decision: the rumor of Callirhoe's beauty arouses in him a prurient curiosity.

The king's reply takes the form of a *subscriptio*, a note typically written by the Roman emperor at the bottom of a petition, rather than a complete letter in itself. It is a simple order: 'Send my slave Dionysius the Milesian', (Διονύσιον ἐμὸν δοῦλον, Μιλήσιον, πέμψον, C 4,6,8). Although Chariton later collectively refers to both Pharnaces' letter and the king's response as ἐπιστολάς (C 5,4,7), which was the Greek translation of the *rescriptio*, perhaps no more than a sentence or two jotted at the bottom of the petition.[24] The king's terse summons accentuates the status differential in the coming trial in Persia: the king has the sole vote; everyone else is a slave.[25] The king's command is an exaggeration of imperial rule.

Both parties leave their homes with large escorts of servants and followers. When Mithridates receives the unexpected summons from the king charging him with plotting against Dionysius' marriage (ἐπεβούλευσας γάμῳ Διονυσίου, C 4,6,8), he first decides to revolt, like his namesake, the infamous Mithridates VI of Pontus. He asks himself, 'Why am a rushing to hand over my freedom to my master's hands; maybe you will win more by staying put. The king is far away and his generals are useless' (C 4,7,2). But, since this is a romance, power is conjoined with love—the 'two finest things' in the opinion of the satrap; however, when Mithridates hears that Dionysius has already left for Babylon with Callirhoe, he decides to go. He hopes the king will pity him, since he did nothing wrong and brings Polycharmus and Chaereas as advocates (συνηγόρους) and witnesses (μάρτυρας) to prove his innocence in the trial (C 4,7,4). This becomes a problem for Dionysius: Callirhoe is a liability. As they journey through Asia, she attracts gawkers along the way (C 4,7,5-6).

---

decision-making in the novels is discussed at greater length in S. Schwartz 2012. Callirhoe's decision to carry her pregnancy is likewise presented as an internal debate at night, in her bedroom in C 2,11.

[24] See Mason 1974, 126. On the difference between two types of imperial *rescripta*, namely the *epistulae* and *subscriptiones*, see Williams 1974, 86-88.

[25] The Greek characterization of high-ranking Persians as δοῦλοι τοῦ βασιλέως, based upon Persian terms for servants (*ba[n]daka* and *libar*), was 'ideologically useful...to the formulation of the polarity between 'free Greeks' and 'enslaved' Persians'; see Missiou 1993, 391.

The Trial, Part I

The statement, 'All Babylon was a law court' (ὅλη ἡ Βαβυλὼν δικαστήριον ἦν, C 5,4,4), marks the commencement of the trial narrative. The Persian capital in this novel is grandiose, opulent, and exotic—consistent with other Greek literary depictions of Persia.[26] This is Mithridates' home turf; like the other satraps, he has a residence there (C 5,2,1). His familiarity with protocol gives him an advantage over his Greek opponent. He cultivates the court officials before the trial (συγκροτῆσαι τὰ πρὸς τὴν δίκην, C 5,2,1). He visits the Persian peers (ὁμοτίμους, C 5,2,2) and bribes Artaxates, 'the greatest and most powerful eunuch by the king's palace', the quintessential Persian factotum.[27] Aware of the importance of appearances, Mithridates formulaically announces his presence to the king via the eunuch: 'Your slave is present to refute the slander of the Greek man and to make obeisance' (C 5,2,2). The eunuch responds with an equally stilted pronouncement communicating the hope that Mithridates is innocent and announcing that the king will pass judgment when Dionysius is present.

Meanwhile, Dionysius' arrival is delayed due to the difficulty of his journey, which allows Mithridates to influence his contacts at the royal court unimpeded. The king rebukes Dionysius for not arriving sooner, because he is accusing a man entrusted with high office. This view of the Persian court may reflect Greek criticisms of the Roman imperial court, where governors had the advantage of powerful social networks in the capital city, networks from which Greek emissaries were excluded.[28]

Callirhoe's fame precedes her arrival to Babylon.[29] As a prelude to the trial itself, Chariton presents a beauty contest, in effect a feminine variant of the trial scene that is called 'face-off' (ἀπάντησις, C 5,3,5), derived from the verb ἀπαντάω, which is also used in legal settings to mean 'appear in court'.[30] The beauty contest establishes a context in which Callirhoe's virtue is tested—wordlessly—against an opponent.[31] Women actively participate by cheering for the

---

[26] Missiou 1993; Briant 2002, 255-301.

[27] Greek authors traditionally identified the chiliarch, the 'Commander of a Thousand' as the most powerful official in the court; see Briant 2002, 258.

[28] Bowie 1982.

[29] As in the trial of Theron (C 3,4,1), rumor draws in men and women alike. Likewise, the rumors of the trial only intensify her fame (ἐνδοξοτέραν αὐτὴν ἐποίει καὶ τὸ τῆς δίκης διήγημα, C 4,7,6); on the significance of Callirhoe's public appearance, see Elsom 1992 and Egger 1994a.

[30] LSJ, s.v. 'ἀπαντάω' def. I,3.

[31] In the visual repertoire of the Hellenistic and Roman world, beauty signified divinity and royalty; see Zeitlin 2003, 79.

respective parties to the trial. The Persian queen collects the varying opinions and oversees a vote 'by show of hands as if in the theater'.[32] Callirhoe remains hidden in her carriage, but the Persian women challenge her to be compared to—literally 'judged with' (συγκριθήτω, C 5,3,6)—Rhodogune, who is described as the 'Asian Callirhoe' (C 5,3,4-7).[33] Callirhoe's appearance in the beauty contest anticipates her appearance in the coming trial scene. She is a 'dazzling light' that stuns the spectators (C 5,3,8-11). Everyone immediately bows to her, and Rhodogune admits defeat. Later in the narrative of the trial scene, a simple Homeric allusion is enough to evoke the impact of her epiphany in the courtroom.[34]

A thirty-day religious festival (ἑορτήν, C 5,3,11) unexpectedly postpones the anticipated trial. It was common in the Greco-Roman world to suspend of public business, including the hearing of trials, during religious festivals. The *locus classicus* for this is the postponement of Socrates' execution until the return of the sacred embassy to Delos. Greek inscriptions also attest to laws forbidding the business of the law courts during festivals; the technical term was ἐκεχειρία.[35] In Rome, festivals were designated as *nefas*. The etymology of this term is the negated form of *fasti*, the days on which all words were permitted to be spoken (*fari*) by the praetors; on days that were *nefas*, the praetor was forbidden to utter the words that were necessary in order to effectuate a legal action.[36] The Roman *iustitium*, an ad hoc suspension of public business could be declared at any time by the senate or by a magistrate with *imperium*.[37]

During the thirty-day interval, both sides prepare the trial as if for 'the greatest war', (C 5,4,1). The trial highlights the class distinctions in Babylonian society. In contrast to Syracuse, where the people, the commander, and the magistrates work in harmony, the 'multitude of barbarians' (τὸ πλῆθος τῶν βαρβάρων) is divided into two factions. The satrapial faction (τὸ σατραπικόν) sides with Mithridates while the popular faction (τὸ δημοτικόν) supports Dionysius. The women, too, actively take sides over the issue of Callirhoe's reputation. The women who had vied with Callirhoe in the beauty contest—that is, the cosmopolitan elite of Babylon—envy her and wish her ill in the trial, whereas the 'masses' (πλῆθος,

---

32 C 5,3,30: χειροτονία δὲ ἦν ὡς ἐν θεάτρῳ. Cf. the interrogation of Theron in Syracuse, C 3,4,1, where women are present during the vote.

33 On Chariton's inspiration for the figure of Rhodogune, see Baslez 1992, 201.

34 C 5,5,9, cf. *Iliad* 3,146 and *Odyssey* 1,366. Reardon 1989, 82 n. 83.

35 Robert 1937, 177-179; Sokolowski 1955, 25-26, 93, 183.

36 Macrobius *Saturnalia* 1,16 and Varro *De Lingua Latina* 6,30, 53.

37 Bund 1964.

C 5,4,2) resent the elite and so cheer for the foreigner's exoneration.[38] The setting for the trial reflects its sensationalism:

> When the assigned day arrived, the king took his position. There is a special hall in the royal palace designated as a law court, outstanding for its size and splendor. There, in the middle, stood the king's throne; on each side were places for the king's friends, those leaders among leaders who held the rank and esteem. In a circle around the throne there stood officers, commanders, and the most honored of the king's freedmen—so that one could well say of that gathering, 'The gods, sitting at Zeus' side, held debate'. (C 5,4,5-6)

The description of the Babylonian courtroom is generic enough to have evoked for Chariton's readers the grandeur of a Roman palatial courtroom, an impressive venue for justice in the Roman world.[39] The opulence and rigid etiquette of the Persian court were proverbial in classical literature, and the visual representation of a king holding court can be seen in a variety of media (such as reliefs and coins) throughout antiquity.[40] The reference to the 'unusually big and beautiful room' may have resonated with the popular understanding of the working of Roman justice for which, beginning with Augustus, the palace became an important locus for the emperor's juridical functions. At a later period, particular buildings were reserved for the dispensing of justice.[41]

The hierarchy of the court is put on display. The king's throne is central, flanked by seats for his friends in order of their 'honors and virtue' (τοῖς ἀξιώμασι καὶ ταῖς ἀρεταῖς, C 5.4.5)—effectively a translation for *dignitas* and *virtus*. The use of the term 'friends' (τοῖς φίλοις, C 5.4.5) does not necessarily indicate a Roman model; their presence near the king was part of the generic image of the palatial courtroom. This detail is mentioned in the Hellenistic practice of kings consulting advisers usually referred to as φίλοι or it may be a translation of *amici principis*, a recognized element of the Roman imperial courts. Their hierarchical

---

[38] There seems to be no meaningful difference between Chariton's use of δῆμος and πλῆθος; see Kaimio 1995, 121-123.

[39] Karabélias 1990, 393 n.104, 394.

[40] Gabelmann 1984. A discussion of Achaemenid scenes of royal audiences may be found in Briant 2002, 204-211.

[41] Millar 1977, 20-22. Cassius Dio (76,11,1) refers to a Palatine building that Septimius Severus used as a courtroom, whose ceiling had been decorated with the constellations under which the emperor was born. Philostratus (*Life of Apollonius of Tyana* 1,25) describes a similar room with domed roof designed to look like the heavens in the men's quarters of the palace of Persian king in Babylon.

ordering suggests the formalization of this institution in the later Hellenistic period; for example, Arrian (*Anabasis* 7,11,8) describes a hierarchical arrangement of Alexander's court at Opis in three concentric circles.[42] The presence of bodyguards and officers suggests the *cohors praetoria*, though it was scarcely unusual for other ancient rulers to include military officials in Chariton's imagined courtroom in their entourages. The inclusion of freedmen (τῶν βασιλέως ἐξελευθέρων τὸ ἐντιμότατον, C 5.4.6) points more specifically to a Roman prototype: early emperors employed freedmen in the imperial administration, some of whom rose to positions of power and influence in the Julio-Claudian era. The public appearance of freedmen waned under Trajan, an emperor who fought against the Parthians.[43] By projecting the employment of hordes of freedman onto a hostile, barbarian empire, Chariton's depiction of the Persian court thus aligns with Flavian critics of the practice of employing imperial freedmen.

Though Chariton's depiction of the Persian court may resemble Roman realities, we cannot discount the possibility that certain features resonated with ideas about Persia. Chariton's knowledge of the Achaemenids hundreds of years before his time would likely have been mediated through book learning, but the existence of the Parthian kingdom on the eastern frontier of the Greco-Roman world could have just as easily have evoked more contemporary notions of the Persian king. Uncertainty about the precise date of this novel precludes our ability to associate features of Chariton's depiction of Persia with specific events in the ongoing conflicts in the east. In any case, it is difficult to separate the Persian or Parthian realities from the representations by ancient Greek and Latin writers, who frequently explained foreign institutions in terms familiar to their readers. For example, while the Achaemenid kings were surrounded by nobles, advisers, bodyguards, and other influential persons, there is little evidence for a formal cabinet (συνέδριον) of advisers.[44] The Parthians, however, may have incorporated Hellenistic institutions into their government. Strabo refers to the two councils from which the Parthian kings were appointed as συνέδρια. In the Roman era, Parthian kings adopted the Hellenistic practice of calling the king's advisers 'friends'

[42] Crook 1955, 21-30.

[43] Eventually, scandals eventually make their presence a liability for the emperor. The significance of freedmen in this particular scene in Chariton is also noted by Karabélias 1990, 393 n. 104. On freedmen in the Roman empire, see Millar 1977, 69-83.

[44] Greek authors relate that the hierarchy of the Persian king's φίλοι was displayed at royal banquets: officials include ὁμοτραπέζοι and σύσσιτοι (tablemates), συμπότοι (drinking companions), σύμβουλοι (advisers), συγγενοῖ (royal kinsmen), and σύνδειπνοι (invited guests); see Briant 2002, 307-315.

(φίλοι).[45] The depiction of the Persian court is informed by stereotypes; however, what is interesting here is that Chariton uses a Persian façade to dissect and indirectly critique Roman imperial dynamics.

The Trial, Part II

The contrast between the initial entrances of the contestants into the majestic courtroom must have tapped feelings of vulnerability that Greek provincials experienced when faced with the power of the Roman imperial administration. Chariton economically sketches the psychological and political dynamics of the Persian court in his description of the opening of the trial:

> The litigants are admitted in silence and fear. On that morning, Mithridates entered first, escorted by his friends and clansmen, he did not appear bright not shining at all, but looked pitiful, like a man under investigation. Dionysius followed afterwards; wearing a Milesian cloak in the Greek style and clutching the letters in his hand. (C 5,4,7)

Mithridates, obviously at home in this milieu, parades his connections. In contrast, Dionysius is patently Greek and so stands alone: in an ironic twist that may have enhanced the Greek reader's sense of alienation, it is Dionysius' appearance that merits comment: his 'Milesian' clothing encodes him as Greco-Oriental.[46] As the foreigner in this venue, Dionysius is without political allies, and therefore relies upon the letters of Pharnaces and the king's reply. His deployment of these documents resembles the way a subject of the Roman Empire might use a *libellus*, a petition addressed to the emperor. Examples of *libelli* that survive in papyri show that they were considered precious documents: the epigraphical and papyrological evidence shows that they were copied and kept with private papers.[47] Dionysius' letters are important documents to counterbalance Mithridates' wealth and personal connections.

---

[45] Strabo *Geography* 11,9,3: τοσοῦτον εἰπόντες μόνον, ὅτι τῶν Παρθυαίων συνέδριόν φησιν εἶναι Ποσειδώνιος διττόν, τὸ μὲν συγγενῶν, τὸ δὲ σοφῶν καὶ μάγων, ἐξ ὧν ἀμποῖν τοὺς βασιλεῖς καθίστασθαι. On the difficulties of using Greek and Latin sources to reconstruct the history of Persian and Parthian institutions, see Frye 1983, 108-109, 220; Briant 2002, 5-9.

[46] A scholion on Aristophanes *Frogs* 542 notes that Miletus was known for its intricate and soft textiles; cf. Theocritus *Idyllion* 15,125–26. A similar type of cloak is also worn by Callirhoe on her wedding to Dionysius (C. 3,2,16).

[47] Millar 1977, 245-246.

The trial begins with the public reading of the petition; the king's response is modeled on the Roman practice of presenting *libelli* at the emperor's *salutationes.*[48] Such moments presented the emperor the opportunity to display his authority and to have it acknowledged by his courtiers. Accordingly, the king orders the letter and his response to be read aloud so that his 'fellow judges' (συνδικάζοντες, C. 5,4,8) may learn the background to the dispute. Under the Roman Empire, it was customary in criminal cases for the emperor to be advised not by a council of advisers but by fellow-judges.[49] Chariton's fictional autocrat, like the Roman emperor, pretends that he is not the sole judge in this case. The listeners applaud the king's prudence and sense of justice (σωφροσύνην καὶ δικαιοσύνην, C 5,4,8). In this simple detail, Chariton sketches the dynamics of a court where those entrusted with helping the king come to a verdict are in fact flatterers rather than judges.

All eyes then turn to Dionysius, the anticipated first speaker, but Mithridates preempts him with a point of order (C 5,4,9). He claims that everyone involved in the trial must be present—particularly 'the woman who is at the center of this trial' (C 5,4,9). The adultery template frames the tension: Mithridates assumes the function of Hephaestus by exposing the wife (Aphrodite/Callirhoe) to be put on display for the judge. As the patron of Chaereas, Mithridates secretly prepares to turn the tables on his accuser. Dionysius responds in a lawyerly fashion (δικανικῶς, C 5,4,11) and construes Mithridates' request as proof of his dishonorable intention 'to parade another man's wife in front of a mob without his consent' (C 5,4,10). Dionysius insists that Callirhoe is neither making an accusation nor being accused (οὔτε ἐγκαλοῦσαν οὔτε ἐγκαλουμένην αὐτήν, C 5,4,10); in an emphatically contrafactual μέν-δέ clause he grants that if she had in fact been seduced, she would have been required to appear in court to account for her deeds, an ostensible allusion to the *lex Julia de adulteriis*. Dionysius refuses to use her as either a witness or advocate, precisely the roles which Mithridates expects Chaereas to play on his behalf.[50] But his plea is rejected because everyone wants to see Callirhoe. The king is 'embarrassed' to order her appearance (C 5,4,12), so his advisers point out that his own letter, the rescript to Dionysius' petition (C 4,6,8), provides the justification for requiring her to appear. Chariton sketches an image of judicial decision-making in a world empire. The ruler forgets what he wrote in his letters, and leaves it to his advisers to find legal justification for doing what the audience expects of him.

---

[48] Millar 1977, 241.

[49] Cassius Dio 76,17; Honoré 1994, 9-10.

[50] C 5,4,10: οὔτε μάρτυρι χρῶμαι τῇ γυναικὶ οὔτε συνηγόρῳ. Cf. C 4,7,4: κἂν [ἐν] τῇ κρίσει Χαιρέαν ἕξω μετ᾽ ἐμαυτοῦ καὶ Πολύχαρμον οὐ συνηγόρους μόνον, ἀλλὰ καὶ μάρτυρας.

Dionysius requests a postponement until the next day so that he can prepare Callirhoe, who is oblivious to the reason why they are in Babylon. The setting shifts to a private conversation between husband and wife. When Dionysius tells her that she must appear in court, Callirhoe laments the 'unjust slander' of adultery (διαβαλεῖν ἀδίκως, C 5,5,2; cf. τὴν ἄδικον διαβολήν, C 1,3,6). A woman implicated in adultery in a court of law would have been particularly vulnerable, especially after Augustus' legislation made it a crime for a husband not to divorce an adulterous wife. Callirhoe's mere appearance in a public courtroom is tantamount to an accusation against her. She says, 'The daughter of Hermocrates is being judged, but without her father as her advocate' (C 5,5,4). Her wish seems to cohere with a custom among the Roman elite for married daughters to remain under the authority of her own *paterfamilias*.[51] Throughout the novel, it is clear that Callirhoe is an extension of Hermocrates; her expectation reveals a closer identification with her father than with her current husband.

The Speeches

When the trial resumes the next day, a crowd gathers outside the palace, a familiar sight in the Roman forum, especially when the trial was a *cause célèbre,* as Callirhoe's is clearly meant to be.[52] The speeches of Dionysius and Mithridates are rhetorical showpieces.[53] Consistent with his characterization as a serious and educated man (φρόνιμος ἀνὴρ καὶ πεπαιδευμένος, C 5,5,1), Dionysius' speech is clearly organized into classical rhetorical divisions: proem (C 5,6,1-5), narration (C 5,6,5-8), proofs (C 5,6,9-10), and short epilogue (C 5,6,10). In a *captatio benevolentiae,* he appeals to the king as guardian of the law and of marriage. He opens by thanking the king for his prudence (σωφροσύνην, C 5,6,1) and praising his sense of justice (δικαιοσύνη, 5,6,4), protection of marriage (γάμοις) and the laws (νόμοις). Next, he restates the charge in Pharnaces' cover letter; namely that the satrap has exploited his office to plot against a private man. He characterizes Mithiridates' behavior as hubris (ὕβρις, C 4,6,4, 5,6,1), insolence (ἀσελγεία, C 5,6,1, 5,6,5), and tyranny (τυραννικός, C 5,6,6).[54] Dionysius contrasts the abundant resources that Mithridates marshals for this trial with his own vulnerability

[51] Hallett 1984, 62-149.

[52] Millar 1977, 21; Bablitz 2007, 34-39.

[53] A thorough rhetorical analysis of the speeches is to be found in Doulamis 2011.

[54] Tyranny is not necessarily linked with the caricature of the barbarian; see Guez 2009, 25-26.

as a foreigner. Because the satrap has the king's trust, he deserves a greater punishment (C 5,6,2), otherwise it will only encourage others to treat the king's authority with contempt (C 5,6,5). This line of argument speaks to the king's interest in displaying mercy (*clementia*, φιλανθρωπία) and reserving his prerogative to punish for the most serious offenses. Mithridates' trial, though motivated by private concerns, becomes a case of treason.[55]

At the crux of the case is the authenticity of the intercepted letter. Dionysius clearly and succinctly (σαφής καὶ σύντομος, C 5,6,5) recapitulates what the reader already knows and zeroes in on the letter allegedly written by Callirhoe's dead husband, calling it a 'most persuasive artifice' (τέχνην πιθανωτάτην) to seduce her. Though Dionysius' attack conforms to the rules of rhetoric, it rests upon a false premise. He follows the Aristotlean recommendation to refute his opponent before he has a chance to speak.[56] The syllogistic demonstration is 'unassailable' (ἀποδείξεις ἄφυκτοι, C 5,6,9): either Chaereas is alive or dead. If he is alive, the letters are authentic and Mithridates is innocent; if dead, the letters are forgeries and Mithridates is guilty. Dionysius assumes that Chaereas is dead: therefore, it follows logically that Mithridates must necessarily be a seducer. Dionysius then brings out the letter as evidence, the type of proof that Aristotle classified as ἄτεχνος, external to the art of rhetoric and therefore self-evident to a degree (*Rhetoric* 1375a). Citing the line, 'I, Chaereas, am alive', Dionysius points out that Mithridates attended Chaereas' funeral (C 5,6,10), and challenges Mithridates to prove that the letter is not a forgery. If he can do it, he is not only an adulterer but a necromancer as well.[57] His epilogue magnifies the absurdity of the situation: 'Consider, King, how shameless an adulterer he is that he pretends to be a dead man' (C 5,6,10).

The speech hits the mark: the listeners are indignant and the king's angry glare amplifies the crowd's response and brings to life the notion that the Persian king, like the Roman emperor, serves as the champion of his subjects in opposition to the aristocrats who serve as his imperial administrators. We are told that 'Dionysius almost carried the vote'. The term ψῆφος (C 5,6,11) normally signified a vote by a popular assembly; the same term was used to describe the jury's verdict in the city of Syracuse.[58] Yet this seems to contradict the premise that the king alone

---

[55] Augustus, generally known for his clemency, imposed punishments for 'serious crimes in which the perpetrators had broken laws of the state or threatened the policies or person of the princeps'; see Dowling 2006, 69-71.

[56] Aristotle *Rhetoric* 1418b: 'The opening speaker should [usually] state his own premises first, then should meet those [expected] of his opponent by disproving and tearing them to pieces before he can make them' (trans. Kennedy).

[57] On the characterization of Mithridates as a magus, see Alvares 2000.

[58] Cf. C 1,6,1; 3,4,15. Mason 1974, 100.

has the authority to decide the case.[59] It is possible that ψῆφος is nothing more than a synonym for verdict. Yet, the use of the term in the Persian trial scene seems odd, until it becomes clear that the crowd of spectators functions as a popular assembly. The transference of the ψῆφος to a monarchical context in effect projects the dynamics of the polis, including its division into democratic and oligarchic factions, onto the glamorous and exotic court of Persia.

Mithridates' speech illustrates how a savvy insider can manipulate arcane legal procedures and run circles around an earnest plaintiff. Gamesmanship overtakes the simple presentation of rival accounts of events. The reader knows that Dionysius' challenge to Mithridates to prove that Chaereas wrote the letter will backfire.[60] Because the reader knows Chaereas is alive, all the arguments are purely theatrical. Mithridates' defense begins with a short proem (C 5,7,1). The main part of the speech is made up of a series of refutations of specific charges made by Dionysius (C 5,7,2-6). These are interrupted by Mithridates' acceptance of the challenge to prove that Chaereas is alive (C 5,7,7). Finally, his epilogue takes the form of an elaborate prayer to the gods (C 5,7,10).

Dionysius' speech gives little space to the narration of the facts, which Aristotle considered a waste of time because the defendant should concentrate on 'whether something happened or whether it was harmful or unjust or unimportant' (*Rhetoric* 1417a). This, however, is precisely where Mithridates concentrates his arguments.

Beginning with topoi standard to defense speeches, Mithridates appeals to the king's justice and mercy (δίκαιος καὶ εἶ καὶ φιλάνθρωπος, C 5,7,1). Calling the accusations slander, he inverts the stereotypical Greek rhetorical attack on barbarians, as well as the Roman prejudice against Greeks, by characterizing his opponent as a 'tricky Greek contriving false slurs against me'.[61] The Persian satrap systematically dismantles Dionysius' attacks. His first approach involves intent, which requires the defendants to prove that he did not have the will to commit the crime of which he is accused. As in the defense of Chaereas by Hermocrates (trial

---

59 The speakers address the judge in the second person singular. See: ἐτίμησας, περιεῖδες, ἐκάλεσας, ἐκδικήσῃς (C 5,6,1); σὺ πᾶσι τηρεῖς (C 5,6,4); λέγε, λόγισαι (C 5,6,10).

60 A motif that we will see later in the second trial in Achilles Tatius' novel, where another overzealous cuckold brings the crimes of the bedroom to the attention of the court; see trial 6, below.

61 C 5,7,1: ἄνθρωπος Ἕλλην, πανούργως συνθεὶς κατ' ἐμοῦ ψευδεῖς διαβολάς. Cicero neatly expresses Roman derision for Greeks, 'For a long time now, a dispute over a word gets those little Greeks (*Graeculos*) in a twist, men who are more avid for argument than for truth' (Cicero *De Oratore* 1,47). For an analysis of Cicero's exploitation of Roman prejudice against provincials as a rhetorical strategy in one particular speech, *Pro L. Flacco*, see May 1988, 81-84.

1), character is the main issue here.[62] Responding to the accusations of insolence and lechery (ὕβρις and ἀσέλγεια, C 5,6,1), Mithridates asserts that he has lived his life temperately (σωφρόνως, C 5,7,20). He says that even if he had been as insolent and incorrigible as Dionysius alleges, being entrusted with office would have made him a better person. Mithridates asks, 'Who would be so foolish as to choose to destroy the benefits of office for the sake of one shameful pleasure?'[63]

In the next section, Mithridates flaunts his superior knowledge of the law by making a motion for a demurrer (παραγραφή, C 5,7,3) a special plea to shut down a groundless suit.[64] His claim that even if he were guilty he could have the case dismissed is clearly a sophistic move to parade his home-court advantage. The use of this strategy was common in the Attic orations. In Roman civil law, this kind of procedural objection would have been introduced during the *in iure* phase of proceedings when the parties appeared before the praetor, who defined the issue and framed the appropriate formula for the procedure before a judge (*apud iudicem*).[65] If successful, it immediately put the accuser on the defensive, thereby shifting the grounds for dispute.[66] In the declamations the move is purely rhetorical, as D. A. Russell observes, 'This plea is clearly often advanced when there can hardly be more than a distant hope of its succeeding, and the speaker has other arguments ready and proceeds to them without much delay'.[67] Mithridates' speech takes a page from the declamations; presumably, the Roman civil trial left a narrower scope for rhetorical grandstanding.

This legalistic ploy brings the distinction between the types of Roman marriage to the foreground. Mithridates turns to Dionysius' emphasis on documentary evidence against him by demanding to scrutinize the accusation's evidence, a move the rhetorical treatises called the ἐλεγχων ἀπαίτησις.[68] Picking up on Dionysius' allusion to Callirhoe's first marriage, Mithridates questions the validity of Dionysius' marriage and claims that 'the law of adultery' (ὁ δὲ τῆς μοιχείας νόμος, C 5,7,3) does not apply to slaves. It is noteworthy that Chariton assumes a 'law of adultery' in his imagined world, as there was in the lived reality of Augustan Rome. Mithridates challenges Dionysius to read aloud the certificate of emancipation (τὸ γραμμάτιον τῆς ἀπελευθερώσεως, C 5,7,4), in order to prove that he freed Callirhoe before marrying her.

---

[62] Russell 1983, 46.

[63] An echo of Creon's defense Oedipus' accusation of treason in Sophocles, *Oedipus Tyrannus* 592-602.

[64] Harrison 1971, 100-124.

[65] Nicholas 1962, 23-25; Crook 1967a, 75-77.

[66] MacDowell 1978, 215.

[67] Russell 1983, 60.

[68] Russell 1983, 45, 138.

The unregistered sale of Callirhoe, described in the second book, now comes back to haunt Dionysius. At that time, he was suspicious when his estate manager purchased a beautiful slave; he immediately questioned the validity of the sale because 'it is impossible for a body to be beautiful which is not free by nature' (C 2,1,5); nevertheless, he swore to marry her according to the Greek laws (C 3,2,8). The attack upon Dionysius' marriage presumes a distinctly Roman, rather than Greek, legal context. In both ancient Greek and Roman law, marriage could only be contracted between two free persons, but the question of who could rightfully obtain justice against an adulterer differed. In Athens, the law against adultery applied only to wives, female relatives, and concubines kept for the purpose of begetting free children.[69] The Augustan laws on marriage and adultery defined adultery as applicable only to certain types of legitimate marriages; the law against *stuprum*, a more generic term for illicit sexual relations, applied to everyone else.[70] In Rome there existed a quasi marriage, called *contubernium*, between two unfree persons or between a free person and a slave.[71] This type of marriage was not subject to the *lex Iulia* against adultery.[72]

In a rhetorical move known as ἀντέγκλημα, 'counter-charge', Mithridates alleges that if Dionysius insists that Callirhoe was free when he bought her then he is a slave-dealer (ἀνδραποδιστής), not a husband (ἀνήρ, C 5,7,4). He undermines Dionysius by repeatedly mentioning the vocabulary of sale (τὴν πρᾶσιν, τὴν τιμήν) even while granting that the marriage is legitimate; in any case, he denies injuring Dionysius 'either as a husband (ἄνδρα) or as a master (κύριον, C 5,7,5)', a masterly use of litotes that emphasizes the existential ambiguity of the marriage's legal status.

Mithridates employs a rhetorical tactic known as the ἀντίληψις or 'counter-hold'.[73] He asserts that even if Dionysius' claim is true, intent to commit adultery is not a crime. If the marriage were legal and he actually attempted to seduce Callirhoe, there would still be no case because what he has done is not forbidden by the law. During the pre-trial negotiation over Callirhoe's appearance in court, Dionysius denied that she was in fact an adulteress (C 5,4,11). Seizing upon this in the trial, Mithridates points out that the charge is for attempted adultery (μέλλουσαν μοιχείαν, C 5,7,5), whereas the laws exact punishment for actual deeds (τὰς τιμωρίας οἱ νόμοι τῶν ἔργων λαμβάνουσι, C 5,7,6). Although it is hard

[69] Demosthenes 23,53.
[70] Treggiari 1991, 263.
[71] Treggiari 1981.
[72] *Digest* 48,5,6.
[73] Russell 1983, 48, 136.

to find explicit references to the Augustan laws on adultery and marriage, the legalistic wrangling over the definition of adultery seems inspired by the complexities and ambiguities that the Augustan legislation must have precipitated.

In conclusion, Mithridates refutes the alleged inauthenticity of the letter upon which Dionysius has staked his victory. We are at the endgame and it becomes clear that Dionysius' rhetorical plea for justice is no match for Mithridates' prowess with procedural technicalities. He imagines what Dionysius might say to him, a technique known as ἠθοποιία.[74] If Mithridates vouches that the handwriting is not his but Chaereas', then it logically follows that Chaereas should be charged with adultery, despite the presumption that he is dead. We know from the earlier narrative that Mithridates is telling the truth, so when he warns Dionysius to drop the charge, he is clearly setting him up for his peripeteia. By invoking the procedure of πρόκλησις, Mithdridates challenges Dionysius to produce evidence in court, typically in the form of testimony by a slave under torture or by a free person under oath. In the Attic orations, the πρόκλησις is used to insinuate that one's opponents were hiding their guilt if they refused the challenge. The nature of this procedure in ancient Athens is the subject of much scholarly discussion. In the four instances in which it occurs in the Attic orations, the speaker typically asserts that his adversary's challenge is inferior to his own, or that the adversary uses it purely as a delaying tactic. In effect, the tactic worked as a dare to force one's opponent to concede an argument and bring an inconclusive trial to swift close.[75] Though Dionysius gambles that Mithridates will balk, the satrap instead testifies (μαρτύρομαι, C 5,7,7) as a 'friend' and urges Dionysius to drop his case because the king will see that Dionysius is the adulterer, not him.

Mithridates gives Dionysius an opportunity to drop the charge. Mutual recriminations ensue. Mithridates makes a pious show and calls on the 'royal, heavenly, and underworldly gods' to help him, a 'good, justly-praying and generously-sacrificing man,' a type of prayer that was commonly invoked by defendants at the end of orations.[76] Then, in a moment that must have been a common fantasy for many real litigants in courtrooms throughout the empire, the defendant's prayer appears to be answered by the gods instantaneously as the supposedly dead Chaereas (C 5,8,1) is revealed and the courtroom becomes a stage:

> τίς ἂν φράσῃ κατ' ἀξίαν ἐκεῖνο τὸ σχῆμα τοῦ δικαστηρίου; ποῖος ποιητὴς ἐπὶ σκηνῆς παράδοξον μῦθον οὕτως εἰσήγαγεν; ἔδοξας ἂν ἐν θεάτρῳ παρεῖναι

[74] Russell 1983, 11-12.

[75] Lysias 4,15-17, Demosthenes 2,38, 53,22-5, and 54,28) See Headlam 1893, 1894; Harrison 1971, 153; Thür 1977, 233-286; Carey 1988; Gagarin 1996, 9.

[76] C 5,7,10; cf. Demosthenes 18,324.

μυρίων παθῶν πλήρει· πάντα ἦν ὁμοῦ, δάκρυα, χαρά, θάμβος, ἔλεος, ἀπιστία, εὐχαι.

Who could accurately describe that tableau in the courtroom? What kind of playwright ever stages such an incredible story? You would have thought that you were in a theater full of a thousand emotions: everything happening all at once: tears, joy, wonder, pity, incredulity, and prayers (C 5,8,2).

The trial between Mithridates and Dionysius turns into a battle between erotic rivals.[77] Callirhoe's bigamy is the kind of insoluble dilemma loved by the declamations, but sexier than the mock trials of fathers and sons. A rapidfire verbal exchange strips away the rhetorical fluff and distills the grounds on which Callirhoe's two husbands base their claims to Callirhoe. One can imagine in the stichomythic style the kind of ripostes a clerk such as Chariton might have heard in court proceedings.[78] There is a structure to the accusations, as shown in Table 2.

Table 2. The Stichomythic Exchange between Callirhoe's Two Husbands

CHAEREAS	DIONYSIUS
I am her first husband.	I am her savior.
I did not divorce her.	You killed her.
Show me the divorce papers.	Look at her tomb.
Her father gave her to me.	She gave herself to me.
You are unworthy.	You were Mithridates' captive.
You keep another man's wife.	You killed your own wife.
You are an adulterer.	You are a murderer.

The exchange distills the essence of the dispute. Chaereas and Dionysius trade accusations over the archetypal crime of the Greek novel: adultery. It is, in effect, an outline for a pair of speeches for a second trial.

The 'brilliance' (λαμπρῶς, C 5,8,6) of Mithiridates' defense renders the verdict a foregone conclusion. For Dionysius, however, the reversal is complete: the accuser in this adultery trial now finds himself in the position of defendant. There is no easy solution to the unexpected revelation of Callirhoe's first husband, so

[77] They are ready for war, C 5,8,4: πρόχειρος πᾶσι τοῖς ἀντερασταῖς πόλεμος. They battle each other, C 5,8,6: πρὸς ἀλλήλους μαχόμενοι.

[78] Hägg 1971, 92 n. 91.

the king dismisses the court and consults his advisers about the necessity of a second hearing concerning Callirhoe. Some of the king's friends assure him that he was right to judge the case because Mithridates was his satrap, but that now that the litigants are private individuals, the dispute belongs in a different venue. The majority of the council advises the king to decide the case on the basis of Hermocrates' reputation for having done a great favor to the king by defeating Athens in the Peloponnesian War. When the king reconvenes the court, he acquits Mithridates and sends him laden with gifts back to his satrapy (C 5,8,8). The bestowal of gifts by the Persian king was associated with the 'politics of gift-giving'.[79] Likewise, the Roman emperor was expected to display *liberalitas* by giving gifts to his *amici* and other members of his government.[80] In Mithridates' case, the gifts function as a form of restitution to the satrap, a gesture restoring him to his previous social status. Mithridates bows and leaves, while the others are left speechless. Dionysius and Chaereas, on the other hand, are told to present formal claims to Callirhoe. The king grants them a five-day extension (διάστημα, C 5,8,9) to prepare their cases.

[79] Briant 2002, 307-323.
[80] Millar 1977, 135-139.

Trial 4.
Trial by Battle: Bigamy
Dionysius v. Chaereas (Chariton, *Callirhoe* 5,10-6,2)

The Story

Once Callirhoe's ambiguous marital status has been exposed, Callirhoe is taken into the custody of the royal harem. The king gives Chaereas and Dionysius five days to prepare their cases. On the day before the trial is set to begin, the king himself is now in love with Callirhoe and stalls for time by suspending all business and lawsuits for a thirty-day festival. In the interval, a rebellion erupts in Egypt and the lawsuit is never brought to trial. The dispute between Dionysius and Chaereas escalates to the battlefield. As Babylon prepares for war, Chaereas, the 'only free man in the city', proclaims, 'I shall get judgment against this judge from the war!' He allies with the Egyptians while Dionysius fights for the king. Eventually the king bestows Callirhoe upon Dionysius as a reward for killing the Egyptian king; however, by a fortuitous turn of events Chaereas captures the Persian king's harem, among whom is Callirhoe. Chaereas and Callirhoe are reunited on Cyprus and return home to Syracuse together.

Analysis

The trial of Mithridates exposed the ambiguity of Callirhoe's marital status, yet there is no indication that she will be subjected to a formal judicial process. Her decision to pass off Chaereas' child as Dionysius' might seem to be an actionable injury of some sort, but in fact the morality of her choice is consistent with the ideal of σωφροσύνη, 'moral self-restraint', from which she never wavers throughout the narrative. In effect, her virtue places her beyond the reach of the law.[1]

[1] Kanavou 2015, 12: 'It can be argued that Kallirhoe practices self-restraint by controlling her motherly instinct in order to take a morally optimal decision for all parties involved (considering also, in a sensible manner, the benefits for her child)'.

Technically, she is simultaneously married to two men, yet the narrative never suggests that she is liable for breaking any law. The fact of bigamy is relevant not to Callirhoe, but to the dispute between two men who have equal claim to be her lawful husband. Accordingly, the judicial procedure in this case is not a trial for adultery or for sexual impropriety (*stuprum*), but an arbitration (διαδικασία, C 5,8,7). This procedure is mentioned by Demosthenes and Plutarch, and is used in the sense of a hearing to evaluate competing claims, usually to the ownership of property—in this case, Callirhoe.[2]

Yet the anticipated hearing never takes place. The legal dispute spills beyond the boundaries of the palace and the entire city of Babylon again becomes a courtroom (τις ὅλην Βαβυλῶνα εἶναι δικαστήριον, C 6,1,5). Formal speeches are dispensed with; instead, Chaereas' and Dionysius' main arguments are ventriloquized through the divided opinions of the Babylonian populace. The men are divided into factions as they were in the first trial (C 5,4). The strengths and weaknesses of both litigants are enumerated. The men on Chaereas' side argue that he was Callirhoe's first husband, she was a virgin when she married him, and they loved each other; her father gave her to him and her fatherland buried her. They also note that Chaereas did not abandon her; Dionysius neither won her nor married her because he bought her from pirates and one cannot buy a freeborn woman from pirates. Dionysius' supporters argue that he rescued Callirhoe from pirates, paid a talent to save her life, and that he married her; whereas Chaereas married her but killed her. It goes unmentioned that Callirhoe continues to be alive. 'Killed' in this instance can only be the equivalent of 'tried to kill'; thus Chariton echoes the central issue or intentionality in Chaereas' trial at the beginning of the novel (trial 1). In contrast to Mithridates' distinction between attempted and actual seduction, here actual murder is not separated from attempted murder.[3] Dionysius' supporters introduce a critical detail that was extraneous to the previous trial: Callirhoe is the mother of his child (C 6,1,3).

The women of Babylon also make speeches 'as if Callirhoe were there'. These arguments are new additions to the course of the conflict. Throughout the earlier trial, Callirhoe functioned as a passive object over which men contended. The women give her advice and assure her that she has the power to select a husband for herself and that her judgment will be as authoritative as the king's. Some tell her to choose the man who first loved her and is a fellow-citizen, while the others advise her to choose her benefactor and savior. The former remind her that she will see her father again; the latter tell her to honor the father of her child. If she

[2] Harrison 1971, 79.

[3] A similar logical impossibility may be found in AT 8,8,4 where Clitophon is punished for Leucippe's murder, even after it is discovered that she is alive; see trial 8 below.

does not choose Chaereas, she will live as a stranger in exile; if she does not choose Dionysius, she may end up back in the tomb. In effect, the men's arguments are projected onto a distinctly feminine dilemma which lays bare a profound schism in her identities as a daughter, wife, and mother: she is torn between her own birthplace and her son's birthplace.

Chariton describes the psychological states of each of the participants through individual conversations with confidants: Callirhoe and the Persian queen (C 5,9,1-7), Dionysius and his child (C 5,9,8-10,6), and Chaereas and Polycharmus (C 5,9,6-10). These speeches encapsulate the various parties' strategies for the upcoming trial. In the meantime, however, the king has fallen in love with Callirhoe. Before the trial, the king, alone in his bedroom, examines himself. Just as the language of sport and war invade the courtroom, the language of justice describes the inner deliberations of the judge. Chariton dramatizes the internal reflections of an absolute ruler and focuses on his process of making judgment. He imagines that 'Eros himself' is his adviser (σύμβουλός, C 6,1,9). Alone in his bedroom, he interrogates himself, 'Who are you? Callirhoe's lover or her judge?' (τίς εἶ; Καλλιρόης ἐραστὴς ἢ δικαστής, C 6,1,10). He rationalizes his own claim over Callirhoe by referring to her as a 'gift from the god'. He rejects having to 'referee' (βραβεύω, C 6,1,11) the marriages of his slaves. He comes back to his senses, and reminds himself of his responsibility to judge the case. He then decides to prolong the trial indefinitely with a procedural device, a power available even to an 'ordinary judge' (ἰδιώτῃ δικαστῇ, C 6,1,12): namely, to declare a thirty-day suspension of all business and lawsuits.

The opening of the anticipated second trial shifts from the judicial formality of the first trial, with the elaborate seating of the members of the king's court, to a more overtly spectacular atmosphere, a continuation of Chariton's escalation of the grandeur of each successive trial scene. As in the second trial in Syracuse, women are active audience members in the second trial in Babylon. The attendees come to see a fight, as if in an arena. Chariton compares the arrival of the contenders with the procession of athletes' entourages at the Olympic games (C 6,2,1). The audience is again divided along class lines; but this time, Dionysius, the former favorite of the people, wins the support of the aristocratic faction (τὸ μὲν δοκιμώτατον Περσῶν πλῆθος, C 6,2,1) and Chaereas wins the support of the popular faction (ὁ δὲ δῆμος Χαίρεας). The audience behaves as a crowd at a sporting event. The sides cheer on the respective champions.[4] When the king arrives, he declares yet another month of sacrifices, thus bringing a symmetry to the

[4] C 6,2,2: συνευχαὶ δὲ καὶ ἐπιβοήσεις μυρίαι τῶν σπευδόντων ἑκατέροις, ἐπευφημούντων 'συ κρείττων, σὺ νικᾷς. See Colin 1965b, 112ff. The verb ἐπιβοᾶν is used when the army elects Chaereas as their leader (C 7,3,10); ἐξεβοᾶν, is used when Syracusan assembly asks

Babylonian trial sequence. The spectacle of the people streaming into the city wearing garlands, singing, and banqueting replaces the spectacle of the games, as the scene shifts immediately to the festive sacrifices to Eros and Aphrodite (C 6,1,4). This is characteristic of Chariton's depiction of the courtroom scene: the trial is supplanted by another ritual. Just as the trial of Chaereas in Syracuse ended in the funeral of Callirhoe, here a religious festival eclipses the expected arbitration between Callirhoe's two husbands.

The experience of litigants waiting for a hearing is not dissimilar to what happened in the Roman Empire. Roman governors of larger provinces traveled to remote communities in a province. This circuit, known as the *conventus*, could be irregular; 'a judicial session could last for three days as well as for three months, and could concern one district or six'.[5] The governor's visit was often timed to coincide with festivals where large crowds usually gathered. Chariton describes such a scene earlier in the novel, when he mentions that Dionysius hosted the Persian satraps at his palatial estate (C 4,1,7). In Babylon, however, Dionysius is the guest rather than the host. He cannot get an immediate appointment with the king as he did with Pharnaces (C 4,6,1). The series of embassies sent by the Greek and Jewish communities to the court of Caligula suggests that litigants could expect to wait in the capital for months before a hearing. The embassies had waited so long in Rome that their cases were left unresolved when the emperor was assassinated; the embassies subsequently had to present their cases again, this time to Claudius.[6]

Dionysius is the first to criticize the Persian legal system he once trusted. He rails against the king for shamelessly delaying the trial while keeping custody of another man's wife (C 6,2,8). The trial itself has compromised Dionysius' position, as new erotic rivals enter the scene: Chaereas is his legal opponent (ἀντίδικον, C 6,2,7) and the king is his erotic rival (ἀντεραστήν). He regrets bringing the case to court and sees himself as embattled from all sides. Chaereas, on the other hand, responds to the limbo in which he finds himself by wishing for his own death. As he did in the first trial in Syracuse, he launches into a lament over his loss of Callirhoe. His grief is of Achillean proportions: just as he stayed up all night torturing the maids, now he refuses to eat. When his friend Polycharmus attempts to intervene, he calls him his 'worst enemy' (πολεμιώτατος, 6,2,8) for saving him from crucifixion. He blames his situation on an evil spirit that tyrannizes him by forcing him to prove he is Callirhoe's husband.

Chaereas to tell his story (C 8,8,2); ἀναβοᾶν is used when the assembly volunteers to help Hermocrates (C 4,3,17).

[5] Fournier 2010, 57.

[6] Harker 2008, 9-24.

In the meantime, the king's growing infatuation with Callirhoe threatens to compromise his authority as the judge. In a private discussion with his chief eunuch, he weighs his options. The character of the Persian king is split: the eunuch personifies the argument for tyranny while the king articulates the argument for kingship, which reflects his attempt to govern himself so as to affirm his authority to govern others.[7] The eunuch, however, undermines this effort. He flatters the king and tells him what he thinks he wants to hear. The king, however, loses his moral bearing. When his chief eunuch suggests that he seduce Callirhoe, the king insists that he must adhere to 'the laws I myself have established and the justice that I practice in all matters' (C 6,3,7). The eunuch suggests that the king distract himself by going on a hunt; however the king is smitten by the vision of Callirhoe as Artemis. Finally, the eunuch offers a sophistic rationalization for the king to do what he wants:

> 'Master', he said, 'you have forgotten the circumstances. For Callirhoe has no husband, and the trial about to whom it is fitting for her to be married remains open. Therefore, keep in mind that you are in love with a widow. So, do not fear the laws, since they were established to protect marriage, and do not fear adultery because it is necessary in the first place that there be a husband who has been harmed before there can be an adulterer who is harming him'. (C 6,4,7)

This ingenious solution hinges on the redefinition of Callirhoe's marital, and hence legal, status. The eunuch characterizes her as a 'widow' (χήρα), though in fact her position is completely the reverse: it is not that she has no husband, but that she has too many husbands. Until the king decides the second trial, Callirhoe is technically without a husband. A woman who once had a husband but is currently unmarried can only be a widow, and therefore not subject to the law against adultery. Thus the eunuch cleverly bends the wording of the law to gratify the king's desire.

The Persian king's impotence as a judge undermines his ability to rule, and so his empire begins to disintegrate when a rebellion erupts in Egypt before the trial begins. Dionysius is recruited to serve the king in the war. When Chaereas learns that the king has awarded Callirhoe to Dionysius, he joins the rebellion, despairing that the case can be settled fairly in this context. The preparations for war eclipse the preparations for the trial (C 6,8-9); the trial and the war are of equal gravity. This shift from courtroom to battlefield is expressed through the transposition of the language of war and the language of the law: the law recedes

[7] Guez 2009, 31-32.

into the realm of metaphor, and the rivalry between Callirhoe's two husbands materializes as a war in which they fight on opposite sides.

Left behind as Babylon prepares for war, Chaereas proclaims, 'I am not the king's slave but the only free man in Babylon' (C 7,1,1).[8] In the most overt criticism of judicial authority in the entire novel, he sarcastically calls the king a 'noble judge' (ὦ καλοῦ δικαστοῦ, C 7,1,5). While Chaereas played by the rules and prepared his case for court, Dionysius won without saying a word (νενίκηκε σιγῶν, C 7,1,5). Chaereas threatens to slit his own throat on the palace steps as a gesture to show the Persians and Medes how their king renders verdicts, but Polycharmus redirects him toward heroic revenge in battle. Chaereas declares: 'I shall get judgment against this judge from the war!' (δίκας ἐν τῷ πολέμῳ λήψομαι παρὰ δικαστοῦ, C 7,1,11).

The trial literally becomes a battle, with Callirhoe as the trophy. The judgment is finally rendered after Dionysius kills the Egyptian king. The king awards him Callirhoe, 'his prize of valor' (τὸ κάλλιστον ἆθλον τῆς ἀριστείας, C 7,5,15), and proclaims, 'War has decided the case' (κέκρικε τὴν δίκην ὁ πόλεμος). In fact, war does decide the lawsuit, but not in the way the king declares. Chaereas also proves himself in battle by leading the Egyptian navy to victory. After he captures the king's harem (which includes Callirhoe), he turns the king's ruling against him:

> Though you were going to decide the case, I have won according to the fairest judge. For this is war, the best judge between the stronger and the weaker. (C 8,4,2)

The decision to resolve the legal dilemma through war shifts the arena for the demonstration of masculinity from the courtroom to the battlefield. The impossible case of the 'virtuous bigamist' clearly cannot be resolved in any legal setting, much less a court where the judge himself is a third contender.[9] It is through war that Chaereas proves his masculinity and gains control over his emotions.[10] He comes into his own as a brilliant general, like his father-in-law. Heroic action on the battlefield, rather than clever argumentation in the courtroom, makes the man.

---

[8] The expression δοῦλος τοῦ βασιλέως was a topos in Greek literature, see Missiou 1993.

[9] G. Anderson 1984, 108.

[10] *Callirhoe* has been interpreted as Chaereas' *Bildungsroman*; see Balot 1998; Scourfield 2003. For a reading of the inculcation of masculinity in the five Greek novels, see M. Jones 2012.

Conclusion

In conclusion, the four trial scenes of Chariton's novel reveal a range of attitudes to the law. In all, the character of the leader—the commander of Syracuse or the king of Persia—determines the integrity of the system of justice. The grandiose and spectacular venues of the Syracusan forum and agora and the Babylonian courtroom speak to of the form of legal consciousness that Ewick and Silbey call 'Before the Law', when the court is perceived as 'an objective realm of disinterested action'. Yet both Hermocrates and the Persian king struggle between their private interests and their duty: Hermocrates yields to the people's demands for Theron's execution, even though it makes the search for his own daughter more difficult. Likewise, the Persian king as he sits in his opulent courtroom in Babylon, represents the majesty of the law, but outside of the courtroom, the king is compromised as an objective arbiter. Both of Callirhoe's Greek husbands, Dionysius and Chaereas, criticize the king for not playing by the rules of the game. In this respect, their attitude reflects the type of gamesmanship that Ewick and Silbey characterize as 'With the Law'. Unfortunately, they are sub par players on the Babylonian turf, where Mithridates and the eunuch are virtuosi at the legal sophistry. The ability to play the game of law, to manipulate the rules to one's advantage, is projected onto barbarians whereas the Greek Chaereas and, to a lesser degree, Dionysius win by their virtue in battle, where courage, not cleverness, wins *gloria*.

In the trial scenes, Callirhoe is passive; however, in the narrative, she demonstrates a great deal of agency over her life. There is a single moment where she makes a judgment that has wide-ranging consequences that deepen the moral complexity of the legal disputes. Specifically, this is her choice not to terminate her pregnancy after a fellow slave on Dionysius' estate notices that she is pregnant. It is no coincidence that that moment of private deliberation is framed as a trial scene, held in the privacy of a bedroom—indeed, in the privacy of Callirhoe's own thoughts (C 2,11,1-3).

The narrative lingers on the process of her decision. 'Callirhoe went up to her room', Chariton tells us, 'and shut the door'. She deliberates with herself, her husband, and her unborn child (βουλευσώμεθα, περὶ τοῦ κοινῇ συμφέροντος,

C 2,11,1). She holds Chaereas' picture next to her womb and first states her opinion (τὴν ἐμὴν γνώμην, C 2,11,1). She says that she wishes to die the wife of Chaereas alone (Χαιρέου μόνου γυνή), in Roman terms, a *univira*. To the fetus she says, 'When you grow up, you will easily be recognized by your family—I am persuaded that when I will give birth, you will be the likeness of your father' (πέπεισμαι γὰρ ὅτι ὅμοιόν σε τέξομαι τῷ πατρί, C 2,11,2). The metaphor of the council continues throughout this internal dialogue. The decision is split: the child casts its vote (ψῆφον, C 2,11,3) against the sentence of death. She then brings in Chaereas, at least in his appearance in her dream. Using the correct legal formula, the vision formally stands by and declares that he entrusts to Callirhoe the custody of the child (αὐτὸς γάρ μοι παραστὰς ἐν τοῖς ὀνείροις 'παρατίθεμαί σοι' φησὶ 'τὸν υἱόν'). And, reciprocally, Callirhoe stands as the witness to the fact that Chaereas has given her in marriage to Dionysius (μαρτύρομαί σε, Χαιρέα, σύ με Διονυσίῳ νυμφαγωγεῖς, C 2,11,3). Callirhoe is judge, defendant, tutor, witness, adoptive parent, and bride in the darkened bedroom that is her private tribunal.

The consequence of this imaginary trial is to give her unborn child legitimacy by agreeing to marry Dionysius 'for the procreation of children according to Greek law' (C 3,2,2). This private trial, conducted by a woman in the darkness of her bedroom, creates a legal dilemma that defies resolution in the courtroom. Although the dispute is settled on the field of battle where men prove themselves to be *virēs,* heroes in the Roman mold, Callirhoe is the ultimate arbiter. Her solitary trial defies the laws of adultery and asserts her control over her own body. She strikes a solution to her dilemma by emulating the matrons of Roman legend. Like Lucretia, she remains virtuous even though she has been forced—by necessity or by violence—to have sexual intercourse with a man who is not her husband. Unlike Lucretia, she chooses not to kill herself and to precipitate the overthrow of monarchy. The child she gives birth to represents the compromise of democracy and monarchy. As the acknowledged son of the leading citizen of Miletus and benefactor of the Persian king, he will also, Callirhoe hopes, one day be recognized as the grandson of Hermocrates. She returns to her home with the man she first married, now a man worthy of being her husband, but not necessarily of being the father of her child.

Callirhoe's inner dialogue with her beloved Chaereas and their son invites the reader to the innermost sanctum—Callirhoe herself—where the truth lies. In the public space of the courtroom, she is an object over which men contend. Chariton's novel obliquely touches upon adultery as a prosecutable crime, but avoids tackling it directly. For to do so would be to damage the idealization of femininity he has created in the character of Callirhoe. In the next section, we shall see how Achilles Tatius similarly probes the limits of the laws of adultery, but at a remove of two or three generations. In *Leucippe and Clitophon*, adulterous triangles proliferate to an absurd degree and generate an avalanche of legal actions.

II

Achilles Tatius, *Leucippe and Clitophon*

Legal Pluralism in Roman Alexandria

Achilles Tatius' novel, *Leucippe and Clitophon*, composed in the later second century C.E., is in dialogue with Chariton's *Callirhoe*. Stylistically, it reflects the Atticism that was the hallmark of educational refinement during the Second Sophistic.[1] Callirhoe challenged the image of the adulteress because her second marriage was paradoxically due to her fidelity to her first husband and their unborn child. Allegations of adultery were made both outside and inside the courtroom, but Callirhoe rose above the fray with her honor intact. Responding to Chariton, Achilles Tatius invests substantial narrative space to an adultery plot, which does not valorize the generic ideal of marriage, but rather serves as a foil to it.

A love affair between Clitophon, the naïf hero of the novel, and Melite, a seductive widow from Ephesus uncouples the components of love and sex, adultery and marriage.[2] Their subversive and over-determined liaison is referred to as γάμος, a problematic term that connotes either marriage or sexual intercourse. The story of the legally ambiguous marriage of Clitophon and Melite tells us more about the complexities of marriage as a formal institution with legal, social, and economic dimensions than does the stereotypical ending in love and marriage. Two trials structure the plot of the 'new beginning' in the second half of the novel.[3] The fifth and sixth books describe the convoluted process whereby Clitophon and Melite hook up, and the seventh and eighth unravel the consequences of that act. Achilles Tatius presumes the existence of a law allowing the prosecution of both the adulterer and the adulteress in a public court. The *lex Julia de adulteriis coercendis*, Augustus' law on adultery, was already over a century and a half old by the time *Leucippe and Clitophon* was written.

The affair unfolds in the cosmopolitan city of Alexandria. Biographical *testimonia* suggest that it was Achilles Tatius' hometown, but this attribution may have been inferred from the prominence the city in his narrative.[4] In this dynamic

---

[1] The significance of the distinction between 'pre-sophistic' and 'sophistic' styles has been challenged by analytical studies of the vocabulary; see Ruiz-Montero 1991.

[2] On Melite as the paradigmatic 'Other Woman', see Cresci 1978; Egger 1990, 75-79; Haynes 2003, 103-106.

[3] Nimis 1998, 109.

[4] Vilborg 1955, 163-168; 1962, 8.

environment, vestiges of prior laws and customs of Egyptians and Greco-Macedonians operated alongside the Roman system. By the late second century, a person living in or passing through this important entrepôt of the Roman Empire would have been aware of the city's reputation for contention among of its various subcultures, an effect of the Roman administration's ad hoc policy of granting differential rights to those groups. Roman magistrates required handbooks of local customs to guide their rulings.[5] The so-called *Acts of the Alexandrian Martyrs*, purportedly official documents generated by the ongoing discord between the Greek and Jewish communities of Alexandria, illustrate the complex politics of within a multicultural society.[6] In a decree preserved on a stele in the Greek city of Cyrene, Augustus had established the principle that provincials be tried in their own courts, and that Roman citizens be tried in Roman courts.[7] In effect, several legal systems operated concurrently within a given social space. Achilles Tatius' delineation of the quasi marriage of Clitophon and Melite illustrates the phenomenon of 'legal pluralism'. The couple performs a series of actions that individually signal that they are married, yet collectively form a pastiche of demotic, Greek, and Roman wedding customs as attested in a variety of sources: papyri and ostraka in Alexandria, vase paintings from Athens, and the legal literature of Rome.[8] Roman *equites* working for the imperial administration presumably formed families with local inhabitants. Not surprisingly, the multiplicity of customs created confusion that lasted well into the Byzantine era.[9] As an institution that created a contractual bond between two individuals, possibly from different socio-economic backgrounds, marriage can be understood as a game where multiple sets of rules were at play. There was potential for confusion—with legal ramifications. A professional advocate—perhaps such as Achilles Tatius, as later scholiasts believed—would have needed to know how to navigate this pluralistic legal environment.[10]

The affair of Melite and Clitophon reflects the variegated legal customs within the Roman Empire on the eve of the Antonine Constitution. By the second decade of the third century C.E., the Antonine Constitution would streamline the administration of justice in the Roman Empire by granting all inhabitants the same rights under Roman law, at least theoretically. Achilles Tatius' novel allows us glimpse into the possible effects the simultaneous processes of the extension of Roman

[5] Modrzejewski 1986A
[6] Musurillo 1954; Harker 2008.
[7] For the full text of the inscription, see J. G. C. Anderson 1927.
[8] For a discussion of the nature of the evidence for Greek weddings, see Vérilhac and Vial 1998, 15-40; Oakley and Sinos 1993. For Roman weddings, see Hersch 2010.
[9] Wolff 1939.
[10] Vilborg 1955, 167-168.

citizenship alongside the growing salience of social class in the administration of penal law of the Roman Empire. The invention of this type of plot presumes a world where clever individuals learned how to exploit loopholes in the patchwork of laws and to 'forum shop' in order to obtain more favorable outcomes. In this pluralistic legal environment forensic acumen was key to survival and preservation of social status.

Trial 5.
Facts Not in Evidence: Murder
Thersander v. Melite and Clitophon
(Achilles Tatius, *Leucippe and Clitophon* 7,7-16)

The Story

Melite, a young widow traveling in Egypt, meets Clitophon and falls in love with him. He, however, is grieving over the death of his beloved Leucippe, whose beheading he witnessed. After a series of disappointingly (for Melite) sexless encounters, Melite brings Clitophon home to her estate in Ephesus, where everyone presumes they are husband and wife. Complications soon arise: first, Leucippe, still alive, is found working as slave on Melite's estate; then, Melite's first husband, Thersander, presumed lost at sea but also still alive, returns home to find his wife dining with the handsome young protagonist. Thersander accosts the presumed adulterer, locks him in a closet in his house, and then leaves to visit a friend, In the meantime, Melite bribes the sentry to allow her into Clitophon's closet, where they finally consummate their presumptive marriage. Melite helps Clitophon escape, but Thersander and his friends collide into him on the street as he escapes disguised as Melite. Before a crowd of onlookers, Thersander loudly denounces Clitophon as an adulterer and cloak thief, and hauls him to the public jail on a charge of adultery.

In prison Clitophon plots his defense. He decides to claim that he was openly married to Melite, and therefore not technically an adulterer. She, on the other hand, defends herself to Thersander in the privacy of their home, claiming that Clitophon was a simple shipwreck victim whom she pitied. Unpersuaded, Thersander bribes the magistrate of the jail to poison Clitophon, but when that does not work, he hatches a scheme to send a stooge into Clitophon's cell to delude him into believing that Melite murdered Leucippe in a fit of jealousy. Distraught over the surprising news, Clitophon resolves to confess to her murder in an effort to be condemned to death.

Thersander and Melite each hire teams of lawyers. In lieu of a defense, Clitophon confesses that he colluded in Leucippe's murder, which throws the court into confusion. His cousin, Clinias, steps up to defend Clitophon, albeit in vain. Thersander's speakers seize upon Clitophon's confession and demand the death penalty. Melite offers her slaves for interrogation and challenges Thersander to hand over his own slave overseer, Sosthenes, who has mysteriously vanished. The president of the jury condemns Clitophon to death, purportedly the statutory penalty for confessed murderers, and announces that Melite will be tried after the slaves are tortured for evidence. Clitophon, who is now a convicted criminal will also be tortured before his execution. Fortuitously, at the moment that the torture implements are wheeled out, the priest of Artemis arrives with a sacred embassy. All punishments are then suspended until after the sacrifices. Clitophon is released into the custody of the priest of the temple of Artemis where he is reunited with Leucippe, who has taken refuge at the goddess' altar.

Analysis

The process whereby Clitophon and Melite come to be recognized as a married couple is fraught with ambiguity. Their liaison evolves gradually through a series of actions that simulate a wedding: oaths, promise to share property, banquets, cohabitation, and their public appearance as a couple—all except sexual intercourse. The event that precipitates a definitional crisis for their marriage occurs a little more than halfway through the fifth book of the novel, when Clitophon suddenly receives a letter from his long lost, presumably dead Leucippe. By a stroke of fortune, she is a slave on Melite's estate. Inferring that Citophon is married to the mistress of the estate, she bitterly congratulates him on his 'unorthodox' wedding (τῶν καινῶν γάμων, AT 5,18,6). Clitophon is at a loss. Satyrus, his slave and go-between, tries to smoothe things over and reassures him that he explained to Leucippe that Clitophon married 'unwittingly' or 'unwillingly' (ἄκων).[1] Coming as it does out of the mouth of a character named Satyrus, the excuse is clearly comic; Clitophon, however, does not get the joke, flatly denying that he is married at all (because, as the reader knows, at this point in the story Clitophon and Melite have not yet had sexual intercourse). Satyrus points to the obvious fact that everyone in town thinks he is married to Melite: after all, she is a local notable whose

[1] AT 5,20,2: κἀγὼ γὰρ αὐτῇ διωμοσάμην, ὡς ἄκων αὐτὴν ἔγημας. An allusion to Oedipus' ex post facto self-defense, where he insists that he married his mother unwittingly. Cf. Sophocles, *Oedipus at Colonus*, 986-7: ἐγὼ δέ νιν | ἄκων τ' ἔγημα.

arrival in Ephesus was celebrated with public tours of her estates, as well as numerous banquets to celebrate their union. When Clitophon denies it, Satyrus asks in disbelief, 'Don't you sleep with her?' (AT 5,20,2)—in answer to which Clitophon admits, 'the deed has never been done' (οἶδα μὲν ἄπιστα λέγων, ἀλλ' οὔπω πέπρακται, AT 5,20,3). Insisting that he remains 'pure' (καθαρός, AT 5,20,3), Clitophon defends himself in a letter to Leucippe: 'Understand that I imitated your virginity, if there is virginity among men'.[2] The reader knows this is true from the preceding narrative of the beautiful and wealthy Melite's futile attempts to seduce Clitophon.

Satyrus' inept excuse and Clitophon's clumsy attempt to refute the obvious truth is the beginning of the conundrum at the heart of the trial scene. The critical term lies in Satyrus' throwaway line that Clitophon married ἄκων, which can be construed in a number of ways: unwillingly, unintentionally, by necessity, or by force.[3] In the moral universe of the Greek novels, this is patently illogical in light of the ideal that marriage is based upon mutual love. As in the murder trial of Chaereas in Chariton (C 1,5,4), the precise definition of ἄκων is crucial to his defense; here in this scenario, it seems silly. In Athenian law, although the consent of the bride was not required, the groom's unquestionably was. Under Roman law, the free consent of both the bride and, *a fortiori*, the groom was the essential criterion that determined the legal validity of a marriage.[4] From the standpoint of Roman law, Clitophon's disavowal of sexual intercourse is irrelevant. All it took for two people to be recognized as a married couple under Roman law was mutual agreement (provided they met the legal eligibility requirements to marry); everything else was subordinate. Of course, it was taken for granted that the couple would consummate their marriage sexually, but that alone did not effectuate a legally binding marital agreement. As long as a man and woman appeared to cohabit, it was taken for granted that they were married. The state was not interested in regulating sexuality in marriage— unless it concerned the wife and another man. In a sense, it was in the breach of marriage that the Roman state asserted an active interest in the bedroom, arguably a legacy of the Augustan law on adultery.

Upon reading Leucippe's bitter rebuke, Clitophon feels like 'an adulterer caught in the act' (ὥσπερ ἐπι' αὐτοφώρῳ μοιχὸς κατειλημμένος, AT 5,19,6). From a legal standpoint, this is nonsensical: according to both Greek and Roman law, a man was only an adulterer if he had an affair with a woman married to

---

[2] AT 5,20,5: μαθήσῃ τὴν σήν με παρθενίαν μεμιμημένον, εἴ τις ἔστι καὶ ἐν ἀνδράσι παρθενία. For a discussion of the complexities of Clitophon's claim to a form of masculine virginity, see Brethes 2007, 249-256.

[3] The term's usage in archaic and classical Greek thought is discussed at length in Rickert 1989.

[4] *Digest* 23,1,7; Raditsa 1980, 307.

another man. It was not adultery if a husband cheated on his wife, and *a fortiori* if a groom-to-be cheated on his fiancée.[5] When Thersander, Melite's first husband, comes into the picture Clitophon becomes an adulterer in the strict sense of the word—with respect to Melite, but not to Leucippe. Clitophon's original defense to Leucippe radically contradicts his defense to Thersander. To Leucippe, Clitophon claims that the marriage is not valid because it was not sexually consummated; to Thersander, Clitophon plans to claim that the marriage is valid because it was openly contracted.[6]

Thersander's irruption into the narrative signals the beginning of the formulaic bedroom showdown, albeit in the dining room. A moment of confusion in the oikos leads directly to the courtroom—except that in the Achilles Tatius' version, the hero is the adulterer and the villain is the cuckold. Like Callirhoe, Melite rushes to embrace her husband, who violently pronounces, 'This man is an adulterer!' (ὁ μοιχὸς οὗτος, AT 5,23,5), the first of twenty times that Clitophon will be referred to as a μοιχός in the subsequent narrative.[7] The encounter turns violent: Thersander smacks Clitophon, grabs him by the hair, throws him down, and beats him. The scene is comic: Clitophon's obliviousness only provokes the cuckold's rage. Clitophon asks, 'Who are you, mister? And why are you hitting me?' (τίς ποτε εἶ, ὦ ἄνθρωπε; καὶ τί με οὕτως ᾐκίσω; AT 5,23,7). Before storming out, Thersander orders his servants to lock up and guard Clitophon in a little room (δωμάτιον, AT 5,23,7) somewhere in the interior of the house.[8]

A subplot ensues that was part of a 'highly ingenious and complex' declamatory scenario that was 'greatly admired' in antiquity: the seduction of a wife by a prisoner in the husband's home.[9] In effect, Achilles Tatius creates the backstory to this set piece, so that the actions of the wife are directly shown to the audience

---

[5] Cohen 1991, 98ff. Treggiari notes that 'some philosophers and later the Christian theologians [tried] to make linguistic usage symmetrical' and cites Augustine *Quaestiones Exodi* 71,4 (=*Corpus Christianorum* series latina xxxiii, 104), where Augustine calls a married man who has sexual relations with a woman other than his wife a *moechus*; see Treggiari 1991, 264.

[6] Discussed in further detail in S. Schwartz 2000-2001.

[7] AT 6,3,5; 6,5,1; 6,5,3; 6,9,1 (twice); 6,9,2; 6,17,1; 6,17,3; 6,20,2; 6,21,2; 8,8,3; 8,8,10; 8,8,11; 8,8,13; 8,10,1; 8,10,3; 8,10,4; 8,10,5; 8,10,11.

[8] Later in the narrative, Clitophon escapes and has to walk through the deserted areas of the house to get to a door that does not open onto the road (AT 6,2,1).

[9] Russell 1983, 51. Regardless of how often the law of adultery was actually invoked in courts in the Roman Empire, the existence of such a law exercised the imaginations of many. For example, in the largely imaginary world of the *controversiae*, there was a law that allowed a person who caught an adulterer with an adulteress to kill them both at once. See Seneca *Controversiae* 1,4; Treggiari 1991, 272.

before her side of the story is distorted through the men's speeches in the courtroom. As a character, Melite is singularly persuasive. Determined to sleep with Clitophon, she convinces the guard to allow her to enter his cell.[10] Once inside, she delivers a pair of persuasive speeches (*suasoriae*) to Clitophon, one spoken out of anger (AT 5,25,2-8), the other out of love (AT 5,26,1-13). She is as eloquent as a philosopher taught by Eros, the 'Divine Sophist'.[11] She releases him from all commitments, assuring him that this will be the first and last time they have intercourse. In a last-ditch effort, she promises she will help him regain his beloved Leucippe. She is so persuasive that she convinces the virginal hero to make love to her, regardless of the fact they are fully conscious that her husband is still alive.

This single action also sets up a dilemma that exercised the imaginations of adultery-obsessed *iurisconsulti* throughout the imperial period.[12] We can see this scenario in an excerpt from a monograph on adultery by the Severan jurist, Papinian:

> A woman, after she had heard that her absent husband had died, married another man; not long after, her husband returned. What steps should be taken against that woman? The reply was that the question raised was not so much one of law as of fact; for if a long time had elapsed without evidence of any fornication [on her part] and she, led by false reports [into believing] that she was free from the earlier bond, contracted a lawful second marriage, the likelihood is that she was [genuinely] deceived, and that there can appear to be nothing deserving punishment. But if the supposed death of her husband shall be proved to have provided an excuse for getting married, [then] since [her] action is offensive to chastity, she ought to be punished in accordance with the nature of the offense committed. (*Digest* 48,5,12,12, trans. Watson)

In this passage, Papinian grapples with the question of *mens rea*: Is a woman guilty of adultery if she truly believed her husband was dead? What if she had been tricked by false rumors? What if the husband's death was a fiction, *ficta*

[10] The figure of the lenient prison guard also appears in Xenophon's novel, in the episode of Amphinomus and Anthia (XE 4,6,5).

[11] AT 5,27,1 ταῦτα φιλοσοφήσασα (διδάσκει γὰρ ὁ Ἔρως καὶ λόγους) ἔλυε τὰ δεσμά. Cf. AT 1,10,1, where Clinias gives Clitophon advice on love: αὐτοδίδακτος γάρ ἐστιν ὁ θεὸς σοφιστής. For an interpretation of the use of φιλοσόφειν in an erotic context, see Goldhill 1995, 94-102. For a rhetorical analysis of Melite's speech, see Ferrini 1987-88.

[12] McGinn 2004, 246.

mariti mors? A corollary to Papinian's question might be, Is a man guilty of adultery if he did not know that his lover was married? This is precisely the paradox imagined by Achilles Tatius.

Melite's seduction of Clitophon has attracted scholarly attention. It has been interpreted as a paradigmatic instance of Achilles Tatius' technique of parodying the genre's over-determined chastity of the protagonists.[13] Another view elaborates upon Clitophon's admission that he had a 'normal human reaction' (AT 5,27,2) and cites the episode as a piece of self-explanatory, emotional realism, something any healthy male would do.[14] Clitophon himself lists the causative factors: the force of Eros' rhetoric, basic human instinct, fear of Eros' wrath, hope for freedom and reunion with Leucippe, and compassion for Melite's love-sickness (AT 5,27,1-2). It recalls the exercise of enumerating the plausible defenses a speaker might make in a declamation, similar to Chariton's list of excuses available to Chaereas in his trial (C 1,5,4). Once the deed is done, Clitophon rationalizes it as 'just like medicine for an ailing soul' (AT 5,27,2).

The playfulness of the scene is undeniable. A single act sets in motion a complex dilemma that defies the logic of the courtroom. The reader knows the romantic hero is in fact not only culpable for breaking his promise of fidelity to the heroine (which seems to be beside the point, as it is elided in the subsequent narrative), but is also technically guilty of the crime for which he had been, until that point, falsely accused.

The formula for the trial scene requires for the innocent protagonist to defend himself against a false accusation. And this was precisely the direction the narrative seemed to be headed—that is, until Melite seduces Clitophon. The fact of the seduction is more juridically significant to Clitophon's relationship to the married couple, Thersander and Melite, than to his relationship with Leucippe. When Clitophon finally has sexual intercourse with Melite, he does so in full knowledge that her husband is alive; from a legal perspective, the act is committed with a *mens rea* or ἑκών. He is instantaneously transformed from an unwitting husband to a conscious, if not deliberate, adulterer. His peripeteia is signaled by a change of costume: he disguises himself as Melite and escapes into the agora, but soon runs into Thersander and his friends. When they discover him, they humiliate him

---

[13] Durham 1938, 11; Cresci 1978, 79; G. Anderson 1982, 23-24; Fusillo 1991, 100; Goldhill 1995, 97; Morales 2004, 59.

[14] Reardon 1994, 88. Foucault (1988,231) reads the novel in a serious vein, explaining away the incident as 'an honorable, minor lapse'. Rattenbury (1926, 69-70) quaintly rationalizes it as a favor 'in return for her service to him, in freeing him from bonds and in saving his beloved Leucippe'.

in front of a gathering crowd a typical treatment of adulterers (AT 6,5,2). Thersander vilifies Clitophon as an adulterer and a clothing thief (τὸν μοιχόν, τὸν λωποδύτην, AT 6,5,3), two crimes that induce shame through the public exposure of nakedness. This time, Thersander takes Clitophon to the public jail to await formal trial on a charge of adultery (ἔγκλημα μοιχείας ἐπιφέρων, AT 6,5,3).

The focus of the trial scene is squarely on the litigants, rather than the scenery and personnel of the court. Achilles Tatius provides relatively few details about the physical setting of the courtroom or the judges; rather, the presence of masses of professional advocates on both sides forms the backdrop. Thersander enlists the help of 'a mass of advocates, no fewer than ten' (πλῆθος ῥητόρων οὐχ ἧττον δέκα, AT 7,7,1) and Melite's defense team is equally well equipped. It was not unheard of in the Greco-Roman world for pleaders to use the services of more than one advocate. For example, the large number of advocates on behalf of Scaurus at his famous trial in 54 B.C.E.—six, including Cicero— was noteworthy; the 'no less than ten' advocates on Thersander's team is an exaggeration, but not entirely implausible.[15] With regard to the factual basis of the charge, the sequencing of the events is critical; the quality of the action, however, demands an argument built from a careful characterization of the nature of the actions. Four complete speeches by Melite, Clitophon, Clinias, and Thersander forming a virtual tetralogy in connection with this trial. Each speaker presents his or her perspective on the preceding events of the narrative. I shall discuss each individually.

The Apologia of Melite

As we have seen from the seduction scene, Melite is a formidable orator in her own right; however, the cultural prohibition of women from speaking in court posed a creative challenge for the novelist.[16] For the author to exclude Melite's voice from the trial scene, when it was so prominent in the earlier narrative, would essentially squander a carefully developed character. Achilles Tatius' solution is to set her formal defense in a domestic context, in a private conversation with Thersander. Melite's speech, described as 'a piece of sophistry mixed with the truth' (ἥτις μεμιγμένην εἶχε τῷ σοφίσματι τὴν ἀλήθειαν, AT 6,8,4), is on the same narrative level as the other three and so functions as the first speech of a tetralogy.

---

[15] Asconius (*In Scaurianam* 20), in his first century C.E. commentary on Cicero's *Pro Scauro*; see Crook 1995, 63.

[16] In the trial scene, one of the speakers, Clinias, apologizes to the jury for seeming to slander a woman, Melite (AT 7,9,9).

More significantly, it is the only speech that actually gives a specific defense to the charge of adultery.

Melite's speech begins as an intimate conversation between spouses in the bedroom. After Thersander confronts her for having a lover, Melite says to him, 'What lover? What is the matter with you?' (AT 6,9,1), and tries to mollify his anger. Her address takes the shape of a formal oration, with a proem (AT 6,9,2), argument (AT 6,9,2-6), short narration (AT 6,9,6-7), and lengthy peroration (AT 6,10,2-6). She opens with a *captatio benevolentiae* in which she addresses Thersander in the same way that a defendant in a trial would appeal to the judge to be 'a fair juror' (δικαστὴς ἴσος). It was a conventional tactic for a defendant to characterize the allegations of the prosecution as slander, and so she urges him to listen by 'purifying [his] ears from slander, pushing anger out of [his] heart, and understanding that reason is an uncontaminated judge' (κριτὴν ἀκέραιον, AT 6,9,2).[17]

Melite asserts that her story is true (AT 6,9,5) and at one level this is perfectly correct. She selects details that are in themselves true and independently verifiable, but combines them in such a way that their sum is false, but plausible. She begins with a syllogistic argument: Thersander was a shipwreck victim; to honor a shipwreck victim is to honor Thersander. Clitophon (whom she does not mention by name) was also a shipwreck victim; therefore, to honor him was to honor Thersander. According to Aristotle the use of syllogism was more laudable than a simple enumeration of examples.[18] She includes a few facts: Clitophon was only one of many shipwreck victims upon whom she showed pity in the pious hope that another woman would do the same for her own lost husband (AT 6,9,2-3). This is another rhetorical strategy praised by Aristotle, who noted that placing a single proof after the enthymeme conveys the impression of 'witnesses giving evidence'.[19] She reiterates the equation of Thersander with Clitophon, whom she calls his 'likeness' (τὴν εἰκόνα) in order to strengthen her argument.[20] In another mostly true claim, she explains that she met Clitophon when he was in mourning for his wife (technically, his posthumous fiancée). She says that someone had informed him that his fiancée, whom he believed dead, was sold to Sosthenes, the estate manager.[21] This is also true: Clitophon learned this from Leucippe herself, although she was disguised as a slave woman at the time. Melite does not say

---

[17] Aristotle *Rhetoric* 1416b5 ff. For an example of this common rhetorical strategy, see Demosthenes 19,1-7.

[18] Aristotle *Rhetoric* 1356b23.

[19] Aristotle *Rhetoric* 1394a14.

[20] Cf. Callirhoe's private council in which she defends her action by imagining that her child will look like Chaereas (C 2,11,2).

[21] Cf. Callirhoe's sale to Leonas, the manager of Dionysius' estate.

specifically when they received this information; the context implies that they learned of this before coming to Ephesus. In her next statement, she says that they confirmed this report when they arrived, which is also true. The only outright falsehood she relates is that Clitophon accompanied her in order to search for his wife (διὰ τοῦτο ἠκολούθησέ μοι, AT 6,9,7); as the reader knows, he accompanied her as a lover.

Overall, Melite's speech creates the impression of truth. She invites Thersander to verify her story: 'Examine each of my statements. If I have told a lie, then I have been committing adultery' (εἴ τι ἐψευσάμην, μεμοίχευμαι, AT 6,9,7). This mixed condition is a subtle piece of sophistry. The verb of the apodosis (μεμοίχευμαι) is in the perfect indicative without ἄν, suggesting a simple statement of fact; however, the aorist indicative of the verb in the protasis (εἴ τι ἐψευσάμην), suggests either a past unreal condition, i.e., 'if I had lied (but did not)'—as Melite means for Thersander to understand—or a simple past condition, i.e., 'if I lied', without any implication about whether it is true or not. The irony is that her statement is true on both counts: she is lying and she is an adulteress. The clever wording of the condition conveys the impression that she is telling the truth.

The Speech of Clitophon

The trial is focalized through Clitophon, the first-person narrator for most of the novel; his entrance into the courtroom initiates the trial scene proper. The speeches of Thersander's and Melite's advocates are not presented in the narrative either directly or indirectly because they presumably occurred when Clitophon was still in prison. Thus, his speech, the first speech to be presented in direct discourse (AT 7,7,2-6) in the narrative of the trial, appears where the speech of prosecution would be expected, a narratological move identical to that of Chariton's placement of Chaereas' speech in the first trial in Syracuse (trial 1).

As Clitophon sits in jail awaiting his trial, he plans to claim that he was openly married to Melite and therefore not an adulterer (AT 6,5,4); however, the plan goes awry when he is told by an informant planted by Thersander that Leucippe was killed by a hitman hired by Melite (AT 7,3).[22] Out of grief, he changes his mind and decides to confess to Leucippe's murder—as well as to all of Thersander's accusations of adultery (AT 7,6,3).

The formula of the self-denunciation (προσαγγελία) appears in the trial of Chaereas in Chariton's novel. In that trial, the court's pity resulted in a verdict

[22] Clitophon has been tricked like this before, notably in the scene of Leucippe's murder by pirates, AT 3,15.

that was congruent with the reader's judgment. It is clear that Achilles Tatius knew the formula: earlier in the novel, there was a story of a traveler, named Menelaus, who had accidentally killed his lover with a javelin during a boar hunt. At the trial for murder, he plead guilty and asked for the death penalty, but the court pitied him and instead sentenced him to three years' exile (AT 2,34,6). Achilles Tatius, however, presents a picture in which the court accepts confession without further investigation. The formula of the προσαγγελία assumes that confession is equivalent to a guilty verdict, a key premise explaining the motivation of the suicidal defendant of the declamations.[23] Clitophon opens with the conventional assertion that all the other speakers are babbling nonsense whereas he will speak the truth (AT 7,7,2); ironically, his false confession rests on a fiction he believes to be true.[24] In the case of Clitophon, the formulaic ending is subverted: he begs for the death penalty and the court gives him exactly what he wants and more: it forces him to submit to humiliating torture before he is put to death.

His surprising confession to Leucippe's murder drives the trial off track. Without any semblance of judicial procedure, the trial convened on a charge of adultery suddenly pivots to a trial for murder, albeit without the evidence of the victim's corpse. It is only after the remaining speeches that the reader learns that the presiding magistrate is in charge of rendering judgment in cases of homicide (AT 7,12,1). Chariton made a similar move when Dionyius' charge of seduction became a case of malfeasance. Paradoxically, the scene of Melite's seduction of Clitophon is not objectionable. The narrator's reticence lies not with the adultery scene, but with its exhibition on the stage of the lawcourt, too titillating for public consumption and inappropriate to the genre's general emphasis on chastity. How far we are from the image of the gods standing at the doorway and laughing at Aphrodite and Ares enmeshed in their lovers' bed!

In deflecting the charge of adultery, Achilles Tatius returns to his strong suit: a gruesome spectacle of death. Clitophon's account is misleading on so many levels: he lies about his involvement in a crime he knows he did not commit and is simultaneously unaware that the story he presents as fact is a fiction. Compared with Melite's defense, where true details are subtly arranged to convey a false impression for an audience of one, Clitophon's narrative is clumsy. He grafts unverified hearsay and outright lies onto the brisk narrative of facts that Melite used

[23] Aristotle is silent about the validity of confession in his section on proofs in the *Rhetoric;* perhaps the omission confirms that in antiquity confession was taken at face value. After late antiquity, confession becomes more central; see Foucault 1978, 58-68; Brooks 2000.

[24] Cf. Melite's apologia (AT 6,9,5) and Clitophon's own response to Leucippe's letter accusing him of infidelity (AT 5,20,5).

in her bedroom defense (AT 7,7,3). When he invites his listeners to make inferences—about Sosthenes' motives, for example— he signposts it with 'I leave it to you to inquire' or 'Why should I not tell the truth?' Midway through his narration, where arguments for his innocence might be expected, Clitophon embellishes the stooge's story with fictitious details about how he was lured into Melite's conspiracy to kill Leucippe (AT 7,7,4). The reader knows that, on the contrary, Melite had offered to help reunite the lovers. Then, in order to lend weight to the prosecution's charge of adultery as well, he claims that Melite promised to make him the 'master of her wealth', another true detail: Melite so vowed at the temple of Isis in Alexandria.[25] Finally, his confession goes over the top: he admits to hiring a murderer for one hundred gold pieces, the precise amount in the cellmate's story. He is honest about his reasons for his confession; namely, he cannot continue to live, still loving the woman he killed (AT 7,7,6). Both statements are true: that is how he feels. Yet it is a lie because he did not kill her.

This bizarre confession throws the court into confusion and upends the normal order of the speeches. Because he included enough of the truth, Melite's own lawyers suspect that she is guilty, while Thersander's lawyers sing a victory song. Here in Ephesus, there is no leader like Chariton's Hermocrates to restore order. Instead, Clinias, Clitophon's cousin, makes a request to address the court on the grounds that it is a 'contest over a man's life' (περὶ γὰρ ψυχῆς ἀνδρὸς ὁ ἀγών, AT 7,9,1).

The Speech of Clinias

As Clitophon's worldlier cousin, Clinias, steps into the role of Clitophon's advocate, a paradoxical position that forces him to rebut the defendant in order to defend him.[26] His speech is twice as long as Clitophon's and serves as the neglected defense speech. Clinias' speech is organized into a proem (AT 7,9,2), a narration in two parts (AT 7,9,3-4 and 7,9,9-13) with intervening arguments (AT 7,9,5-8), and a peroration (AT 7,9,14). Its purpose is to set the record straight so that it coheres with the main narrative in which this trial is embedded. The first part of the narration is consistent with Clitophon's, diverging only when it comes to the 'unexpectedly undetectable' (ἐξαίφνης ἀφανής, AT 7,9,4) evidence of Leucippe's murder. There is no explanation of how Clinias came to know these details, nor does it matter because Clinias' speech is aligned with what the reader knows,

---

[25] AT 7,7,5: τῶν ἑαυτῆς με κύριον ἀποφαίνειν ὑπισχνεῖτο. See also AT 5,14,2.

[26] On the contrast between the knowing Clinias and the gullible Clitophon, see Whitmarsh 2003.

thus marking this speech as 'true' within the context of the narrative framework and inviting the reader to identify with him as the champion of the novel's protagonist.

Clinias argues that his 'opponent'—Clitophon—falsely claimed responsibility (αἰτίαν) for the crimes in order to get the 'drug for the unlucky', the 'punishment for the unfortunate' (AT 7,9,2).[27] He demands evidence. Normally, this tactic, known as the ἐλέγχων ἀπαίτησις, was used to embarrass one's opponent by asking for evidence the speaker knows does not exist.[28] Yet, because the reader knows the facts of the case, Clinias' strategy is transparent. Carefully couching his challenge in the form of a conditional sentence, Clinias challenges Clitophon—'if he in fact plotted the deed'—to name the person he bribed to conceal the victim's body. He asks, 'Who has ever heard of a murder without a killer or a corpse?' (AT 7,9,7). In fact, this is precisely the subject of Antiphon's famous oration, *On the Murder of Herodes*, where the prosecution makes a case that the defendant was paid to murder the victim and that a slave helped him dispose of the body. The organization of Clinias' speech is analogous to Antiphon's: after the brief narration of the facts of the case, he moves to an argument based upon probability.[29] Clinias, like Antiphon's speaker, presents the arguments for the defense as facts, while characterizing the prosecution's case as 'a speculative reconstruction of events that can only be discussed in terms of probabilities'.[30]

It is axiomatic in the Greek novels that lovers are willing to die for each other. The corollary is that a lover will do anything, even committing perjury, in order to be with his beloved. Clinias deconstructs this generic cliché with a series of oxymorons. He punctures the absurdity of his opponent's claim that Clitophon killed Leucippe because he loved Melite (AT 7,9,7): 'How can he accuse Melite, whom he loved, but now wish to die for Leucippe, whom he killed?' and 'Who would so hate the object of his love and love the object of his hate?' He argues that if Clitophon meant what he said, under cross-examination he would be forced to deny the murder in order to protect the woman he claims to love (i.e., Melite) to avoid being pointlessly executed on behalf of a dead girl (AT 7,9,8). The logical conclusion is elided, thus leaving the impression of the validity of the argument that Clitophon could not have murdered Leucippe. The reader realizes that Clinias is getting close to discovering the truth. Clinias' only blind spot is that he is unaware that the cellmate's story is a fiction created by Thersander. We see him work

---

[27] This is consistent with the declamatory theme of the προσαγγελία, where poison is usually the mode of suicide the speaker requests of the Council; see Russell 1983, 35.

[28] Russell 1983, 138.

[29] Antiphon 5,25-8; 43-45. See Gagarin 1988, 47-56.

[30] Gagarin 1988, 49.

to corroborate his theory, as he urges the court to interrogate the prisoner, the estate manager Sosthenes, and Melite's maids (AT 7,9,14)—all of whom, it is interesting to note, are unfree, thus underscoring the importance of the testimony of slaves in the world of the novels.[31] Clinias predicts what the outcome of the testimony will be: Sosthenes will testify to Leucippe's enslavement; the slave women will testify to her disappearance; and the prisoner will testify to her murder (AT 7,9,14). Even missing a piece of the puzzle, Clinias' story 'seemed persuasive to many' (AT 7,10,1).

Clinias' formal challenge (πρόκλησις) provokes another flurry of activity among the rival teams of professional speakers. Thersander's advocates demand the death penalty for Clitophon on the grounds that a person who condemns himself 'with the god's providence' is to be executed. On the other side, Melite's advocates' rise to the call by formally issuing a counter-challenge to produce testimony (πρόκλησιν, AT 7,10,2) and offering her slaves for interrogation, in order to pressure Thersander to hand over his own slave, Sosthenes.

The Speech of Thersander

Although Thersander initiated the trial, Clinias' demands for evidence put him on the defensive. His speech contains a proem (AT 7,11,1), in which he dismisses Clinias as 'whoever this guy is' and calls him a liar and 'a wizard'.[32] Thersander deflects suspicion onto his opponents while biding time to send Sosthenes away (AT 7,10,3), whom he will later claim was also murdered by the defendants. He refuses Clinias' demand for Sosthenes' torture, attempts to undermine the value of the proffered testimony of Melite's maids, and doubts the existence of the Clitophon's fellow prisoner. The reader knows that Thersander has custody of Leucippe, who is guarded by Sosthenes. The circumstance is identical to Mithridates' concealment of Chaereas as a surprise witness; here, however, Leucippe's appearance will foil Thersander's plans.

The main focus is upon Clitophon's confession. Thersander asserts that 'confession is stronger than the discovery of the crime'.[33] He mentions a law that commands a confessed murderer to be put to death (τὸν νόμον, ὃς ἐκέλευσε τὸν αὑτοῦ

[31] Cf. Antiphon *On the Murder of Herodes* 40-42.

[32] AT 7,11,1: γόητος ἀκούοντες πιθανῶς μὲν ὑποκρινομένου, πιθανῶς δὲ δακρύοντος. Dionysius makes a similar remark about the satrap Mithridates in the trial in Babylon in C 5,6,10.

[33] AT 7,11,1: μεῖζον γὰρ τῆς φωρᾶς τὸ αὐτὸν ἑαυτοῦ κατεῖπεν.

κατειπόντα φόνον τεθνάναι, AT 7,12,1). Accordingly, Thersander argues, Clitophon must be punished with at least the same severity as a murderer caught red-handed. In Thersander's interpretation of the law, apprehension in flagrante delicto is separate from confession, which is the stronger indicator of guilt. By this logic, the 'stronger' indicator of guilt deserves the stronger punishment. Implicit is the idea that speech (a confession) is more convincing evidence than action (commission of the crime), an inversion of the traditional valuation of ἔργον over λόγος.

In both Athenian and Roman law, the moment a confession was made, guilt was acknowledged; because the purpose of a trial was to determine culpability, a confession obviated the need for a formal verdict.[34] The Athenian procedure of summary arrest (ἀπαγωγή) may have been familiar to readers of the Attic orators in the second century C.E. A criminal who was caught in the act (ἐπ' αὐτοφώρῳ) was brought before the Eleven, a board of magistrates in Athens; if he confessed, then the Eleven had the power put him to death without trial.[35] Referring to this procedure in *Against Timocrates*, Demosthenes notes, 'Concerning other kinds of evil-doers, the law orders that those who confess be punished without trial'.[36] Taken out of context, Demosthenes seems to confirm that the Athenian law ordered the summary execution of confessed criminals; what is elided is the requirement that they first be caught in the act and brought before the magistrate. Capture, confession, and execution were all part of a single legal action in Athens. In Roman law, under the formulary system as set out in the Twelve Tables, a confession before a magistrate was equivalent to a judgment, thus theoretically permitting a magistrate to execute a confessed criminal without trial.[37]

The prospect that a defendant might subvert the purpose of a trial by falsely confessing to the crime fueled the imagination of declaimers, as we have seen above in Chaereas' trial.[38] The dramatic potential of a law that guarantees that the confessor will be automatically punished is illustrated by a *controversia* of Seneca the Elder, in which a bereaved woman, having been frustrated in her attempt to hang herself, tries to commit suicide by confessing to a sacrilege that had recently been committed in the city. Seneca the Elder explains the assumption underlying this principle:

---

[34] Maffi 1986.

[35] Todd 1993, 80; Hansen 1976, 34.

[36] Demosthenes 24,65: τῶν περὶ τἄλλα κακούργων τοὺς ὁμολογοῦντας ἄνευ κρίσεως κολάζειν οἱ νόμοι κελεύουσιν.

[37] Jolowicz 1952, 184-186.

[38] Bonner 1949, 103.

> *Confessio conscientiae vox est. Confessio coacti et quae fecit agnoscentis verbum est. Omnium vox erat: 'sacrilegus latere non poterit: quisquis est, non ipse bonum exitum non quisquam suorum; etsi nemo fuerit accusator, ipse narrabit'.*
>
> Confession is the voice of conscience. Confession is the word of one who is coerced and who acknowledges what he has done. It used to be the voice of everyone: 'A desecrator will not be able to remain hidden: whoever he is, he and his people will come to no good end; even if no one will have been his accuser, he himself will tell the tale'.[39]

The speaker conceives of the confessor as driven by the gods and by the spirits of the ones violated. According to this interpretation, confession is merely the manifestation of divine punishment. Thus, in justifying his plea that Clitophon be put to death as a self-confessed murderer, Thersander asks the jury, 'Do you suppose that this man confessed in any way other than by the god's will?' (AT 7,11,8).

Thersander's hyperbolic enumeration of murders is a red herring, a ploy to circumvent Melite's challenge for evidence (πρόκλησις). He employs a common tactic known as the 'counter-charge' (ἀντέγκλημα) and tries to argue that because Leucippe was his slave, he is the victim of property damage.[40] He twists Clinias' emphasis on Sosthenes' unknown whereabouts into proof that his opponents killed him for denouncing the adultery to him. It was typical in the Attic orations for a speaker to challenge his adversary to present evidence that would be embarrassing or impossible to get; the adversary's refusal would be construed as concealment of information.[41]

Throughout his speech, Thersander presents probabilities as facts. He accuses Melite of maliciously issuing the challenge for him to produce Sosthenes for questioning, when she herself knew he was killed. And even if he were alive, his testimony would be useless, at least according to Thersander. Later, he casuistically argues that his estate manager testifies through him that Leucippe was bought legally and so was Thersander's slave.[42] He speculates that Melite's maids' testimony will be useless because Melite and Clitophon wanted to reduce the number

[39] Seneca *Controversiae* 8,1.

[40] Russell 1983, 136.

[41] Thür 1977, 233-261.

[42] Cf. Mithridates' questioning of the legitimacy of Dionysius' marriage to Callirhoe, whom he bought as a slave. Thersander does not oppose the torture of Melite's maids; he assumes that they will contradict her story.

of witnesses by leaving Leucippe near a den of bandits (AT 7,11,7).[43] Finally, Thersander alleges that the testimony of Clitophon's fellow prisoner (and Thersander's own plant) is a fiction invented by his opponent. Thersander argues that the existence of the informant 'who says nothing to the magistrate, but confides the secret details of the murder to Clitophon' (AT 7,11,8), suggests that he was a co-conspirator.

This brings Thersander's speech back to where it began: Thersander returns to Clitophon's confession. He appeals to the jurors to stop treating so important an affair so lightly. He swears that he knows nothing about Sosthenes' whereabouts—which is true, because during the trial, Thersander sent Sosthenes away toward Smyrna (AT 7,10,4). Because Thersander controls the missing pieces of the puzzle, he runs rings around the defense. Furthermore, by spinning hearsay as truth, Thersander avoids being put in a position where he might perjure himself. His perverse belief in the sacredness of oaths highlights the extreme importance of verbal acuity in the lawcourt.

The three speeches are the centerpiece of the trial scene. It is only after they are done that the details of the courtroom come into focus. Up until this point, all we know is that the audience is addressed, like any classical jury, simply as 'gentlemen of Ephesus' (Ἄνδρες Ἐφέσιοι, AT 7,9,2); details of the jury's composition are described at the moment of the verdict:

> ἔδοξε τῷ προέδρῳ τῶν δικαστῶν—ἦν δὲ τοῦ βασιλικοῦ γένους καὶ τὰς μὲν φονικὰς ἐδίκαζε δίκας, κατὰ δὲ τὸν νόμον συμβούλους ἐκ τῶν γεραιτέρων εἶχεν, οὓς ἐπιγνώμονας ἐλάμβανε τῆς γνώσεως—ἔδοξεν οὖν αὐτῷ διασκοπήσαντι σὺν τοῖς παρέδροις αὐτοῦ θάνατον μὲν ἐμοῦ καταγνῶναι κατὰ τὸν νόμον, ὃς ἐκέλευσε τὸν αὑτοῦ κατειπόντα φόνον τεθνάναι.
>
> The president of the jurors—for he was of the royal clan and judged cases of homicide and according to the law had advisors selected from the elders, whom he took as arbiters of the verdict—thus decided that in his view, upon consulting with his assessors, that I was condemned to death according to the law which ordered that a self-confessed murderer be put to death. (AT 7,12,1)

The description of the presiding judge seems over-determined and confused.[44] The 'president of the jurors' is a member of the royal clan who, as it is explained,

[43] That outlaws actually would carry out a crime engineered by someone else has a precedent in the novel: in the second book, Callisthenes, a rejected suitor of Leucippe, hired a band of (incompetent) pirates to kidnap her (AT 2,16).

[44] Vilborg 1962, 122.

usually judged cases of murder; this recalls the classical Athenian ἄρχων βασιλεύς, the magistrate responsible for conducting pretrial hearings for cases of murder.[45] Accordingly, the 'council of advisors selected from the elders' corresponds to the court of the Areopagus, a jury of elder statesmen who tried cases of premeditated homicide. It is uncertain whether in Classical Athens the ἄρχων βασιλεύς merely presided over the proceedings of the Areopagus, or voted with the other members of the jury.[46] In Achilles Tatius' rendition, the president comes from distinguished family and consults elders selected by law as 'arbiters' of the verdict (ἐπιγνώμονας ἐλάμβανε τῆς γνώσεως, AT 7,12,1), apparently something inspired by the Roman model of the legal advisers (*iurisconsulti*), who were increasingly becoming fixtures in Roman courts in the second and third centuries. Achilles Tatius refers to the president's action as to 'examine' (διασκοπεῖν, AT 7,12,1), something like the process of the provincial governor who invites his advisers to review his judgment, and then issues a verdict under his sole authority. In this fictional courtroom, the judge and jury may wear the tunics of the Athenian archons, but they speak the language of Roman law—with a heavy accent.

The verdict is elegant. In an ironic subversion of the generic προσαγγελία, the 'suicide by jury', the hero asks for death but, instead of pitying him, the court throws the book at him. Clitophon is condemned to death according to the letter of law. The ancillary judgment is presented as a tricolon: there will be a second trial for Melite, a deposition for Thersander, and torture for Clitophon. In essence, the presiding judge calls the bluffs of all three parties. In the subsequent trial, the evidence of Melite's slaves will be admitted and Thersander will swear in writing that he does not know where Sosthenes is.[47] Achilles Tatius mentions this detail as a matter of course, as part of the president's official duties in bringing the case to a close. Finally, now that Clitophon is a condemned criminal, the president orders that he be tortured for evidence to be used in the next trial. This appears to be more consistent with Roman practices than Athenian. In Athens, public execution was relatively rare and prisons had minimal security; often prisoners simply

---

[45] MacDowell 1963, 33-38.

[46] The confusion is stems from the use of the verb δικάζειν to describe the activity of the ἄρχων βασιλεύς. This is the same verb that Achilles Tatius uses here. It is also used in a few other literary passages such as Lysias 26,12 and Andocides 1,78. The latter is a decree, a ψήφισμα, which is probably not an authentic fifth-century document; if spurious, it may be a manifestation of the same memory of the Athenian democracy upon which Achilles Tatius draws. On the other hand, both *Athenaiōn Politeia* 57,4 and Draco's law on homicide (*IG* I^2 115,11-13) distinguish between the actions of the ἄρχων βασιλεύς and the jury. His function was likely analogous to that of magistrates who presided over other cases MacDowell 1963, 37-38; Harrison 1971, 37-83.

[47] The use of writing at this point in the proceedings seems to reflect the Roman habit of documenting an increasing range of legal acts; see Meyer 2004, 174.

went into exile or committed suicide out of public view.[48] The next worst punishment was ἀτιμία, disenfranchisement; however, that did not necessarily entail automatic degradation to slave status. Under Roman law, conviction for a capital crime resulted in various gradations of punishment according to social status. In Clitophon's case, he is fettered, stripped, and hung from ropes while the whips, fire, and wheel are prepared for his torture (AT 7,12,1). The drastic punishment that is envisioned here is something roughly equivalent to the Roman *summum supplicium,* a cruel death with protracted suffering.[49]

The throng of eager spectators that typically forms the emotional wallpaper of the trials in Chariton's novel is nowhere to be seen. In this courtroom, the only crowd consists of advocates (AT 7,7,1). When there is an outcry, it is limited to the courtroom (AT 7,9,1); it does not spill into the streets of the city as it did in Chariton's Syracuse and Babylon. Clitophon's sentencing is businesslike— that is, until the spotlight shifts to the hero's anticipated torture.[50]

Achilles Tatius holds out the prospect of a ghastly spectacle, but then pulls back at the last moment by introducing the arrival of a religious embassy led by a priest of Artemis and including Sostratus, Leucippe's father. A suspension of public business goes into effect: Clitophon's torture and punishment must wait until after the ambassadors have finished their sacrifices (AT 7,12,3). It is only at this point that an excited crowd gathers around Clitophon, an object of intense interest as a result of his fortuitous, last-minute escape from punishment.[51] At the same time, a messenger interrupts with news that a 'beautiful foreign girl' (i.e., Leucippe) has taken refuge at the altar of Artemis (AT 7,15,1). As Clitophon tries to rush to the temple, the guards seize him. When they insist that they cannot release a convict condemned to death, the crowd physically intervenes to shield the novel's hero.[52] The priest of Artemis then personally guarantees Clitophon's appearance at the next trial, which will expose the tension between the jurisdiction of the city and that of the goddess.

---

[48] Allen 2000, 232-237.

[49] Grodzynski 1984; Bauman 1996, 151.

[50] Elsewhere in the novel, Achilles Tatius does not shy away from description of violence: the case in point is the spectacle of Leucippe's disembowelment by pirates. Xenophon of Ephesus vividly describes Habrocomes' torture (XE 2,6,3-4). On violence in the novels and its relationship to early Christian martyr acts, see Chew 2003.

[51] This also happens with Habrocomes (XE 4,2,9) and Charicleia (trial 9, below).

[52] The crowd similarly intervenes in the arrest of Daphnis (Longus 2,14,4) and the rescue Charicleia from her execution (H 8,9,15).

Trial 6.
Iudicium Deorum: Sacrilege
Thersander v. Priest of Artemis and Associates
(Achilles Tatius, *Leucippe and Clitophon* 8,7-15)

The Story

While Clitophon's execution is temporarily stayed by the arrival of a sacred delegation, Leucippe flees to the shrine of Artemis, where the lovers are reunited. The rules of asylum specify that only men, virgins, or abused slaves may enter the shrine. Intent on pursuing his case, Thersander issues a summons to Clitophon that devolves into violence and insults. As the crowd drags Thersander away from the temple, he ominously proclaims that 'the syrinx will punish Leucippe'.

At the sacrificial rites the next day, Thersander approaches the president of the city council and formally requests an immediate hearing on the grounds that the convict has been freed and a key witness has disappeared. The president schedules the trial for the following morning.

Thersander's accusations are many: first, he requests that Clitophon be duly executed. He then accuses the priest of Artemis of sacrilege and overstepping his authority. Because the charge of adultery against Melite remains unresolved, he also demands that Melite's maids be tortured for evidence. In closing, he announces his intention to prosecute Leucippe and her father on an unspecified charge.

The priest defends himself by launching an invective against Thersander. One of Thersander's lawyers, a speaker named Sopater, rebuts the priest's speech with an invective of his own, culminating with a simple syllogism: if the husband is dead, then the wife is not an adulteress; Thersander is alive, therefore, Melite is an adulteress. Thersander rashly makes two challenges. First, Melite must swear by the spring of the Styx that she did not commit adultery while Thersander was away. Second, Leucippe must enter the cave of the syrinx. The court is adjourned and the scene shifts to the precinct of Artemis, the site of the two ordeals. Leucippe successfully passes the virginity test and Melite is exonerated due to a cleverly worded condition in the oath she swears. Thersander flees Ephesus in defeat and is ultimately condemned in absentia to banishment.

Analysis

In the second trial scene in Ephesus, Achilles Tatius anatomizes how a legal dispute may devolve into chaos when litigants speak on their own behalf while teams of professional advocates coach them from the sidelines. The temple of Artemis, a world-renowned landmark, is the backdrop for the finale of Achilles Tatius' novel. Although specific physical details of the temple are scarce, the myths of the place underscore the contrast between the temple and the civic court.[1] The priest of Artemis emerges here as a pivotal figure. At the end of the first trial, the arrival of a sacred embassy temporarily suspended Clitophon's execution for murder. The priest is drawn into the trial when he takes custody of Clitophon. At the same time, Leucippe, still alive but enslaved, seeks refuge from her master at the goddess' altar. The priest explains the temple's strict laws of purity: entrance is permitted only men and virgins; married women and other non-virgins are excluded under penalty of death. The sole exception is when a female slave has a complaint against her master. In such a case, she may seek asylum at the shrine while the case is being adjudicated in the courts. If the court finds that the master has done nothing wrong, the master must take an oath that he will not retaliate against his slave; if the judges decide in favor of the slave, she remains a servant of the goddess (AT 7,13). As we shall see, the temple serves an auxiliary role to the civic court while at the same time claiming to derive its authority from the goddess.

Thersander and his retinue approach the temple and demand a retrial, based on a hyper-legalistic assertion that a verdict is a verdict, and that the court must follow through on its allegedly sacrosanct promise to put Clitophon to death. The fact that Leucippe is alive and ipso facto not murdered is immaterial to his claim. What begins as a personal dispute escalates into a manifesto against tyranny when Thersander belligerently accuses the priest of illegally releasing a convicted murderer and commandeering his slave girl (AT 8,1,1-2). A fistfight ensues and Thersander punches Clitophon, who tragically laments (τραγῳδῶν, AT 8,1,5) the bully's incursion into the goddess' precincts as an act of tyranny and concludes by asserting his status as 'a free man from a not insignificant city'.[2] The crowd witnesses the summons, but protects the hero by hauling Thersander away from

[1] On the description of Ephesus in the novel, see Saïd 1994, 227. On realia in the depiction of the temple and priest of Artemis, see Edsall 1996, 43-49.

[2] On asylum, see AT 8,2,1: ἐν τοῖς τῆς ἀσυλίας παιόμεθα χωρίοις, ... σὺ δὲ αὐτῶν ἐν ὄψει τυραννεῖς τῶν θεῶν. On free status, see AT 8,3,1: 'ὦ ἄνδρες, πέπονθα, ἐλεύθερός τε ὢν καὶ πόλεως οὐκ ἀσήμου. Cf. Chaereas' declaration on the steps of the king's palace that he is the only free man in Babylon (C 6,7,1).

the temple precinct. Thus the temple represents not only a space where slaves and citizens of other cities are protected, but also a space for the expression of popular justice.[3]

The second trial of the novel places the institutions of the polis at the center of debate. Thersander, a native Ephesian, uses his insider's privilege to shift the legal dispute to an alternate playing field. He cryptically warns Clitophon, 'Your case has been decided and you will pay the penalty; but the syrinx will avenge that pseudo-virginal whore' (AT 8,3,3). As the outsider in this context, Clitophon must rely upon a native informant—the priest—to explain the procedural details of the ordeals of the syrinx and the water of the Styx, both of which displace the civic spaces of justice and projects the judicial process onto the divine sphere. Narratively, the aetiologies of the ordeals bracket the trial scene proper.

In the midst of the religious festival that suspended Clitophon's execution, Thersander approaches the president of the council during the sacrifices and demands that his case be resumed immediately, on the grounds that the convict has been freed and that his slave, Sosthenes, has disappeared. To convey a sense of urgency, the temporal transition between the request for the trial and the trial scene itself is marked by a single sentence: 'The trial was scheduled for the next day' (προγέγραπτο μὲν οὖν εἰς τὴν ὑστεραίαν ἡ δίκη, AT 8,7,6). The setting immediately shifts to the 'appointed time' (ἡκούσης δὲ τῆς κυρίας AT 8,8,1) and the narrative proceeds directly to the speeches in the trial.[4]

Three speeches, by Thersander, the priest of Artemis, and a professional advocate named Sopater, form a virtual tetralogy that models rhetorical strategies to argue that crimes against individuals are equivalents to crimes against the city and its institutions. In the first two speeches, allegations of illicit sexual activity are inseparable from tyranny. The tone of this trial seems to be inspired by Attic invective. For example, in *Against Timarchus*, Aeschines argues that the prostitution of his foe, Timarchus, compromised the institutions of the state. Aeschines labors to justify his strategic choice to pursue a public indictment (γραφή) over a private suit (δική).[5] His rationale is that an acquittal of such a depraved person will undermine the authority of the law, encourage immorality, foster tyranny, and overthrow the democracy. Demosthenes uses a similar tactic in *Against Meidias*, where he emphasizes the symbolism of Meidias' assault on the sponsor and producer of the public chorus (χορηγός) at the civic festival of Dionysus, and argues that if Meidias goes free, the citizens can no longer trust in the security of their

---

[3] Cf. Thersander's earlier arrest of Clitophon in the streets during an all-night festival (see trial 5). On popular justice, see Forsdyke 2008.

[4] Cf. Chariton's introduction to the second Babylonian trial (C 6,1).

[5] Aeschines 1 *Against Timarchus*, 1, 5, and 191.

government.[6] Thersander uses the same angle of attack to warrant casting a wider net to prosecute anyone and everyone associated with Clitophon.

The Speech of Thersander

The scope of Thersander's accusations expands beyond the original charges of adultery in the first trial in Ephesus. Melite's retrial for murder, as announced in the prior verdict, temporarily recedes from the narrative. Once again, the original charge is eclipsed by new accusations against the priest of Artemis for desecrating the temple by harboring an unchaste woman (i.e., Leucippe) and for tyranny by defying the verdict of the previous trial. Thersander's prosecution consists of a proem (AT 8,8,1-3), an argument for executing Clitophon (AT 8,8,4-8), the presentation of the case against the priest (AT 8,8,6-11), and an epilogue that vaguely alludes to further accusations against Melite, Sosthenes, Leucippe, her 'holy hypocrite' of a father (AT 8,8,12-14).

To justify the continuation of his lawsuit, Thersander magnifies the scale of criminality and admits he does not know where to begin (AT 8,8,1; cf. Demosthenes 18,129). Essentially, he makes a 'slippery slope' argument, listing the crimes in a crescendo to reinforce their magnitude:

> ὅταν μὲν γὰρ φονεύωσι τοὺς ἀλλοτρίους οἰκέτας οἱ μοιχοί, μοιχεύωσι δὲ τὰς ἀλλοτρίας γυναῖκας οἱ φονεῖς, λύωσι δ' ἡμῖν τὰς θεωρίας οἱ πονροβοσκοί, τὰ δὲ σεμνότατα τῶν ἱερῶν μιαίνωσιν αἱ πόρναι, τὰς ἡμέρας δὲ λογιζόμεναι ταῖς δούλαις καὶ τοῖς δεσπόταις, τί δράσειε τις ἔτι, τῆς ἀνομίας ὁμοῦ καὶ μοιχείας καὶ ἀσεβείας καὶ μιαιφονίας κεκρασμένης;
>
> For whenever adulterers kill other men's slaves, and killers commit adultery with other men's wives, and pimps destroy sacred embassies, and prostitutes pollute the great solemnity of temples and arrange trial dates between slave women and masters, what is a person to do, given that lawlessness is nevertheless overwhelmed by adultery and sacrilege and bloodshed? (AT 8,8,3)[7]

It is worth pointing out the self-conscious use of several rhetorical figures in this purple passage: isocolon, anastrophe (οἱ μοιχοί, μοιχεύωσι), chiasmus (φονεύωσι

---

[6] Demosthenes 21 *Against Meidias*, 32, and 219-222.

[7] For the translation of τὰς ἡμέρας δὲ λογιζόμεναι as 'arrange trial dates', I follow Vilborg 1962, 131.

οἱ μοιχοί and μοιχεύωσιοί φονεῖς, λύωσι τὰς θεωρίας and τὰ δὲ σεμνότατα τῶν ἱερῶν μιαίνωσιν), alliteration (ταῖς δούλαις καὶ τοῖς δεσπόταις, and τί δράσειε τις ἔτι), and homoioteleuton (ἀνομίας, μοιχείας, ἀσεβείας, μιαιφονίας). In each clause, the impression of wrongdoing is compounded by the use of nouns for criminals (μοιχοί, φονεῖς, πορνοβοσκοί, πόρναι) as the subjects of verbs describing the types of crimes (φονεύωσι, μοιχεύωσι, λύωσι, μιαίνωσι). The last item in the sequence occupies an emphatic position: specifically, the insinuation that Leucippe is a prostitute and therefore guilty of polluting the temple of Artemis.

The second trial revisits the crisis of confession raised in the first. Thersander argues that it is an affront to the authority of the court for Clitophon to defy its earlier conviction (AT 8,8,4). The fact that the victim of the murder to which he confessed is alive after all is immaterial to Thersander's claim. His demand that Clitophon be put to death devolves into an absurdly legalistic argument over procedural details.[8] A half a century or so after Achilles Tatius' time, the third-century jurist Paul ruled, 'One who admits liability is in the position of one against whom judgment is pronounced; for, in a way, he is condemned by his own decision'.[9] He cites a civil suit that equated confession with conviction:

> *Si is, cum quo lege Aquilia agitur, confessus est servum occidisse, licet non occiderit, si tamen occisus sit homo, ex confesso tenetur.*
>
> If someone sued under the *lex Aquilia* admits that he killed the slave, he will be liable on his own admission, even though he did not kill him, if the slave in fact has been killed. (*Digest* 48,2,4, trans. Watson)

Due to issues of chronology, it is doubtful that Achilles Tatius knew of these rulings. Yet, perhaps the issue of confession had become problematic for Roman courts around this time, and the novel simply reflects a broader social phenomenon as illustrated by reports of Christians who freely confessed when they were charged before Roman courts. In the previous trial, Clitophon admitted that he killed Leucippe, Thersander's slave (AT 7,11,4). Of course, the key qualification in Paul's ruling is 'if the slave has in fact been killed'. In this trial scene, however, the facts are clear that the slave is very much alive, which ought to render the case

---

[8] This may have been a subject of debate in law courts in Achilles Tatius' time. In the third century, Roman jurists weighed in on the contingencies that might affect the validity of a confession. In a situation that fits Clitophon's situation exactly, Ulpian wrote that a confession was invalid if it was based on factual error, but not on ignorance of the law (*Digest* 48,2,2). Yan Thomas suggests that confession was a 'juridical fiction', the purpose of which was to advance a suit to discussion of compensation; see Y. Thomas 1986, 94.

[9] *Digest* 48,2,1: *Confessus pro iudicato est, qui quodammodo sua sententia damnatur.*

moot. Nevertheless, the fact of the confession remains the central point of contention.

The main thrust of Thersander's attack moves from the letter of the law to the moral character of Clitophon and the priest. He points to the danger of pollution by allowing a convict to stand in court wearing a white robe instead of chains (AT 8,8,4). According to him, the real danger is that Clitophon, a convicted murderer arrogates the right to speak in public.[10] Thersander calls for the earlier 'decree of the presidents and the councilors' to be read, a commonplace in the Attic orations, when the speaker would ask the clerk to read aloud the law so as to portray his opponent as attacking the law itself.[11] He urges the judges to carry out the death sentence against Clitophon, who is already technically dead as far as the laws are concerned because his conviction is overdue (ὑπερήμερος, AT 8,8,6).[12]

Next comes the accusation against the priest for tyranny. Thersander deploys many of the standard tropes associated with such a line of attack:

> τί λέγεις, ὦ σεμνότατε καὶ κοσμιώτατε ἱερεῦ; ἐν ποίοις ἱεροῖς γέγραπται νόμοις τοὺς ὑπὸ τῆς βουλῆς καὶ τῶν πρυτάνεων κατεγνωσμένους καὶ θανάτοις καὶ δεσμοῖς παραδοθέντας ἐξαρπάζειν τῆς καταδίκης καὶ τῶν δεσμῶν ἀπολύειν, καὶ κυριώτερον σαυτὸν ποιεῖν τῶν προέδρων καὶ τῶν δικαστηρίων;
>
> What do you say, O most august and genteel priest? In what sacred laws is it inscribed that you have the authority rescue from their sentence those condemned by the council and the presidents and relegated to execution and imprisonment, to loosen their chains and to make yourself more sovereign than the presidents and the courts? (AT 8,8,6)

The aggregation of words for political entities (τῆς βουλῆς, τῶν πρυτάνεων, τῶν προέδρων, τῶν δικαστηρίων) emphasizes the city's alleged supervision over the temple. References to the priest's release of Clitophon are pleonastic; there is little substantive difference between 'to snatch away people condemned by the council

---

[10] AT 8,8,4: τάχα δὲ τολμήσει καὶ φωνὴν ἀφεῖναι καὶ ἐπιρρητορεῦσαί τι κατ' ἐμοῦ. Cf. Aeschines 1,29: τετόλμηκε Τίμαρχος δημηγορεῖν.

[11] AT 8,8,5: Λέγε δὲ ὧδε τῶν προέδρων καὶ τῶν συμβούλων τὸ δόγμα; cf. Aeschines 1,33-5. The plural προέδρων, literally 'presidents', must refer to the jurors despite the fact that in AT 7,12,1, the decision seems to be made by a single president of the jurors under the advisement of the elders. Vilborg (1962, 131) notes that 'Thersander expresses himself a little carelessly; what he wants to say is 'the decision of the juridical authorities'.

[12] LSJ, s.v. 'ὑπερήμερος' usually refers to default on a loan.

and the prytanies and handed over to death and chains' and 'to release from conviction and imprisonment'. The chiastic order of the clauses thus yields a sentence beginning and ending with the allegation that the priest considers himself above the law.

A key concept in this section is κυρία, legal authority. The president's official chair (θώκου, AT 8,8,7) becomes a symbol for the contested authority. Thersander argues the president is no longer κύριος of anything and calls on him to cede his office and the courtroom to the priest because he is powerless to enforce the court's judgments against criminals. He invites the priest to take the president's place—now called a 'throne' (ἐν τῷ τοῦ προέδρου θρόνῳ, AT 8,8,8)—so that he can assume the power to judge and command. He urges the priest to assume Artemis' role as well, because he has also usurped her power. He declares that the goddess alone is able to absolve defendants—but only before the judgment of the court has been given; that is, the goddess does not release prisoners before trial.[13]

Thersander seems to be splitting hairs, and it is uncertain whether any of this corresponds to reality. Customarily, there was a performative dimension to asylum. Traditionally a suppliant had to take physical hold of an object connected with a sanctuary. It would not usually be simple for people sentenced to capital punishment to have the opportunity to seek sanctuary before being taken to prison pending execution. All of this is subordinate to Thersander's overall point that the priest is guilty of hubris against both the state and the goddess. His line of reasoning veers back to the subject of sexual deviance: he alleges that the priest is defiling the shrine by using the temple as a jail, a brothel, and a room for adulterers (AT 8,8,10-11).

Returning to the original charge of adultery, Thersander responds to Melite's challenge (πρόκλησις). He casts the potential torture of Melite's slaves as something that he—and not Melite—had demanded, a move to deflect attention from the reciprocal expectation that his own slaves are also subject to torture.[14] He frames the question to be put to the torture as a pair of alternative conditions, and stipulates that Melite forfeit her dowry if the torture validates his claim that she is an adulteress:

---

[13] AT 8,8,9: αὐτῇ μόνῃ τοὺς ἐπ' αὐτὴν καταφεύγοντας ἔξεστι σώζειν, καὶ ταῦτα πρὸ δικαστηρίου γνώσεως.

[14] The tactic was used in trials in classical Athens; see Mirhady 1996. On forfeiture of of a fraction of the dowry in convictions of adultery under the *lex Iulia de adulteriis coercendies*, see McGinn 1998, 143.

> ἐν γὰρ τῇ τῶν θεραπαινῶν βασάνῳ τὴν ἐξέτασιν γενέσθαι δέδοκται. ταύτας οὖν αἰτῶ, αἳ κἂν βασανιζόμεναι φήσωσιν οὐκ εἰδέναι τοῦτον τὸν κατάδικον χρόνῳ πολλῷ συνόντα αὐτῇ καὶ < ἐν > ἀνδρὸς χώρᾳ ἐν τῇ οἰκίᾳ τῇ ἐμῇ, οὐκ ἐν μοιχοῦ μόνον, καθεστηκότα, πάσης αἰτίας αὐτὴν ἀφίημι. ἄν τοίνυν τοὐναντίον, τὴν μὲν κατὰ τὸν νόμον ἀφεῖσθαι τῆς προικός φημὶ δεῖν ἐμοί, τὸν δὲ ὑποσχεῖν τὴν ὀφειλομένην τοῖς μοιχοῖς τιμωρίαν· θάνατος δέ ἐστιν αὕτη.
>
> In the first trial it was decided that there be an investigation by torture of the maids. I therefore now request them. And if they confess under torture that they have no knowledge that this convict was cohabiting with her for an extended time and had taken the place of a husband — not merely an adulterer— in my house, then I will release her from the entire charge of adultery. But if otherwise, I declare that she must forfeit to me her dowry in accordance with the law and he must suffer the prescribed punishment for adulterers: namely, death. (AT 8,8,13)

Essentially, the case hinges on a simple factual question: Were Melite and Clitophon married? Given the fluid nature of their liaison, the answer to this simple question is anything but straightforward. By adding the superfluous qualification, 'the place of a husband and not merely an adulterer', Thersander has unwittingly muddied the waters. In any case, he says, Clitophon will be condemned to death, either as an adulterer or as a murderer (ὡς μοιχὸς ἢ ὡς φονεύς, AT 8,8,13).[15] It is immaterial that there was no death penalty for adultery under Roman law. In the universe of the Greek novels, adultery is the ultimate crime and therefore deserves the ultimate punishment.

The Speech of the Priest

The priest is an insider who understands how the legal system works amidst a whirlwind of accusations of adultery and sexual debauchery. Like Mithridates in Chariton's first Babylonian trial, both figures blend civic and religious functions: the satrap was characterized as a *magus*, whereas the priest of Artemis champions the laws of the polis. Both hold the male protagonists in their custody: Chaereas was Mithridates' client, and Clitophon is a suppliant at the temple of Artemis. At

[15] Evans Grubbs (1995, 217) adduces Thersander's remark as evidence that adultery was a capital crime as late as the second or third century. Given the demands for melodrama in the fiction, I am inclined toward skepticism on this point.

the end of the trial, both produce the key person whose testimony refutes the prosecution's case *in toto*.

The priest's speech addresses the issue of the relationship between court and temple in the polis. As we have seen in Thersander's speech and will see in the priest's, the speakers do not position themselves as defending one authority against the other; rather, they compete over the boundaries between these spheres and thereby reveal alternate notions about the respective roles of the two institutions.

As can be seen in Table 3, the priest's speech is a carefully crafted rebuttal to Thersander. Both speeches are of roughly equal length, with fourteen sub-sections each. The main points are identified by letter so as to highlight the close correspondence between the two speeches. Each speech has a *proem* (A) and a brief *narratio* (B). Thersander's two main attacks center around the theme of authority: the first argument (C-G) is that the authority of the court must be upheld in the face of the priest's efforts to subvert it. The second argument extends the argument to apply to the priest's own sphere of authority (H-J). Finally, they both conclude by leaving the door open for further accusations and speeches (K-L).

The priest's refutation carefully reflects the structure of the accusation. A proem (A-B) and an epilogue (K-L) bracket his arguments. The priest turns each of the charges against Thersander in two sections. In both, he begins with Thersander's second assertion, followed by his final assertion of that subsection, and concludes the subsection with Thersander's initial allegation. The schema is XY...Z versus YZ...X. For example, Thersander asserts that 'Artemis alone has the power' (H), then alleges that the priest misuses a public space (the temple) for private purposes (sex, I). The priest inverts it: Thersander uses a private space (his house) for public purposes (to administer justice, I′). Thersander ends with the allegation that the priest was sleeping with Leucippe (J), whereas the priest ends by emphasizing the power of Artemis (H′).

Table 3. Comparison of Speeches of Thersander and the Priest of Artemis

	THERSANDER (AT 8,8)		**THE PRIEST (AT 8,9)**
	Proem		
A	So many unrelated crimes, I am tongue-tied. (1-2)	A′	Such abuse is a sign of an unclean mouth. His tongue is full of hubris. (1-2)
	Brief Narration		
B	The priest neglects his duty. (3)	B′	Thersander pretends to be cultured. (3-5)
	Argument 1: The Power of the Court		
C	(To the court) You condemned Clitophon to death; now he is free. (4)	D′	(To the court) You honored me with the priestly office. I need not defend my life. (6)
D	Read the sentence. The execution is overdue. (5)	G′	According to Thersander, a tyrant is someone who protects the innocent. (7)
E	(To the priest) Where is it written that you can free a convict? (6)	E′	(To Thersander) By what authority did you throw Clitophon in jail? (8)
F	(To the presiding judge): Get off the bench. (7)	F′	Shut the law courts! (9)
G	(To the priest) Step up and be the tyrant you are. (8)	C′	(To the court) You have never condemned a man to chains, but Thersander has. (10)
	Argument 2: The Power of Artemis		
H	Artemis alone has the power. (9)	I′	Thersander holds court at night in his house. (11)
I	(To priest) You are turning her temple into a brothel. (10)	J′	Conviction for murder is moot because Leucippe is alive. (12)
J	You dined and probably slept with the slave girl. (11)	H′	Artemis has saved them both (12).
	Epilogue		
K	Punish both men now. (12)	K′	(To Thersander) You have killed two people by false accusation. (13)
L	The other two charges: let maids be tortured. I will charge my slave girl and her father later. (13-14)	L′	I have said enough: let the foreigners speak. (14)

In response to the prosecution's hyperbolic accusation that the priest has desecrated the temple of Artemis, the priest launches an invective, 'in the style of Aristophanic comedy' (τὴν Ἀριστοφάνους ἐζηλωκὼς κωμῳδίαν, AT 8,9,1). Invective has been characterized as 'an inverted form: it should be organized in the same way, but with the topics turned to vituperation instead of praise'.[16] The priest's speech is a showpiece; hearing the invective coming out of the mouth of a religious official has jarred some modern commentators.[17] The most common topics of invective were age, physical appearance, sexual deviance, criminality, bankruptcy, barbarism, gluttony, madness, violence, autocratic tendencies, tyranny, treachery, dangerousness to the state, evil associates— all inversions of behavioral norms for cultivated men.[18] The priest's speech paradoxically reinforces the genre's ethos of παιδεία and σωφροσύνη by demonizing its antithesis. The priest's retorts—often obscene—echo items in Thersander's own speech and are subsumed to his pious defense of religion. He says that it is the mark of an impure mouth to abuse the things and persons connected with the goddess, thus suggesting that things and persons not associated with the goddess (i.e., Thersander) are fair game (AT 8,8,10). Five of the fourteen sections that comprise the speech are devoted to the subject of attacking the character of Thersander, a rhetorical strategy which was not only condoned, but also encouraged in rhetorical handbooks, particularly in cases where the sole issue was one of fact.[19]

By parrying Thersander's characterization of the priest as an accessory to all sorts of debauchery, the priest portrays Thersander as a sexual pervert in the mold of Aeschines' Timarchus.[20] For example, the priest's comment that Thersander's 'tongue is full of hubris' (τὴν γλῶτταν μεστὴν ὕβρεως, AT 8,9,2) answers Thersander's apology to the jury for being 'tongue-tied' in enumerating every detail of the crimes (τῆς τῶν ἄλλων μνήμης τὴν γλῶτταν ἐφ' ἕκαστον ἑλούσης, AT 8,8,2). The allegation that Thersander 'performed solemnity and pretended prudence' (σεμνότητα δ' ἔδρακε καὶ σωφροσύνην ὑπεκρίνατο, AT 8,9,2) snidely corresponds to Thersander's closing line, in which he referred to Leucippe's father as a 'holy hypocrite' (σεμνὸν τοῦτον πατρὸς ὑποκριτήν, AT 8,8,14). The

[16] Long 1996, 78.

[17] For example, Gaselee comments, 'In the whole of the first part of the good bishop's speech there is a series of double meaning, insinuations, and plays upon words which are not without wit, but...are not pleasing to Northern and Christian ears'; see Gaselee and Warmington 1969, 419 n. 411. Vilborg calls it 'witty' and parses the sexual puns; see Vilborg 1962, 132-133.

[18] Long 1996, 66-67.

[19] Russell 1983, 46-47.

[20] For examples of Achilles Tatius' explicit allusions to Aeschines *Against Timarchus,* see Brethes 2007, 21 n. 60.

vivid image of Thersander bending over and lying down for lovers is a retort to Thersander's taunting the priest to receive obeisance (ὑποκύπτων καὶ ὑποκατακλινόμενος, AT 8,9,2; cf. μετὰ τῆς Ἀρτέμιδος προσκυνοῦ, AT 8,8,8). The priest's assertion that Thersander rented for himself a 'little alleyway' where he had a 'shack' (ὀλίγον ἑαυτῷ μισθωσάμενος στενωπεῖον, εἶχεν ἐνταῦθα τὸ οἴκημα, AT 8,9,3) answers Thersander's allegation that the priest is using the temple as a 'shack' (οἴκημα τὸ ἱερὸν ἐποίησας, AT 8,8,11).

The attack on Thersander's pretense to be a man of παιδεία is a retort to his vilification of the priest as a fraud. The equivalence between the priest and the cultured gentleman (πεπαιδεύμενος) indicates that both identities were understood as acquired through careful practice and recognized in the eyes of the community. The priest points out to the presiding judge and council that they themselves honored him with the office. In other words, the priesthood is a civic office rather than a religious calling. In this light, it is not completely anomalous for the priest to speak in an 'Aristophanic' manner. He presumably claims to be a cultured man himself, one whose worthiness has been validated by the city's representatives. The priest comments that Thersander 'pretends to be in love with education' (παιδείας προσποιούμενος ἐρᾶν, AT 8,9,2). He then turns to two aspects of παιδεία: the care for the soul and the exercise of the body. On one level these become the basis of double entendres for Thersander's sexual deviance. On another level, they allude to the Platonic education in virtue, where the faculties of the body are applied metaphorically to the training of the soul.[21] Seen in this light, the priest's attack on Thersander is inseparable from the inherited traditions of παιδεία. Like Plato, Homer was central to Greek education. The priest transforms this into a verb, 'doing Homer' (ὁμηρίζων) which Vilborg construes as a pun on ὁμός, 'same, joint', and μηρός, 'thigh'. Likewise, musical education is subordinated to his sexual pursuits in a word play on the verb περιβαίνειν (AT 8,9,4), which refers to a style of strumming a lyre as well as 'to straddle'; in combination with the direct object, a πλῆκτρον (a pick as well a euphemism for penis), it forms yet another double entendre.[22] Thersander's gymnastic education is an obvious target for this kind of character slur. The priest says that Thersander wrestled suggestively at the gymnasium in his youth; when he grew older he flaunted his ruined physique and shamelessly exercised only his tongue and mouth, metonymy for the rhetorical exercises of a gentleman as well as a metaphor for sexual practices (AT 8,9,5). Thersander symbolizes the degeneration of culture or ἄσκησις,

---

[21] Brethes 2006, 181.

[22] Vilborg 1962, 133. Whitmarsh (2001, 134) translates it as 'Homer-eroticism'.

the regimen of moderate exercise of the body and of the voice that was prescribed for mature men during the imperial period.[23]

Moving to the refutation of the charge of tyranny against him, the priest contrasts himself to his opponent. He says that Thersander has 'illiterately' (ἀπαιδεύτως AT 8,9,5) slandered him, a person honored with the priesthood by none other than the people of Ephesus. But, whereas Thersander insists upon complying with the court's verdict, the priest draws upon his cultural capital; namely, his popularity with the citizens of Ephesus. The priest thus avoids a defense of his own character (AT 8,9,6; cf. Demosthenes 18,10).

The next section demonstrates how to dismantle an accusation via the ἀντίληψις, a form of rebuttal in which a defendant claims that he did nothing illegal.[24] He turns Thersander's allegations against him into two separate charges: that he released a prisoner and that he released someone sentenced to death. On both counts, the priest notes that Clitophon was wrongfully imprisoned and convicted; therefore, the priest's protection of him is not illegal. Whereas Thersander blames the priest for illegally freeing a convict, the priest now accuses Thersander of illegally imprisoning him in the first place on the basis that only the law has the authority to forcibly restrain a person (ὁ νόμος αὐτόν, ὁ καὶ σοῦ καὶ πάντων κύριος, δησάτω, AT 8,9,8), thus implying that it is Thersander—not the priest—who has usurped the powers of the state:

> This noble gentleman is everything unto himself: assembly, council, president, and general. In private he punishes and judges and orders people to be fettered, and the trial date is after dark. The midnight judge is just fine and dandy! (AT 8,9,10-11)

The proper time for trials is, of course, during the day; the allusion to a nighttime trial refers to Clitophon's arrest, earlier in the narrative, during an all-night festival, with connotations of conspiracy and debauchery.[25] Typically, the convening of a governing council at night was normally considered unusual, if not improper. Aulus Gellius (14,7,8) reports that it was illegal for the Roman senate to pass a decree before dawn.[26] In Plato's *Laws*, the council of ten magistrates responsible for the Guardians' education and the security of the state, meets nightly. The priest alleges that Thersander appropriates all the important functions of the state under

---

[23] Gleason 1995, 84-91.

[24] Cf. Mithridates' defense in trial 3; Russell 1983, 48-49.

[25] Vilborg 1962, 134.

[26] Talbert 1984, 190.

cover of darkness by playing 'the midnight judge'.[27] While it is not inconceivable that Achilles Tatius drew upon the concept of some kind of night court, in the novels an arrest or beating in the house at night is a prelude to a civic trial.

The priest becomes the mouthpiece for the general principle of the city's authority to limit an individual's right to take revenge. In upholding the principle of due process, the priest presumes that the cuckold's right to self-help, as strenuously asserted by the speaker of Lysias' *Against Eratosthenes,* was no longer recognized as legitimate. While there is evidence from the Attic orations that the husband's privilege was already limited in the classical period, as it was under Augustus' legislation, the concept of the vigilante husband lived on in the imaginary universe of the declamations.[28] In direct response to Thersander's challenge of the right to offer asylum to a prisoner (AT 8,8,6), the priest states the legal principle that 'without a trial, no individual is more powerful than another' (οὐδενὸς γὰρ οὐδείς ἐστιν ἄνευ κρίσεως δυνατώτερος, AT 8,9,9). The priest applies the same principle to Thersander's actions upon discovering Clitophon in his home. He asks, 'According to what laws did you imprison the young foreigner? Which of the councilors (τίς προέδρων) condemned him? Which court (ποῖον δικαστήριον) ordered the man to be bound?' He asserts that even if the person is guilty, he must first be cross-examined, judged, and allowed to speak; only the laws have the power to restrain a person.[29] Although such an argument is not without precedent in the classical orations, it suggests that vigilantism and false imprisonment remained an issue in Achilles Tatius' time.[30]

The decisive evidence that exonerates Clitophon of Leucippe's murder is saved for the grand finale: namely, the obvious fact that the victim, Leucippe, is alive. Logically, this fact ought to obviate the trial; however, literarily the objective is to prolong the trial scene is to defer the ending with as many twists as possible. It is similar to Mithridates' strategy in the first Babylonian trial in Chariton's novel, where he concealed his most compelling witness—i.e., Chaereas—until after the conclusion of his rhetorically brilliant speech of defense. In the form of an imaginary cross-examination of Thersander (ἠθοποιία), the priest speaks the

[27] AT 8,9,11: ὁ νυκτερινὸς δικαστής. Cf. Plato *Laws* 968a: τὸν τῶν ἀρχόντων νυκτερινὸν σύλλογον. Liviabella Furiani 1985 understands this detail as a 'winking allusion' to Plato.

[28] Classical Athens: Cohen 1991, 12ff. Declamations: Russell 1983, 51.

[29] AT 8,9,8: ἀλλὰ καὶ κριθήτω πρῶτον, ἐλεγχθήτω, λόγου μεταλαβών· ὁ νόμος αὐτόν, ὁ καὶ σοῦ καὶ πάντων κύριος, δησάτω.

[30] For example, the speaker of Antiphon 5,17 discusses in some detail the laws regulating imprisonment in connection with an incident in which the prosecutors refused the defendant bail; the speaker uses their actions as evidence of his opponents' bad faith and evasion of the law; see Hansen 1976. Likewise, Roman law limited the power of individual to imprison people; see *Digest* 2,7.

unspoken: he is not guilty of releasing a person sentenced to death, because Clitophon is not guilty of the murder for which he was sentenced, because that murder never actually happened. To underscore the absurdity, the priest points to Leucippe and turns the charge against Thersander, holding him liable for three metaphorical murders: he killed Leucippe in speech, intended to kill Clitophon in deed, and is responsible for Sosthenes' mysterious disappearance. As Clinias did in the first trial, the priest—also speaking in second position, in defense of Clitophon—comes closest to the truth as the reader knows it.

The Speech of Sopater

After the priest is finished speaking, once again there seems to be some confusion in the courtroom over the order of speakers. The priest yields the floor to his fellow advocates for a defense speech on behalf of Clitophon and Leucippe. An unnamed man identified as 'a not dishonorable speaker and a member of the council' steps up to speak but is interrupted by Thersander's advocate (συνήγορος, AT 8,10,1), a man named Sopater, who addresses the first speaker as 'Nicostratus'.[31] He argues that because Thersander's accusation was directed against the priest, who gave already his defense, the trial has moved to the next phase, the prosecution against the adulterers. Sopater insists that Nicostratus will have the opportunity to rebut the charges afterwards. It is important to note the absence of a magistrate to ensure due process. The courtroom is a jousting arena in which the speakers make claims that seem to have no bearing on actual law.

Sopater is portrayed as a speaker who is so clever that he is inept. His lack of self-awareness is signaled by his exaggerated gestures—such as rubbing his face, an inappropriate movement, according to Quintilian's handbook on rhetoric.[32] He begins with a rebuttal of the priest's attack on Thersander (AT 8,10,3-6). Then, after a brief defense of Thersander's life (AT 8,10,7), he builds his case against Melite for adultery (AT 8,10,8-11). Sopater's inflated self-confidence eventually

---

[31] J. Schwartz 1967, 547 misidentifies 'Nicostratus' as the name of the priest. Sopater, on the other hand, shares a name with a family of philosophers and rhetoricians, one of whom wrote one of the most important surviving collections of rhetorical 'questions', the Διαίρεσις Ζητημάτων. Unfortunately, this Sopater lived two or more centuries after Achilles Tatius, so any identification of the fictional rhetor with this family is purely speculative.

[32] Quintilian *Institutio Oratoria* 11,3,121-3. Vilborg considers this as an echo of Aeschines' *On the Embassy,* a speech against Demosthenes, where Aeschines ridicules his opponent's gestures in an almost identical fashion: Aeschines 2,49: ἐφ' ἅπασι δ' ὑμῖν ἀνίσταται τελευταῖος Δημοσθένης, καὶ τερατευσάμενος, ὥσπερ εἴωθε, τῷ σχήματι καὶ τρίψας τὴν κεφαλήν.

misleads Thersander into posing a disastrously worded question for Melite's trial by ordeal. Sopater glosses over the adultery charge, apparently distracted by the priest's recent accusation that Thersander is liable for two, maybe three, deaths (δυσὶ θανάτοις ἔνοχον ὄντα, AT 8,10,2). Sopater simply turns the charge against Clitophon, even though the fact has been undeniably established that Leucippe is not dead, but alive. The speech is a comic muddle of different objectives: to continue to accuse Clitophon of murder, to discredit the priest, and to pursue the charge of adultery against Melite.

In contrast to the priest's speech, Sopater's retorts are tedious and shallow. For example, he repeats almost verbatim the priest's allegation that Thersander 'uses his tongue for insolence' (AT 8,9,5), yet does so without recognizing the salaciousness of the accusation. Sopater is unimaginative: he uses 'tongue' as a conventional metonym to underscore the priest's shocking language. He announces that he will use the priest's own words against him, even after he has criticized the priest for shifting the blame to Thersander. Sopater is stupid as well. He mentions 'riddles' in the priest's speech, which he is not clever enough to parry. He can only assert that Thersander is telling the truth and the priest is lying. He tautologically argues that 'the false accusations he so shamelessly made by ridiculing Thersander's lifestyle are not at all removed from the imputation of false accusation' (AT 8,10,3). Gaselee suspects that the text is not sound; Vilborg calls the sentence 'flat'.[33] I prefer to believe that Achilles Tatius intentionally designed an awkward sentence to highlight the stupidity of this professional orator.

Although Sopater presents himself as an expert on procedure, he digresses into the same type of character assassination as the previous speakers. He insinuates that the priest has been bribed for his testimony (AT 8,10,4) and repeats Thersander's point that the priest has turned 'the temple of Artemis into a temple of Aphrodite'—i.e., a brothel (AT 8,10,6). He alleges that the priest lusts after the 'adulterer and prostitute', whose beauty Sopater pruriently dwells on at length (AT 8,10,5). Expanding upon Thersander's reference to the priest's symposium, Sopater asserts that they all slept and drank together throughout the night without chaperones. His solution is to propose yet another trial over the priest's fitness to hold the office (AT 8, 10,6).

Sopater then pivots to his next point: Melite. Echoing the priest's aposiopesis about his own character, Sopater points out that 'everyone knows Thersander's character' (AT 8,10,7). He depicts his client as a fine and prudent young man who grew up and, after having carefully selected a wife for her lineage and wealth,

---

[33] Gaselee and Warmington 1969, 427 n.421; Vilborg 1962, 135.

married Melite according to the laws. In the process of characterizing Melite as a flagrant adulteress he uses many of the same terms that he used to discredit the priest.[34] The word for adultery (μοιχεία) and its derivatives appear ten times in Sopater's speech (twenty-five lines in Vilborg's text): the effect is overkill. He claims that Melite took advantage of her husband's long voyage to engage in affairs and 'found a young, low-class, male prostitute who played the role of a husband with women, and a wife with men' (AT 8,10,9).[35] He denounces Melite in a polysyndeton of her alleged vices: she consorted with her lover with impunity, in a foreign country, blatantly on the seas, in a boat, on land and sea, and from Egypt to Ionia and that she advertised her affair 'with the help not only of a trumpet, but also with a herald' (AT 8,10,10). In anticipation of the argument that Melite thought her husband was dead, Sopater formulates the following ultimatum:

> εἰ μὲν τέθνηκεν, ἀπήλλαξαι τῆς αἰτίας· οὐδὲ γὰρ ἐστιν ὁ τὴν μοιχείαν παθών, οὐδὲ ὑβρίζεται γάμος οὐκ ἔχων ἄνδρα· εἰ δὲ ὁ γάμος τῷ τὸν γήμαντα ζῆν οὐκ ἀνῄρεται, τὴν γαμηθεῖσαν διαφθείραντος ἄλλου λελῄστευται.

> If he is dead, she is absolved of blame, for there is no party aggrieved by adultery, and a marriage is not violated when there is no husband. But if the marriage has not been annulled because the husband is still alive, then it has been destroyed because another man has stolen the wife. (AT 8,10,12)

The first proposition is similar to the eunuch's advice to the Persian king in Chariton's novel, where he argues that the king need not worry about being an adulterer because Callirhoe technically had no husband. Sopater's characterization of Melite's affairs is so devastating—to his own client—that Thersander impulsively interrupts Sopater and proposes that Melite be tested by ordeal. In effect, the advocate alienates his client and forces him into an impossible position. Sopater's vehement denunciation of Melite leads Thersander to pose the wrong question for the oath challenge, thereby undermining his own lawsuit.

---

[34] Shamelessness (AT 8,10,8 ἀναισχυντίας πεπλήρωται and 8,10,11 οὐκ ᾐσχύνετο; cf. 8,10,2 ἀναισχύντως ὑποκριναμένου), insolence (AT 8,10,12 ὑβρίζεται; cf. 8,10,4 ὕβρεως), sleeping together (AT 8,10,10 συγκαθεύδουσα; cf. 8,10,6 κοινῇ...ἐκαθεύδετε), blatancy (AT 8,10,9 φανερῶς ἀσελγαίνουσα; cf. 8,10,4 οὕτω φανερῶς), spectators or lack thereof (AT 8,10,9 πάντων ὁρώντων; cf. AT 8,10,6 οὐδεὶς γέγονε θεατής), wantonness (AT 8,10,9 ἀσελγαίνουσα: cf. AT 8,10,2 ἀσελγῶς), purchase and sale (AT 8,10,9 ἐωνημένη; cf AT 8,10,6 ἐωνήσατο).

[35] Cf. Clitophon's capture in Melite's clothing in AT 6,5. For an analysis of the insult that a man behaves as a woman, see Dover 1989, 103-109.

Ordeals

Through two trials-by-ordeal, Melite and Leucippe, debarred from speaking in court because they are female, silently defend themselves before the community. Thersander's challenge invokes the two goddesses, Artemis and Aphrodite, who oversee aspects of female sexuality. These puzzling ordeals have attracted scholarly commentary. Rattenbury, who had presumed that Achilles Tatius was the latest of the novels, reads the ordeals in this novel as an attempt to humanize the conventional chastity ordeal as presented in Heliodorus (H 10,8-9), and to illuminate 'certain apparent absurdities in the conventions on which the literary forms were built'.[36] Segal's structuralist approach informs his view that the ordeals of the two women reflect a fundamental dichotomy between Aphrodite and Artemis that runs throughout the narrative.[37] On the other hand, Morgan has reintroduced the issue of the novels' 'didacticism', and argues for a reading of the novel as 'a statement of moral and erotic values'.[38]

The ordeals represent a fantasy of justice that is consistent with the style of the Greek novels. Nevertheless, it is worth thinking through what these fictional ordeals might have signified to readers in the second or third centuries. After all, it was around this time that stories of miracles and wonders (paradoxographies) and of Christian martyrs being put on trial (martyrologies) circulated around the Roman world. Historians of Greek and Roman law have tended to dismiss ordeals as vestiges of a primitive sense of justice.[39] Indeed, the usage of trial by ordeal (derived from the Germanic *Urteil*) was more prominent in medieval law than in classical Greek and Roman law. Glotz argues that the Greeks used the ordeal, which he defined as 'the judgment of a god', as a religious procedure that coexisted with judicial procedures. Because the ordeal conflated proof and punishment, it had a double function: if the subject passed it successfully, then it served as proof of his innocence; if the subject failed, then it served as both proof of guilt and punishment. According to Glotz, the ancient Greeks did not necessarily conceive of the ordeal as the verdict of a particular god, but rather as the judgment of magical powers or supernatural forces.[40] For example, Herodotus (Herodotus 1,86,2) suggests that one of Cyrus' motives for putting Croesus on the pyre was to test whether 'one of the spirits' (τίς δαιμόνων) would save him. While

---

[36] Rattenbury 1926.

[37] Segal 1984. The mythological and symbolic dimension to these ordeals has been examined in great detail in Laplace 1983; S. Bartsch 1989, 92-93.

[38] Morgan 1996, 72-73.

[39] Wolff 1951, 50 n. 52; Gernet 1981, 90; Bartlett 1986; Cantarella 1991a, 227-230.

[40] Glotz 1904, 5 (page citations are to reprint edition).

technically outside the scope of the normal judicial process, the ordeal could be invoked when normal judicial procedures failed to yield a satisfactory result. It served much the same purpose as the oath, which continued to be used in classical Greece despite the growing authority of the courts to make judgments and enforce them.[41] Achilles Tatius uses a term commonly used to refer to a trial (κρίσις, AT 8,12,9 and 8,14,2) to refer to these ordeals, signifying that they function along a continuum that runs from courtroom proceedings to divine judgment, where the discovery of truth transcends rhetoric.

The ordeals address two charges: adultery (for Melite) and unchastity (for Leucippe). The sites of the ordeals are in vicinity of the temple of Artemis, where the entire demos can witness the rites (AT 8,13,1). The jurors and the president of the previous trials not only attend as spectators to the ordeals, but also participate in their administration.[42]

Thersander reads out two challenges, the wording of which is critical. At the core is a simple pair of mutually exclusive conditions: if the defendant is guilty, then let her suffer X; if innocent, then let her not suffer X:

> Μελίτην μέν, εἰ μὴ κεκοινώνηκεν εἰς Ἀφροδίτην τῷδε τῷ ξένῳ παρ' ὃν ἀπεδήμουν χρόνον, εἰς τὸ τῆς ἱερᾶς Στυγὸς ὕδωρ εἰσβᾶσαν καὶ ἐπομοσαμένην ἀπηλλάχθαι τῶν ἐγκλημάτων.
>
> If Melite has not had sexual relations with this stranger during the time while I was away, let her step into the water of the holy Styx and, after making an oath, she will be cleared of the charges (AT 8,11,2).

In response, Melite asks what the consequences of the ordeal will be. In a very subtle shift, she refers to the penalty that Thersander will pay if she succeeds, rather than by her if she fails (σὲ δὲ τί δεῖ παθεῖν, ἂν συκοφάντης ἁλῷς; AT 8,11,3). She thereby turns the ordeal into a test not of her fidelity, but of his candidness in making his accusations. Melite readily agrees to the oath challenge and repeats Thersander's words:

> 'Ἀλλὰ καὶ ἔγωγε', ἔφη, 'ταύτην δέχομαι τὴν πρόκλησιν, καὶ ἔτι πλέον αὐτὴ προστίθημι· τὸ δὲ μέγιστον, οὐδὲ εἶδον τὸ παράπαν οὔτε ξένον, οὔτε πολίτην ἥκειν εἰς ὁμιλίαν, καθ' ὅν λέγεις καιρόν'.

---

41 Plescia 1970, 41-43.

42 Jurors: 'καὶ ὧν...σε δεῖ παθεῖν, ἂν συκοφάντης ἁλῷς;''Ὅ τι ἄν', ἔφη, 'δόξῃ προστιμῆσαι τοῖς δικασταῖς', AT 8,11,3-4. President: τὴν μὲν ὁ πρόεδρος δεξιωσάμενος, ἐκ τοῦ ὕδατος ἐξάγει, AT 8,14,5.

> 'And I, for my part', she said, 'accept this challenge, and I add one more thing, chiefly this: that I absolutely did not allow any man, neither foreigner nor citizen, to have sexual contact with me during the time which you specify'. (AT 8,11,3)

The specification of a particular window of time is the solution to the enigma of Melite's miraculous vindication at the conclusion of the trial. Leucippe's challenge, regarding her virginity, is also phrased as a pair of conditions:

> τὴν δὲ ἑτέραν, εἰ μὲν τυγχάνει γυνή, δουλεύειν τῷ δεσπότῃ (δούλαις γὰρ μόναις γυναιξὶν ἔξεστιν εἰς τὸν τῆς Ἀρτέμιδος ναὸν παριέναι), εἰ δὲ φησιν εἶναι παρθένος, ἐν τῷ τῆς σύριγγος ἄντρῳ κλεισθῆναι.

> If Leucippe is a woman [i.e., not a virgin], then let her serve her master (because female slaves were the only women able to approach the shrine of Artemis); if she says that she is a virgin, then let her be shut in the cave of the syrinx. (AT 8,11,2)

As soon as Melite and Thersander agree upon the terms of the challenge, the court is adjourned and the ordeals are scheduled for the next day (AT 8,11,4). Achilles Tatius proceeds immediately to a paradoxographical description of the ordeal of the water of the Styx.

A point of comparison for the ordeals appears in Xenophon of Ephesus' novel, *Anthia and Habrocomes*, where the hero's crucifixion evolves into an instance of divine intervention. As Habrocomes mounts his cross, he makes a prayer, the structure of which merits close attention.[43] Addressed to the god of the Nile, it is phrased as a pair of alternative conditions: if I am guilty, let me die; if I am innocent, let me live:

> ὦ θεῶν...φιλανθρωπότατε, ὃς Αἴγυπτον ἔχεις, δι' ὃν καὶ γῆ καὶ θάλασσα πᾶσιν ἀνθρώροις πέφηνεν, εἰ μέν τι Ἀβροκόμης ἀδικεῖ, καὶ ἀπολοίμην οἰκτρῶς καὶ μείζονα τιμωρίαν εἴ τις ἐστὶ ταύτης ὑπόσχοιμι· εἰ δὲ ὑπὸ γυναικὸς προδέδομαι πονηρᾶς, μήτε τὸ Νείλου ῥεῦμα μιανθείη ποτε ἀδίκως ἀπολομένου σώματι, μήτε σὺ τοιοῦτον ἴδοις θέαμα, ἄνθρωπον οὐδὲν ἀδικήσαντα ἀπολλύμενον ἐπὶ τῆς σῆς ἐνταῦθα.

---

[43] Prayers were a conventional component of Christian martyrologies; however, the structure of Habrocomes' prayer differs slightly from the prayers of martyrs. Numerous examples may be found throughout the texts assembled by Musurillo 1972.

> O most benevolent of the gods, you who possess Egypt, through whom both land and sea have been revealed to all humanity: if Habrocomes has done anything wrong, then may I die pitifully and suffer a greater punishment, if there is one greater than this; but if I have been betrayed by an evil woman, then may the currents of the Nile never be polluted with a corpse of an unjustly killed man, nor may you see such a sight, a man who did nothing wrong dying there in your land (XE 4,2,4-5).[44]

The invocation of the god and the land of Egypt at the beginning and end of the prayer, the conditional phrases in a μέν-δέ construction, the amplification of the δέ-condition with two apodoses introduced by μήτε, and the repetition ἀδικεῖ-ἀδίκως-ἀδικήσαντα convey the impression that this is a formulaic opening of an ordeal.

The same basic formula can be seen in the Athenian challenge to torture, πρόκλησις, a type of procedure that is in certain respects analogous to an ordeal.[45] It was generally formulated in a μέν-δέ construction balancing two conditions: the μέν-condition expresses the penalty if guilt is determined and the δέ-condition expresses the results if the torture proves otherwise. A representative formula may be found in Demosthenes' speech, *Against Neaera:*

> Καὶ εἰ μὲν ὁμολογεῖν ἐκ Στεφάνου εἶναι καὶ Νεαίρας τούτους τοὺς παῖδας, πεπρᾶσθαι Νέαιραν κατὰ τοὺς νόμους καὶ τοὺς παῖδας ξένους εἶναι· εἰ δὲ μὴ ὁμολογοῖεν ἐκ ταύτης εἶναι αὐτοὺς ἀλλ' ἐξ ἑτέρας γυναικὸς ἀστῆς, ἀφίστασθαι τοῦ ἀγῶνος ἤθελον τοῦ Νεαίρας, καὶ εἴ τι ἐκ τῶν βασάνων βλαφθείησαν αἱ ἄνθρωποι, ἀποτίνειν ὅ τι βλαβείησαν.

> And if the slave women agree that these are Neaera's children, Neaera is to be sold in accordance with the laws, and her children are to be classified as foreign. If, however, they agreed that they are not Neaera's children but from another woman, an Athenian, I was willing to abandon my case against Neaera; and if the women were injured in the torture, I was willing to pay compensation for the injuries. (Demosthenes 59,124, trans. Bers)[46]

---

[44] I have chosen O'Sullivan's reading for ἀπολοίμην. Papanikolaou preserves the transmitted reading ἀπολομένου σώματι. O'Sullivan (1986, 87) remarks that the corpse (σῶμα) must not be the subject of the participle since it is the ἄνθρωπος and not his corpse that perishes unjustly (i.e., without having committed any crime).

[45] Thür 1977, 95.

[46] Bers 2003. See also Aeschines 2,127, Demosthenes 37,27, and 39,40. On the formula, see Thür 1977, 128-129.

The procedure was applied to persons who did not have civic rights and who therefore were incapable of testifying in court: while torture was restricted to slaves, as Glotz notes, 'the ordeal existed as a means of proof for women and for those who were *capite minores*, domestics or slaves, bastards or foreigners'.[47] The supposed mystery inherent in ascertaining the sexual purity of women—or men, for that matter—meant that appeals to divine judgment served as a respectable pretense to resolve a socially awkward dilemma. This phenomenon is not unique to the ancient world, but also appeared in medieval Europe, where 'the evidence of laws and legal cases shows that ordeals were deemed particularly appropriate in deciding charges of sexual misconduct'.[48] Women and men alike submitted to the ordeals of the red-hot iron and cauldron in cases involving not only adultery, but bestiality and paternity as well.

Melite is subjected to the ordeal of the water of the Styx, which is used for people 'accused in the affairs of Aphrodite'.[49] There are two aspects to this ordeal: the oath and the submersion in water. Its aetiology, explained before the scene of the ordeal (AT 8,12,1-7), is connected with two devotees of Artemis who fell in love and broke their vows of chastity; as punishment the goddess transformed the girl into a small spring. The ordeal consists of the following: the woman writes an oath on a tablet, ties it around her neck with string, and then steps into the spring for a prescribed amount of time. If she is faithful to her oath, the spring stays low. If not, the spring bubbles up to her neck and covers the tablet (AT 8,12,9). Melite's oath falls under the category of 'decisory' oath, which Plescia defines as typically

> taken when one of the parties to a suit, being unable to prove his charge, offered to refer the decision of the case to the oath of his opponent, who was bound either to accept or to tender the same challenge back; otherwise his refusal was tantamount to a confession. Such an oath was the deciding evidence and constituted the whole trial: proof, judgment, and penalty.[50]

He also notes that there is no evidence for the use of this type of oath, functionally an ordeal, in Athenian courts. Melite's ordeal conforms to other water ordeals

47 Glotz 1904, 124-125.
48 Bartlett 1986, 19-20.
49 AT 8,12,8: ὅταν τις αἰτίαν ἔχῃ Ἀφροδισίων.
50 Plescia 1970, 13.

known from Greco-Roman and other cultures.[51] Bodies of fresh water, specifically streams and rivers, were associated with rituals of virginity.[52] The water of the Styx, a river of the underworld, had a special relationship with oaths in the literary tradition. For example, according to Hesiod, gods who swore falsely by the Styx were punished by being cut off temporarily from divine society.[53] The ordeals of the Styx involve drinking and submersion (of objects) in its waters.[54] A parallel use of an ordeal to prove marital fidelity is to be found in an anecdote related by the sophist Alciphron concerning an oath of marital fidelity that a husband forced his wife to swear at the well of Callichoros at Eleusis.[55]

The ordeal of the cave of the syrinx, as the priest earlier explained to the protagonists, is used when a woman is accused of not being a virgin (ὅταν οὖν αἰτίαν ἔχῃ τις οὐκ εἶναι παρθένος, AT 8,6,12). Although the scenario may seem fantastical, there is evidence that less spectacular virginity tests existed in reality. These took the form of background interviews, perhaps conducted by a midwife. They were useful in circumstances where questions about an unwed girl's virginity might have legal ramifications, such as when she was fatherless and her guardian's reputation was at stake.[56] The legend of the syrinx could have been invoked as an old wives' tale, a cautionary legend designed to teach girls the value of virginity without going into too much detail.[57] It is also the culmination of a long series of tests for Leucippe throughout the course of the narrative that mark her transition from a 'well-guarded virgin' (AT 1,9,3) to a marriageable woman.[58]

The priest explains the process to the couple: the demos sends the girl to the door of the cave and the pipes judge the matter. The girl enters, dressed in the proper garment. If she is a virgin, the music of the pipes is heard, the doors open automatically, and she comes out wearing a wreath on her head. If she is not a virgin, instead of music a scream is heard. She is left in the cave for three days, after which the priestess enters and finds only the pipes, the girl having disappeared. In effect this is a live burial, a type of ordeal generally reserved for

[51] For analogous rituals in Bithynian, Hindu, Czech, and Anglo-Saxon cultures, see Glotz 1904, 79 n. 71; Lea 1968, 279-283.

[52] Glotz 1904, 79ff.

[53] Hesiod *Theogony* 793ff. See also *Iliad* 2,755, 14,271, 15,38; Apollonius Rhodius 2,291; Virgil *Aeneid* 6,323-4, 12,814-5.

[54] Glotz 1904, 114-116.

[55] Alciphron 3,69, cited by Glotz 1904, 79 n. 72.

[56] Evans Grubbs 1995, 199-202.

[57] A more indirect allusion to virginity test appears in AT 3,25, in the ekphrasis about the phoenix. Morales argues that the description of how the phoenix reveals 'the secret mysteries of its body' (trans. Whitmarsh 2001, 61.) to an Egyptian priest prefigures the virginity test; see Morales 2004, 190-195.

[58] Lalanne 2006, 146-149.

women. In Rome Vestals who betrayed their vows of chastity were subjected to a similar test: as in the ordeal of the syrinx, the Vestal would be veiled and taken to an opening of a cave near one of the gates of the city. A few items, such as a lamp, bread, water, oil, and milk, would be placed in the cave with her. In effect, this was a form of punishment since a miracle from the goddess would be required for the priestess' survival.[59] The punishment of the Vestals by other means was a popular theme in the Latin declamations.[60] In Greek tradition, Antigone is the most salient example of a girl who is punished by being buried alive. Glotz describes Achilles Tatius' ordeal of the cave of the syrinx in connection with these cases, but finds no precise parallels and notes that the author applies this type of ordeal 'non sans modification'.[61]

The tempo of the narrative, as measured by the frequency of temporal markers, quickens in the final part of the eighth book of the novel. The scene of the ordeals opens 'on the following day' (AT 8,13,1) and the narrative emphasizes select, concrete details. The scene of the ordeals is the climactic moment of the trial. Whereas the courtroom gave the actors leeway to manipulate, suppress, and misrepresent the truth, the ordeals reveal the truth immediately and unequivocally; their judgment is incontestable.

The return of the first-person narration, which had been displaced by a voice closer to that of the omniscient narrator, underscores the emotionality of the spectacle. The ordeals are focalized through Clitophon, as he watches the trembling Leucippe (AT 8,13,2) and prays to Pan to honor his 'contract' with Artemis to allow his beloved to survive (AT 8,13,2-4). The reference to Pan as a god notorious for his love of virgins (θεός ἐστι φιλοπάρθενος, AT 8,13,3) calls to mind other situations in which Leucippe has been exposed to violence. Given the precedent set by the other spectacles centering on Leucippe and witnessed by Clitophon such as her sacrifice by the brigands (AT 3,15,1-5) and her feigned death at the hands of the pirates (AT 5,7,4-9), the outcome of the ordeal remains uncertain. Thersander had earlier scoffed at the possibility that she could have remained a virgin after spending so much time in the company of pirates (AT 6,21,3), the reader cannot be entirely sure he is wrong. The details of what happened between her

59 Glotz 1904, 96-98; Mommsen 1899, 928-929.

60 Plutarch *Numa* 10 and *Quaestiones Romanae* 96; Dionysius of Halicarnassus 2,67. For the theme of the Vestal's punishment in the declamations, see Seneca *Controversiae* 1,3 and 6,8.

61 Glotz 1904, 101.

having been sacrificed at sea and her reappearance on Melite's estate are presented to the reader only in the final chapters of the novel, after she has successfully passed the test (AT 8,16).[62]

The ordeals are a spectacle (θέα, AT 8,14,3), a 'macroscopic event in which a few individuals or a group of people form the focus of interest, whether deliberately or not, for an emotive crowd that functions as an audience'.[63] In this scene the audience consists of the entire citizen body (δῆμος, AT 8,13,1, 14,2, 14,3, 14,4), which performs the critical function of confirming Clitophon's subjective impressions. Whereas descriptive details in the trials were suppressed in favor of verbal virtuosity, the description of the ordeals lingers on the visuality of the moment: the participants' facial expressions, their physical gestures, costume, the attendant sounds, and other sensations.[64] As the doors of the cave open to reveal Leucippe, alive and intact, the spectators' cheers cue Clitophon's response:

> ὡς δὲ ἐξέθορεν ἡ Λευκίππη, πᾶς μὲν ὁ δῆμος ἐξεβόησεν ὑφ' ἡδονῆς καὶ τὸν Θέρσανδρον ἐλοιδόρουν, ἐγὼ δὲ ὅστις ἐγεγόνειν οὐκ ἂν εἴποιμι λόγῳ.
>
> As Leucippe sprang out, all the people shouted out from pleasure and reviled Thersander, and I could not put into words what kind of state I had been in. (AT 8,14,2)

The use of a μέν-δέ construction to describe the response to the sight of Leucippe suggests that the audience reacts to the spectacle (μέν), and Clitophon reacts both to the spectacle and to the audience's reaction (δέ). The demos expresses its emotions vocally through cheers and hisses; in contrast, Clitophon is completely inarticulate, having been deceived twice before in spectacles where his fellow viewers proved unreliable corroborators of the truth. The conditions of the spectacle of Leucippe's ordeal are different. Set in a civic context, it is a ceremony witnessed by the population of the city of Ephesus. The audience validates the truth for Clitophon; nevertheless, the intense emotion he feels renders him mute.

---

62 Segal notes the 'virginal-violated' doubling in Leucippe's characterization; see Segal 1984, 84-85; Ormand 2010.

63 S. Bartsch 1989, 109.

64 Facial expressions: of Thersander, AT 8,13,1; of Melite, AT 8,14,3. Physical gestures: Leucippe enters calmly, AT 8,13,2; president leads Melite out of the water, AT 8,14,4. Dress: of Leucippe, AT 8,13,1. Sounds: Clitophon's murmur, music heard from the cave, AT 8,14,1. Touch: description of the water of the Styx, AT 8,14,4. The virgin's dress (κεκοσμημένη στολῇ τῇ νενομισμένῃ, AT 8,6,12) and the 'clear' note of the panpipes (λιγυρόν τι μέλος, AT 8,6,13) reiterate earlier details of the ordeal's aetiology.

In contrast, Melite's ordeal is described succinctly. After she stands in the water for her allotted time, the president helps her out. As the heroine's rival, Melite ought to get her just deserts. Yet she survives her ordeal unscathed. The reader knows that she had intercourse with Clitophon after her husband reappeared on the scene, making her a deliberate and completely knowing adulteress. The outcome of her ordeal poses a riddle that invites the reader to backtrack over the previous narrative, yet the solution to the puzzle subverts the generic message of the ideal romance. Achilles Tatius both valorizes and subverts the generic ideal of 'rightful love and lawful marriage', by celebrating adultery and subversion of the legal process.

Melite's emergence from her ordeal precipitates the denouement of the novel. The slave, Sosthenes, bears the brunt of the punishment while his master, Thersander, runs away 'afraid the crowd would stone him' (AT 8,14,4). Sosthenes confesses as soon as he sees that he is going to be tortured and is sent to jail before serving his punishment. Thersander is condemned in absentia to banishment. In the final chapter of the novel, Clinias explains the legal details that wrap up the trial, as well as the novel: Thersander appealed the case not with the intention of actually fighting it, but in order to defer interrogation. Clitophon says that they waited the prescribed three days before the president, who has Thersander's quitclaim read aloud (AT 8,19,2). Exonerated, the lovers leave the law courts of Ephesus behind and sail to Byzantium to their generically happy ending.

Conclusion

As we have seen in the trial scenes in *Leucippe and Clitophon*, the ambiguities of Clitophon and Melite's liaison are observed in the breach rather than in the act, thus revealing the fault lines dividing custom from law, and public appearances from private realities. Paradoxically, in Achilles Tatius' world, the fact of sexual intercourse was more pertinent to ascertaining the crime of adultery than to consummating the legal act of marriage. The over-determination of the intimate act of sexual intercourse runs counter to the law's definition of marriage, which traditionally was first and foremost an economic contract. Yet, through the trials in Ephesus, we can begin to gauge how popular attitudes might have changed over the course of the century and a half after the Augustan formulation of marriage—and adultery—was enshrined in Roman law and seeped into the consciousness of citizens and subjects of the Roman Empire. Achilles Tatius' portrayal of an adultery trial that is subverted through legalistic technicalities represents a jaded view of the unintended consequences of legislation that had once seemed sensible at another time and place. Rather than eradicate the perceived problem of adultery and other sexual transgressions, Augustus' laws created other problems, not the least of which was a heightened sense of legal gamesmanship that undermined the original intention to regulate the sexuality of the elite classes of Rome and of the provinces.

Achilles Tatius constructs his trial scenes as elaborate tetralogies. Both trials revolve around sets of three speeches. Both sets begin with a speech of accusation: in Clitophon's case, he is his own accuser. The second speeches of each set are defenses delivered by a supporter of Clitophon (Clinias, the priest). Finally, the last speech to be delivered in *oratio recta* in each trial leads into misconceived arguments culminating in muddled procedure and legalistic quibbling. The organization of the speeches is inspired by the declamations. The substance of speeches reveals a parody of the legal process and, especially, the futility of pursuing charges of adultery through the courts of the Greek city.

The prominence of the priest in the second trial illustrates an awareness of the political tensions inherent in the dynamics of asylum. Achilles Tatius depicts a situation where human actors, frustrated in one forum, play in the interstices between various civic spaces in order to attain their objectives. The debate revolves around the issue of the authority of the priest and the sanctity of the temple. The right of fugitives to seek asylum at sacred sites was highly contentious, not least because it threatened to undermine the authority of the city's juridical institutions. Ancient sources reveal an anxiety that temples, rather than being sanctuaries for the falsely accused or unjustly prosecuted, would become havens for outlaws and runaway slaves. In the classical and Hellenistic periods, sites of asylum could challenge the civic law's power to enforce verdict. Temples offering sanctuary to convicts, runaway slaves, and debtors could house crowds of refugees who needed to be fed. During the Roman civil wars in the first century B.C.E., the Artemesion became a flashpoint for rebellion. Brutus and Cassius sought asylum there, as did Marc Antony, who doubled the size of the temple grounds to accommodate the many fugitives who sought protection there. After Actium, Octavian reestablished the earlier, smaller precinct by having a wall built around the temple of Artemis. As a consequence, limitations were placed on the types of criminals that could seek asylum.[1]

In Rome, sites and persons, such as the *flamen Dialis* and the Vestals, were recognized as having the power to grant asylum; eventually, Augustus appropriated the title and power of the *pontifex maximus* and used it as a mechanism for granting of *clementia*.[2] Statues of the emperor were subsequently used as sites of asylum for abused slaves.[3] In Ephesus, there was a tradition that the Amazons had founded the temple of Artemis as a place of refuge; subsequent rulers affirmed the temple's privileged status.[4] Perhaps it was in connection with that privilege that individuals who served as the 'Megabyzos', the chief temple official, displayed a 'feeling of self esteem and importance that is rather unique among Greek temple officials'.[5] In the imperial period, the office disappeared as other types of priesthoods were created by the civic elite.[6] Shrines and temples dedicated to Augustus, Julius Caesar, Domitian, and Hadrian were built in the urban center of Ephesus as well as near the Artemesion itself, suggesting that the privilege of asylum was jealously watched by the imperial power.[7]

The world of Achilles Tatius' novel celebrates the indeterminacy of trials that overlap multiple jurisdictions: the private verbal contracts and oaths in Alexandria, the civic courts of Ephesus, and the precincts of the temple of Artemis. Mis-

---

[1] Chaniotis 1996.

[2] Freyburger 1992; Dowling 2006, 160-163.

[3] Price 1984, 192-193.

[4] Rigsby 1996, 386-387.

[5] Bremmer 2008, 42.

[6] Bremmer 2008, 48; J. O. Smith 1996; C. M. Thomas 1995, 98-105; Dmitriev 2005, 25-26.

[7] Price 1984, 254-257; Rigsby 1996, 391-393; Rogers 2012, 96-102.

information, overblown rhetoric, specious arguments, clever phrasing, and sophistry subvert the generic expectations of the trial scene. It is clear that the author understood the intricacies of how to play the game of legal brinksmanship, the form of legal consciousness that Ewick and Silbey identify as 'With the Law'. The Ephesian characters—Melite, Thersander, and the priest of Artemis—are resourceful and tactical in their navigation of the legal system. Clitophon and Clinias, outsiders to Ephesus, do not have the same inside knowledge of local rules, regulations, and networks of personal relationships. Thus, their attempts in court backfire. Hoping for death, Clitophon makes a false confession that adds torture into the sentence. Clinias gets close to the truth, but his careful deductions are overshadowed by Thersander's bluster. It is not until the priest takes up the mantle of Clitophon and Leucippe's case that they get the results they want: proof, via the ordeals, that they both are eligible to be legally married.

III

Heliodorus, *Aethiopica*

Patria Potestas after the Antonine Constitution

In 212 C.E., the emperor Caracalla issued an edict, known as the *Constitutio Antoniniana,* that extended Roman citizenship to all free inhabitants of his empire, thereby formally eliminating the distinction between citizens and non-citizens. The intent and immediate consequences are debated. By the third century, there were many (how many is impossible to know precisely) people with Roman citizenship living throughout the empire. Theoretically, the Edict of Caracalla initiated a gradual reduction of the kind of legal pluralism and the attendant confusion that Achilles Tatius' trial scenes reflect. By opening the Roman judicial system to all inhabitants of the empire, the *Constitutio Antoniniana* theoretically obviated whatever effective judicial authority remained at the local level. Petitioners and litigants who were involved in cases that might be appealed now had incentive to formulate their legal claims within a Roman conceptual framework.

A fundamental notion in Roman family and property law was *manus*, the peculiarly Roman construction of paternal authority and was more far-reaching than the Greek κυρία.[1] The traditional Roman ideal of the father's power, *patria potestas,* was associated with the legendary *ius vitae necisque*—life and death power—over his children. It had become obsolete by the reign of Hadrian, who placed limitations on the father's absolute authority over his dependents; nevertheless, it continued to thrive in the imaginary worlds of the declamations and literature.[2]

Heliodorus' *Aethiopica* dramatizes the concept of *patria potestas* in a climactic trial scene set in the exotic kingdom of Meroe in Ethiopia. Although the precise date of the novel remains uncertain, a date after Caracalla's edict coheres with the general consensus that it was written no earlier than the third century C.E.

In the final book of the *Aethiopica,* Charicleia, the novel's heroine, is to be sacrificed in the triumphal rites for the Ethiopian king. The irony is that she knows

---

[1] Gaius, *Institutes,* book 1 in *Digest* 1,6,3: 'Also in our *potestas* are our children whom we have begotten in lawful wedlock. This right over our children is peculiar to the Romans (*quod ius proprium civium Romanorum est*)'.

[2] *Digest* 48,9,5; discussed below in trial 7.

that she is his daughter. Approaching the altar, she suddenly falls at the knees of the gymnosophists, the sages who counsel the king, and demands a trial,

> ‘ὦ σοφώτατοι’ ἔλεγε ‘μικρὸν ἐπιμείνατε· δίκη γάρ μοι καὶ κρίσις πρόκειται πρὸς τοὺς βασιλεύοντας, ὑμᾶς δὲ μόνους καὶ τοῖς τοσούτοις δικάζειν πυνθάνομαι’.
>
> O wisest of men, wait a moment: for I have a lawsuit and a trial to bring against the rulers, and I hear that you alone judge such cases. (H 10,10,1)

The reader already knows that the case she will present is the culmination of her quest to reclaim her birthright as the daughter of the king and queen of Ethiopia. Although the sages agree to hear the case, the king remains skeptical:

> ‘δῆλον μὲν’ εἶπεν ‘ὡς οὐδὲν ἐρεῖ σπουδαῖον, ἀλλ’, ὅπερ ἴδιον τῶν τὰ τελευταῖα κινδυνευόντων, λόγων ματαίων ἔσται πλάσματα πρὸς ὑπέρθεσιν’.
>
> It is clear that she will say nothing serious, rather—as is so typical of people who are in danger of dying—it will be a fabrication of silly stories to stall for time. (H 10,10,4)

His prediction that what she is about to say will be a ‘fabrication’ (πλάσματα) alludes to the entire genre itself. The word, πλάσματα, is one of the terms used to describe prose fiction, most famously by the emperor Julian, who was dismissive of fictional stories presented in the guise of history.[3] The intention that the king attributes to Charicleia corresponds to that of the authors of the Greek novels, who weave a theoretically limitless string of invented episodes, the main function of which is to postpone closure for as long as possible.[4] In fact, Charicleia faces a formidable obstacle: her claim, though true, will seem patently false because she is white-skinned and the king and queen are black-skinned. As it happens, Charicleia's argument confounds the king's expectations. Her speech is not a piece of fiction, but rather a well-constructed case in which she, with the calculated timing of a masterful playwright, presents irrefutable proof that in fact she is the king's daughter.

---

[3] Julian *Epistles* 89,301b. On ancient terms for the novel, an otherwise under-theorized genre in antiquity, see Morgan 1993, 176-193.

[4] Reardon 1991, 80; Konstan 1998, 34; C. M. Thomas 1998, 280.

Throughout the novel, we see that Charicleia's status as a daughter is overdetermined: she has a biological father (Hydaspes), an adoptive father (Charicles), a foster father (Calasiris), and a guardian (Thyamis). Heliodorus' choice to frame the revelation of her identity as a trial, rather than in any number of other settings suitable for a recognition scene, speaks to an overriding concern with the resolution of paradox and the establishment of clear legal definitions.[5] Threats to the marital relationship, central themes of the trials in Chariton and Achilles Tatius, are subordinated in the *Aethiopica* to the relationship between parents and children. Heliodorus' problematization of fatherhood, I posit, reflects a larger cultural process whereby Greeks absorbed Roman ideas of paternal authority that were becoming standardized in the imperial legal system.

Although Caracalla's edict may not have been revolutionary, it formally established the concept of a single jurisdiction and accelerated the pace at which local laws were replaced by the universal law of the Roman Empire. Third-century legal sources indicate that a consequence of the edict was the blurring of boundaries between slaves and free persons, and between *honestiores* and *humiliores*. The political instability of the later third century C.E. only exacerbated the ability of *decuriones* to shoulder the burdens of municipal finance.[6] City dwellers in the Greek East adjusted to the distinctive treatment of property in Roman law, guided by the principles that the *paterfamilias* was the sole owner of the family's property except for the *peculium,* an allowance he might grant to a son or a slave, and that the father's theoretically absolute authority lasted until he died or emancipated his son. The papyrological evidence suggests that people living in Greco-Roman Egypt had many ways of working around these parameters in order to legitimize their own customs surrounding family law and inheritance; yet the notion of *patria potestas* remained entrenched in legal thought.[7] By the sixth century, the *Digest* of Justinian shows that this cornerstone of Roman law was more or less successfully absorbed into the legal cultures of the eastern half of Roman Empire.

In order to place Heliodorus in historical context, we immediately face the decades-long scholarly debate over the date of the *Aethiopica.* Two likely windows for its composition and initial reception have been identified: either the middle of the third century or the last quarter of the fourth—a difference of three or four generations. In order to adduce possible legal comparanda for the trials in Heliodorus, it is necessary to consider briefly the evidence and arguments for the

---

[5] Charicleia's recognition scene is discussed more fully in Cave 1988, 19-20; Montiglio 2013.

[6] Garnsey 1970, 266-271; Alföldy 1974; Corcoran 1996, 101-111; 2006, 50-51; Zuiderhoek 2009.

[7] Arjava 1998, 165.

novel's date. The sixth-century *terminus ante quem* provided by the single surviving papyrus fragment of the *Aethiopica* is not particularly useful; we must therefore rely on other evidence, both internal and external, that might point to the author's contemporary reality and to literary dependencies between the novel and other works.[8]

The subscription appended to the last book of the *Aethiopica* is the starting point for dating the novel. The author identifies himself as 'a Phoenician man from Emesa, from the clan descended from the Sun, Theodosius' child, Heliodorus'.[9] There is no indication of a specific date, nor should we expect it; Chariton likewise identified himself only by his hometown and his occupation. Circumstantial evidence points to the connection with Emesa, the hometown of the family of Julia Domna, the wife of Septimius Severus and mother of Caracalla, as well as the great-aunt of the emperor Elegabalus.[10] Its destruction during the rebellion of Zenobia in the 270's might suggest a *terminus ante quem* for Heliodorus' date, assuming that the city never recovered after the upheaval.[11] Byzantine *testimonia* place Heliodorus in the reign of Theodosius I (379-395).[12] In the nineteenth century, stylistic considerations led Erwin Rohde to believe that the *Aethiopica*, which he judged the most refined of the extant novels, was therefore the earliest; he placed the other novels after it, on the assumption that literary genres decay

---

[8] Stephens 1994, 409-410.

[9] H 10,10,41: ὃ συνέταξεν ἀνὴρ Φοῖνιξ Ἐμισηνός, τῶν ἀφ' Ἡλίου γένος, Θεοδοσίου παῖς Ἡλιόδωρος.

[10] Rohde 1914, 300-309. In an assessment of the intertextual relationship between Heliodorus and another author from Emesa, L. Flavius Philostratus, John Morgan argues that they shared the same cultural milieu, although which one came first is uncertain; see Morgan 2009.

[11] Weinreich 1962, 33-34.

[12] Socrates, an early church historian who lived in the late fourth/early fifth centuries, identifies the novel's author with a bishop of Tricca in Thessaly. Another *terminus ante quem* is supplied by a marginal note in the earliest manuscript (from the eleventh century) that claims Heliodorus lived under Theodosius I, who reigned from 379 to 395. Socrates' *testimonium* has been called into question on the grounds that Heliodorus was a common name, easily confused with another individual, and that this is just the first of many Christianizing details which had been grafted onto the novelist's biography in order to legitimize a relatively widely-read novel; Achilles Tatius was also identified as a bishop in the Suda; see Vilborg 1962, 8. The marginal note in the manuscript is not as obviously revisionist, but may be explained as a confusion between the Roman emperor Theodosius and the author's father named in the subscription at the end of the novel (H 10,41,1); see Easterling and Knox 1989, 249.

over time.[13] Even after Rohde's chronology was overturned by papyrological discoveries, the dating of Heliodorus' novel to a century or more after the presumed peak of the literary form in the second century C.E. seemed difficult to reconcile with the aesthetic truism that the highest quality works of art and literature are produced within a narrow temporal window.[14]

Given the paucity of secure external evidence for the date of the *Aethiopica*, internal evidence has received the preponderance of scholarly attention. A signal debate concerns the resemblance between Heliodorus' description of Hydaspes' siege of Syene by flooding the outside of the city and turning it into an island (H 9,2-6) and Julian's panegyric description of the historical siege of Nisibis, which was repelled by the Emperor Constantius II in the middle of the fourth century.[15] At bottom it is a question of the direction of influence: did the novelist draw upon the historical event for details, or did the future emperor present a fictionalized account of an actual incident of which his audience, none other than the emperor himself, was no mere onlooker but indeed its mastermind?[16] Other sig-

[13] Rohde 1914, 493-498.

[14] Velleius Paterculus 1,17,4; Sinko 1940/46, 41-45.

[15] Van der Valk 1941, 97-100. Morgan argues Heliodorus relied heavily on literary sources—including late literary sources such as Julian—in his depiction of Syene and Meroe; see Morgan 1982, 221-265.

[16] Julian's derogatory reference to the novels in *Epistle* 89 (p. 141 Bidez) proves that he not only knew they existed, but also had enough interest and intellectual energy to form an opinion of them, making him one of the few ancient literary critics who even acknowledged their existence; see Weinreich 1962, 35. Colonna (1950, 79-87) confirmed Van der Valk's dating, thus reinforcing the position that Heliodorus had imitated Julian's account of the historical siege, therefore supporting the fourth-century date; nevertheless, scholarly opinion remained divided for the next two decades. Other proponents of the later date are: Keydell 1966, 345-350; J. Schwartz 1967, 549-552; Lacombrade 1970, 70-89; Reardon 1971, 334-336 n. 357. For the third-century date, see: Szepessy 1957, 241-259; Weinreich 1962, 32-55; Lesky 1966, 865-866; Perry 1967, 349 n. 313. In the 1970's, Szepessy upset this chronology by comparing Julian's account with an independent Syriac account referring to the siege, written by Ephraem of Nisibis; Szepessy saw evidence that Julian's account was more similar to Heliodorus' novel than to historical fact, as far as could be discerned through comparison with the Syriac text; see Szepessy 1972, 279-287; 1976, 247-226. He argued that it was Julian who was derivative, and that Heliodorus had to have written before the mid-fourth century. This view continued to have its proponents; see Maróth 1979, 239-243; Lane Fox 1987, 137, 704 n. 152; Lightfoot 1988, 119; Bowie 1989, 123-124, 249-150. Arguments for and against the evidentiary value of the siege of Syene have become extremely technical, involving not only the analysis of military tactics and source criticism, but also the interpretation of Syriac documents, and establishing the chronology of the *Historia Augusta*. For source criticism, see Lightfoot 1988, 106-125. The Syriac documents are discussed in Maróth 1979, 239-243. For parallels with the *Historia Augusta,* see Bowersock 1994, 149-160.

nificant clues include Heliodorus' description of Delphi, the treatment of war captives, the presence of heavily armed cavalry, and the constellation of states bringing tribute.[17] The novel's religious atmosphere has been scrutinized for traces of the Severan cult of Helios, Christian influence, or a pagan reaction to Christianity.[18] Morgan suggests that the *Aethiopica* is 'the youthful production of someone who later became a bishop in Thessaly', who was part of a 'rearguard reassertion of paganism from around the time of Julian the Apostate, who himself wrote a Hymn to the Sun'.[19] The evidence remains inconclusive.[20]

Heliodorus wrote for a world in which near-universal citizenship shapes the legal context of the trial scenes. The question remains open, however, as to whether we can also see traces of the legislative reforms of Diocletian and Constantine in the Tetrarchic age (284-324), when imperial pronouncements eclipsed juristic opinions. In an effort to centralize the empire and strengthen the bureaucracy, the emperors commissioned law codes. The tradition of Roman law was upheld; however, the more centralized judicial administration of it may have ameliorated the confusion caused by legal pluralism before 212 C.E. illustrated by the

---

17 Points of close correspondence between Heliodorus' depiction of Delphi and what is known about Delphi of the high imperial period may suggest a date in the second or early third century; see Pouilloux 1983, 285-286; Feuillâtre 1966, 147-150. Hydaspes' examination (ἀνάκρισις) of the war captives has been examined in light of documented legal practices with inconclusive results; see Papathomas 2010, 631. The description of a soldier 'like a man of iron or a moving hammered metal statue' (H 9,15,6), may reflect knowledge of cataphracts, the heavily armed Persian cavalrymen whom the Romans first encountered at the Battle of Strasbourg in 357; see Bowersock 1994, 158-159. The unusual constellation of states bringing tribute to the Ethiopian king in the novel points to close relationship with the *Historia Augusta*, a work which has been securely dated to the fourth century and more likely to be the source of Heliodorus than *vice versa*; see Bowersock 1994, 152.

18 Rohde (1914, 493-498) proposed that the prominence of the Sun-god in the novel corresponds to the popularity and promotion of the cult of Helios first by the Severan emperors in the third century, specifically under Aurelian (270-275). Other scholars have seen links with the reigns of Severus Alexander and Elegabalus (circa 220-240); see Altheim 1948-1950, 93-124; Rattenbury and Lumb 1935, 1:vii-xv; Weinreich 1962, 32-40. Chuvin (1991) places Heliodorus among the last pagans; however, the role of the Sun-god in the novel is less prominent than has been claimed; see Morgan 1978, xli-xlviii.

19 Morgan 2009, 280. The line between pagan and Christian cultures in the fourth century was very fluid would weaken the validity of using religious atmosphere to determine a date; see Cameron 2011, 4-13.

20 Bowie and Harrison (1993, 160) have expressed optimism that a 'systematic linguistic analysis' of Heliodorus in comparison with texts from the third and fourth centuries might resolve the dilemma of the date of his novel. The current *communis opinio* seems to have settled in the middle, though leaning slightly toward the later date; see, for example, Whitmarsh 2008, 381. Bowie, at first persuaded by the earlier date, has left open the possibility of a later date; see Bowie 1989, 123-124, 249-150; 1994, 446; 1996.

gamesmanship of Achilles Tatius' trial scenes. A quarter of Constantine's legislation concerned family law, which indicates his emphasis on the restoration of morals, inspired by the model of Augustus and influenced by Christianity. Under Constantine, Augustan laws that had become obsolete or counterproductive were amended. These included laws still on the books that penalized celibacy and childlessness in inheritance law and granted the right to anyone to denounce another for adultery. At the same time Constantine's legislation extended restrictions on permissible marriages while also granting the right of wives to divorce husbands on specific (and limited) grounds. Finally, Constantine shored up the power of the *paterfamilias*, particularly as it related to the status of children who were abandoned or sold.[21] In the following analysis of the *Aethiopica*, careful consideration will be given to the possibility that the laws of Constantine—particularly laws on family and marriage—shaped the way Heliodorus constructs the legal dilemmas that launch trial scenes.

---

[21] Evans Grubbs 1993 and 1995.

Trial 7.
In the Name of the Father: Patricide Aristippus v. Cnemon (Heliodorus, *Aethiopica* 1,9-14)

The Story

The first trial of the novel is set in Athens, where Cnemon is a teenager living in the home of his father, Aristippus, a member of the civic elite. Aristippus is married to his second wife, a seductive young woman named Demaenete, who falls in love with Cnemon, her stepson. When Cnemon rejects Demaenete's sexual overtures, she denounces Cnemon to Aristippus: she falsely claims he kicked her in the abdomen and insulted them both. Aristippus punishes his son with a beating. Demaenete's lust is insatiable, so she enlists the help of her handmaid, Thisbe, to entrap Cnemon. Thisbe seduces him and intimates that his step-mother has a lover. She leads him to his parents' bedroom in order to catch the adulterer red-handed. With sword in hand, Cnemon bursts into the room , but finds that the man in bed is not an adulterer but his own father. Thus, Cnemon's error ironically substantiates Demaenete's false allegations. Aristippus locks him up for the night, and brings him to the assembly the next morning.

The case is heard by a jury of 2,700 citizens. Aristippus speaks first, claiming that though he has the legal right to kill his son, he prefers to have his son tried rather than summarily executed. Throughout the proceedings, Demaenete wails. The secretary asks Cnemon whether he drew a sword on his father. Cnemon acknowledges he did. There is a loud outcry and the court prohibits him from speaking further. He is immediately found guilty. Three punishments are proposed: death by stoning, death by hurling off a cliff, and exile. Cnemon pleads through the noise of the crowd. A majority of the jury votes for the death penalty, but the 1,700 votes are evenly split between death by stoning and death by cliff); as a result, the 1,000 votes for exile prevail. Cnemon then goes into exile on Aegina, where his mother's family lives.

Analysis

The *Aethiopica* is the longest and most complex narrative of the extant Greek novels. The story of the first trial scene is part of a lengthy inset narration by Cnemon, the defendant in the trial. It is rightly termed a 'novella', in that it includes many of the typical motifs of the genre—love, exile, return—but rearranges them so as to establish a foil to the chaste love of the novel's protagonists, Charicleia and Theagenes. The following analysis of the Athenian trials builds on seminal narratological interpretations of this novel by J. R. Morgan and J. J. Winkler.[1] Both focus on contrasting narrative styles in the *Aethiopica:* the 'proairetic', in which the events of the story are told in the sequence they originally occurred and the 'hermeneutic', in which the bits of the story are presented out of order for the reader to piece together. Theorists of narratology refer to the sequence of events as they unfold over time as the *fabula, histoire,* or story; however, because the narrator is not bound to tell the story in linear order, the events can be rearranged in order to create effects of pleasure, surprise, and suspense for the reader. The arrangement of the events in the narrative is termed the *sjužet*, *récit*, or plot. Heliodorus employs both types of narrative styles in Cnemon's tale. The first segment (H 1,9-1,14) culminates in the trial of Cnemon; it is told in a straightforward manner, as if Heliodorus intended to demonstrate to his reader that he knew well the generic conventions.[2] Cnemon's novella thus represents a skeletal version of what the reader of romance expects: a fine young man, a lustful older woman, an adultery scene, and a trial. The second portion of the novella (in two parts, H 1,14-17 and 2,8-11) presents the trial of Aristippus and Cnemon's pursuit of justice in the hermeneutic mode, unfolding as a complex puzzle. For the sake of simplicity, I shall discuss the novella in two parts: the relatively linear plot of Cnemon's trial (trial 7) and the complex plot of Aristippus' trial (trial 8).

Cnemon's narrative depicts classical Athens as a perilous place where domestic intrigue leads to a torrent of lawsuits. Massive juries of common citizens are susceptible to passions and yield unpredictable verdicts. Select allusion to the canonical Attic orators lends plausibility to Heliodorus' construction of Athenian democratic institutions.[3] We must remember that this Athens is a fiction of the Roman age, when certain details figured more prominently in cultural memory—in particular, the notorious litigiousness of democratic Athens familiar to readers

---

[1] Morgan 1989c; Winkler 1999.

[2] Winkler 1999, 300.

[3] Pouilloux 1983; Oudot 1992; Rougemont 1992, 93-99; Saïd 1994.

in the imperial period.[4] The popular courts are portrayed as an antiquated institution. When a domestic dispute escalates to the courts of the polis, justice eludes all parties. The democratic trials transpose the romantic ideal of domestic harmony into a tragic mode (H 2,11,2): father and son, both victims of the schemes of uncontrolled women, are convicted and punished by the erratic and emotional Athenian demos for crimes they did not commit. The final punishment and restitution are brought about outside of the Athenian judicial system, which is depicted as vulnerable to the proliferation of untruths. The story is presented to the reader in discontinuous segments two or three levels removed from the main level of narration. In the following analysis, I will limit discussion of the intricacies of the narration in order to focus primarily on Heliodorus' adaptation of the formulaic adultery scene to emphasize the relationship between father and son.

Like other novelistic heroes, Cnemon is the adolescent son of a gentleman of Athens. Cnemon's father, Aristippus, is described as a member of 'the upper council' (H 1,9,1)—i.e., the Council of the Areopagus.[5] As a member of the civic elite, he owns property and slaves in the country, in addition to his city house (H 1,12,1). Because he is a widower with only one son, Aristippus remarries a younger woman named Demaenete (H 1,9,2), who is herself from an upper-class clan (H 2,9,2). She has her own slave girl, named Thisbe, whose prettiness and skill at the harp (H 1,11,3) signify the family's wealth.

The incident that precipitates the trial of Cnemon originates from within the confines of the house. At the beginning of his tale, Cnemon describes himself as an ephebe (H 1,10,1), a designation not merely of age but, more importantly, of social status.[6] He is essentially a *filiusfamilias*, subordinate to his father while he is being groomed to become his father's heir. Yet, he is still impressionable. He

---

[4] On Athens' reputation, see Theron's comment in Chariton's novel that the demos of Athens is 'talkative and litigious' (δῆμός ἐστι λάλος καὶ φιλοδίκος, C 1,11,6). See Oudot 1992, 102; S. D. Smith 2007, 61-63. On meddlesomeness (πολυπραγμοσύνη) as a metaphor for reading the novels, see Hunter 2009.

[5] Aristippus is also the representative of his polis on the Amphictyonic Council at Delphi (H 2,26,3), an institution that was revived in the Roman era; see Pouilloux 1983, 271-274. Both of these councils underwent an important revival in the imperial period; discussed in Oliver 1980, 1-33. Aristippus is prominent enough to dine regularly in the Prytaneion (H 1,10,3), a distinction which, in the classical period, was awarded to honored speakers and magistrates, a privilege famously ironized by Socrates (Plato *Apology* 36d); in later periods, it retained its historical resonance while being bestowed to greater numbers of people; see Miller 1978, 4-8; Hansen 1991, 314. His upper-class status is also hinted at by his remark that he introduced his son to his clansmen, γεννήτας (H 1,13,1), a social organization that in classical Athens suggested aristocratic ties. During the imperial period, this institution was revived; noted by Morgan 1989a, 363 n. 315. On clans in imperial Athens, see Oliver 1980.

[6] Lalanne 2006, 75.

mistakes his stepmother's kisses for motherly feelings. Only after she addresses him as 'the new Hippolytus' (H 1,10,2), does he realize— to his shame—that she wants to seduce him. Demaenete does not take rejection well. Like Phaedra of Euripides' *Hippolytus*, she denounces her stepson to her husband, saying that Cnemon kicked her in the abdomen in a fit of jealousy when he learned she was pregnant.[7] Her story convinces Aristippus, who makes no further inquiry nor offers Cnemon the opportunity to make a defense. He beats Cnemon, who asks why he is being punished: Aristippus interprets this as a sign of Cnemon's arrogance.[8] Aristippus orders his servants to whip him, a domestic punishment typically inflicted upon slaves but here used by servants against the master's son.[9] This harsh treatment is less noteworthy for the rage Aristippus feels by this perceived attack upon his wife's sexuality—a legitimate cause for anger—than for the abject degradation Cnemon suffers. Aristippus stops when he has 'satisfied his rage'.[10]

Demaenete, still intent on seducing Cnemon, enlists the help of her maid, Thisbe, a *serva callida,* who 'falls in love upon command' (H 1,11,3). As ordered, Thisbe ingratiates herself to Cnemon and becomes his lover. Cnemon, however, prudishly worries about the propriety of his affair with a household slave.[11] Worried about being caught, he asks her to be discreet; she then intimates that she knows of a much more scandalous affair:

> 'Cnemon', she said, 'you seem to me a complete fool! If you suppose that it is dangerous to be caught sleeping with a purchased handmaid like me, what kind of punishment would you think a woman deserves who says she is well-born and has a lawfully wedded husband, and is aware that death is the penalty for breaking the law, but has an extramarital affair anyway?' (H 1,11,4)

[7] Cf. Chaereas' kicking of the pregnant Callirhoe (C 1,4). On Euripidean resonances, see Rattenbury and Lumb 1935, 15 n. 11. For a more extensive analysis of parallels with Euripides' lost *Hippolytus Velatus*, see Rocca 1976, 25-31. On the stereotype of the 'wicked stepmother' (*saeva noverca*) in the declamations see van Mal-Maeder 2001, 62-66.

[8] Cf. AT 5,23,5 where Thersander catches Clitophon in his home.

[9] Saller 1991. Cnemon describes this beating as 'lacerating' (ξαινοίμην H 1,11,1). The infliction of physical wounds was characteristic of the discipline of slaves. For example, the scars on Leucippe's back suffice as proof of the overseer's abuse (AT 5,17,6). The whipping of Habrocomes in Xenophon of Ephesus' novel is similarly gruesome (XE 2,6,2-3); see Halm-Tisserant 2013, 127.

[10] H 1,11,2: ὡς δὲ ἐνεπέπληστο τῆς ὀργῆς. Violence between fathers and sons is not mentioned in Stoic discussion of anger, either because it was taken for granted or because it was rare; see W. V. Harris 2001, 310-311.

[11] Konstan 1994b, 147-148; Haynes 2003, 114.

When Thisbe implies that Demaenete is the woman in question, Cnemon is outraged and is 'prepared to slay them both' (ὡς ἄμφω διαχειρισόμενος, H 1,12,2). The false notion that death was the penalty for both members of an adulterous couple had deep roots in popular imagination. In Roman law, the nearest reference to putting the couple to death is subsumed under the right of the *paterfamilias* to put his daughter to death immediately after killing her lover, but only if they were caught in her father's house or her husband's.[12] Heliodorus may have been familiar with the Athenian statute concerning justifiable killing of an adulterer in Demosthenes' oration *Against Aristocrates*:

> If a man kills another unintentionally in an athletic contest, or overcoming him in a fight on the highway, or unwittingly in battle, or in intercourse with his wife, or mother, or sister, or daughter, or concubine kept for procreation of legitimate children, he shall not go into exile as a murderer on that account. (Demosthenes 23,53)

The law of justifiable homicide cited by Demosthenes permitted a husband, a son, a brother, a father, or a concubine's mate to kill a perpetrator with impunity; however, no mention is made of a stepson punishing a stepmother. Likewise, Lysias' *On the Murder of Eratosthenes* links adultery with justifiable homicide. As we have already seen in Chariton, Lysias was an influential model on rhetorical exercises in the imperial period. The speaker of that oration had a powerful interest in convincing the jurors that the law did not just permit but actually exhorted him to kill Eratosthenes.[13] It is interesting that neither Demosthenes nor Lysias expressly mention the killing of the adulteress. In the later Republic and early Principate, rhetorical exercises commonly presupposed an adultery law that stated, 'If a man is caught in the act of adultery, let him be killed'.[14] A declamatory scenario in Seneca's *Controversiae* (1,4) declares that a man who catches an adulteress with an adulterer is permitted to kill them, as long as he kills them both.[15] This exercise constructs a dilemma in which a father orders his son, à la Orestes, to kill an adulteress who is also the son's mother. Susan Treggiari argues that the rule

> that anyone catching adulterers in the act could kill them with impunity...is a far more extreme custom than anything claimed for in actual law in the pre-

[12] Ulpian, *On Adultery*, book 1 in *Digest* 48,23,2-4.

[13] E. M. Harris 1990.

[14] Cohen 1991, 98-132.

[15] Seneca the Elder refers to a speech made by Cicero on a variant of this theme; see *Controversiae* 1,4,7. On the popularity of the theme in rhetorical exercises, see Bonner 1949, 119-122.

> Augustan period. It does not seem logical to argue from the rhetoricians that statute or custom conferred on husbands or fathers the right to kill without trial the adulteress, adulterer, or both when taken in the act.[16]

Augustus limited the husband's right to self-help by prohibiting him from killing an adulterous wife and by restricting his right to kill the lover.[17] Heliodorus' imagined adultery law is closer in spirit to those found in rhetorical exercises than in actual law, either Athenian or Roman.

Nevertheless, certain aspects of Heliodorus' adultery scene echo discussions that were taking place in legal circles in the centuries following Augustus' legislation. Questions arose over who had the right to prosecute, how long after the incident a case could be brought to trial, what court would rule in such cases, and the permissible degree of relation between the avenger and the adulteress.[18] Stepmothers tread the fine line between insider and outsider: the animosity of stepmothers toward their stepchildren was proverbial in ancient myth and literature, yet the stepmother is the wife of the *paterfamilias*.[19] The ambiguity of her status is reflected in the Roman law of patricide, the *lex Pompeia de parricidiis,* which excluded stepmothers from the set of relatives covered by the law.[20] Second-century jurists, however, asserted that stepmothers, as well as betrothed persons, were covered by the spirit of the law.[21] Seneca's *Controversiae* take for granted that the *filiusfamilias* would always assume the father's interests.[22] Cnemon is representative of the ideal son—so much so that when Thisbe urges him to 'be a man' (ἀλλ' ὅπως ἀνὴρ σκέψαι, H 1,11,5), Cnemon takes it literally and naïvely appropriates the role of husband (ἀνὴρ).

Cnemon's confrontation of Demaenete and her imaginary lover follows the formula of the bedroom showdown; however, Cnemon unwittingly assumes the role of the cuckold while ironically appearing as the adulterer to the married couple. One night, Thisbe alerts Cnemon to the lover's presence in the house and urges him to ready his sword for revenge (H 1,12,1). Details of light and darkness signal that this is a formulaic adultery scene: Thisbe illuminates the path through

---

16 Treggiari 1991, 274.

17 *Digest* 48,5,25; see Evans Grubbs 1995, 214 n. 240.

18 *Digest* 48,5.

19 P. A. Watson 1995.

20 *Digest* 48,9,1.

21 *Digest* 48,9,3: Marcian *Institutes*, book 14: It must be known that first cousins are included under the *lex Pompeia*, but that others of an equal or closer degree of kindred are not similarly covered. Stepmothers and betrothed persons are left out, but covered by the spirit of the law'.

22 Noted by Bonner 1949, 121-122. Further developed in Gunderson 2003.

the darkened house and Cnemon notices a light inside his parents' bedroom. Sword in hand, he bursts through the closed bedroom doors and orders the alleged culprit to show himself (H 1,12,2). Cnemon, ready to kill his stepmother and her supposed lover, sees his own father crawl out of bed, begging for mercy (H 1,12,3). Anagnorisis and peripeteia coincide as Cnemon, intending to catch an adulterer in the act, is caught in the role of the avenging cuckold. Cnemon's recognition of his father instantaneously transforms a noble intention to avenge his father's honor into the creation of prima facie evidence of attempted patricide. Aristippus disarms him, and orders the servants to tie Cnemon's hands (H 1,12,4). Demaenete says something to the effect of 'I told you so', referring to her earlier allegation that Cnemon was out of control, thereby appearing to validate her previous (false) accusation. The *paterfamilias* responds, 'Yes, but I didn't believe you'.

The trial scene proper begins, as typical, in the morning, when Aristippus takes Cnemon in chains to the popular assembly on a charge of attempted patricide (ἐπὶ τὸν δῆμον ἦγε, H 1,13,1). Heliodorus conflates the technicalities of legal procedure in classical Athens, which he and his readers knew primarily through the Attic orations. Modern philologists and legal historians have worked to clarify the legal nomenclature that distinguished procedures by the type of injury and the venue for judgment, of which there were several in classical Athenian democracy.[23] How much more difficult would it have been for lay readers of the orations in the Roman Empire to decipher the complexities of democratic procedural law, long made obsolete in the third or fourth centuries of the empire? There were at least five terms for actions that would initiate trial, depending on the venue. The γραφή, a public charge tried by jurors, and the δίκη, a private charge tried by judges, are the most common.[24] Other terms refer to procedures that go directly to the assembly or council: the προβολή was a preliminary accusation before the Assembly, the εἰσαγγελία was a formal indictment before the Assembly and the Council of 500, whereas the ἀπόφασις was the presentation of an investigative report, often with a request for action, to the Assembly or the Areopagus. Other procedures refer to the filing of a charge with the Eleven, the elected magistrates in classical Athens who controlled the prison and had limited judicial power.[25] The ἀπαγωγή, discussed above in the trial of Clitophon (trial 5), was the term used when the prosecutor remanded the wrongdoer to a magistrate for summary arrest,

[23] 'The Athenians took much more interest in procedural than in substantive law'. See Hansen 1975, 21.

[24] Hansen 1975, 9.

[25] Harrison 1971, 17-18; Hansen 1976; Todd 1993, 117-119.

typically for culprits caught in the act (ἐπ᾽ αὐτοφώρῳ) of committing crimes classified as κακουργία because of the malicious or stealthy nature of the infraction (such as burglary, theft, and adultery).[26] A cuckold who caught an adulterer in the act had the option to kill him with impunity or to bring him before the Eleven for summary judgment. If the criminal acknowledged his guilt, he would be immediately executed; but if he pled innocent, then he would stand trial.[27] A related procedure, referred to as ἐφήγησις, was used when the prosecutor made a denunciation to a magistrate who would then in turn arrest the wrongdoer.[28]

The immediacy with which Aristippus arrests Cnemon for violently breaking and entering the bedroom evokes the ἀπαγωγή; however, no magistrates are mentioned. Cnemon's fetters do not tell us much: the image of a defendant being led in chains from prison into the courtroom recurs across a wide range of genres, from the Attic orations to Christian martyrologies.[29] Aristippus, however, takes Cnemon straight to the popular assembly (H 1,13,1 δεσμῶν ἐπὶ τὸν δῆμον ἦγε), rather than to the law court, which suggests the procedures of either προβωλή or εἰσαγγελία.[30] Unlike the γραφή, the routine procedure for prosecuting a public crime, the εἰσαγγελία did not penalize the prosecutor for failure to obtain a certain percentage of the votes.[31] The purpose of the exemption was to ensure that there would be no impediment to the prosecution of the most serious crimes such as treason, official misconduct, the abuse of orphans, and parental abuse, the crime of which Cnemon is accused. The Athenian law is cited in Demosthenes' *Against Timocrates*:

> If anyone is arrested after having been caught for mistreatment of his parents or for desertion from the army, or for entering any forbidden place proclaimed barred to him by the laws, let the Eleven imprison him and bring him before the Heliaia, and let whoever, among whom it is possible, prosecute him. If he is found guilty, let the Heliaia assess the penalty he must pay or suffer. (Demosthenes 24,105)

---

26 Cohen 1983, 52-61. On the range of meanings for 'ἐπ᾽ αὐτοφώρῳ', see E. M. Harris 1994.

27 Harrison 1971, 221-229; MacDowell 1978, 148-149; Cohen 1991, 114-120.

28 Hansen 1976, 26.

29 Cf. Demosthenes 24,105: δησάντων αὐτὸν οἱ ἕνδεκα καὶ εἰσαγόντων εἰς τὴν ἡλιαίαν. In Chariton's novel, Theron is led in chains to the theater (C 3,4,7). See also *Martyrdom of Ptolemaeus and Lucius* 11-12, *The Martyrs of Lyons* 8-9, *The Martyrdom of Perpetua and Felicitas* 6,1.

30 In the extant Athenian orations, δῆμος almost always refers to the popular assembly and never to the law courts; see Hansen 1978.

31 Harrison 1971, 49-59; MacDowell 1978, 183-186.

Heliodorus' vision of the trial is inspired by a procedure similar to that described by Demosthenes: the size of this court (2,700 judges, as the reader is later told) suggests that Heliodorus imagines something like the convening of the fourth-century Heliaia, whereby the popular assembly convened as a court to hear political trials.[32] Valerius Maximus offers a parallel case from Roman history. During the period of the Late Republic, a high-ranking senator named L. Gellius suspected his son of sleeping with his stepmother and plotting patricide. Rather than summarily punishing him, Gellius opted to take 'almost the entire senate into his council (*concilium*)' in order to give his son the opportunity to make a defense. After the matter was investigated, the senate voted to acquit him. As Valerius Maximus concludes, 'If having been incited by his angry impulse, he had rushed to violence, he would have committed a crime rather than avenged one'.[33] Similarly, as a respectable member of the Areopagus, the Greek analog to the Roman senate, Aristippus may have done something similar to Gellius by taking the matter to an aristocratic venue, instead of presenting a private, familial dispute to the masses in the popular assembly. It is a move that would have been unusual under the Roman Empire, but typical—at least as imagined by Heliodorus—for the democracy of classical Athens.

The aura of democracy is created via the minutia of procedure. Aristippus claims that Cnemon's nocturnal ambush compelled him to denounce his son (προσαγγέλλω τοῦτον, H 1,13,2) under the court's protection. In the classical period, the verb προσαγγέλλω generally meant 'to make a report'; in post-classical sources, however, it meant to 'denounce' to a governmental authority.[34] As we have seen in the trials of Chaereas (trial 1) and Clitophon (trial 5), προσαγγελία was the name given in rhetorical handbooks for the strategy of self-indictment.[35] Although in the present case Aristippus denounces not himself but his son, with the verb προσαγγέλλειν, Heliodorus has hit upon a *mot juste* that has a classical Athenian ring to it but carries the full rhetorical nuance of 'denounce' expected at the opening of a novelistic trial scene.[36]

---

[32] Dinarchus 1,52 mentions 2,500 citizens; *Athenaion Politeia* 68,1; see Hansen 1991, 191, 215.

[33] *Facta et Dicta Memorabilia* 5,9,1, translation adapted from Shackleton Bailey 2000.

[34] For example, Demosthenes 18,170 καὶ μετὰ ταῦθ' ὡς ἦλθεν ἡ βουλὴ καὶ ἀπήγγειλαν οἱ πρυτάνεις τὰ προσηγγελμέν' ἑαυτοῖς. Most of the citations in the LSJ under the entry 'προσαγγελία, προσαγγέλλω' where it is used as 'denounce' come from post-classical sources, both literary and epigraphic. *Denuntiare* is also translated as καταγγέλλειν and εἰσαγγέλλειν; see Laffi 2013, 20, 50 and 55.

[35] Russell 1983, 35-36.

[36] This is also the verb used to describe Charicles' self-indictment to the assembly at Delphi: H 4,19,6 ἴσως μὲν, ὦ Δελφοί, προσαγγεῖλαί με βουλόμενον ἐμαυτὸν ἥκειν εἰς μέσους καὶ ταύτην συγκεκληκέναι τὴν ἐκκλησίαν ἡγεῖσθε.

Aristippus' denunciation trots out the clichés of the declamatory motif of maltreatment of parents.[37] His head is covered with dirt, a symbol of grief. His proem consists of the short statement that he raised his son with the conventional hope that he would support him in his old age. Aristippus claims to have done everything expected in the rearing of a free man, specifically by teaching him to read, introducing him to his phratry and to his clansmen, enrolling him as an ephebe, and proclaiming him a citizen according to the city's laws. It echoes Plato's *Crito* 50d-51a, in which the personified Laws remind Socrates that they are responsible for his life, education, and identity; in effect, the father is the personification of the power of laws in the *Crito*. This interpretation of *patria potestas* runs throughout Latin declamatory exercises, in which threats to the *manus* of the father result in the literal amputation of the son's hands.[38] In Greek declamations, disowning the son is more typical.[39] In both, however, the power of the father was emphatically reinforced in exercises for training young men to assume their adult roles.

The second part of Aristippus' narration, introduced by an adversative δέ (H 1,13,2), contrasts the son's behavior with his own. The description of Cnemon's hostility against his father parallels Aristippus' benevolence toward his son. He cites four specific instances of his son's hubris in ascending order of severity. First, he wantonly assaulted Aristippus. Secondly, he assaulted his father's 'lawfully wedded spouse' (τὴν κατὰ νόμους συνοικοῦσαν μοι, H 1,13,2). Thirdly, Cnemon intruded 'armed and at night' (τέλος δὲ καὶ ξιφήρης νύκτωρ ἐπῆλθε, H 1,13,2) into his father's room. The emphasis on the detail of time ('at night', νύκτωρ, H 1,13,2) characterizes Cnemon's crime as a one of stealth (κακουργία). In Athenian law, as in most other legal systems, particular circumstances contributing to the potential for a violent confrontation between criminal and victim (such as breaking and entering), distinguish a crime as aggravated rather than simple, and therefore subject to summary punishment. As Aristippus describes it, all of those elements are present in the bedroom showdown.[40] In conclusion, Aristippus asserts that his son nearly became a patricide (καὶ παρὰ τοσοῦτον γέγονε πατραλοίας, H 1,13,2).

In forensic oratory, the use of the term patricide is freely applied to a variety of situations as a rhetorical trope for exaggerating the gravity of certain crimes. In Athenian law, patricide was tried in the same courts and by the same procedures

---

[37] A typical example may be found in Seneca *Controversiae* 9,4

[38] Gunderson 2003, 59-72.

[39] Russell 1983, 30-33.

[40] For a discussion of the factors contributing to the flagrance of a crime, see Cohen 1983, 40, 58-68.

as other types of homicide.[41] Similarly in Rome, cases concerning patricide were tried before the *quaestio de sicariis et veneficiis,* one of the standing courts established during the Republic to try cases of homicide.[42] The charge against Cnemon is further complicated because it concerns attempted, rather than actual, patricide.

As we have seen in the novels of Chariton and Achilles Tatius, the genre of the Greek romance tends to gravitate to crimes that are intended, but not carried out. In Chariton's novel, Mithridates is accused not of actual seduction, but only of attempted seduction. For the novels, intention alone constitutes grounds for legal action. Cnemon's crime might have fallen under the rubric of βούλευσις (conspiracy), which covered a wide variety of acts, ranging from intentional killing, to killing by means of an agent, or forming a plan to kill which either fails or remains unrealized.[43] There existed a trial for wounding with intent to kill (δίκη τραύματος ἐκ προνοίας) before the Areopagus, the same court charged with cases of intentional homicide; however, in the surviving instances of such procedures, the cases involved actual injuries.[44] Excessive violence was covered under other procedures, such as private suits for assault (δίκη αἰκείας) or public indictments for insolence (γραφὴ ὕβρεως).[45]

In Cnemon's case, no one was actually injured: he simply brandished a sword. Naturally, this threatening act would be seen as self-evident proof of premeditation. In Lysias 4,6, the speaker argues that if he had entered his opponent's house carrying a sword, then his opponent would have better grounds for arguing that he intended to kill him; as it happened, the speaker wounded his opponent with a potsherd, an ordinary household item. Roman law, on the other hand, was more straightforward. A rescript of Hadrian equated attempted murder with actual murder. It is mentioned in the *Digest* in connection with the *lex Cornelia de sicariis et veneficiis:*

---

[41] An anecdote related by Cicero *Pro Roscio Amerino* 70 and Diogenes Laertius 1,59, which claims that Solon did not fix a penalty for patricide, had led MacDowell to suggest that patricide was treated under the normal laws of homicide MacDowell 1963, 116; Treston 1923, 220-221.

[42] Lassen 1992.

[43] MacDowell 1963, 60-61.

[44] Lysias 3, 4, Todd 1993, 272.

[45] Demosthenes' *Against Conon*, in which the prosecutor argues that he almost died at the hands of Conon, is a δικὴ αἰκείας: see Demosthenes 54,11 κἂν ἔμπυος γενόμενος διεφθάρην and 54,12 καὶ παρηκολούθησέ μοι τοιαύτη νόσος ἐξ ἧς εἰς τοὔσχατον ἦλθον, ἐξ ὧν ὑπὸ τούτων ἔλαβον πληγῶν). Antiphon's *Third Tetralogy*, also concerns an incident of physical violence; since this resulted in death, it is prosecuted as a murder case, a δικὴ φόνου.

> The deified Hadrian wrote in a rescript that he who kills a man, if he committed this act without the intention of causing death, could be acquitted; and he who did not kill a man but wounded him with the intention of killing ought to be found guilty of homicide. On this account, it should be laid down that if someone draws his sword or weapon, he undoubtedly did so with the intention of causing death. (Digest 48,8,1,3, trans. Robinson)

Roman law recognized the mere drawing of a weapon as a crime, regardless of whether or not it resulted in injury. Thus, Aristippus' emphasis on Cnemon's armed appearance (ξιφήρης, H 1,13,2) as he opened the bedroom door is offered as proof that he intended to kill him. A similar case appears in Apuleius' *Metamorphoses* 3,1-12: the novel's narrator, Lucius, accidentally stumbles upon a group of robbers in the act of breaking into his friend's house one evening and is tried in Hypata for killing three men.[46] According to R. G. Summers, 'this great attention to a single detail makes no sense unless the charge and the defense are not for murder but for the intent to commit murder'.[47] Here we see that Apuleius grafts onto his Greek model a detail inspired by Roman law. Likewise, Heliodorus' emphasis on the detail that Cnemon is armed presumes a distinctly Roman legal reality.

Aristippus closes his speech with the assertion that he had a right to kill Cnemon but chose not to do so because it is 'better to obtain justice by means of the law than by a child's death' (H 1,13,2). If he had killed Cnemon in self-defense when he burst into the bedroom, then he would have had a case for justifiable homicide (δίκαιος φόνος) under the law of Athens.[48] Alternately, Aristippus may equally be asserting the *ius vitae necisque*, his right as *paterfamilias* over the life and death of his son. This power, attested mostly by literary authors, was probably not exercised over grown children in Roman law during the Principate.[49] Yet, it was a common theme in the Latin declamations and certainly loomed large in the imaginations of schoolboys.[50] By the time of Hadrian, limitations were imposed upon this right. The *Digest* refers to a case that shares many features with the story of Cnemon and Aristippus:

---

[46] Apuleius *Metamorphoses* 2,18, 2,32, 3,4, 3,5.

[47] Summers 1970, 517.

[48] MacDowell 1963, 70-71.

[49] Nicholas 1962, 109-110; Y. Thomas 1984; W. V. Harris 1986; Saller 1994, 115-117.

[50] Gunderson 2003.

> It is said that when a certain man had killed in the course of a hunt his son, who had been committing adultery with his stepmother, the deified Hadrian deported him to an island [because he acted] more [like] a brigand in killing him than as [one] with a father's right; for paternal power ought to depend on compassion, not cruelty. (*Digest* 48,9,5: Marcian, *Institutes*, book 14; trans. Robinson)

In classical Athens, a father did not hold the same power over his family.[51] It was a right associated with Roman law in particular and rarely mentioned by classical Greek authors. Later Greek authors, however, were aware of the Roman practice and frequently expressed their astonishment at it.[52] One of the few places in which this right is associated with Athenian law is found in Sextus Empiricus. Writing in the late second century C.E., he attributes to Solon a law allowing the father to kill his children:

> Cronos decided to destroy his own children, and Solon gave the Athenians the law 'concerning things immune' by which he allowed each man to slay his own child; but with us the laws forbid the slaying of children.[53]

There is no reason to take this statement as evidence of an actual practice; what it does show, however, is that in the imperial era, Greek writers disassociated themselves from this practice by ascribing it to the exotic or legendary past, and implicitly to Rome. Aristippus' conscious decision to bring Cnemon to trial rather than exercise his right to punish Cnemon echoes similar crises in Euripides' *Orestes*. For example, Tyndareus censures Orestes for not availing himself of legal remedies instead of taking the law into his own hands by killing his mother Clytemnestra.[54] Similarly, when Pylades enters and announces that he has been exiled from Phocis by his father, Orestes asks whether this was a result of a private accusation, or whether his father brought a public charge before the citizens of Phocis.[55] From these literary examples, Aristippus aligns himself with the law by renouncing his right to self-help.

At the end of his speech, Aristippus weeps. This conventional gesture is then amplified by Demaenete, whose loud wailing throws the courtroom into confu-

---

[51] Crook 1967b, 113; Harrison 1968, 70-78.
[52] Y. Thomas 1984, 500.
[53] Sextus Empiricus 3,211; see Saller 1994, 102-103.
[54] Euripides *Orestes* 496-506.
[55] Euripides *Orestes* 766: ἴδιον ἢ κοινὸν πολίταις ἐπιφέρων ἔγκλημά τι;

sion. The Athenian orators note (often pejoratively) the practice of winning sympathy by parading one's weeping children into the courtroom.[56] Demaenete is an illustration of the persuasive power of emotional display. In fact, her weeping is remarkably articulate: she testifies, affirms the charge, shows sympathy for Cnemon, claims that he threatened his parents, and laments that he was possessed by avenging spirits (H 1,13,3). The jury in this trial, as juries in other novelistic trials, proves itself highly susceptible to this type of emotional suasion.

In contrast to Demaenete, who in effect makes a public statement without actually speaking, Cnemon is again denied the chance to make a defense. When he rises to speak, an official asks him an unambiguous and direct question: 'Did you attack your father with a sword?' (ὁ γραμματεὺς προσελθὼν ἠρώτα στενὸν ἐρώτημα, εἰ τῷ πατρὶ ξιφήρης ἐπῆλθον, H 1,13,4). Two details point to a Roman, rather than Athenian, context. Firstly, the title of the official is the γραμματεύς. His role in interrogating Cnemon seems to accord with administrative practices in the Greek cities under the Roman Empire. A similar official, called the γραμματεὺς τοῦ δήμου, is mentioned in connection with the narrative of Paul's experiences in Ephesus (*Acts* 19,35) and also appears in imperial inscriptions. This official, elected annually, came to supplant the στρατηγός as the eponymous magistrate in city decrees.[57] Secondly, there is the significance of the sword. Among his other legal reforms, Hadrian clarified the definition of attempted murder by specifying the drawing of a sword as the determinative criterion (*nam si gladium strinxerit...indubitante occidendi animo id eum admisisse, Digest* 48,8,1,3). Cnemon answers the official question truthfully—that is, affirmatively—but his explanation is cut short by a general outcry. This simple answer is enough to convict Cnemon without further examination. The assembly affirms the clerk's ruling by denying Cnemon his defense.

The voting procedure is vague, with different factions calling for different punishments. The overall impression forms a composite of stereotypes of Athenian democracy that were in circulation in the Roman period. There is an abundance of seemingly technical detail, yet what Heliodorus gets wrong is interesting for what it reveals about how Roman Greeks understood Athenian democracy. Three details stand out in particular: the number of jurors, the method of voting, and the form of the proposed punishments.

The jury that Heliodorus imagines is a distinctly pre-imperial, democratic institution. It is called the demos, which means the 'people' in general but was a

---

[56] For example, Lysias 20,34, Demosthenes 21,99 and 186-8, Andocides 1,48; parodied by Aristophanes *Wasps* 568-74 and 976-8. See Harrison 1971, 63-64; MacDowell 1988, 258.

[57] Sherwin-White 1963, 86-87; A. H. M. Jones 1940, 238-240.

synonym for the democratic assembly of the city. In classical Athens, the assembly admitted all citizens, whereas the judges sitting in the δικαστήρια, or popular courts, were citizens selected by random lot. Both the assembly and the popular courts represented the will of the citizen body as a whole.[58] In the Roman period, such juries were distant memories. The size of Cnemon's jury of 2,700 judges is hyperbolic; it is more than triple the size of the imperial Roman senate.[59] In classical Athens, the total number of men who were eligible to serve on a jury in a given year was 6,000. The actual size of juries varied. There is evidence for figures of 201 and 401 for private lawsuits; public cases typically involved juries comprised of multiples of 500 plus one.[60] Deinarchus (1,52) cites a figure of 2,500 in reference to an earlier case in which the court ruled in the speaker's favor. Likewise, Andocides (1,17) refers to a case of a γραφὴ παρανόμων, a charge for proposing an illegal law, which was heard by '6,000 Athenians', likely an exaggeration for rhetorical effect.[61] Heliodorus likewise inflates the number of jurors in order to dramatize Cnemon's narrow escape from execution. Although the number is fictional, it reflects an awareness that classical Athenian juries were made of multiples of 500. Even the figure of 1,700 may be broken down into standard jury sizes: 500 times three, plus 200. The overall impression is that Cnemon's case is exceptionally important and that Athens is so extremely democratic that a private lawsuit can be tried by the assembly, an image consistent with the stereotype of Athenian litigiousness.[62]

The voting procedure described by Heliodorus conflates three different methods of voting: acclamation, show of hands, and ballot. Six different verbs are used for the process: ἀνεβόησαν, κρίναντες, ἐδοκίμαζον, διεχειροτόνουν, καταχειροτονήσαντες, and ψηφισαμένων (H 1,13,4-14,1). In contrast to the noun θόρυβος, or 'uproar' (H 1,13,5) the verb ἀναβοᾶν means 'to shout' in a general sense, as well as the more specific sense of 'to acclaim', which in the imperial period was a common method of gauging popular opinion and carried the force of an official vote.[63] The jury immediately proceeds to vote upon the penalty, suggesting that the shout of the crowd is equivalent to a guilty verdict. Of course, it was not unusual for audiences to cheer or hiss to express their response to events, often quite loudly. For example, in classical Athens the trial of the generals at the Battle of Arginusai before the popular assembly of Athens was derailed by shouting and

---

[58] On the overlapping functions of the popular courts and the assembly in classical Athens, see Hansen 1975, 51-57.

[59] Talbert 1984, 131-134.

[60] Hansen 1991, 187.

[61] Hansen 1982, 20.

[62] Discussed above in connection with the trial of Theron (trial 3).

[63] Colin 1965b; Aldrete 1999.

general uproar.[64] At the same time, the use of the verb κρίνειν, 'to decide' (H 1,14,1), suggests that the assembly is acting in a judicial capacity, which confirms that ἀνεβόησαν refers to an official vote. Similarly, δοκιμάζειν ('to choose, approve') conveys the sense of an official judgment. The use of the verb χειροτονεῖν as well as its compounds (διεχειροτόνουν, H 1,13,5 and καταχειροτονήσαντες, H 1,14,1) implies that the vote was conducted by a show of hands.[65] This was the normal method of voting in the classical Athenian assembly; however, when the assembly was sitting in its judiciary capacity, bronze ballots were used. Here, the reference to a ψῆφος suggests some other type of vote.[66] Heliodorus uses the terms interchangeably; later in the novel, in the assembly at Delphi, the expression 'with one vote and the hand of all' seems to be a figure of speech to mean 'unanimously' (μιᾷ ψήφῳ καὶ χειρὶ, H 4,21,2). The round numbers of the tally in Cnemon's case reflect the regular practice of a vote by show of hands, in which the president would rapidly estimate whether or not a motion passed. Most importantly, the description of the vote is simply a lead-up to the story of how Cnemon is saved when a third alternative arises to upset the vote count.

In classical Athens, when the jury voted in favor of the prosecution and the law did not fix a specific penalty for the crime, there was a second round of voting. In this later round, called the τίμησις, the prosecution and the defense each proposed a penalty; the jurors then chose one or the other.[67] In Cnemon's case, the first vote concerns whether or not to allow Cnemon a defense speech. As in the trial of Clitophon (trial 5), the defendant's confession is incontestable; therefore, because Cnemon's guilt is clearly established, his defense is precluded. As we have seen in other trial scenes in the novels, the nature of the proceedings is typically fluid. In this trial, the second vote is a choice between penalties proposed not by the prosecution and defense, but by different factions in the assembly.

At first, the assembly is unanimous about the death penalty, but the vote is divided as to the method of execution. Some vote for stoning (λίθοις βάλλειν, H 1,13,4 and καταλεῦσαι, H 1,14,1), an archaic punishment associated with crimes against society, such as patricide. The mythic tradition provides many precedents. In Euripides' *Orestes* (914-915), the Argive assembly condemns

---

64 Xenophon *Hellenica* 1,7; MacDowell 1978, 186-189.

65 Hansen 1977, 124.

66 Staveley 1972, 83-88, 95-100. By the classical period, the term ψῆφος had acquired the more general and metaphorical sense of 'vote', rather than specifically 'vote by ballot' as opposed to a show of hands. Hence the use of the term ψηφίσματα to denote regular decrees of the assembly, decrees which in all likelihood were voted upon by a show of hands; see Hansen 1991, 147.

67 Harrison 1971, 80-82; MacDowell 1978, 252-253; Hansen 1991, 202-203; Todd 1993, 133-134. A well-known illustration of the process of the τίμησις is the trial of Socrates.

Electra and Orestes, found guilty of matricide, to death by stoning. Similarly, in Sophocles' *Oedipus at Colonus* (434-435), Oedipus expresses a wish to be stoned to death.[68] Herodotus (9,5,3) mentions the historical incident of the stoning of Lycides and his family after he proposed that Salamis surrender to the Persians. The speaker of one of the pseudo-Quintilian *Declamationes* (12,12) suggests that if the judges do not punish an official for mismanagement of the grain dole during a famine, the people will stone him.[69] As far as we know, stoning was not an official penalty in Greek or Roman law; if it did happen, it was more likely a popular form of justice, rather than one determined by a judge's ruling.[70] In early Roman law the legendary punishment of a patricide was to be 'flogged with blood-colored rods, then sewn up in a sack with a dog, a dunghill cock, a viper, and a monkey; then the sack is thrown into the depths of the sea' (*Digest* 48,9,9). A later law, the *lex Pompeia*, however, made patricide subject to a relatively less gruesome, but still dreadful penalty: burning at the stake and being thrown to the beasts (*Digest* 48,9,1). Compared to these sensationalistic legal penalties for patricide, the more proverbial punishment of stoning seems relatively mild.

A different faction among the jurors urges that Cnemon be thrown into the βάραθρον (H 1,13,4 and 1,14,1), a 'man-made chasm northwest of the Hill of the Nymphs' that was specifically associated with the topography of Athens—just as the Tarpeian Rock, another site of execution, was associated with Rome.[71] It is unclear whether the precipitation into the pit was itself the means of execution, or whether it was the place where the bodies of slain convicts were hurled as a way of denying them proper burial. Most of the classical evidence seems to suggest that it constituted both execution and burial; however, a reference by Plutarch to a place in Athens 'where now the public officers cast out the bodies of those who had been put to death' has been interpreted as evidence that the pit was used for

[68] Instances of stoning in myth are collected in Cantarella 1991a, 73-84. In Mosaic law (Deuteronomy 21,21) stoning was the prescribed punishment for a number of crimes, including neglect of a parent and incest; see Hirzel 1909, 251-253; Barkan 1935, 44-49.

[69] Pease 1907, 17; Cantarella 1991a, 84-87, 326-329.

[70] On stoning as a form of mob violence, see Forsdyke 2008, 25-26.

[71] Wycherley 1978, 269; Cantarella 1991a, 232-263. Other references to the exact location are collected by Barkan 1935, 55-59. The term βάραθρον is found in fifth century authors; from the fourth century, this term is superseded by a more generic word, ὄρυγμα, signifying 'excavation'. See Barkan 1935, 56; Cantarella 1991a, 102. According to the Suda (s.v. 'μητραγύρτης'), the βάραθρον was filled in at the end of the fifth century to expiate the murder of a priest who had introduced the cult of Cybele to Athens; see Barkan 1935, 52-53.

the disposal of corpses of people executed by other means.[72] Like stoning, precipitation was a legendary form of punishment that also had a certain expiatory dimension.[73] It was an exceptional form of punishment reserved for religious or political crimes.[74] The similarity of both modes of execution to scapegoat ritual is reflected in their occasional conflation in literary texts. For example, in Euripides' *Ion*, Creusa is charged with plotting to poison Ion. The officials at Delphi search for her in order to stone her (1111-2) and vote unanimously to throw her from a cliff (1222-5). The tradition concerning Aesop, who was executed by the people of Delphi, is similarly divided regarding whether he was pushed off a cliff or stoned to death.[75] It is clear that Heliodorus specifically conceives of precipitation into the pit and stoning as interchangeably dramatic modes of execution.[76]

Although the process of the τίμησις was criticized because it deprived the jury of the freedom to assess whatever penalty it saw fit, Aristotle pointed out that it was impracticable to leave the specific sentencing in the hands of a large jury.[77] Cnemon's imagined trial bears this out. In Athens, proposals put forth to large voting assemblies had to be presented as simply as possible, typically as a choice between two options. Otherwise, a minority of votes might determine the outcome—precisely the situation that Heliodorus envisions. During the course of voting a third penalty, exile, arises as some people begin to doubt Demaenete and take Cnemon's protests seriously. Exile was the typical penalty for the brandishing of a weapon with intent to kill. Athenian law punished criminals convicted of conspiracy to kill with the same penalty as actual homicide: exile if the crime was unintentional, execution if intentional; however, the interval between conviction and τίμησις allowed the convict to flee Athens; thus, exile was a *de facto* alternate penalty.[78] The jurist Marcian noted that the penalty for homicide was deportation for *honestiores* and crucifixion or being thrown to the beasts for *humiliores* (*Digest* 48,8,3,5). Patricide, however, was special: it was the only crime for which Hadrian permitted *decuriones* to be subjected to capital punishment (*Digest* 48,19,15).

---

72 Plutarch *Themistocles* 22. See Barkan 1935, 59-62; Cantarella 1991a, 99-100; Todd 1993, 14.

73 Gras 1984, 75-89; Cantarella 1991a, 91-95.

74 It is mentioned in Plato, *Gorgias* 516e; see Todd 1993, 141.

75 Nicole Loraux, comment to Gras 1984, 88-89.

76 A parallel expression found in Lysias' *Against Agoratus* makes it clear that both verbs, though separated by καί, refer to a single action (θάνατον δικαίως καταψηφισάμενοι τῷ δημίῳ παρέδοτε καὶ ἀπετυμπανίσθη, Lysias 13,56).

77 Todd 1993, 134-135.

78 Demosthenes 23,71-2; MacDowell 1963, 113-115; 1978, 120; Todd 1993, 274.

In Cnemon's trial the opinion of the majority of the judges decides upon execution but the vote is evenly split between the first two proposals of execution (stoning and precipitation); consequently, the third proposal for sentencing him to exile carries the day. Cnemon is convicted of a crime he did not intend to commit, but is saved in the end by a procedural technicality—not unlike Orestes' acquittal in Aeschylus' *Eumenides* (748-53).

After Cnemon is exiled, Aristippus discovers the truth concerning Demaenete's scheme and tries to appeal the verdict. The procedural details are realistic, drawn from Athenian, rather than Roman, laws of pardon and appeal. Aristippus reports everything to the demos and obtains a pardon for Cnemon, again by a slim margin. He then canvasses his friends and relatives and petitions (πρυτανευόμενος, H 1,17,6) for Cnemon's return; the participle has an appropriately Attic sound to it and conforms to one of the known functions of the presiding magistrates (πρυτάνεις) in democratic Athens—namely to convene assemblies.[79] Aristippus' enlisting the support of his friends and relatives vaguely reflects the Athenian law on intentional homicide, which allowed the relatives of the victim to pardon his exiled killer.[80] According to Athenian law, the judgment of the courts was not usually reversible; the assembly was the only body with the power to reverse the decision of the court.[81] Aristippus' consultation with the demos is logical, not only from the standpoint of its being the court in which Cnemon was originally tried, but also from the standpoint of actual Athenian practice. It reflects awareness on the part of an imperial Greek author that the demos was the supreme authority in classical Athens and did not easily comply with private requests.

The trial of Cnemon reveals a portrait of an erratic Athenian judicial system that is the obverse of the ideal of a stable legal system supervised by a leader who embodies justice and surrounds himself with wise advisors. This was a powerful component of ideologies of rule throughout world history. In the case of Heliodorus, the implicit comparandum is the Roman emperor, who answered petitions, served as the ultimate court of appeal, and guaranteed law and order.[82] The love

---

79 Hansen 1991, 132-133.

80 MacDowell 1963, 117-125. This law is cited in Demosthenes 23,72; *IG*² 115, Draco's law on homicide, also refers to pardon but Heliodorus was unlikely to have consulted it. The decision of a court could also be reversed if a δίκη ψευδομαρτυριῶν, a case for giving false testimony, were brought; see MacDowell 1978, 244. In addition, there was also a procedure known as ἔφεσις, whereby the decision of an arbitrator could be appealed; see Harrison 1971, 72-74. The circumstances of Cnemon's case do not seem to warrant the latter; the former, however, might be used on the grounds that the evidence which Aristippus used to come to the conclusion that Cnemon intended to kill him was false.

81 Demosthenes 24,55; MacDowell 1978, 258.

82 This argument is developed further in S. Schwartz 2010.

affairs of the characters in Athens represent the antithesis of the protagonists' true love.[83] The same is true for the depiction of the legal system. Athens is a polis where democratic courts are dominated by mobs: politicized, unpredictable, and ungovernable.

[83] Winkler 1999, 299; Morgan 1989c, 107.

Trial 8.
The Fury's Whip: Entrapment
Kinsmen of Demaenete v. Aristippus
(Heliodorus, *Aethiopica* 1,14-17 and 2,8-11)

The Story

Demaenete's infatuation with Cnemon remains unabated, despite his court-ordered exile. To deflect her mistress' growing frustration, Thisbe promises to arrange a secret tryst with Cnemon in a house belonging to a flute-girl named Arsinoe. Thisbe then confesses to Aristippus her responsiblity for Cnemon's awkward incursion into his bedroom and promises to provide Aristippus with evidence of his wife's infidelity. She leads him to Arsinoe's house, where he finds Demaenete waiting for her lover. He apprehends his wife and takes her back to the city for trial, but she thwarts his plans by hurling herself into a crevasse that was the traditional site of executions in Athens. Aristippus declares, 'I have obtained justice from you even before the laws' and duly reports the incident to the demos and secures a pardon for Cnemon.

Meanwhile, Arsinoe informs Demaenete's family of Thisbe's scheme, hoping thereby to make Thisbe, her rival, suffer. The kinsmen of Demaenete hire speakers to charge Aristippus for using adultery as a pretext for murdering his wife. They issue a demand for Thisbe's torture; however, she runs away, thus leaving Aristippus unable to meet the challenge. Consequently, the demos convicts him not of murder, but of conspiring against Demaenete and arranging to have his own son exiled. Aristippus is sentenced to property confiscation and exile. In order to exonerate his father, Cnemon attempts to find Thisbe and bring her back to Athens to give exculpatory testimony, but his hopes are dashed when he finds her dead body in an underground cave in the marshes of the Nile.

Analysis

The continuation of Cnemon's Athenian saga hinges on the trial of his father. As we have seen in the other novels, it is typical for a trial scene to segue into another. After Cnemon finishes the story of his own trial, Theagenes and Charicleia (like the reader) sense that the verdict of exile cannot be the end of his story and beg him to continue the tale, saying, 'You will destroy us if you let the evil Demaenete go unpunished!' (H 1,14,2). His audience's existential investment in seeing the villain of the story punished compels Cnemon to continue. On one level, the ensuing story shows that schemes of uncontrolled women defy simple resolution and ultimately lead to their extrajudicial deaths; however, it is simplistic to look at the sequence as a simple morality tale that women who try to subvert the rules will suffer in the end. On a deeper level, we see Heliodorus deconstruct the conventional trial scene, rearranging it so as to present an alternative way of narrating the nature of justice.

The continuation of Cnemon's tale is markedly more complex than the first portion. Logically, Cnemon cannot know what happened in Athens after he left; Heliodorus is usually deliberate about explaining how his characters come to know something.[1] Cnemon was the homodiegetic narrator of the previous trial scene, which was written in a straightforward, chronological, proairetic style. The second half of his tale, as we shall see, is narrated in the 'hermeneutic', or puzzle-solving, mode. J. R. Morgan has shown that Heliodorus alternates between these two narrational modes throughout the novel; Cnemon's 'novella' illustrates this technique in miniature.[2] Through a series of nested narratives Cnemon becomes a heterodiegetic narrator as he relates the events to Theagenes and Charicleia: more precisely, he reports stories that were reported to him by two different people. Cnemon's narrative is already one degree removed from the main narrative; thus the others' reports in turn are embedded at two removes. The story of Thisbe is told in fragments by three different narrators: Charias (H 1,14,2-1,17,6), Anticles (H 2,8,3-2,9,4), and finally by Thisbe herself through the medium of a written tablet tied to her lifeless body (H 2,10). The effect of these doubly embedded narratives is to blur the conventional markers of the trial scene.

The fragmented perspectives allow the analeptic narrative of Cnemon's life in Athens to catch up with the plot of his journey with Theagenes and Charicleia as the three Greeks navigate the confusing and alien world of the Egyptian marshes. The 'Athenian tragedy' of Cnemon's homodiegetic narrative of his own trial and exile serves as an oasis of familiarity in the midst of the mysterious,

---

[1] Winkler 1999, 289.

[2] Morgan 1989c, 99.

corpse-strewn seashore of the *Aethiopica's* opening tableau. As Athens recedes into the distance, the rest of Cnemon's narrative becomes progressively weirder. References to the Furies bracket the sequence of metaphysical crime and punishment.[3] The uncanny appearance of Thisbe's corpse marks the moment when Cnemon's narrative converges with the main level of narration.

Taken together, the sub-narratives relate the story of Thisbe. She is the author, director, and stage manager of the conspiracy to entrap her mistress in a 'bedtrick', a ruse whereby one person is substituted for another in bed.[4] The first segment is narrated by Cnemon's friend, Charias, who has come from Athens to Aegina and informs him that Demaenete has died. Though Cnemon is elsewhere a skeptical narratee, he anticipates a poetically just ending: his first response is to worry that her death was random, unconnected to her actions. To allay Cnemon's fears, Charias announces sententiously, 'Justice has not abandoned us entirely; she may overlook something small and refrain from immediate vengeance, but on the lawless ones she casts a swift eye' (H 1,14,4).[5]

Charias first establishes that he learned everything from Thisbe, the agent of the plot, but not its narrator—at least, not yet. Charias' narrative reiterates the basic outline of the adultery scene that led to Cnemon's conviction in the first trial in Athens; in the present instance, it leads to his father's conviction. Both episodes end tragically for men who believe they are avenging an act of adultery. The symmetry between the two Athenian trials is shown in Table 4. Thisbe again fabricates allegations of adultery where there is no actual adulterer. Just as Cnemon's fortunes were reversed when the lamp revealed Demaenete in bed with Aristippus, here Demaenete is discovered in a darkened bedroom with a non-existent lover. The men's gullibility results in the conviction of both father and son by the demos of Athens.

According to Thisbe via Charias, after Cnemon's exile, Demaenete elegiacally blames Thisbe for losing her beloved. Thisbe, on the other hand, strategizes about how to save herself. Reprising her role as accessory to her mistress' desires, she offers to arrange a tryst between Demaenete and Cnemon. Thisbe builds her scheme upon two deceptions and a truth. To Demaenete, she reports that Cnemon is in Athens; to her friend, Arsinoe, she says that she needs a place to meet her lover, 'Teledemos'; and to Aristippus, she confesses the truth that she induced Cnemon to burst into his bedroom. Aristippus is beguiled by Thisbe, just as he

[3] H 1,14,6: τὴν δὲ εὐθὺς Ἐρινύες ἤλαυνον and H 2,11,1, τιμωρὸς Ἐρινὺς.

[4] The motif of the bedtrick is widespread in world literature; see Doniger 2000. For a more detailed discussion of the bedtricks in Heliodorus' novel, see S. Schwartz 2012.

[5] Morgan 1989a, 364 n. 317.

was previously by Demaenete. Thisbe corroborates his suspicions and volunteers to provide hard proof of his wife's infidelity.

Table 4. Comparison of the Athenian Trials

TRIAL OF CNEMON	TRIAL OF ARISTIPPUS
Intrigue of Demaenete against Cnemon	Intrigue of Thisbe against Demaenete
Thisbe tells Cnemon that Demaenete has a lover	Thisbe tells Aristippus that Demaenete has a lover
Cnemon finds Demaenete with Aristippus in their bedroom	Aristippus finds Demaenete alone in a hetaira's bedroom
Aristippus takes Cnemon to the demos	Aristippus takes Demaenete to the demos (thwarted)
	Intrigue of Arsinoe against Thisbe
Trial and conviction of the innocent Cnemon	Trial and conviction of the innocent Aristippus
Death of Demaenete avenges injustice against Cnemon	Death of Thisbe avenges injustice against Aristippus

The description of a darkened bedroom and a maid's involvement sets up a second bedroom showdown. Thisbe is the subject of thirteen active verbs and seven participles in the description of the bedtrick itself (H 1,17,1-4). She brings Demaenete to Arsinoe's house on the pretext of a rendezvous with Cnemon; she then brings Aristippus to meet Demaenete. Once inside the darkened room, she directs his attention to the presence of the lover, to whom he declares 'I have you!' (ἔχω σε, H 1,17,3). Thisbe fabricates evidence of the (non-existent) adulterer's escape by slamming the doors and urging Aristippus to catch him. Although the plan was for Aristippus to apprehend the lover, he declares that he has the culprit he wants: namely, his wife (τὴν ἀλιτήριον καὶ ἣν μάλιστα ἐβουλόμην ἔχω, H 1,17,4).

Typically the bedroom showdown results in the arrest of the male intruder. In Lysias 1, the punishment of the adulterer is the main issue, while that of the adulterous wife is treated as a private matter to be settled behind closed doors. Aristippus' arrest of Demaenete defies that formula. The confrontation between the spouses is brought to public attention: Aristippus treats his wife as a criminal to be punished by the demos, not by her husband. He makes the same mistake as in the first trial by abrogating his right as the paternal authority to discipline his dependents and instead remanding them to the public authorities. Thus, as a dutiful citizen, he apprehends his wife, brings her to the city, and submits his grievance to the civic authorities (H 1,17,4).

Although the setting is Athenian, the situation reflects a concern raised by Quintilian with the application of Roman adultery law. He wondered whether a husband had the right to kill an adulterer if the act of adultery took place outside of the marital home.[6] The location of Arsinoe's house is specified thrice: 'in front of the city' (H 1,15,6), on the 'outskirts of town' (H 1,16,4), and in the vicinity of the garden of the Epicureans (H 1,16,5). It is clearly significant that Aristippus' wife is not only outside oikos, but in a location outside the city, such as the Kerameikos, or 'Potter's Quarter', through which the road from the agora to the Academy passed as it exited Dipylon Gate and continued toward a district of workshops; later writers suggest that it was a busy, crowded, and slightly seedy 'red light district'.[7]

In the world of the novels, desire is conflated with fact; therefore, Demaenete is guilty of adultery in intention, but not in fact. Her arrest in the hetaira's house represents her degradation from wife to prostitute. Charias narrates Demaenete's thoughts: realizing the full implications of her crime and its consequences, she takes matters into her own hands. A tricolon encapsulates the personal, social, and legal consequences of her act:

> And she comprehended the entire situation at once, as it seems: the disappointment of her expectations, the dishonor in the future, the punishment of the laws. (H 1,17,4)

The use of the term ἀτιμία (H 1,17,4) is evocative of classical Athenian law, where it meant disenfranchisement, the punishment prescribed for a man who did not divorce his adulterous wife; however, we do not hear as much about the adulteress' punishment in Athenian law. In Roman law, the adulteress lost her social standing; her husband was required to divorce her; she lost her dowry and could not remarry. As a sign of dishonor, she was prohibited from wearing the *stola* of a matron and forced to wear the toga. Like a prostitute, she was debarred from religious rituals restricted to honorable women.[8] Disgrace was certainly a consequence of adultery for women throughout the ancient world (and later), but the presumed punishment of Demaenete for being caught in a brothel seems to come from the world of the Roman Empire, rather than from classical Athens. The style of her suicide, throwing herself into a crevasse, known as the βόθρος, near the

---

[6] Quintilian *Institutio Oratoria* 7,3,10; Treggiari 1991, 263.
[7] Wycherley 1978, 234, 254-235; Keuls 1985, 158-160.
[8] McGinn 1998, 156-171.

Academy is reminiscent of the punishment of unchaste Vestals, who were thrown from the Tarpeian Rock, a well-known theme found in declamations.[9]

The situation would seem to offer an opportunity for Heliodorus to elaborate upon the interesting legal dilemmas that Quintilian explored; however, Demaenete's suicide preempts the expected adultery trial. Aristippus finally asserts his authority over his wife. He stands in contrast to the other cuckolds of the Greek novels. Unlike the jealous Chaereas, the suspicious Dionysius, and the raving Thersander, Aristippus remains levelheaded. When Demaenete plunges headlong into the βόθρος, Aristippus pronounces what is in effect a quitclaim: 'I have obtained justice from you before the laws' (ἔχω παρὰ σοῦ καὶ πρὸ τῶν νόμων τὴν δίκην, H 1,17,6), an echo of Euphiletus' statement in Lysias' *Against Eratosthenes*, 'It is not I who will kill you, but the law of the city' (οὐκ ἐγώ σε ἀποκτενῶ, ἀλλ' ὁ τῆς πόλεως νόμος, Lysias 1,26). Aristippus defends his actions as justifiable, rather than premeditated, and dutifully reports everything to the demos. He petitions to have Cnemon pardoned now that the truth of Demaenete's scheme is patent.

The expected closure that Demaenete's death represents is illusory. Heliodorus takes a radical departure from the regular novelistic pattern, in which the narrative leads directly from crime to trial. In this case, we have something that is closer to a cliffhanger in a murder mystery. Charias' sub-narrative ends with an admission that he left Athens before he learned of the outcome of the vote regarding Cnemon's pardon. Cnemon, Theagenes, and Charicleia then fall asleep. A lengthy battle sequence in the haunts of the bandits (H 1,18-2,7) interrupts Cnemon's tale and separates Theagenes from Charicleia. The morass of Athenian trial procedure intrudes into the Egyptian section of the novel, signified by the ghoulish discovery of a woman's corpse in a cave, which poses a new mystery. At first, Theagenes assumes the corpse is Charicleia's, but when she emerges from the depths of the cave, Cnemon realizes that the body belongs to Thisbe. Suddenly, a bit player deeply embedded in the Athenian digression emerges at the top-level of the narrative.

This unexpected appearance of a character who was seen only through the eyes of a series of Athenian males, is a brilliant device. Charicleia innocently gives voice to the implied reader's questions: 'Who is this woman? How did she get here? Why did we not meet her on the way?' (H 2.8.1). The questions initiate the next segment of the Athenian tale up to the exile of Aristippus. In response,

---

9 Cantarella 1991a, 262. This pit is, as the narrator notes parenthetically, the site of national sacrifices performed by the polemarchs of Athens: H 1,17,5 ἐπειδὴ κατὰ τὸν βόθρον ἐγένετο τὸν ἐν Ακαδημίᾳ (πάντως γινώσκεις, ἔνθα τοῖς ἥρωσιν οἱ πολέμαρχοι τὸ πάτριον ἐναγίζουσιν). Heliodorus is fairly accurate here; see Morgan 1989a, 368 n. 321.

Cnemon admits, 'I do not know the answer, but I can tell you the following story' (H 2,8,3), which he heard from another friend Anticles, who fills in the gap after Aristippus was tried and convicted of Demaenete's death.

The usually vivid description and direct speech that are characteristic of extended scenes are minimal in this episode. In short, Cnemon learns that another love triangle developed when Arsinoe became jealous of Thisbe's musical skill and the attention it won from a wealthy client. An expert machinator, she plots her revenge by having Thisbe tortured for evidence in yet another trial. When she informs Demaenete's relatives that Thisbe abetted Demaenete's suicide, they hire the cleverest speakers (H 2,9,2) to sue for justice in the assembly. The extra-legality of Aristippus' quitclaim comes to haunt him. His in-laws accuse him of killing Demaenete without a trial or an investigation (ἄκριτον καὶ ἀνέλεγκτον) and using adultery as a cover (τὴν μοιχείαν προκάλυμμα τοῦ φόνου, H 2,9,2), the very scenario that Euphiletus in Lysias 1 so assiduously tried to avoid by portraying the adulterer's death as a spontaneous response to the shock of finding an intruder in his home.[10] The prosecution demands proof of an adulterer, 'dead or alive', and calls for the torture of the maids (cf. trial 1, above), a routine procedure in the case of adultery. As in Cnemon's trial, the fact that there is no evidence of an actual adulterer leads to Aristippus' trial.

The fate of his trial turns upon the challenge for evidence, the πρόκλησις εἰς βάσανον (cf. trial 5, above). Thisbe flees from Athens to avoid torture, leaving Aristippus unable to meet the prosecution's challenge.[11] The demos angrily convicts him not of murder, but of complicity in both the plot against Demaenete and Cnemon's unjust exile (συναίτιον τῆς τε εἰς Δημαινέτην ἐπιβουλῆς καὶ τῆς ἐμῆς ἀφίκου φυγῆς, H 2,9,3). In effect, the accusation instantly metamorphoses from adultery to murder in the midst of proceedings; Aristippus is charged for murder, but convicted of another crime (cf. trial 5, above). As in the first trial in Athens, the judgment of the popular court proves to be erratic, resulting in a conviction that confounds the reader's expectations of justice.

Heliodorus' Athens conveys an impression unending legal vendettas. The roles of father and son are reversed; the burden of seeking justice is shifted to Cnemon to bring Thisbe back to Athens to give the testimony that will exonerate his father. That becomes impossible once it is obvious that Thisbe is dead. In an echo of his father's quitclaim to Demaenete, Cnemon declares, 'In my eyes, she has paid the price for her crimes' (H 2,9,3).

[10] Lysias 1,37-42; see also Carey 1989, 61-62.

[11] Other slaves who flee before they can be tortured for evidence in a lawsuit are Clio (the slave of Pantheia, Leucippe's mother) and Sosthenes, in Achilles Tatius' novel.

Yet, the ending is again a mere illusion. The mystery of Thisbe's corpse lingers. When Cnemon discovers a tablet hanging from her neck, the lifeless Thisbe paradoxically emerges as a narrator in her own right, telling her own story only posthumously. Through the mechanism of a written letter, she informs Cnemon that Demaenete is dead (H 2,10,1-4; cf. Charias in H 1,14,2) and confesses her love for him. She alludes to her experience on the island—how she was taken captive by the bandit chief's lieutenant, who was in love with her. Finally, she tells Cnemon that she freely committed all her crimes in order to avenge him (H 2,10,3) and invites him to listen to the rest of the story—now, a futile gesture.

Although Thisbe's letter appears to be the coda to the Athenian saga, Cnemon remains appropriately wary (H 2,11,2). His suspicion is grounded upon her capacity to 'speak' after death through the tablet. He cannot test the truth of her tale now that she is dead. He pronounces the case closed, declaring that a Fury pursued Thisbe to Egypt and to her death. As Cnemon and Theagenes mull over the mystery, Thermouthis, Thisbe's bandit-lover appears (H 2,12). The suddenness of his entrance evokes a macabre bedroom showdown. The dark, labyrinthine cave functions as the conjugal bedroom; the grisly bandit, angry and naked, immediately leaps to the superficial conclusion that Cnemon killed Thisbe (H 2,13).[12] Unlike the first time when he was lured into a bedroom showdown, here Cnemon keeps his wits about him and defends himself by showing the murder weapon, an ivory-handled sword dripping with warm blood (H 2,14). Thermouthis recognizes it as belonging to Thyamis, the leader of the bandits. Cnemon offers it as proof of Thyamis' guilt—and his own innocence, a symbolic compensation for the first adultery scenario in which a sword implicated him in attempted murder. In the end, the savage bandit dissolves in a pool of tears, cries himself to sleep, and dies by snakebite.

Cnemon's story concludes in accordance with the conventions of the genre. Like Alcinous in Homer *Odyssey* 7,308-28, who offers his new guest-friend the hand of his daughter in marriage (H 6,7,8), Cnemon becomes a guest at the home of Nausicles of Naucratis, who eventually reveals that he was Thisbe's lover and the cause of her departure from Athens. Nausicles accepts liability (ὑπόδικος, H 6,8,1), for everything that happened to Cnemon's father (now vanished, never to be resurrected in the subsequent narrative) as a result of her disappearance compensates him by giving him money and passage home. We have shifted back to a scene of domestic justice wherein a benefactor takes in a young Greek man who flees from persecution in his hometown (cf. Phoenix in *Il.* 9.444-59).

---

[12] S. Schwartz 2012, 175-177.

The Athenian trial scenes are episodes in an escalating cycle of errors of judgment, literally and figuratively. The tangled personal enmities in Athens culminate in its popular courts. As the narrative moves further from Athens, stories of trials are presented to the reader as fragments by different narrators; the only continuous forensic oration to be presented in *oratio recta* in the text is Aristippus' accusation of his son. Cnemon's entire tale functions as the defense he was prevented from delivering at his trial. As the quest for justice propels the characters beyond Athens and into Egypt, morally ambiguous minor characters become catalysts for ending the tale: Arsinoe, Nausicles, and Thermouthis. The arbitrariness of the popular law courts of Athens drives Cnemon and Aristippus, the protagonists of Cnemon's novella, into exile. Efforts to evade the law lead to the deaths of a series of antagonists: Demaenete, Thisbe, and Thermouthis. Nevertheless, the novella has a characteristically conservative, happy ending: Cnemon marries a nice, Greek girl whose father is a successful businessman. He is reintegrated into the polis—albeit not into Athens but into Naucratis, an oasis of Hellenism in Egypt, and an adumbration of Charicleia's trajectory from Delphi to Meroe via Memphis—both of them sites for trials to come.

Trial 9.
Innocents Abroad: Poisoning
Arsace v. Charicleia
(Heliodorus, *Aethiopica* 8,8-15)

The Story

Arsace, the wife of the Persian satrap of Memphis, lusts for Theagenes, and Charicleia is an obstacle on her path to seducing him. Plotting to get her out of the way, Arsace resolves upon ordering her execution; however, it is against the law of Memphis to kill someone without a conviction by the Persian authorities. Arsace's chambermaid, Cybele, offers to poison Charicleia. When Cybele accidentally drinks the poison herself, she points to Charicleia as her murderer. The heroine is arrested and taken to Arsace's court for interrogation. She defiantly confesses and is thrown into prison next to Theagenes. The next morning, Arsace duly summons the Persian nobles to a trial. She charges Charicleia with poisoning. Charicleia falsely confesses to the murder and claims that she intended to do the same to Arsace. The judges sentence Charicleia to be burned at the stake. The spectacle of her execution draws a crowd and Arsace watches from atop the city wall. While the pyre is being lit, Charicleia proclaims her innocence and calls for Arsace's downfall. There is an outcry for a retrial, but Charicleia is miraculously saved from the flames, which leads the demos to proclaim her innocence. Arsace, surrounded by her entourage of bodyguards, scolds the demos. After the botched execution, Charicleia is sent back to jail, pending a second trial on a new charge for sorcery, which never materializes.

Analysis

Heliodorus brings his protagonists from the dysfunction of Athenian democracy, through the disorderly world of the boukoloi, and into the fantastical realm of barbarian kings and queens. The power dynamics of this world were arguably more familiar to imperial age Greeks who inhabited a world where the image of the emperor adorned temples and civic spaces, and circulated on coins. His word was the law. Heliodorus uses the imperial courtroom to draw a moralistic contrast between good kings and tyrants. Two monarchies, the Persian Empire and the kingdom of Ethiopia, form the backdrops for contrasting trial scenes.

The virtue of the emperor was central to his public image throughout the empire. In the novels, a trial of an innocent defendant serves as the litmus test of the monarch's virtue.[1] We have already discussed this in the context of Chariton's novel, where the king struggled to control his passions and eventually came to an expedient verdict. Heliodorus, too, uses the royal courtroom to differentiate between the tyrant and the virtuous king. Priests stand as a check on the power of the monarch. How well the monarch survives the priests' challenge determines whether he will keep his authority.

The seventh and eighth books of the *Aethiopica* are set in the sixth-century B.C.E., when Egypt was a province of the Persian Empire. A trial scene set in Memphis highlights the tension between the imperial court and the indigenous cult of Isis. The satrapy of Memphis, which lies geographically between Athens and Meroe, serves as an intermediate political space. The reader is introduced to Memphis from the perspective of a returning exile, Thyamis, the leader of an army of brigands. With Theagenes as his second-in-command, he comes to reclaim his birthright to the priesthood of Isis, currently held by his younger brother, Petosiris. The episode is laden with literary allusions to two epic sieges of the Greek literary tradition: those of Thebes and of Troy. Yet it also has certain structural features of a trial scene. Like the duel between Dionysius and Chaereas at the end of the Babylonian segment of Chariton's novel, this trial-by-combat unravels before it can develop into a full-blown trial scene. This brief episode highlights the basic moral polarities that govern Memphis and serves as the exposition for the trial of Charicleia in the Persian imperial courtroom.

Heliodorus delineates an adulterous triangle within the context of the palace at Memphis. Charicleia and Theagenes are under the control of the imperious and menacing queen Arsace, the sister of the Persian king and the wife of the satrap Oroondates. She is the doppelgänger of Demaenete, a powerful married woman who strives to seduce the young hero. Like Cnemon, Theagenes becomes the object of a *domina*'s erotic quest. Arsace's servant, Cybele, like Thisbe, facilitates her mistress' scheme. But whereas Thisbe was sexy, Cybele is an older woman and mother of an adult son who is also a slave in the royal court; she uses the

---

[1] On moralization in Heliodorus, see Dowden 1996.

power of suggestion and her knowledge of drugs to gratify her mistress' desire.[2] Whereas Cnemon's saga unfolded in the interstices between the jurisdictions of Athens, Aegina, Naucratis, and the marshlands of the outlaws, Charicleia and Theagenes are trapped within a tyrannical state controlled by a powerful woman who sees justice as instrumental, as explained by Cybele,

> Keep in mind that she is of the Persian race and of royal blood (this is what you said in your greeting), and that she is endowed with great resources and power and thus has the license to reward cooperation and to punish disobedience. (H 7,20,4)

Like Clytemnestra in Aeschylus' *Agamemnon*, Arsace transforms the state into a tyranny in the absence of the male head of the household.[3] Heliodorus builds the scene upon the topoi of luxury, despotism, as well as justice of the Persians. Memphis, a province of the Persian Empire, conforms to the literary stereotype of the palace of the 'Oriental' despot.[4]

This potent political stereotype was deployed against powerful women during the Roman Empire. Tacitus' history of the early Principate describes similarly libidinous and cruel women, such as Agrippina the Younger, Statilia Messalina, and Poppaea Sabina, who were the wives and sisters of emperors.[5] The topos persisted long after the Julio-Claudian dynasty. At the turn of the third century C.E., the historian Herodian incorporated a tale of palace intrigue in his history of the fall of the Antonine dynasty after the death of Marcus Aurelius. He explains that Commodus' transformation from a well-behaved youth to a tyrant was due to an attempted assassination masterminded by his sister, Lucilla, the haughty and jealous widow of the co-emperor Lucius Verus, and carried out by her lover.[6] The figure of Arsace fits the pattern: she exploits her access to channels of political power to vent her frustrations and pursue vendettas. As we shall see, the trial of Charicleia for the poisoning death of Cybele provokes a popular uprising against the tyranny of Arsace.

---

[2] Cf. Plangon, the slave in Chariton's novel, a mature woman who tells Callirhoe that she is pregnant and manipulates her maternal instincts to induce her to marry her master; see S. Schwartz 1999, 42.

[3] The idea that the degeneration of the Persian monarchy was due to the absence of the male heads of the household and consequent influence of the women is also found in Plato *Laws* 694d-696a.

[4] The characterization is found in the tale of Deioces in Herodotus 1,96. On the stereotype of the despot, see Futre Pinheiro 1989, 18-26; Egger 1990, 67-94; Haynes 2003, 110-112.

[5] Vidén 1993, 13-65.

[6] Herodian *Ab excessu divi Marci* 1,8,3-6.

The status of Charicleia and Theagenes as they enter the court of the satrapial palace is ambiguous. When they first arrive, they are under the tutelage of Calasiris, a former priest of Isis who assumes the role of their guardian and escorts them from Delphi to Memphis. When he dies, he entrusts them to his son and heir, Thyamis; however, the religious laws of the temple of Isis require that the foreigners vacate the holy precincts until the mourning period is over. In the interval, the young Greeks are invited to stay as Arsace's guests. They are vulnerable in this context; Heliodorus analogizes them 'to prisoners of war who have been captured under the pretense of kindness and hospitality' (H 7,12,2). In contrast to the world of the outlaws, where the dangers of anarchy and violence were palpable, in Memphis the power of the tyrant is exerted through the complicated laws and customs of the palace, with its rituals, formal audiences, prostration, eunuchs, bodyguards—the stock details we have already seen in Chariton's depiction of the Persian court. As foreigners who have lost their native guide, they do not understand Persian etiquette and become dependent on Cybele, a Greek slave who has successfully assimilated to the Persian court (H 7,12,6).

Theagenes is degraded to slave status when Arsace discovers that he was taken prisoner by the commander of the Persian garrison in the Nile Delta in the battle against the boukoloi. She summons him for formal interrogation and casuistically asserts that he is her slave and must obey her orders even if he is unwilling to do so (H 7,24,4). She places him under the supervision of another servant, Achaemenes, to whom she betroths Charicleia (H 7,24,4). Theagenes complies under duress, but asserts to Arsace that because Charicleia is technically not a prisoner of war, she is not her slave.[7] Regardless, Charicleia 'chooses to submit to serving at [Arsace's] pleasure' (H 7,24,6). Arsace holds out the prospect of freedom for good behavior, but warns Theagenes that if he disobeys, he will be subjected to the worst and most dishonorable condition of servitude (H 7,25,2).[8]

The conflict between the protagonists and Arsace is framed by the larger cultural paradigm of the philosophical contest between the sage and the tyrant. Thyamis, the heir to the high priesthood of Isis, acts as a counterbalance to Arsace. As we have seen with the temple of Artemis in Achilles Tatius' novel (trial 6), the temple of Isis stands in opposition to tyranny. In a city dominated by the palace of the Persian satrap, the temple is an island of lawfulness, where Calasiris is buried according to the ancestral law (κατὰ τὸν πάτριον νόμον, H 7,11,5). Theagenes and Charicleia leave the temple in obedience to the law (τῷ νόμῳ πειθόμενοι, H 7,11,6) and the custodian of the temple warns Theagenes and Charicleia that it is illegal to mourn for a priest (οὐκ ἔννομα, H 7,11,8).

---

[7] Cf. C 7,1,1 where Chaereas is called the only free man in Babylon.

[8] A similar threat is made by Manto to Habrocomes, the hero of the *Ephesiaca;* see XE 2,5.

In his transformation from bandit king to high priest, Thyamis is not unlike the Stoic philosophers who opposed Roman emperors on a moral, rather than political, basis:

> The position of emperor is acknowledged by Seneca, Lucan, Curiatius Maternus, and Tacitus, all counted more or less among the opposition. They will grant the emperor an eminence above the law of the state so long as he remains accountable to the laws of nature and reason; citizens, for their part, must retain a freedom no longer political but moral. A good ruler and, by consequence, a legitimate ruler in the Stoic sense, is one who does not corrupt his subjects, does not insist on servile behavior or adulation or betrayal of friends.[9]

The philosopher's freedom of speech (παρρησία) is his weapon against the tyrant. Freedom of speech was an important Greek ideal as least as old as Aeschylus' *Prometheus Bound.* In the Roman Empire, the philosopher took on the attributes of a holy man.[10] One such example is the Pythagorean sage, Apollonius of Tyana, depicted by Philostratus as a philosophical hero who repeatedly confronts rulers, both Roman and foreign. His trial before the tyrannical Domitian is the climax of his biography.[11] Apollonius challenges the tyrant with his rhetorical versatility; when Domitian demands that the sage subject himself to interrogation, the sage responds by disappearing, thus subverting the judicial procedures set up under the emperor's authority.

The agon between Thyamis and Arsace belongs to this tradition. Both assert competing rights over custody of Theagenes and Charicleia. Thyamis characterizes his relationship to the heroes in technical, legal terms. He calls them his 'deposit' (παρακαταθήκην, H 8,3,5), a word normally used to refer to money or valuables entrusted to a temple for safekeeping; here it is extended to children entrusted to guardians.[12] He speaks of his formal obligation to Theagenes and Charicleia as his inheritance (κληρονόμον, H 8,3,7). Arsace counters Thyamis' legal language by invoking the 'law of war' (πολέμου νόμῳ, H 8,3,8), that declares captives the property of the victor. She insists that her status as master

---

[9] MacMullen 1966, 63-64.

[10] G. Anderson 1994.

[11] Philostratus *Vita Apollonii* 8,1-5; see Henderson 2003, 32.

[12] Demosthenes 28,15. Chariton also uses it in this sense to apply to the child of Callirhoe in C 2,9,6, 8,4,5, and 8,4,8; discussed in S. Schwartz 1999, 33.

(τὸ δεσποτεύειν) trumps Thyamis' mere 'concern' (τοῦ προνοεῖν).[13] Thyamis rebuts her reasoning with a sermon on ethical kingship in which he draws an antithesis between war and peace, enslavement and liberation, the tyrant's will and the king's judgment (H 8,4,1-2). When he questions the propriety of Arsace's feelings for the 'young foreigners', Arsace flies into a rage— 'Proof', the narrator adds, 'of her soul's guilt' (H 8,5,1). She threatens to bring Thyamis to justice for killing the commander of the Persian guard (H 8,5,1) and asserts that her will defines what is right; namely, that she rightfully owns Theagenes, the object of her desire.[14]

Arsace relies on her slave, Cybele, to implement her wishes. The strategy to seduce Theagenes is simple: eliminate Charicleia. Arsace immediately issues an order for Charicleia's death; however, Cybele reminds her that the laws of Persia forbid execution without the decision of the Persian authorities (H 8,7,1).[15] The topos can be traced to Herodotus, who praises a Persian law forbidding anyone, including the king, to execute a person on a single charge.[16] We have already seen in Chariton's novel the common conception that the power of the Persian king was constrained by the law. Heliodorus probes the tension between private power in the domestic sphere and the the formal power of the sovereign. Arsace is the inverse of Aristippus, who forfeits his right as *paterfamilias* to punish his son in the privacy of his home and lawfully pursues the charge in the democratic court of Athens. Arsace, on the other hand, is ready to use everything in her power (πάντων γὰρ ἐν ἐξουσίᾳ σοι τυγχανούσῃ, H 8,7,1) to execute Charicleia, but is compelled by the law to take the case to court.

Cybele devises a strategem to use the laws to Arsace's benefit.[17] She suggests falsely implicating Charicleia, their legal opponent (τὴν ἀντίδικον, H 8,7,2) in a capital crime so that the authorities will execute Charicleia on behalf of Arsace.

---

13 The expression 'law of war' is found elsewhere in the Greek novels. In *Leucippe and Clitophon* it is applied to rape, which is cast as a right awarded to the victor in war (AT 2,24,3). Longus uses it in a slightly different sense when the Methymnean boys attempt to inflame the anger of the assembly by alleging that the Mytileneans stole their ship by the 'law of war' (L 2,19,2).

14 Ironically, Thyamis had earlier made a similar claim when he was the leader of the outlaws; see H 1,21,1: εἰ μὲν γὰρ ἔδει τῷ τῆς ἀρχῆς ἀποχρήσασθαι νόμῳ, πάντως ἐξήρκει μοι τὸ βούλεσθαι.

15 Cf. AT 7,1,2-3, where Thersander attempts to persuade the prison warden to poison Clitophon; the warden refuses on the grounds that the polis executed his predecessor for committing a similar crime; see Colin 1965b, 62-63.

16 Herodotus 1,137: αἰνέω μέν νυν τόνδε τὸν νόμον, αἰνέω δὲ καὶ τόνδε, τὸ μὴ μιῆς αἰτίης εἵνεκα μήτε αὐτὸν τὸν βασιλέα μηδένα φονεύειν.

17 Cf. C 6.4.7 (trial 4): The eunuch legalistically redefines Callirhoe as a widow, so that the king does not become an adulterer.

But Cybele quickly dismisses the plan and suggests a stealthier approach: poison. The plan, however, backfires when Cybele accidentally drinks the poison herself. As she dies, she reverts to the first plan and, with her dying breath, she indicates before witnesses that Charicleia as her murderer (H 8,8,2).

Heliodorus recycles the formula of the slave who cannot testify, which figures so prominently in the second part of the Athenian trials. Because the key witness and the victim happen to be one and the same, it is impossible to cross-examine Cybele's false testimony. This procedural dilemma is explored in Antiphon 1 and 5,30-35, and now poses a rhetorical challenge for Charicleia. Not only is the key witness dead, but her last words confer an aura of truth to her accusation. This parallels the discovery of Thisbe's tablets (H 2,10) where the dispositive proof of the accused's guilt is the testimony of a person who is dead. Charicleia is placed at a severe disadvantage in the trial due to her low status. Already dependent as a foreigner and a guest of Arsace, she is charged with a crime in a jurisdiction where she has no rights. She is manacled and led to Arsace, who convenes an inquest within the privacy of her palace. She threatens Charicleia with punishment and torture (κολαστήρια καὶ βασάνους, H 8,8,3) while onlookers gaze at the 'strange spectacle' of Charicleia (καινὸν ἦν ἡ Χαρίκλεια τοῖς ὁρῶσι θέαμα). She is permitted to make a statement, ambiguously phrased as a pair of propositions:

> 'καὶ ὦ θαυμασία' ἔφη, 'εἰ μὲν ζῇ Θεαγένης, καθαρεύω κἀγὼ τοῦ φόνου· εἰ δέ τι πέπονθεν ὑπὸ τῶν σῶν ἀνοσίων βουλευμάτων, οὐδὲν δεῖ σοι τῶν κατ' ἐμοῦ βασάνων. ἔχεις με τὴν φαρμακίδα, τῆς καὶ θρεψαμένης σε καὶ πρὸς τὰ κάλλιστα τῶν ἔργων παιδευσαμένης'
>
> 'Your Majesty', she said, 'if Theagenes is still living, then I am innocent of murder. But if he has suffered anything because of your unholy plans, then you need not have me tortured: you consider me the poisoner of the woman who nurtured you and taught you such fine deeds'. (H 8,8,5)

This is not so much a confession as a cleverly worded gamble. The logic of her statement evokes the procedure of an ordeal, already discussed in the context of Tatius' novel, where Melite swears an oath that consists of a pair of alternate conditions (trial 6, above). Infuriated by Charicleia's defiance, Arsace orders her beaten, chained, and guarded until the next morning when the Persian authorities will try her and give her the death penalty. When the truth concerning Cybele's death by poison comes to light after a servant who accidentally mixed up the cups attests to Charicleia's innocence, Arsace has the informant put in chains as an accomplice.

At Arsace's command, a trial is convened the next day. The judges are the leading Persians, suggesting an aristocratic body, perhaps something like the kind of advisory council that magistrates had throughout the provinces of the Roman Empire.[18] They seem to have a degree of independence; as Cybele warned Arsace, they are the sole body empowered to sentence people to death, a power denied even to the satrap. The reader is meant to understand that they serve as a check on the satrap's power. Heliodorus enumerates their functions: to give advice concerning public matters, to render judgment, and to set punishments.[19]

It is unlikely that actual Achaemenid, Parthian, or Sassanid institutions lay behind the depiction of this court. As we have seen in Chariton's novel, Heliodorus' Persia can be read as a cipher for empire—that is to say, Rome, the only empire of which imperial age Greeks had any experience. In this light, the Persian court at Memphis is analogous to the *praetorium* of a governor of a Roman province.[20] The physical details of the court do not get much attention: the judges arrive at dawn and sit in front. The reference to the time of the trial is conventional: it was common for public business to begin at dawn.[21] The placement of the judges suggests the custom of seating high-ranking spectators in the first rows at theatrical performances.[22] Christian martyr acts likewise indicate the presence of an audience in the *praetorium*, smaller than an audience to a trial held in the agora or in an amphitheater.[23] At the end of the trial, Arsace addresses the demos, which has gathered to watch the trial. As with all trials in the novels, it promises to be more spectacular than any other trial.

The narrative presents the speeches in this trial in indirect discourse, so as to proceed quickly to the highlight of the scene: Charicleia's expected execution. Arsace contrasts the sad death of her beloved servant with the murderer's wicked exploitation of her generosity, a rhetorical trope that appears in Aristippus' contrast between his own paternal devotion and Cnemon's ingratitude (H 1,13,2). Like Demaenete's appearance in the trial of Cnemon, Arsace's accusation is highly emotional and patently false. She is depicted as a most bitter accuser (πικροτάτη κατήγορος, H 8,9,7), who cries unceasingly (συνεχὲς ἐπιδακρύουσα, H 8,9,6). She calls the judges to witness her generosity as a host to the stranger

[18] H 8,7,2 and 8,9,1: τῶν ἐν τέλει Περσῶν and H 8,9,5: τούς τε δυνάστας Περσῶν. In Chariton's novel, the Persian king was advised by a council of friends (C 5,4,5), analogous to the Hellenistic συνέδριον of the king's φίλοι or the Roman emperor's *consilium principis*. Other Roman magistrates also had advisory councils; see Peachin 1996, 46-48.

[19] H 8,9,5: τὸ βουλεύεσθαι ὑπὲρ τῶν κοινῶν καὶ δικάζειν τε καὶ τιμωρίας ὁρίζειν.

[20] Comparable scenes in Christian narratives are discussed in Aubert 2010.

[21] Hansen 1987, 33; Talbert 1984, 189-190.

[22] Talbert 1984, 43.

[23] Aubert 2010, 291.

(H 8,9,6), a role she had earlier disavowed (H 8,3,8). In response, Charicleia resorts to self-denunciation (προσαγγελία), a formula familiar to us from the confessions of Chaereas (trial 1) and of Clitophon (trial 5). Charicleia admits to all the false charges in order to precipitate her execution (ἀλλ' ὡμολόγει καὶ αὖθις τὸ ἔγκλημα, H 8,9,7). All of this is reported in indirect discourse.

While Chariton and Achilles Tatius exploit the pathos of self-denunciation through highly wrought speeches, Heliodorus is more controlled. The interest of the trial scene shifts from rhetoric to spectacle. Two strands of the Persian mirage come together: lawfulness and cruelty, a topos found throughout Greek literature.[24] The judges are inclined to sentence Charicleia to a cruel Persian execution (ὠμοτέρᾳ τε καὶ Περσικῇ τιμωρίᾳ, H 8,9,9); precisely what that entails is left to the reader's imagination. Her appearance moves them to pity and she receives the (ironically) mitigated penalty live immolation (πυρὶ καταναλωθῆναι κατέκριναν H 8,9,9).[25] Cruel punishments, usually merely threatened, have ample precedent in other novels.[26] Live cremation appears in Xenophon of Ephesus' novel (XE 4,2,8), where Habrocomes miraculously survives crucifixion, only to be sentenced to *crematio* or *vivicomburium* by the authority of the prefect of Egypt. Yet cruelty is more than a literary commonplace; it may simply reflect the general escalation in the severity of judicial punishments in the third century C.E.[27] Under the Roman *lex Cornelia de sicariis et veneficis* the penalty for lethal poisoning was property confiscation and deportation to an island for *honestiores*, and crucifixion or being thrown to the beasts for *humiliores*.[28] *Crematio* was a particularly horrific mode of execution that emphasized the gravity of the crime as well as the infamy of the criminal.[29] In early Roman history, crimes such as arson, treason, and violation of the oaths of the Vestals were punished with live burning.[30] As

---

[24] Surviving Persian inscriptions suggest that cruelty in punishment was part of Achaemenid propaganda; see Briant 2002, 122-123. Herodotus relates many incidents of bodily mutilation and beheading by the Persian king, incidents which naturally struck the Greeks as abhorrent (mutilation: 3,69, 154; beheading, with or without impalement: 3,79; 7,35, 238; 8,118, 9,78-9); see Hartog 1988, 332-333. On the Greek abhorrence of mutilation, see the anecdote in Arrian 4,7 concerning Alexander's proposal to punish Bessus by cutting off his ears and nose and sending him back to the Persians for execution: this proposal is interpreted as a sign of Alexander's increasingly objectionable Orientalism.

[25] The motif of Persian cruelty recurs in H 8,15,2, H 9,6,6.

[26] Chew 2003.

[27] MacMullen 1990, 204-217; Coleman 1990, 44-73.

[28] *Digest* 48,8; also discussed in connection with the trial 7, above.

[29] *Paulys Real-Encyclopädie der classischen Altertumswissenschaft*, s.v. 'vivicomburium' and 'crematio'. See also Cantarella 1991a, 224.

[30] Cantarella 1991a, 224-230.

forms of execution became progressively more severe after around 200 C.E., *crematio* replaced decapitation by blow of the sword for crimes such as offences against the emperor, temple-robbery, plotting against, or murder of, a master by a slave, and (after 300 C.E.) performing magic or nocturnal rites in a temple.[31] Christian martyrologies provide many examples of individuals who were condemned to be burned alive.[32] Convicts were fodder for spectacles presented in the arenas and amphitheaters in the imperial period. Both Lucillius (reign of Nero) and Tertullian (Severan period) mention the spectacle of criminals who were dressed as Hercules' live immolation on Mount Oeta.[33] By the end of Constantine's reign, the number of capital crimes greatly increased, and horrific new punishments were invented, such as pouring molten lead down the convict's throat. At the end of the fourth century, many of the laws of the emperors Valentian and Valens specified the penalty of mutilation, torture, as well as *crematio.*[34]

Charicleia's *crematio* is thus meant to be a grand spectacle (τὴν θέαν, H 8,9,10). We see it through the eyes of the onlookers (αὐτόπται, H 8,9,10). As in Achilles Tatius' depiction of the ordeals in Ephesus (trial 6), sensory perceptions are emphasized: sight, sound, as well as a heightened sense of physicality. The executioners 'seize' her (ἥρπαστο, H 8,9,10)—the same verb routinely used to denote violent abduction. She is taken outside the city walls, the traditional place for executions in the Greco-Roman world, while a herald proclaims that she is being executed for poisoning. Arsace takes her place on the city walls in order to 'gorge herself on the sight' (τὴν ὄψιν ἐμφορηθείη, H 8,9,10) of Charicleia's punishment.

Charicleia inverts the power dynamics of the execution by transforming it into an ordeal in which she challenges the authority of the tyrant. She announces that she will climb onto the burning pyre voluntarily (ὡς ἑκοῦσα ἐπιβήσεται τῆς πυρᾶς ἐπαγγειλαμένη, H 8,9,11), similar to Iphigenia's self-sacrifice on behalf of the state in Euripides' *Iphigenia at Aulis*. The optics make it clear that Charicleia's action is a political statement: she lifts her hands and offers a prayer to 'the Sun and Earth and spirits, the overseers and avengers (ἔφοροί τε καὶ τιμωροί, H 8,9,12) against abominable (ἀθεμίτων) people on the earth and beneath it'. A comparable scene appears in the novel of Xenophon of Ephesus, in which Habrocomes is condemned to execution by the prefect of Egypt. He, too, raises his hands

---

31 MacMullen 1990, 209, 359.

32 Polycarp 11-16; Carpus, Papylus, and Agathonice 36 (Greek recension) or 6,3 (Latin); Martyrs of Lyons 57; Potamiaena and Basilides 1; Pionus 18, 21; Fructuosus and Companions 4; Montanus and Lucius 3; Agape, Irene and Chione 4-7. Texts in Musurillo 1972.

33 Lucillius *Anth. Pal.* 11,184 and Tertullian *Apol.* 15,4-5; discussed in Coleman 1990, 60-61.

34 MacMullen 1990, 211-212.

and offers a prayer phrased as a simple pair of alternative outcomes: 'If I am guilty, let me die; if I am innocent, let me live' (XE 4,2,4). The question of his guilt or innocence is left open for the ensuing ordeal to prove. He is proven innocent and the prefect of Egypt emerges from the episode as the hero's benefactor, his authority intact, in much the same way as the authority of the Persian king is relatively unscathed in Chariton.

Charicleia's prayer, by contrast, conforms more closely to the dynamics of vision and the subversive potential of public execution that Foucault described:

> In punishment-as-spectacle a confused horror spread from the scaffold; it enveloped both executioner and condemned; and, although it was always ready to invert the shame inflicted on the victim into pity or glory, it often turned the legal violence of the executioner into shame.[35]

Unlike Habrocomes' prayer, Charicleia's contains a pointed criticism of the ruling authority. She openly asserts her innocence (literally, her 'purity', καθαρὰν, H 8,9,2), summons the spectators to be witnesses, and insists that she voluntarily accepts her fate. The second part of her prayer explains her choice to die: she prays for the punishment of Arsace, 'the wretched, immoral adulteress' (ἀλάστορα καὶ ἀθεμιτουργὸν καὶ μοιχαλίδα, H 8,9,12). The convict thereby subverts a public display of the state's power by redefining it as a public display of individual virtue—even glory—in the face of tyranny.

While the crowd clamors for a retrial, Charicleia climbs onto the pyre and defiantly—even enthusiastically—meets her death. Her behavior echoes that of Christian martyrs and other figures who made names for themselves by freely facing spectacular deaths. Peregrinus Proteus was one such figure; his self-immolation is described by Lucian.[36] As instances of martyrdom began to make an impact upon Greco-Roman consciousness during the High Empire, Heliodorus may well have been influenced by literary accounts of trials and executions that circulated in the second to fourth centuries.[37] In most martyr acts, the convicted Christians die, although occasionally their bodies miraculously remain intact.[38] Charicleia's execution, however, is significantly different from most accounts of martyrs' immolation: she survives when the flames appear to violate the basic laws of nature by avoiding her wherever she steps. Her survival of this ordeal is not attributable to the judgment of the gods nor to her personal virtue but, similar

---

[35] Foucault 1979, 9.

[36] Lucian *De morte Peregrini*. MacMullen 1966, 99-100.

[37] Bowersock 1994, 143; 1995, 24.

[38] For example, *Polycarp* 16 and *Pionus* 22.

to the clever wording in Melite's oath (trial 6), is a trick of a magical stone amulet she wears.

For the time being, the reader is as amazed as the spectators; the explanation of this magical phenomenon is postponed until after the end of the trial scene. Within the context of the scene of execution, it is characterized as an act of defiance against the ruler, in the vein of Christian martyrologies and the semi-fictional trial of Apollonius of Tyana for sorcery and divination by Domitian.[39] Apollonius refuses to bow down to the Roman Emperor, Domitian. Likewise, Charicleia openly attests to her innocence and the tyrant's injustice, thereby winning the audience's sympathy. Apollonius' exit, on the other hand, is surreal: he literally vanishes from his trial. His defense speech is presented as an addendum to the narrative, a 'document' of what he would have said had he not disappeared. Charicleia, however, remains present. As Arsace browbeats the executioners to throw more fuel on the fire the audience, now referred to collectively as a polis and a demos (H 8,9,15), she actively influences the proceedings. Led by Thyamis, who had previously challenged Arsace's authority, the spectators physically insert themselves between Charicleia and Arsace. They interpret Charicleia's immunity from the flames as a divine sign of innocence and thus rush forward to rescue her. As she leaps out of the fire, the entire city cheers the gods in unison.

The trial and execution of Charicleia end with the prospect of revolution. Faced with the angry cries of the crowd (ἐκβοῆσαι, H 8,9,16), Arsace immediately recognizes that her authority is being threatened and descends from the wall with a phalanx of bodyguards and Persian nobles. She seizes Charicleia and scolds the demos for rescuing a 'self-confessed poisoner and murderer caught in the act' (φαρμακίδα καὶ φόνων ἐργάτιν ἐπ' αὐτοφώρῳ ληφθεῖσαν καὶ ὁμολογήσασαν, H 8,9,17) and bluntly accuses the spectators of overturning all the powers of the state: Persian laws, the king, the satraps, the nobles, and the judges (H 8,9,17). Charicleia's miraculous rescue is characterized as proof of her powers of witchcraft that she allegedly used in her poisoning of Cybele (τῆς γοητείας, H 8,9,18). Some of the incredulous spectators are swayed that sorcery is at work. The element of uncertainly prompts a new investigation. Arsace thus invites the people to the council house (πρὸς τὸ συνέδριον, H 8,9,18) in the morning for another hearing of the matter. Arsace sends Charicleia back to jail pending a second trial for sorcery.

The popular rebellion does not overthrow the Persian Empire—nor should it be expected to do so. As we see in Chariton's novel, Persia, like Rome, is strong

[39] Philostratus *Vita Apollonii* 7,32-8,5. Other parallels between the *Aethiopica* and Philostratus' *Vita Apollonii* have been noted, and it has been suggested that Heliodorus had read Philostratus; see Morgan 2009.

enough to withstand insurrection. The anticipated second trial never takes place because the protagonists are fortuitously summoned to the satrap, Oroondates, on campaign in Syene. When the heroes finally understand that they are being released and not tortured again, Theagenes says,

> How nicely…Arsace supposes that she can hide her immoral deeds under cover of night and darkness. But the awe-inspiring eye of justice shines its light and exposes secret abominations. (H 8,13,4)

Vision and sight, so important in the spectacle of Charicleia's execution, is recalled in this invocation of 'the eye of justice', an abstraction that reflects the view that the ideal of justice transcends the institutions of the state.

Arsace's ultimate demise takes place on the level of the narrative. The eunuch who escorts the protagonists to Syene tersely reports to them, 'Your enemy has paid the penalty. Arsace is dead'—a nearly verbatim echo of the report of Demaenete's death.[40] Like Cnemon's stepmother, Arsace kills herself in the end to avoid punishment from Oroondates or the king. Demaenete fears the dishonor or disenfranchisement (ἀτιμία) she would suffer in the future; Arsace likewise fears 'bringing discredit upon herself' (ἐνασχημονοῦσα, H 8,15,2). The eunuch assures the protagonists that they are innocent (οὐδὲν ἠδικηκότες, H 8,15,3) and free of the woman who wronged them. Their innocence is vindicated by their enemy's punishment. The characters construe this as an act of 'the great gods and justice' (H 8,15,5).

The appearance of a *deus ex machina* reinforces the schema that the innocent will be acquitted and the guilty will be punished, if not by the state then by the transcendent force of divine judgment. In the end, Heliodorus' portrait of tyranny stops short of revolution. Arsace represents a permissible target for attacking the state. As a woman and usurper of her absent husband's power, which emboldens her to pursue her adulterous desires. Feminine, lustful, short-tempered, and 'Oriental', she is a caricature of Cleopatra, the antithesis of the ideal of the Roman emperor. The popular priest/sage/philosopher may supplant the tyrant, but not the king. Thyamis' rebellion against Arsace establishes a paradigm against which the reader will judge Sisimithres, the president of the council of gymnosophists, when he too supports Charicleia in the coming agon with the Ethiopian king, Hydaspes.

---

[40] H 8,15,2: 'Ὦ ξένοι' ἔφη 'θαρσεῖτε. δίκην ὑμῖν ὑπέσχεν ἡ πολεμία· τέθνηκεν Ἀρσάκη. Cf. H 1,14,3: ἔχεις παρὰ τῆς πολεμίας τὴν δίκην· Δημαινέτη τέθνηκεν'.

Trial 10.
A Royal Paternity Suit: Infanticide
Charicleia v. Hydaspes
(Heliodorus, *Aethiopica* 10,9-17)

The Story

After the battle between the Persians and the Ethiopians at Syene, Charicleia and Theagenes are captured with a group of youths to be sacrificed in the triumph of Hydaspes, the king of Meroe. Upon spectacularly passing a virginity test, a prerequisite for the sacrifice, Charicleia suddenly announces that she has a lawsuit against the king. She appeals to the council of gymnosophists, the sages of Ethiopia, to judge the case. The king scoffs, but Sisimithres, the leader of the council, prevails upon the king to grant her an audience.

Charicleia asserts that it is a violation of nature and the law for Hydaspes to sacrifice her, on the grounds that she is not only a native Ethiopian, but also a member of the royal house. However, one glaring obstacle belies the truth of her claim: her skin color. She is white, but the king is black. She presents a number of proofs to support her claim. The first is a band embroidered by Queen Persinna in the royal Ethiopian script telling the story of Charicleia's birth and exposure. Sisimithres then attests to his part in saving the baby from exposure and giving her to a Greek diplomat he met in Egypt. Charicleia displays her birth tokens; Hydaspes recognizes them, but is skeptical that he and his wife could produce a white child. Persinna's band explains the anomaly as the effect of her having gazed at a painting of the white-skinned Andromeda when Charicleia was conceived. Servants bring out the painting and the resemblance to Charicleia is unmistakeable. Finally, a distinctive birthmark on Charicleia's arm clinches her lawsuit.

Despite the success of Charicleia's lawsuit, Hydaspes insists that he has a duty to conduct the sacrifice regardless. When the crowd makes it clear that it is prepared to block Hydaspes, he happily admits defeat.

Analysis

Charicleia's parentage is central to the final two trials in Heliodorus' novel. In the first, Charicleia attempts to have her biological father acknowledge his paternity. Her case is founded upon claims to indigeneity, citizenship, and, more importantly, blood-kinship to the king himself. In a subsequent trial (trial 11, below), Charicleia's adoptive father attempts to assert the priority of his parental rights over her. Unlike Chariton and Achilles Tatius, whose protagonists ultimately return to the Greek city, Heliodorus self-consciously reconfigures notions of center and periphery by having Theagenes and Charicleia end their journey beyond the edge of the oikoumene.[1] As we have seen in Chariton's novel, the court of a foreign king is the arena where the protagonists' identity as Hellenes is most severely tested—and vindicated.[2] In Meroe the protagonists are strangers without rights and personal connections, as they were in Memphis. Charicleia must beg the king's councilors to permit her to make a formal claim against the king himself. To readers living in the third-century Roman Empire, after the Edict of Caracalla theoretically created universal citizenship, Charicleia's situation may have seemed anachronistic in probing the distinction between 'foreign' and 'citizen' in a universal empire.

The fundamental dilemma of this trial hinges upon Charicleia's abandonment at birth, the effect of a mother's terror that the physical appearance of her infant would incriminate her of adultery.[3] Charicleia's lawsuit dramatizes the troubling indeterminacy of paternity, a conundrum inextricably connected to the spectre of adultery. The test of the heroine's identity is thus intertwined with her parents' σωφροσύνη: that is, the queen's chastity and the king's self-control.

By the tenth book of the novel, the reader already knows the answer to the riddle of Charicleia's birth when Calasiris read the embroidered band aloud (H 4,8); the impending mystery is, 'What kind of king is Hydapses?' On the one hand, he is characterized as just and pious, obedient to the law; on the other hand, he is a barbarian who presides over human sacrifice. In Memphis, the tyrannical Arsace flouted Persian law by planning to kill Charicleia; in contrast, the pious king of Meroe dutifully upholds the ritual laws of human sacrifice, a barbaric practice. If we follow Photius' definition of the genre as one in which the heroes are vindicated and the villains are punished, then the present trial queers the genre's moral valence: any monarch, whether tyrannical or pious, spells doom for

---

[1] Whitmarsh 1998.

[2] Whitmarsh 2011, 115-128. The motif is not limited to Greek literature; see also Wills 1990.

[3] The sexual triangularity of Charicleia's conception is discussed in Olsen 2012, 310-318. On maternal recognition, see Montiglio 2013, 130-140.

the heroes. Charicleia's performance in the trial will transform the king from *triumphator* and *pater patriae,* for whom his subjects feel 'a dripping gentle, filial eros' (ἵλεών τε καὶ ἥμερον πατρικόν τινα ἔρωτα, H 10,3,3), into an actual father, the *paterfamilias* of a marriageable daughter.[4]

Heliodorus bases the idealized kingdom of Meroe upon a literary commonplace going back to Homer (ἀμύμονας Αἰθιοπῆας, *Iliad* 1,423*)* characterizing the Ethiopians as exceptionally pious, wise, and just.[5] Hydaspes embodies attributes of the good king as commonly evoked in panegyric: he is generous, law-abiding, peaceful, and fair.[6] For example, when Hydaspes suspects the priests of Syene of treachery, he does not use coercion in his interrogation of them, but appeals to their consciences. Whereas Arsace demanded obeisance and tried to dominate the priest of Isis, Hydaspes prostrates himself before the gods of his defeated enemy (H 9,12,3). In the distribution of the spoils of the battle, Hydaspes displays his benevolence, even over the objections of the crowd, by bestowing the satrap's extravagant sword belt upon the soldier who captured the enemy commander. He justifies his gift by citing the 'law of war', which allows the conqueror—in this case a lowly soldier— to take anything from the person of the captive (H. 9,23,5). This is in distinct contrast to Arsace, who invoked the 'law of war' to assert ownership over her free guests (H 8,3,8). Hydaspes' piety radiates to his subjects, who loudly cheer his proclamations (H 9,27,1). Like their king, the Ethiopians have a highly developed sense of morality and justice, particularly in war. During the siege of Syene, an Ethiopian archer shot a Persian soldier who threatened to kill the satrap, because he considered it an affront to justice that the soldier used the retreat as an opportunity to take revenge on a personal enemy (H 9,20,6). Even the defeated satrap is so impressed with Hydaspes' kindness that he prostrates himself before him, explicitly violating Persian custom because 'it is not illegal to honor the most law-abiding of all mankind' (H 9,27,2).

---

[4] Morgan notes that the description of eros is 'not one would normally choose to define the feelings of a child for its father or of subjects for their king'; Morgan 1978, 262. Cf. Thucydides' characterization of the Athenians' enthusiasm for Alcibiades' proposal to go to Sicily (Thucydides 6,24,3).

[5] One fourth (25 of 103) of the instances of δίκη and its derivatives are found in the last book of the novel. In my discussion of the trials in Memphis, I am deeply indebted to the meticulous yet unpublished commentary on books 9 and 10 by Morgan 1978. On the literary image of Ethiopians, see Lesky 1959; Nadeau 1970; Treloar 1972. On the association of the gymnosophists with Ethiopia, see Robiano 1992.

[6] For example, Menander Rhetor *Περὶ Ἐπιδεικτικῶν* 373,7-8 organizes the panegyric of a king around four virtues: courage, justice, self-control, and prudence (ἀνδρεία, δικαιοσύνη, σωφροσύνη, φρόνησις), along with humaneness (φιλανθρωπία) from which justice is derived.

Yet, underlying the exterior image of the king is the painful and emotional dilemma of the abandonment and sale of children. It was an ancient motif in myth and literature, as well as a matter that drew the attention of the Roman jurists. Classical Roman law protected *patria potestas* when a child was sold or abandoned. A freeborn child who was exposed or sold kept his or her right of free birth and could later be reclaimed by his or her parents. The real-life legal complexities inherent in the event that an abandoned child was reared by someone else appear in thousands of imperial replies to petitions.[7] The confusion persisted even after the Edict of Caracalla theoretically superseded local laws regarding the status of such children. In 331 C.E., Constantine issued a ruling that *patria potestas* was terminated when a father exposed or sold a child; the person who rescued the child retained legal rights over it. At this time, Christian writers condemned the exposure of infants, a decision to which parents in desperate straits were sometimes driven. It is possible that Constantine's law was influenced by the growing attention to the practice.[8] The exposure of Charicleia as an infant was not caused by economic exigency, but rather by the need that the queen be above suspicion of adultery. The problem of infanticide and child abandonment is projected onto a larger-than-life setting, where the facets of this delicate dilemma can be fully explored.[9]

The physical setting for Hydaspes' triumph in Meroe receives considerable attention in the narrative. Its opulence, even greater than that of the Persian palace at Memphis, is augmented by the aura of religiosity surrounding the first-fruit sacrifice of the captive youths. The royal family sits under a square, canopied pavilion (σκηνὴν, H 10,6,2) on the plain outside the city walls, near a holy glade. Prominently located, it is suggestive of a theatrical set as well as the headquarters of a Roman general.[10] There, Hydaspes dispenses prizes and accepts tribute from his allies and subjects. The spatiality of the setting suggests limits: Hydaspes maintains a distance from his subjects, who are excluded from the inner circle around the sacrificial altars. A second pavilion nearby houses the images of Ethiopian gods and heroes on an elevated dais; on a lower step sit the gymnosophists. All of this is ringed by foot soldiers holding their shields vertically so as to occlude the crowd from the space where the ceremony is performed (H 10,6,3-5).

The setting is reminiscent of Arsace's opulent pavilion (also called a σκηνήν, H 7,3,2) where, surrounded by bodyguards, she presided over the execution of

---

[7] Evans Grubbs 2010, 301.

[8] Evans Grubbs 1993, 133-136.

[9] For a discussion of the scholarship on child exposure, see W. V. Harris 1994. On the novelists' use of this mythic and literary motif, see Kudlien 1989.

[10] Southern 2007.

Charicleia (trial 9). Hydaspes, too, oversees a lethal ritual performed before a crowd of spectators—in effect, a show in a Roman arena. The reader is not yet sure that he is not a despot. Yet, the moral and political landscapes are differently configured: whereas in Memphis the spectators angrily threatened rebellion against the ruler, the people of Meroe identify with the ruler and demand the sacrifice of Charicleia, piously cheering, 'Let the ancestral rites be performed!' (τὰ πάτρια τελείσθω, H 10,7,1). The reader is left to wonder, Will this king be a demagogue? Will he, like Arsace, march angrily through a crowd in order to drag the heroine away by her neck? Will the people of Meroe restrain the *triumphator*, or will they behave as mercurially as the populaces of Athens and Memphis?

The protagonists' theatrical entrance into the Ethiopian camp marks a new beginning in the novel; it is analogized to 'the prologue and prelude in a play', (H 8,17,5).[11] The detail of their riding on horses, as if they are masters rather than captives, is significant: it points back to the opening tableau of the novel, when they were mounted on horseback (H 1,4,3) before their identities were revealed to the reader. At that time, we remember, Cnemon hears Charicleia's cry to Apollo, 'No judge is harsher than you!' and recognizes them as fellow Greeks who would be a receptive audience to the tale of his own trial in Athens.

Now, in the final book of the novel, the protagonists are themselves subjected to trials-by-ordeal. After Hydaspes receives the embassies and tribute, the first order of business is to verify the purity of the sacrificial victims. This is done by means of a contraption referred to as a grid (ἐσχάρα, H 10,8,2) made from interwoven golden skewers imbued with special powers whereby they burn the feet of anyone—male or female—who has had sexual intercourse or committed perjury. The fantastical grid is a literary device, equivalent to the ordeal of the cave of the syrinx in Achilles Tatius' novel (trial 6). Heliodorus' use of the expression 'with a radiant expression' to describe the heroine's appearance seems to be an intertextual allusion to Achilles Tatius' description of Leucippe after her ordeal.[12] After Theagenes passes the test, he points out the obvious irony that the reward for their virtue is to be sentenced to death. Charicleia, on the other hand, confidently faces the imminent 'contest' (ὁ ἀγών, H 10,9,3). Reprising her spectacular rescue from the burning pyre in Memphis she is dressed as Artemis, 'like a statue of a goddess' (ἀγάλματι θεοῦ, H 10,9,3) as she walks over the grid. This phantasmagorical test shares many properties with ordeals by fire, particularly the variety that required the subject to hold a red-hot iron and swear an oath. The virginity

[11] Nimis 2003.

[12] AT 8,14,3 and H 10,7,3: φαιδρῷ τῷ προσώπῳ; Morgan 1978, 305, 313. Rattenbury, assuming that Achilles Tatius was later than Heliodorus, thought that the ordeal of Leucippe was a parody of Heliodorus; see Rattenbury 1926.

test represents a shortcut to publicly establishing definition in lieu of the elusive mystery of sexual and/or spiritual integrity.[13]

As we have already seen, Achilles Tatius used the virginity ordeal as a *deus ex machina* in order to bring a convoluted series of legal dilemmas to a clean and swift resolution. In contrast, Heliodorus inverts the relationship between trial and ordeal. Trial scenes typically include surprising twists and turns that derail the expected ending and heighten the drama of spectacle. The legendary judiciousness of the Ethiopians may be mirage; the Persians, too, were renowned for their sense of justice, yet under Arsace Persian justice devolved into tyranny. By choosing to present the trial after the scene of the ordeal, Heliodorus shifts the focus from the metaphysical level of divine justice to the human level of the institution of the trial. The judicial process, not the ordeal, will ultimately determine the truth and the heroine's fate.

The moment Charicleia leaps, unscathed, off the grid, she announces that she has a suit to bring against rulers (δίκη γάρ μοι καὶ κρίσις, H 10,10,1), 'a contest for her life' (καὶ τὸν περὶ ψυχῆς ἀγῶνά, H 10,10,2).[14] The Ethiopian law requiring human sacrifice underscores the political dangers of hyper-legalism. It can easily lead to tyranny unless the power of the king is counterbalanced by other voices. The first voice is that of his wife, who instinctively empathizes with the girl on the basis of her beauty and her age. The second voice belongs to the gymnosophists who object to the 'unlawful' sacrifice of human beings, as well as all other forms of animal sacrifice. The deliberation is conducted in the foreign language of Greek, which excludes the Ethiopian audience and privileges the reader of the novel. As the gymnosophists withdraw into the temple, Sisimithres reminds the king of his duty to correct the arbitrary impulse of the masses, thereby articulating the fundamental principle that distinguishes a tyrant from a good king.[15] In the eighth book, the tyrannical Arsace tried to disperse the crowd that came to Charicleia's rescue; now, paradoxically, the crowd in Meroe demands her sacrifice, which poses a dilemma for Hydaspes. Sisimithres reminds the king that he must perform the sacrifice because of the 'overpowering, inexorable, ancestral custom of Ethiopian law'.[16]

---

13 For example, Sophocles *Antigone* 265; discussed in Glotz 1904, 104-109; Cantarella 1991a, 227-236. On the inherent vagueness of the concept of virginity, see Goldhill 1995, 115-131.

14 Cf. Clinias' defense of Clitophon: περὶ γὰρ ψυχῆς ἀνδρὸς ὁ ἀγών, AT 7,9,1.

15 H 10,9,7: ἐπάναγκες γὰρ βασιλεῖ καὶ ἄκριτον ἔστιν ὅτε πλήθους ὁρμὴν θεραπεύειν.

16 H 10,9,7: διὰ δὲ τὸ προκατειληφὸς τοῦ Αἰθιοπικοῦ νόμου πάτριον ἀπαραίτητον. On the other hand, he also notes the circle of light around the strangers and interprets it as 'evidence' (τεκμαιρομένῳ, H 10,9,7) that they are protected by a higher power.

The trial scene is the telos of Charicleia's—as well as the narrative's—wanderings. It is essentially a recognition scene, in which Hydaspes experiences a transformational anagnorisis. Charicleia must not only present the evidence of her identity, but she must also perform in the context of a trial and an agon.[17] The gymnosophists gladly agree to hear the case, but all parties must agree whether Charicleia should be allowed to speak. The exchange which follows between Sisimithres and Hydaspes highlights the conflict between what is right and what is legal, parallel to the agon between Thyamis and Arsace, in which a sage-like figure advises a ruler concerning the just treatment of a prisoner. The gymnosophists champion philosophical truth—what is right; whereas Hydaspes insists upon constitutional formalism—what is legal.[18] As Arsace did in Memphis, Hydaspes pulls rank, thereby reinforcing distinctions of the social and political hierarchy. In this case, Charicleia again faces several disabilities: she is (or appears to be) a foreigner, a captive, a non-citizen, and a young woman. Overcoming these hurdles is preliminary to the recognition. Hydaspes raises a series of procedural objections, which are in turn refuted by witty, philosophical responses by Sisimithres. The sage asks the king, 'Do you hear the challenge (πρόκλησις, H 10,10,2) proffered by this stranger?' Hydaspes scoffs at the suggestion that she has any ground for claiming that her rights have been deprived. When Sisimithres suggests that Charicleia herself can answer the questions, the king invokes the differential between himself and the girl, objecting that 'it is not a trial but insolence' (οὐ κρίσις ἀλλ' ὕβρις, H 10,10,3) for a captive to sue him.

Sisimithres dispassionately reminds the king that 'Justice has no regard for prestige. In trials, only one person is king: he who wins with the more logical arguments', (H 10,10,3): an echo of the Stoic dictum, 'Only the wise man is king'.[19] Hydaspes then objects that the law permits the council to judge cases only between the king and his subjects, not foreigners (H 10,10,4). Sisimithres retorts with another maxim: 'In the eyes of the prudent man, the strength of one's claims lies not in appearance but in character' (H 10,10,4), a direct allusion to the single most important obstacle Charicleia must overcome in her case—namely, the color of her skin.

Hydaspes preemptively dismisses her pleas as 'preposterous speeches that people facing mortal danger concoct to stall for time' (λόγων ματαίων ἔσται πλάσματα πρὸς ὑπέρθεσιν, H 10,10,4)—a playful jab at the formulaic trial scene with its cliché of rhetorical showpieces. The trial begins as if it were a verbal

---

[17] Whitmarsh 1998, 115.
[18] Morgan 1978, 331.
[19] Morgan 1978, 333.

boxing match: Charicleia opens strongly, even joyfully, whereas Hydaspes reluctantly turns to Sisimithres to referee. The heroine invokes the gods as her witnesses and accomplices (μάρτυρες, συλλήπτορες H 10,11,3), a proem more appropriate to an ordeal than to a forensic speech. She forgoes a narrative, and instead poses questions followed by assertions to Hydaspes that seem to be outrageous claims, but which instead add up to riddle for him to solve.

Charicleia's evidence is presented as an escalating tricolon of statements rejected by Hydaspes. Returning to the issue of her social status and legal standing, discussed by Hydaspes and Sisimithres, she first asks him whether the law commands him to sacrifice foreigners or natives. When he answers, 'Foreigners', she suggests that it is time for him to find another victim, because he will find out that she is a native-born Ethiopian. This only confirms his initial expectations; amazed, he accuses her of fabricating stories (τοῦ δὲ θαυμάζοντος καὶ πλάττεσθαι λέγοντος, H 10,12,1). Charicleia compounds his bewilderment with the startling claim that she is his daughter; a string of superlatives evokes the emotional intensification (τὰ μικρότερα, τὰ μείζονα, τὰ πρῶτα καὶ ἐγγύτατα, H 10,12,1). Hydaspes expresses his shock and Charicleia answers him for a third time by outright calling him, 'Father!' (H 10,12,1). Angrily ignoring her, the king complains to Sisimithres and dismisses her speech as an arrogant and theatrical attempt to forestall the sacrifice (H 10,12,2). As he orders her to be taken away, she resorts to a procedural technicality: namely, that only the judges (οἱ δικάζοντες, H 1,12,3) can dismiss her, because the king is a party to the present case and cannot cast a vote (σὺ δὲ δικάζῃ τὸ παρόν, οὐ ψῆφον φέρεις, H 10,12,3). In the other trials of the novel, these roles have been conflated. In Athens, family members become opponents. Cnemon, believing he is acting in defense of his father, is instead prosecuted by him; Aristippus, seeking to bring his wife to justice, is accused of putting her to death. Here, a girl accuses her father: 'Perhaps, O King, the law allows you to kill foreigners, but neither the law nor nature allow you, Father, to commit infanticide' (τεκνοκτονεῖν, H 10,12,3). It is a powerful indictment, a final attempt not only to reclaim her biological identity, but also to redeem her parents for infanticide.

The rest of the scene concentrates on Charicleia's presentation of the formal proofs of her claim. In essence, it is a recognition scene cast as a trial. Technical jargon underscores Charicleia's command of forensic technique. She announces that she will show that she is in fact his daughter with the most important types of evidence (τὰς μεγίστας ἀποδείξεις, H 10,14,2): documentary proof (τάς τε ἐγγράφους πίστεις) and confirmation of the facts by the testimony of witnesses (τὰς ἐκ μαρτύρων βεβαιώσεις). Specifically, she alludes to two compelling proofs she will introduce: the band embroidered with the story of her birth described in

Calasiris' narrative (H 4,8) and the testimony of Sisimithres. The use of proofs in a speech was a central concern to ancient rhetoricians. Aristotle (*Rhetoric* 1375a) distinguished between 'artificial' (ἔντεχνος) and 'artless' (ἄτεχνος) proofs, similar to the contrast we might draw between arguments and evidence. Under the category of artless proofs he placed laws, witnesses, agreements, torture, and oaths because these could not be refuted through rhetoric. From Aristotle's perspective, the invented proofs required expertise in the technique of logical argumentation.[20] For Charicleia, however, the most important (μεγίστας) proofs are artless; because her claim appears so improbable, she constructs a syllogistic argument in order to transform the pieces of evidence she will present into τεκμήρια, the incontrovertible signs that Aristotle admitted as a premise for a syllogistic argument.[21] Alluding to Sisimithres' ability to vouch for her, she explains that the strongest proof is the judge's opinion (μεγίστη δ' ἔοικε τῷ λέγοντι πίστις ἡ τοῦ διαιτῶντος γνῶσις, H 10,12,4). Hers is the speech not of a rhetor but of a philosopher, as is evident in the way she styles her speech as a philosophical interrogation.

Hydaspes scrutinizes each of Charicleia's claims, heightening the suspense about how she will demonstrate that two black Ethiopians are the parents of a white child. She first presents Persinna's embroidery, a narrative that risks incriminating the queen. Persinna anticipates that she will be under a cloud of suspicion when her husband reads it, and will become a target of his mistrust, anger, and repudiation (H 10,13,1). More than a birth token, the band is a mechanism, like Thisbe's tablet, to give voice to a woman whose sexuality lies at the crux of a legal dilemma. It is also a conundrum: given the cultural repression of women's speech in the courtroom, how can she craft and apologia for herself against allegations of adultery once it becomes a matter for the court to decide?

The actual text of Persinna's letter is presented much earlier in the novel, when Calasiris tells Cnemon the story of when he first read it to Charicleia and Theagenes (H 4,8).[22] Persinna's band is a story within a story within a story. When it is produced as documentary evidence in the context of Charicleia's paternity suit, it functions as Persinna's speech of defense (ἀπολογοῦμαι, H 4,8,2) to her daughter. What appeared as a legalistic metaphor at first becomes intelligible in retrospect. Persinna writes that she exposed her child without Hydaspes' knowledge, but not because she was guilty (οὐδὲν ἀδικοῦσα, H 4,8,2). The band

---

[20] Eden 1986, 7-24.

[21] Eden 1986, 20.

[22] The rich imagery of weaving and writing on Persinna's band and how they relate to the complex narrative structure of the novel and themes of Hellenism and identity, has been discussed elsewhere; see M. J. Anderson 1997; Whitmarsh 1998.

relates that she and Hydaspes were childless for ten years until one lazy summer afternoon when Hydaspes, 'commanded by a dream', made love to her. She knew immediately that she had become pregnant. The child, the much-anticipated 'successor in the royal clan' (H 4,8,5), was born with bright white skin, a trait the queen attributes to the fact that she was gazing at the painting of Andromeda when she conceived and the image of the pale figure was impressed upon the fetus.[23] She realized that no one would believe her, and that it would be interpreted as evidence of adultery (πεπεισμένη τὴν σὴν χροιὰν μοιχείαν ἐμοὶ προσάψουσαν, H 4,8,6). And so, as she explains on the band, she exposed her baby.

Hydaspes' reaction to the unfolding recognition echoes those of another king confronted with the discovery of true paternity. Persinna, like Jocasta in Sophocles' *Oedipus Tyrannus,* knows the solution to the enigma of the exposed child before the king does. Persinna hands the evidence over to Hydaspes to figure out the truth himself. He reads the band and accepts the fact of the infant's exposure, yet remains skeptical. He asks the inevitable question of how the exposed infant survived and what happened to the precious gems that were her birth tokens. Like Oedipus, who accuses Creon of masking his intention to usurp power (ἦ τοσόνδ' ἔχεις τόλμης πρόσωπον, Sophocles, *Oedipus Tyrannus* 532-535), Hydaspes immediately detects a conspiracy and suspects that the girl is an imposter (ὥσπερ προσωπεῖον, H 10,13,4) who has been bribed with the gems to pose as his daughter in order to usurp the royal succession. On the other hand, Sisimithres is a composite of Teiresias, who cannot lie, and the messenger from Corinth, who testifies to the survival of the child. The gymnosophist relates that he saved the exposed infant and gave her to a Greek man while he was on a diplomatic mission in Egypt. He points to the band and notes that the script is Ethiopian royal script, but that only Hydaspes would be able to tell whether it is Persinna's.[24] The reference to the band leads Sisimithres to acknowledge the other tokens he gave to the Greek man (ἕτερα συνεκτεθέντα γνωρίσματα, H 10,14,2), which Charicleia then presents. Persinna recognizes them and Hydaspes asks her whether she has more to say. Once again, she refuses to speak in public and suggests that they discuss it in the privacy of the palace. Charicleia then presents her next 'document', the pantarbe ring inscribed with holy letters (γράμμασι δὲ ἱεροῖς τισιν ἀνάγραπτος, H 8,11,8). Hydaspes recognizes it, but is still unconvinced.

It is finally Sisimithres' duty to explain Charicleia's skin color, the overriding piece of evidence that seems to contradict her claim to be the biological daughter of the king. And so he points to the biological facts of her age, her skin color, and

---

[23] On the theory of 'maternal impression', see Reeve 1989.

[24] H 10,14,1. On Ethiopian forms of writing, see Morgan 1978, 351-352.

her beauty—the most telling evidence of her nobility. Hydaspes now chides Sisimithres for being an advocate rather than a judge (συνηγορῶν μᾶλλον ἢ δικάζων, H 10,14,5). The king remains fixated on the complete improbability that he and his wife could produce a white child. Sisimithres prepares for the grand finale when the truth will be revealed. He smiles ironically (H 10,14,6)—perhaps we are meant to read it as Socratic —and states that the gymnosophists are always right and owe nothing to anyone, except to live in accordance with virtue. He redefines a 'judge' (δικαστήν, H 10,14,6) as 'the advocate of justice' (τὸν τοῦ δικαίου συνήγορον). In the present case, justice equates to saving and defending the king's daughter; therefore, Sisimithres becomes Hydaspes' advocate (τί δὲ οὐχὶ σοὶ μᾶλλον ἢ τῇ κόρῃ συνηγορῶν φανήσομαι, H 10,14,6). The king's interest, Charicleia's interest, and the interest of justice are congruent.

Once the palace attendants bring out the painting of Andromeda, everyone notices that Charicleia looks exactly like Andromeda. The audience, which until now had no understanding of what was being said because the trial was in Greek, cheers in astonishment. It is this visual proof which persuades the crowd. As a final proof, Sisimithres notes the baby he rescued had a birthmark on her arm. Just as Odysseus' scar, the lock of Electra's hair, and Oedipus' ankles, the proof of Charicleia's identity is inscribed on her body. He bares her arm and displays the mark, at which point Persinna melts into tears and Hydaspes, seeing his wife's reaction, is finally persuaded.[25]

At last, paternal feelings get the best of Hydaspes, and he too embraces Charicleia. Yet, there remains the law ordering Charicleia and her fellow captives to be sacrificed. The relationship between Hydaspes and the crowd fully develops in the remainder of the scene. Before he takes any further action, he looks at the crowd and assesses its emotions. The spectators are as moved as he is; they weep at the grand spectacle with a mixture of pleasure and pity—and then they raise an outcry, despite the heralds' call for silence (H 10,16,3). Just as the people did not understand the trial, now it is the king who is unable to interpret the meaning of the outcry (οὔτε τὸ βούλημα τοῦ παράχου προδήλως ἐκφαίνοντας, H 10,16,3). Up until this moment, the trial is conducted in a public pavilion at a distance from the crowd. From the spectators' perspective, the trial is a wordless pantomime. The interrogation is conducted in the privacy of the king's tent, resembling a judicial proceeding before a Roman magistrate advised by a council of jurists. The trial thus simultaneously represents two very different venues for the pronouncement of a verdict: the ruling in chambers and the public dissemination of the verdict

---

[25] For a discussion of the birthmark, see Morgan 1978, 367-368. Cf. Leucippe's display of the lashes 'written' on her naked back, AT 5,17,6.

(especially condemnation) in a spectacle. The trial is not over until its significance is understood by the entire city.

Hydaspes' address to the crowd is fairly long (H 10,16,4-10). It begins with an address to the spectators (H 10,16,4-8), in which he declares that he shall put aside his paternal interests and perform the sacrifice as required by law. He then turns to his daughter to invite her to be sacrificed (H 10,16,9-10) and concludes with a prayer to the gods (H 10,16,10). The reader is led to believe that as soon as Charicleia proves her identity, she will be safe from sacrifice—only to realize that the opposite is about to happen. Ancient rhetorical treatises call this tactic of reverse psychology the 'disingenuous argument' (ἐσχηματίσμενος λόγος), typified by the famous address of Agamemnon to the Achaeans in *Iliad* 2,110-141.[26] In a rhetorical showpiece of pathos Hydaspes portrays himself as a father torn between his desire to see his newly found daughter live and his duty to perform the traditional rite. Again looming in the background is Agamemnon qua conflicted father in Euripides' *Iphigenia at Aulis,* who is obligated to perform the sacrifice of his own daughter in the interests of the people. Unlike the Achaean soldiers, the Ethiopians sympathize with the king. In Hydaspes' case, the force compelling him to sacrifice his daughter is not the pressure of public opinion, but the law. Most of the speech consists of a disquisition upon the ambivalence of child sacrifice. The point is to overturn a traditional religious ritual—to mark a separation from the ancestral rites of the Ethiopians to a more enlightened era informed by the teachings of the gymnosophists, who would abolish all animal sacrifice altogether. Hydaspes milks the emotionality of the moment: he consoles the masses, but insists that she must be sacrificed.

Finally, he challenges the people to determine whether it will be pleasing to the gods to sacrifice his daughter. As he pretends to lead Charicleia to be sacrificed, the crowd stops him with a loud outcry. Heliodorus seems to have in mind the kind of vote by acclamation that was common in arenas and other large public gathering spaces in the Roman Empire.[27] The crowd is moved to chant:

> 'Save the girl', they shouted, 'save the royal bloodline, save the one who was saved by the gods! We are gratified. The decree has been fulfilled in our eyes. We recognized you as our king: you too, recognize yourself as a father. May the gods be gracious to us for our apparent transgression. We will transgress even more by resisting their will. Let no one kill the girl who was saved by

[26] [Dionysius of Halicarnassus], 'Περὶ ἐσχηματισμένων', in Usener and Radermacher 1904-1929, 295-358.; Russell 1983, 36, 138. See also Clitophon's speech in trial 5.

[27] Colin 1965b, 109-152.

> them. O, father of your people, be a father in your home as well!' (H 10,17,1-2)

The remarkably articulate chant enters into a dialogue with the king's gestures. In the Roman Empire, structured acclamations between emperor and people helped manage moments of potential crises in public relations.[28] As in the trial in Memphis, the spectators physically stop Charicleia's 'killer' by blocking his path to the altars (H 10,17,2). Hydaspes happily admits defeat, and lets the people continue with their shouting and celebrations over 'their' success. Thus, with the help of the entire assembly, Charicleia wins the 'trial and contest' (κρίσις καὶ ἀγών) for her life. In the process, Meroe becomes more civilized and more just by abolishing human sacrifice.

More importantly, the king has shown that he is open to persuasion by his advisers, by the crowd, and by his own child. As we have seen, at the outset of the trial the council of advisers had sole authority to judge cases involving the king although the separation of powers seemed tenuous; the king's dominant role in the proceedings held out the possibility that Hydapses may be a tyrant in the mold of Arsace. There is a dynamic tension in the relationship between council and king: the council feels free to admonish the king when he oversteps his role, and the king is strong enough to push the council to define its position. Unlike Arsace, who is dominated by the mob, Hydaspes' powers of oratory enable him to redirect the crowd's rebellious energy toward a noble end.[29] The government of Ethiopia is guided by a sense of lawfulness without legalism, and piety without ritualism.

---

[28] Aldrete 1999, 199.

[29] On the importance of oratorical training of emperors, see Aldrete 1999, 85-97.

Trial 11.
Lost and Found: Abduction
Charicles v. Theagenes
(Heliodorus, *Aethiopica* 4,17-21 and 10,34-38)

The Story

After the protagonists fall in love during a ritual procession in Delphi, Theagenes leads an armed band of Thessalian youths in 'erotic battle' to abduct Charicleia, who is complicit in her elopement. The Egyptian priest, Calasiris, acts as chaperone for them on their self-imposed exile as 'captives of chaste love'. He requires Theagenes to vow not to touch Charicleia until she recovers her nation and parents. Meanwhile, the heroine's adoptive father, Charicles, receives news of her abduction and at first construes his loss as divine punishment for some ritual transgression; however, once he learns that Theagenes and the Thessalians are responsible, he demands an emergency meeting of the citizens of Delphi.

The magistrates summon the assembly, which becomes a midnight council chamber. Charicles' plea for help moves the demos to tears. Hegesias, the strategos, proposes hunting down the criminals, impaling them, and disenfranchising their descendants. The assembly passes a decree that henceforth bans the Thessalians from participation in the sacred mission. As the meeting is adjourned, the entire populace—men, children, ephebes, women, and old men—rush out of the city to capture the culprits. As the narrative follows the protagonists' flight, Charicles recedes from the main narrative at the end of the fourth book.

Six books later, after Charicleia has successfully reclaimed her birthright, a mysterious beggar appears in Meroe with a group of ambassadors from the city of Syene. He presents a petition from the Persian satrap to Hydaspes to allow the bearer to search for his lost daughter among the captives taken in the siege. Out of sympathy for this father bereft of his child, Hydaspes grants his request. As the man scans the group of captives huddled by the sacrificial altar, he notices Theagenes and seizes him. At this point, the protagonists recognize the beggar as Charicles. He charges Theagenes for sacrilege and kidnapping his daughter. Interrogated by Hydaspes, Theagenes pleads guilty to all the charges and alleges that the king himself is an accomplice, thus throwing the courtroom into chaos. Calling herself a patricide, Charicleia rushes forward to embrace Charicles. The crowd cheers this second father-daughter reunion. Theagenes' performance proves that he is a worthy husband for Charicleia. They are then married and inducted into the priesthood of the Sun and the Moon.

Analysis

The solution of a final enigma ties up the various loose ends of the *Aethiopica*. It revolves around the figure of Charicles, Charicleia's adoptive father in Delphi. He was introduced into the narrative as a character in the tale of Calasiris, as told to Cnemon over the course of a long night at the house of Nausicles in Naucratis (H 2,21,3-5,2,5). With the end of Calasiris' tale, this tertiary character is dropped from the main narrative, as others have been (cf. Aristippus, Arsinoe, Nausicles). The appearance of an unnamed 'old man' in Meroe sparks a number of recognitions within the framework of a second trial scene.

The bipartite structure of this trial scene spotlights the pursuit of a lawsuit across geographic space, narrative time, and legal jurisdictions. Theagenes is accused of a crime that was committed in Delphi and is now brought to the court of the Ethiopian king for adjudication.

The abduction of Charicleia is the crime for which Theagenes is put on trial.[1] Whereas Charicleia proved that she was the daughter of Hydaspes in her trial; in this subsequent trial Theagenes will prove that she is the daughter of Charicles. This is his agon: he must demonstrate his worthiness to marry Charicleia in the eyes of not one potential father-in-law, but two. Although her identity remains the central to the proceedings, Charicleia withdraws from the public space of the pavilion and is sequestered in the palace with her mother.

Bride theft loomed in the cultural consciousness in the fourth century, as reflected in an edict of Constantine in 326 C.E. that attempted to eradicate the practice of marriage by abduction (*raptus*).[2] The edict called for the harsh punishment of not only the abductor, but also the abductee and any accomplices. The girl's capacity to consent to this type of marriage was devalued and, moreover, she was held guilty by association and was obligated to pay the same penalty as the abductor. A slave who denounced an abductor would be promoted to a higher social

---

[1] On the literary background of abduction marriage see Lateiner 1997.

[2] Evans Grubbs 1989, 59-61.

status; on the other hand, parents who condoned the abduction were subject to deportation. The seriousness of Constantine's purpose is reflected in the proviso that a guilty verdict could not be appealed.[3] Christian sources discuss abduction marriage as well, though they tend to be more lenient.[4] In 349 C.E., an amendment to the law of Constantine reduced the penalty from the *summum supplicium* (condemnation to a degrading execution by beasts or fire) to *capitalis poena* (death penalty or exile). Twenty-five years later, another law imposed a five-year limit for prosecuting a case of marriage by abduction.[5] In light of the amelioration of the severity of Constantine's original legislation on *raptus*, it is tempting to speculate that the novel's focus on abduction perhaps reflects a broader cultural debate on the nature of this crime in the fourth century C.E.

Abduction of a marriageable girl subverted customary ways of contracting marriages. If the victim was unwilling, then abduction was essentially equivalent to rape. If, however, the girl was a willing participant in her own kidnapping (as Charicleia is in this episode), then the abduction was in effect an elopement.[6] Staged abduction or 'bride theft' could be a practical solution to an unconsummated love affair. Anthropologists have observed that it occurs in societies where marriages are arranged and a high value is placed on virginity.[7] The abductor is typically a prospective husband who has either been rejected by the girl's family or who has decided for other reasons to take matters into his own hands. The Greek novels provide other examples of frustrated, young, unmarried men and the stratagems they use to accomplish their objectives.[8] In cultures where male honor is linked to the sexuality of the women in his family, it is automatically assumed that a girl who has been abducted has been raped. Since her reputation and future marriageability are permanently damaged, the girl's family would discretely try to arrange a marriage with the abductor rather than risk public prosecution and the concomitant dishonor to the family. A Byzantine law (perhaps semi-fictional) mentioned in Achilles Tatius' novel declares that a man who abducts a woman is to have marriage as his penalty (AT 2,13,3). Whether an actual law or simply an adage disguised as a law, the extension of this line of reasoning is that a rape must be legitimized as a marriage to remedy the damage to the girl's reputation and the family's honor. This is what happens at the end of Achilles Tatius' novel, with

---

[3] Codex Theodosianus 9,24,1.

[4] Evans Grubbs 1995, 88-89.

[5] Evans Grubbs 1995, 186, 192.

[6] Charicleia's cooperation is made explicit in H 4,17,4: καὶ τὴν Χαρίκλειαν εὐτρεπῆ καὶ ἅπαντα προειδευῖαν καὶ τὴν βίαν ἑκοῦσαν ὑφισταμένην ἀναρπάζουσιν.

[7] Evans Grubbs 1989, 64.

[8] For example, the tyrant of Acragas (C 1,2), Callisthenes (AT 2,13), and Lampis (L 4,28).

the wedding of Calligone, Clitophon's sister, to Callisthenes, her kidnapper (AT 8,17-18).

Bride theft, like adultery, was understood as an attack against the authority of the male head of the household. In classical Athens, the question of the woman's consent in rape or adultery was less dispositive than the fact that the privacy of the oikos was violated.[9] Under Roman law, the spouses' consent determined the fact of a marriage, which presumably gave children some leverage over the selection of a marriage partner. For instance, in Delphi Charicles had arranged for Charicleia to marry his nephew, but was unable to win the consent of his lovesick daughter (H 4,7,9). Her departure from her father's oikos is staged as an armed attack: Theagenes 'marshals' (ἐστρατήγει, H 4,17,3) an armed band (ἔνοπλος κῶμος) in an erotic battle (ἐρωτικὸν πόλεμον). The young men raise a battle cry, break through the gates of the house, and burst into Charicleia's bedroom (H 4,17,5).[10] In this way, Theagenes' courage and display of military leadership mitigates the apparent threat of sexual violence. Calasiris says that she was ready and willing to be taken.[11] The lovers in turn declare that their 'persons are hostage to fate' (τύχης λοιπὸν ἀγώγιμα σώματα, H 4,18,2).[12] The adjective ἀγώγιμα has a technical, legal meaning. It is applied to objects which are capable of being carried, portables; when applied to persons, it can mean 'liable to seizure'. For example, Demosthenes (23,11) uses the term ἀγώγιμος in the sense of 'liable to arrest', ἀγωγή. Theagenes calls himself and Charicleia 'prisoners of a chaste love' (σωφρονοῦντος ἔρωτος αἰχμάλωτας, H 4,18,2), foreshadowing their status when they are brought as captives to Meroe. Charicleia objects to being left alone with Theagenes on the grounds that it will be the beginning of injustice and even 'treason' (προδοσίας, H 4,18,4).[13] The couple's relationship is sanctified with a private oath; the taint of criminality is glossed over with a quasi-legal agreement.

Charicles' effort to seek justice for this daughter's kidnapping is inspired by the world of the *Iliad* and by the world of Demosthenes in the era of the Sacred Wars against the Phocians at Delphi. Charicles, a priest of Apollo, like Homer's

---

[9] On the woman's consent in classical Athens, see Omitowoju 2002.

[10] The reference to the tampered lock on the door (H 4,17,3) seems to be a stock element in the description of scenes of staged abductions. For example, the lengthy description of the layout of the women's bedrooms in the house of Hippias and the procedures for locking them (AT 2,19). The use of military metaphor in connection with love is a trope seen in other novels (C 7,1, 7,4; AT 1,11).

[11] H 4,17,4: καὶ τὴν Χαρίκλειαν εὐτρεπῆ καὶ ἅπαντα προειδυῖαν καὶ τὴν βίαν ἑκοῦσαν ὑφισταμένην.

[12] The noun σώματα takes the force of 'captive persons' when linked with a verb signifying 'to lead', from which the adjective ἀγώγιμος is derived; Ducrey 1968, 26-27, 39-40.

[13] Clitophon and Melite also swear oaths at the temple of Isis before embarking on their journey from Alexandria to Ephesus (AT 5,14,2-3).

Chryses, speculates that his daughter's abduction is a punishment he pays 'because of the wrath of the gods' (ἐκ θεῶν μήνιδος ταυτηνὶ τίνω τὴν δίκην, H 4,19,3). After the abduction of his daughter, his first recourse is to self-help, a kind of vigilante justice. An informal crowd gathers around his home after the attack; these are the first people to whom Charicles appeals for help. He urges them to chase and punish 'the enemies and transgressors' (H 4,19,2). When Calasiris informs him that Theagenes was the architect of the raid, Charicles requests an emergency meeting of the assembly. The magistrates summon the people of Delphi to the theater in the middle of the night, with trumpeters—the scenario is borrowed from a section of Demosthenes' *De Corona* (18,169), in which an emergency meeting of the Athenian council was convened when Athens heard the news that Elatea had been taken by Philip II of Macedon. Charicleia is equated with the temple's treasure, plundered by the Thessalians (H 4,19,8). Charicleia's abduction is an insult to the entire polis; finding and punishing the person responsible for harming her is a matter of the greatest civic importance.

As the injured party, Charicles delivers a speech that is equivalent to a prosecution. Dressed in mourning, his head covered with dirt and ashes, his appearance is similar to Aristippus' in the trial of Cnemon (H 4,19,5). Both fathers symbolize the empty oikos, the household that has lost its heir. In the proem (H 4,29,6-7), Charicles begins with a *captatio benevolentiae*, in which he explains why he called the assembly. He says that it was not in order to denounce himself (προσαγγεῖλαί με βουλόμενον ἐμαυτόν, H 4,19,6), an allusion to the formulaic self-denunciation; nevertheless, he hyperbolically claims he 'deserves to die many times over', (H 4,19,6). He deploys the stereotypical claim that the city is also the victim, a standard rhetorical strategy found among the Greek orators, particularly when the prosecution had to justify bringing its case to the attention of the people (in a democratic jury or assembly) by claiming that the accused has attacked the entire city. Charicles' real motive for summoning them is to not to get his daughter back but to see that the criminals are punished. The injury to his own family is an affront to the city (ἥ τε κοινὴ πάντων ἀπάτη, H 4,19,79); he characterizes it as temple robbery, a particularly serious crime for Delphi, whose accumulated treasures were famously plundered in the Amphictyonic Wars, as readers of Demosthenes would have well known.[14]

Charicles' characterization as a helpless father bereft of his offspring specifically evokes the pathos of Oedipus in Sophocles' *Oedipus at Colonus*. Because his family was destroyed, he must beg the city for support. He takes for granted

---

[14] H 4,19,8: καὶ τὸν νεὼν τοῦ Πυθίου τοῦ τιμιωτάτου κτήματος ἀποσυλήσαντες. In the Attic orators, it seems that the term, ἱεροσυλία, came to connote general sacrilege; see Cohen 1983, 104-105.

that the audience in Delphi is already familiar with his misfortunes, an echo of Oedipus' notoriety. Earlier in the novel (H 2,29,3-5), the reader learned from Calasiris' tale that Charicles' first wife and young daughter had died tragically by an unfortunate blaze in his daughter's bedroom—a metaphor for the destructive power of eros. Like Oedipus, Charicles went into exile after his family was destroyed. He refers to his daughter as his eyes (H 4,19,8), a term of endearment by which Oedipus calls two daughters after they are abducted by Creon. Without them, Oedipus is truly blind; Antigone and Ismene are referred to several times as κόραι, a word that means both 'girls' and 'pupils (of the eyes)'.[15] In the same vein, Charicles refers to his daughter as his 'anchor and sole consolation'.[16] He is pursued by a 'strife-loving' (φιλονεικίας, H 4,19,8) daimon, a play on the name of Oedipus' son, Polyneices. The culmination of this pathetic speech is a description of Charicleia as a bride stolen before her wedding, echoing the death of his first daughter. At this point, Charicles melts down in grief.

In lieu of a defense speech, the strategos rallies the demos to action. Like Hermocrates in Chariton's first trial scene in Syracuse, Hegesias issues a call to arms against the attackers (πολέμιοι, H 4,20,2); namely, Theagenes and his band. His speech is punctuated with hortatory subjunctives (μὴ συμβαπτιζώμεθα, μηδὲ λάθωμεν) and other verbs in the first-person plural (παρασχοῖμεν, κινήσαιμεν), as well as by first-person plural adjectives and pronouns (ἡμεῖς, τῆς ἡμετέρας παρασκευῆς, ἐκ τοῦ δημοσίου τοῦ ἡμετέρου). A sense of urgency pervades Hegesias' speech, as it did in Hermocrates' exhortation to the Syracusan people not to waste time in the trial and delay Callirhoe's burial further (C 1,5,7). Likewise, Hegesias admonishes the audience not to wallow in sorrow with Charicles, lest they miss the opportunity to pursue the enemy (H 4,20,1).

The image of Delphi and Thessaly at war with one another is inspired by the Attic orators, where the exclusion of citizens of other cities from participation at Delphi was a means of influencing the domestic policy of a rival power, as seen in the complex litigation between Demosthenes and Aeschines as well as the diplomatic negotiations between Philip II and the other Greek cities concerning membership in the Amphictyonic League.[17] The type of retaliation Hegesias encourages is not an orderly arrest followed by a lawful trial, but an act of state-sanctioned vigilantism. He proposes to strip the criminals of their rights and take

---

[15] Sophocles, *Oedipus at Colonus* 866, 902, 1009, and 1097; *LSJ* s.v. 'κόρη', defs. I,1 and III.

[16] H 4,19,9: μόνη παραψυχὴ καὶ ὡς εἰπεῖν ἄγκυρα. Cf. Sophocles, *Oedipus at Colonus* 345-52.

[17] Demosthenes *De corona*.

vengeance on their family, a punishment that makes sense within the novel's conception of justice as an intergenerational phenomenon: children are punished for crimes against their fathers, and so parents must suffer for the crimes their children commit.[18] The positive outcome of Charicleia's lawsuit against Hydaspes represents the corollary of this view of justice. When a child is virtuous (and knows how to speak in court), the family is restored. Yet, no sooner does Hegesias propose the punishment than he qualifies it by proposing that the Thessalian boys be prohibited from participating in future festivals, with the expectation that it will cause the assembly of Thessaly to penalize its own citizens (H 4,20,3). Hegesias additionally proposes to ban the temple attendant from passing the torch to the armed runner (H 4,21,1), the moment in the religious festival that Theagenes (the runner) and Charicleia (the temple attendant) met each other.[19] The assembly enthusiastically endorses Hegesias' proposals 'with one vote and the hand of all' (H 4,21,2). Like the Syracusans in Chariton's novel, once the assembly is adjourned, the entire city—including women, children, and old men—rushes out of the theater and off to overtake Charicleia's kidnappers (H 4,21,2).[20]

Were this storyline to end at this point, it would not technically be a trial scene. The fifth book opens with the scene as viewed through the eyes of Calasiris. He describes the assembly as it appeared in the rear-view mirror, so to speak, as he and the protagonists escape prosecution. The story of what happened next is left unresolved: Calasiris says, 'The city of Delphi was in such a condition, but what happened next, I do not know' (H 5,1,1). It is at this point that Charicles vanishes from the narrative. Yet, as we have seen in the complicated story of Cnemon and Thisbe, Heliodorus is meticulous about gathering loose ends. He takes a similar strategy with Charicles.

Charicles is re-introduced into the narrative six books later as an unnamed petitioner among the embassy from Syene during Hydaspes' official audience with his subjects and allies. This procedure is vaguely similar to the imperial practice of addressing *libelli* and other official business during the Roman emperor's *salutationes*.[21] He carries a letter written by Oroondates, which serves the same function as Pharnaces' letter of recommendation for Dionysius in Chariton's

---

[18] H 4,20,3: διαβιβάσαντας καὶ τοὺς ἐξ αὐτῶν ἀτιμῶσαι, καὶ εἰς τὸ γένος τὴν τιμωρίαν. On the continuum between lawful punishment and vigilantism, see Forsdyke 2008.

[19] It has been suggested that Heliodorus added this final proposal, in order to minimize an ahistorical detail inserted for the purposes of the narrative and believed his readers would notice was an outright fabrication; see Pouilloux 1983, 269.

[20] A similarly generalized zeal for doing something after the assembly meeting appears at the end of the trial of Chaereas (trial 1) in Chariton's novel when the entire city of Syracuse attends Callirhoe's funeral (C 1,6).

[21] Millar 1977, 241. Cf. Dionysius' petition in trial 3, above.

novel (trial 3).[22] After the standard opening address to the 'merciful and fortunate king of the Ethiopians', Oroondates' letter (H 10,34,2-4) congratulates Hydaspes for his recent victory and thanks him for his generosity. He requests one small favor: the gift of the captive girl who was en route to him during the recent war. The satrap vouches for the bearer of the letter, a man (as yet unidentified), whom he met in Elephantine. The contrast in moral values between Chariton and Heliodorus is made clear in this small detail of letters of commendation: whereas the letter of Pharnaces in Chariton's novel cited Dionysius' status as the first man of Miletus, Oroondates cites Charicles' fatherly devotion in searching for his lost child. He refers indirectly to the unnamed man's prestige: 'his nobility shows in his manners, but his misery shows on his face'. The letter closes with an appeal for Hydaspes to send the man back to him 'a father not only in name, but in fact', (πατέρα μὴ μόνον ὀνομαζόμενον ἀλλὰ καὶ γεγενημένον, H 10,34,4). The petition strikes a chord with the king, recently reunited with his own daughter and so, unaware that Charicleia is the girl in question, he magnanimously grants the request of the unnamed man, who gratefully prostrates himself and kisses the king's feet.

The man vainly searches the group of captives who stand around the altar, but does not find his daughter (because she is inside the palace with her mother). Suddenly, he throws his cloak around Theagenes' neck and arrests him.[23] This is a dramatization of the procedure of summary arrest, known as ἀπαγωγή in classical Athenian law and *manus iniectio* in Roman law, whereby a criminal was caught red-handed and literally hauled before a magistrate for punishment. In Roman law the arrest was effectuated by physically holding the criminal and declaring in Latin '*teneo te*', or in Greek, 'ἔχω σε' (H 10,35,1)—'I have you'.[24] The man grasps Theagenes; even the guards cannot pry him away. He drags (ἀγαγεῖν, H 10,35,2) Theagenes before the council and the king, and makes an accusation: 'This is the one who kidnapped my daughter'. In case the reader has not yet figured out that the mystery man is Charicles, he characterizes Theagenes' crime with three participles that appeared six books previously to describe the heroine's kidnapping in Delphi.[25] In an objection familiar to us from the trial of the priest

[22] Charicles' letter is a loose simulation of a letter of introduction; see Morgan 1978, 549.

[23] Cf. AT 7,12,4, where Leucippe's father, while looking for his daughter, chances upon Clitophon, who is also about to be executed; see Morgan 1978, 553.

[24] Morgan 1978, 562. It is an echo of the first Athenian trial, when another father, Aristippus, had hauled a younger man (Cnemon) to court (H 1,17,3).

[25] 'Despoil' (συλαγωγήσας, H 10,35,2, cf. ἀποσυλήσαντες, H 4,19,8); 'strip' (ἐρημώσας, H 10,35,2; cf. ἔρημος, H 4,19,6), and 'seize' (ἀναρπάσας, H 10,35,2, cf. τὴν τῆς κόρης ἁρπαγὴν, H 4,19,1).

of Artemis in Achilles Tatius' novel (trial 6, above), Charicles presumes that Theagenes seeks asylum at the gods' altars, obviously unaware of Theagenes' impending sacrifice.

The councilors and king understand his appeal, but the spectators, who can only see what is happening, guide the reader's response to this surprising twist (H 10,35,2). The initial effect is meant to be one of surprise, an unexpected complication raised just at the moment when the story appears to have reached its happy ending. Heliodorus prolongs the revelation of the mystery until the king invites him to tell his story. Virtually resuming where Charicles left off in his earlier speech to the assembly at Delphi, he retells the story of the abduction (H 10,36,2-3), with only a few minor deviations from the version related in Calasiris' tale.

Charicles delivers a formal accusation, thereby reopening a cold case of abduction.[26] He emphasizes Charicleia's status as the temple attendant (ζάκορος) and Theagenes' status as the leader of the Thessalian delegation to the festival at Delphi. The abduction is again cast as a temple robbery (ἀποσυλήσας, H 10,36,3). He argues that it is in the interest of the Ethiopians to punish Theagenes for his crime. By equating Apollo with the Sun god, he argues that Theagenes is guilty of sacrilege against the god of the Ethiopians as well, because he attacked the shrine and priest at Delphi, a reminder to the reader of the equation of the two gods.[27]

In order to fill in the missing gaps in his narrative, Heliodorus has Charicles tell the backstory of how he came to Meroe. He explains that he attempted to find redress in Oeta, Theagenes' hometown. The people of Oeta 'gave him up for slaughter' (εἰς σφαγήν, H 10,36,4); that is, they disenfranchised him, the outcome Hegesias intended.[28] Charicles had identified Calasiris, the 'pseudo-prophet', as Theagenes' accomplice (συνεργοῦ δε͂ αὐτῷ, H 10,36,4).[29] In conclusion, he claims that he was too overwhelmed by grief at the assembly at Delphi to do anything, and therefore now supplicates the king to help him find his daughter. Again Charicles sobs when he is finished speaking, as he did at Delphi.

At this point, Heliodorus closes the temporal gap in the narrative between Delphi and Meroe. The frequency of justice-related words intensifies (such as ἄδικος, ἔνδικον, ὁ ἀδικήσας, τὸ ἀδίκημα, δίκαιος). Hydaspes is de facto the judge

---

[26] Morgan 1978, 563-583.

[27] For a discussion of the religious background of the equation of Apollo with Helios, see Morgan 1978, xxxviii-lx, especially xliv-xlv.

[28] Likewise, in Athens persons who were found in places from which they were outlawed were liable to ἀπαγωγή; see MacDowell 1978, 74-75.

[29] Cf. Thersander's charge against the priest of Artemis (trial 6).

in this case. Having heard Charicles' speech, Hydaspes offers Theagenes an opportunity to respond ('τί' ἔφη 'πρὸς ταῦτα ἐρεῖς;' H 10,37,1), the functional equivalent to the procedure used in the earlier trial of Cnemon (see trial 7), where the magistrate asked a simple question of whether or not what has been said is true. Whereas Cnemon confessed accidentally, in this instance Theagenes confesses deliberately. He proudly pleads guilty as charged and denounces himself as a bandit, a kidnapper, and a violent, unjust man vis-à-vis Charicles (ληστὴς ἐγὼ καὶ ἅρπαξ καὶ βίαιος καὶ ἄδικος περὶ τοῦτον, H 10,37,1), but Theagenes subverts his confession by turning it around and seeming to attack the judge himself. He claims that by committing the crime with which he is now charged, he has become Hydaspes' benefactor (εὐεργέτης, H 10,37,1). The paradox is symmetrical to Charicleia's earlier accusation of the king in her trial scene. Without comment, Hydaspes sentences Theagenes to 'lawful slaughter of execution' (τὴν ἐκ τῆς τιμωρίας ἔνδικον σφαγὴν, H 10,37,2). He orders Theagenes to surrender the girl to her father and to be happy that he will die as a sacrifice rather than as a criminal condemned to execution.

Theagenes then concocts a clever legal argument. He indicates to Hydaspes that the person who is legally obligated to give back the girl is 'not the man who committed the crime, but the man who profits from the crime'.[30] Essentially, Theagenes distinguishes between degrees of culpability. Kidnapping is conceived of as a kind of theft: in Athenian law (probably) and in Roman law (definitely), a person who knowingly received stolen property was liable for theft.[31] Unaware that Charicleia is the 'stolen goods' in question, Hydaspes objects to the charge. Theagenes' cryptic declaration that the king himself is an accomplice to the crime heightens the suspense. In the end, this legalistic reasoning dissolves when Theagenes dramatically names Hydaspes as the possessor of the stolen property and identifies Charicleia as the daughter of Charicles. The crowd reacts with jubilation to this second father-daughter reunion.

Sisimithres reprises his role as the figure whose virtue gives him the authority to redefine what is procedurally proper. He intervenes to set things straight, as he had done in Charicleia's lawsuit. He embraces Charicles and identifies himself as the Ethiopian man who had originally entrusted the girl to him. Charicleia then runs to Charicles and melodramatically begs him to punish her as a patricide, an action that mirrors Cnemon's innocent conviction for patricide at the beginning of the novel. Her hyperbolic confession and apology highlight her filial devotion,

30 H 10,37,2: ἀλλ' οὐχ ὁ ἀδικήσας...ἀλλ' ὁ τὸ ἀδίκημα ἔχων ἀποδιδόναι δίκαιος. See Morgan 1978, 585-586.

31 The Athenian law is discussed by Cohen 1983, 84-86; E. M. Harris 1994. For the Roman law, see *Digest* 47,2,3,35.

now doubled. At this point, the trial dissolves as the theatrical metaphor takes over. Persinna articulates what is in effect the final judgment in the trial: she asks her husband to truly acknowledge (ἀληθῶς γίνωσκε) Theagenes as a worthy bridegroom for their daughter who, despite her boldness in the courtroom, was too shy to speak (μόλις ἐξαγορευσάσης, H 10,38,2) when it came to love. The novel then ends with the betrothal of Theagenes and Charicleia and their assumption to the high priesthood of the cults of the Sun and Moon, and their marriage.

Conclusion

From a formal perspective, Heliodorus' courtroom scenes are highly sophisticated constructions. The trial of Theagenes represents most clearly the technique of presenting the background for the trial in discontinuous narrative segments. Heliodorus revitalizes clichés of the novelistic trial scene—domestic discipline, self-accusation, ordeals, stays of execution—in the service of constructing a telos for the novel's progression through differing juridical cultures. Pairs of set speeches, such as in Achilles Tatius' novel, are rare in the *Aethiopica*; instead, the author prefers to relate the content of speeches indirectly, thereby focusing upon the characters' actions upon the stage of justice. Heliodorus thus creates an aura of suspense in the saga of the trials in Athens. Despite the tragic ending for Aristippus, Cnemon ultimately wins his happy ending by leaving Athens and settling in Egypt, prefiguring the happy ending for the novel's protagonists. The ambitious scope of this novel allows extensive delineation of legal tableaux in three distinctly different political contexts: democracy, tyranny, and monarchy. In the world of the *Aethiopica*, harmony between parents and children is at least as essential as harmony between lovers. In the Athenian trials, the democratic courts interfered with the relationship between father and son. Memphis was a place where authority was divided between the acting satrap and the priest. The individuals holding these positions were insecure in their authority: Arsace, ruling in lieu of her husband, abused her office while Thyamis, the son of Calasiris and successor to the priesthood, was preoccupied with performing his filial duty to mourn his father. Tyranny forces the unprotected protagonists to use their wits to survive. In the spectacle of her execution Charicleia turns the Persian system against itself through her appropriation of her birth tokens. In doing so, she emerges as an individual who knows how to speak in court, a skill with which she finally wins her father's acknowledgment. Through learning to play the game of legal argumentation, the protagonists mature into their proper social roles as the leaders of Meroe.

General Conclusion

Educated Greek readers during the Roman Empire had a taste for elaborate trial scenes. We do too, as is clear in the popularity of law-related narratives in our own culture. Stories of trials inform and—are informed by—a common understanding of the law, which is not necessarily the perspective of legal professionals. To live in any society requires a basic awareness of the governing rules. The more complex the rules become, the more stories proliferate about circumventing them. During the first centuries C.E., the legal culture of the empire was gradually shifting from a variegated patchwork of local and imperial jurisdictions toward an ideal of universal law. Much remains to be learned about how this complex and haphazard process affected the inhabitants of the Greco-Roman oikoumene in lived experience. The fictional trial scenes present distorted reflections and composite sketches rather than direct evidence of substantive and procedural laws under the Roman Empire. The novels of Chariton, Achilles Tatius, and Heliodorus, with their evident fascination with the life of the law, can only tell a portion of the story of the evolution of how Greeks used, subverted, and reinforced the evolving playbook of the Roman imperial fora.

The novelists' interest in trials is easily explained by the educational culture with its great emphasis on rhetoric, but that is only part of the picture. Hypothetical and melodramatic legal dilemmas in Greek and Roman rhetorical education fostered the habit of ingenuity at outwitting opponents. Performance mattered more than substance. Even when the Roman conceptualization of crime and punishment seems to lie under the surface of the trial scenes, the Greek novels studiously avoid directly engaging with Roman law, and use instead an oblique approach that privileges personal virtue as defined within and by Greek culture. The Byzantine scholar, Photius, clearly recognized this dynamic in the fictional narratives with which he was familiar: heroes are exonerated because of their paideia, while villains are ultimately punished because they lack self-control. In this sense, the trial scenes themselves are not about law at all, but about morality and virtue. The 'contest of narratives' (ἀγών λόγων), a template deeply embedded Greek thought, provided the structure for the demonstration of personal character through rhetoric alone. The main narrative that leads up to the trial, on the other hand, elaborates the kind of theoretical scenarios that generated innovative interpretations of existing laws, particularly the laws of Augustus on adultery, which were particularly apt for a literary genre extolling an ideal of symmetrical and mutual love culminating in matrimony. Embedded within a larger narrative, the contest of speeches in the courtroom becomes consequential rather than pure intellectual gamesmanship. Even when the trial scenes devolve into rhetorical ostentation, the narrative arc of the novel sustains the pretense that events in the courtroom matter. Something real is at stake: punishment of the wicked, the reward of the innocent, and the happy ending in love and marriage.

The trials of the Greek novels exhibit a revitalized interest not only in the debates, but more importantly, in the psychological dynamics that provided the context for those debates to take place. The phenomenon of the extended, literary depiction of courtroom scenes addressed Greek audiences' interest in peering behind the scenes of the operation of the law courts of the Roman Empire. Detailed narratives in the Greek language about trials began to circulate beyond the courts themselves during the first three centuries C.E. The most well-known to us are early Christian texts, yet there were others as well, such as the so-called Acts of the Alexandrian Martyrs, a collection of semi-fictional documents surrounding the ongoing stasis between the Greek and Jewish communities of Alexandria.

Over the course of the Roman Empire, the mechanisms for rendering justice moved from public spaces and into the controlled spaces of the magistrate's chambers. As punishments concomitantly became more spectacular, there arose an audience for reports and then narratives that purported to reveal what really occurred in the inner sanctum of the magistrate's tribunal.

Once we start from the point that the trials are works of fiction, it is established that every detail of the narrative reflects a decision by the author. In order to create the illusion of reality, the authors include details drawn from the world, either experienced directly or mediated through books. Authenticating statements aside, the novelists make no commitment to historical accuracy. The world created in the novels is an artificial construct, but the readers' engagement with this world tells us something about what they were ready to believe, at least temporarily. The outlines of the story world had to have been recognizable to contemporary readers in order to create an effect of verisimilitude. Given the fragmentary nature of what has survived antiquity, we can piece together a general semblance of that reality by drawing upon other types of sources: in this study of the trial scenes, sources related to the world of the law, both Greek and Roman.

In the novels, trials are depicted as entertainment for the masses. In the courtroom, knowledge of the law is less important than oratorical performance. The technicalities of the law—rules of order, evidentiary procedures, jurisdiction of officials, statutes, precedents—are less important than the spectacle of trying innocent heroes for dreadful crimes and even more dreadful punishments. The formalities of the law set the stage for the moment when something extraordinary will be exhibited for all to see. The reader is expected to share the same reactions as the trial's fictional spectators: not necessarily to decide upon what is expedient or just, but to gaze with pity, wonder, astonishment, and delight.

Certain general facts emerge from this study. First of all, trials provide the ideal occasion for the novelist to flaunt his mastery of the techniques of rhetoric. The speeches in the trial scenes support the position that rhetoric was alive and well under the empire, and people continued to find entertainment value in watching the staged conflict between combatants who used words as their weapons. The frequency of speeches—both the lengthy speeches presented in *oratio recta* as well as indirectly narrated speeches—suggests that imperial audiences expected at least one pair of speeches in any courtroom scene. Even when Chariton takes pains to specify that the procedure of Theron was a summary interrogation, a distinctly different procedure from the trial of Chaereas, Theron nevertheless delivers a speech-length response to the interrogator's question. In a number of scenes, the elision of the second speech always spells mortal danger for the hero: Chaereas is condemned in absentia to crucifixion and Cnemon is denied the opportunity to make his defense in court. Speeches are the essence of the trial scenes and the ability to speak in court is critical for survival—and victory.

Another commonality to be found among the trial scenes is that the narrative of the crime almost always precedes the narrative of the trial. That is, the reader first is told of some injury, mistake, or plot which sets the judicial proceedings in motion. This may seem an obvious point, but it is different from the experience of the reader of, for example, isolated speeches of the Attic orators. In orations, the speaker relates what had happened prior to the courtroom or assembly proceedings in the course of his speech. The narrative is subordinated within a broader rhetorical framework, the primary aim of which is to win a majority of votes. Such narrations are immediately suspect; in the interest of persuasion, orators emphasize some facts and, presumably, suppress others. The reader of an oration must reconstruct the scenario of the crime through the highly biased account of only one, or sometimes two partisans to the dispute. Even with the *controversiae*, where both sides of a case are represented, the facts of the case are presented in a skeletal form. The readers of the novels, however, do not have to work so hard: the authors fully develop the circumstantial background of the trials. Seldom is there any ambiguity about who is in the right and who is in the wrong. For example, in Chariton's novel, it is clear from the beginning that Theron the pirate is guilty. Similarly, we know that Charicleia has been innocently entrapped by the conspiracy of Arsace and Cybele. There are many other examples of this pattern.

The point of the trial scene is to manipulate and confound readerly expectations with surprising twists and turns: in other words, to create paradox. When the readers know the truth of the events preceding the trial, they gain a perspective on the trustworthiness of the speakers. Heliodorus undermines the anticipated conclusion in the Athenian trials and in the trial of Theagenes by postponing the revelation of key information or by reintroducing long lost minor characters, such as Thisbe and Charicles, as critical actors in trial scenes. For the most part, however, the narrative contextualizes the rhetorical moment; although the speeches in the trial scenes exhibit the techniques of other rhetorical works, they are not really rhetorical works per se. That is, one cannot extricate them, even the most complex and fully developed ones, such as those in Achilles Tatius' novel, from their context and hold them up as stand-alone specimens of rhetoric. The contextualization of speeches and the ironic play on the differing degrees of knowledge among the characters would seem to offer an opportunity for commentary on the efficacy of rhetoric; however, the overall impression one gets from studying the trial scenes is that they end in ambiguity as often as they come to definite closure. The spectators' emotional reactions of surprise, pity, and jubilation guide the reader's response to the events portrayed. The larger narrative shifts the reader's attention to other objects: the pathos of the protagonists, the unscrupulousness of the villains, the unpredictability but ultimate beneficence of Tyche and Dike, Fortune and Justice.

If trial scenes highlight larger issues of morality and justice, the way the trial scenes are constructed reveals something of the legal consciousness of authors and audiences. Photius had a simple view of justice in the novels: it is the punishment of the wicked and the vindication of the innocent. It is important to distinguish between the verdict of the trial and the end of the plot. The verdict is the vote that occurs subsequent to the speeches in the trial, whereas the end is what ultimately happens to the characters within the larger narrative. On a purely functional level, the novelists' strategy is to perpetuate the dramatic conflict as long as possible; a trial scene in which both sides presented their cases and a judge then rendered a mutually satisfactory decision would stop the plot dead in its tracks. Therefore, the novelists use the unexpected event, the insoluble dilemma, or the supernatural phenomenon to disrupt trials and sustain the dramatic tension long after the characters leave the courtroom. The correspondence between the verdict of the court and the resolution of the dramatic conflict sheds light on the question of whether the audience actually believed in the efficacy of the courts. It is worthwhile to review whether Photius' characterization of the genre is congruent with the twelve trial scenes we have looked at:

1. Syracuse v. Chaereas (C 1,4-6). In this trial, both the verdict and the end are just. Despite Chaereas' best efforts to force the court to punish him, the hero is acquitted of accidentally causing the death of Callirhoe. In this trial, the system works.

2. Chaereas v. Theron (C 3,4). Again, both the verdict and the end are just; but it is the moral inverse of the trial of Chaereas. Despite Theron's best efforts to persuade the court to let him off, the truth comes out and the villain is punished for kidnapping Callirhoe. The system once again works.

3. Dionysius v. Mithridates (C 5,4-9). This trial, which takes place in a very different juridical venue from the first two, nevertheless has the same outcome. Both the verdict and the end are just: Mithridates is acquitted, because he never actually seduced Callirhoe. In the end, he returns to his province lavishly rewarded by the king. Yet, this ending is not as morally satisfying as the first two trials. The reader knows that Mithridates was in love with Callirhoe and that he planned to use Chaereas as a pawn in his scheme to undermine Dionysius' legal strategy. In this respect he would seem to fit the role of villain; however, by virtue of his opposition to Dionysius, Chaereas' rival, and because he was instrumental in (almost) reuniting Chaereas and Callirhoe, he can be seen as a neither good nor bad, but as an instrumental character. The end of this trial seems to reinforce the image of a Persian Empire where the operative values are loyalty to the king and the king's lavish patronage of his satraps.

4. Dionysius v. Chaereas (C 5,10-6,2). This trial has no formal verdict. The dilemma of Callirhoe's simultaneous marriage to two men, both of whom have legitimate claims to be her husband, poses a situation which is too difficult to solve. The trial is aborted when war erupts, and so the competition shifts from the arena of rational discourse in the courtroom and moves to the battlefield, where chance and valor figure more prominently. In other words, justice is realized through deeds, not words. Although the Persian king awards Callirhoe to Dionysius as a prize of valor, Chaereas wins her when he captures the Persian harem, thus proving himself on the battlefield rather than in the courtroom. He is a general worthy of being the son-in-law of the famous Hermocrates of Syracuse.

5. Thersander v. Melite and Clitophon (AT 7,7-16). Achilles Tatius constructs a kaleidoscopic legal case. On the one hand, the anticipated verdict would be just: Clitophon is guilty of adultery, the original charge, and so deserves to be punished. However, because the charge shifts in the middle of the trial from adultery to murder, a crime of which he is innocent, the verdict is unjust. He deserves to be punished, but not for the crime of killing Leucippe, thus contradicting the generic convention that the hero is by definition 'blameless'. The situation in this case is too complicated and leaves the room for profound ambiguity regarding the hero's morality and the justice of the ending.

6. Thersander v. Priest of Artemis and Associates (AT 8,7-15). In the second trial, both verdict and end are just in the sense that the outcomes are favorable to the protagonists. Melite, and thereby Clitophon, are exonerated for adultery. Leucippe's ordeal proves she is a virgin. Nevertheless, there is a sense that the verdict of Melite's ordeal is not exactly right: Melite was an adulteress, in fact and in intention, but survives her ordeal, thereby not only saving herself, but also vindicating Clitophon's ostensible chastity. Both get away on a legalistic technicality.

7. Aristippus v. Cnemon (H 1,9-14). The verdict of this trial is unjust, but ultimately justice prevails in the end. The marriage of Cnemon to the daughter of Nausicles comes only after a complicated series of turnabouts. In one of these, Thisbe, Cnemon's seductress, is stabbed by a bandit who mistakes her for his own girlfriend. Cnemon's final discovery of the truth that will save his father is fortuitous, but too late to alter the outcome of the demos' vote.

8. Kinsmen of Demaenete v. Aristippus (H 1,14-17; 2,8-9). The result of this trial is similar to the trial of Cnemon: the court's condemnation of Aristippus is utterly unjust—even tragic— the result of the opportunism of devious women. Aristippus is an innocent victim of the schemes of one hetaira to gain revenge on another. Demaenete, the originator of the plot to seduce Cnemon, thwarts a trial by committing suicide. As far as Aristippus' ultimate end, the reader is left in the dark. He is simply dropped from the narrative, as is the character of Arsinoe, the flute-girl who instigated the trial.

9. Arsace v. Charicleia (H 8,8-15). The conviction of Charicleia by the Persian court for poisoning Cybele is unjust, but paradoxically in accordance with Charicleia's wishes. Her glorious rescue from the flames represents an upheaval of the court's mistaken verdict and sentence.

10. Charicleia v. Hydaspes (H 10,9-17). The verdict confirms what the narrative had indicated would be its telos. Charicleia is recognized as Hydaspes' daughter. The truth in this trial is demonstrated through logical argumentation.

11. Charicles v. Theagenes (H 4,17-21; 10,34-38). Since all shreds of juridical or formal proceedings dissolve into a tearful recognition scene once Charicleia reveals herself to Charicles, it is impossible to speak of a formal verdict. The end, however, is just: Charicles is reconciled with his daughter and Theagenes proves that he is worthy of being her husband.

Aside from the dynamics of eros, one of the foremost concerns of the Greek ideal romance is certainly love's dark side, adultery. In Chariton's novel, a husband's fear that Callirhoe has been seduced triggers not one, but two, trials. Chaereas accidentally 'kills' Callirhoe when he believes that he will find her in flagrante delicto with her lover. Likewise, her second husband becomes paranoid that Mithridates is plotting against his marriage, thus leading him into the tangled politics in the Persian Empire. In Achilles Tatius' novel, a cuckolded husband initiates a complex lawsuit encompassing not only the propriety of Clitophon's relationship with Melite, a married woman, but also the purity of Leucippe, his fiancée.

In Heliodorus' novel, neither Charicleia nor Theagenes comes close to being implicated in unchastity, let alone adultery. Only in relation to the patriarchal figures in the novel, Aristippus, Oroondates, and Hydaspes, does adultery come into play. Demaenete is painted as an adulteress, even though her passion for Cnemon is never sexually consummated. Arsace represents an extreme version of the adulteress who, like Demaenete, is frustrated in her attempts to seduce a young man (Theagenes). Both would-be adulteresses commit suicide before their husbands are able to bring them to justice.

The irony of Charicleia's virginity ordeal in Meroe is that in order to reclaim her patrimony and save her life, she must prove that she is the daughter of Hydaspes, and thereby implicatinh her mother in a potential charge of adultery. The cause of her separation from her birth parents was her mother's fear that the infant's unusually light-skinned appearance would be misunderstood as evidence of adultery. Charicleia's identity—her Greek name, her Greek education, and Greek manners—are the result of Persinna's initial decision to place marital fidelity over maternal instinct, a choice similar to Callirhoe's. Yet, as Charicleia's lawsuit reveals, there was no adultery at all. The theory of maternal impression explains away all suspicion about the queen's honor.

Narrative allows the reader to peer behind the veil that excludes feminine speech from the courtroom. Certain female characters are depicted as orators in their own right. We see them deliberating, arguing, and defending themselves against the allegations of adultery that swirl around them. In Chariton's first trial scene, we have seen how Callirhoe is left speechless (more specifically, comatose) after Chaereas violently accuses her of adultery. When she is a slave and discovers she is pregnant, she is presented as deliberating aloud to herself in the privacy her bedroom over whether to abort the child conceived on her wedding night to her beloved Chaereas, or to pass it off as the son of another man in order to establish his freeborn status. When a similar accusation brings her to the king's courtroom in Babylon, she is reluctant to appear in the court for fear of incriminating herself by simply showing her face in public. With Melite, Achilles Tatius has created a female character who takes initiative in arranging her own re-marriage, yet in the courtroom she is represented by speakers-for-hire. Her apologia is set in the bedroom of her home and delivered to her husband as if to a judge. In the courtroom, even her lawyers' speeches are elided from the trial narrative. In the penultimate trial of the *Aethiopica,* Charicleia recruits the support of the advisors of the king of Meroe and then brings a lawsuit against the king himself. Yet, on only one occasion, the trial of Melite, are the accusations of adultery factually valid. In other trials, the mere suspicion of adultery drives characters toward the courtroom, even when the charges seem to deal with entirely other matters, such as murder, malfeasance, and parricide. The novelists show that even the suspicion of sexual misbehavior brings a cascade of other problems.

Magic plays a role in the trials. Mithridates' carefully calculated theatrics enable him to orchestrate the 'miraculous' reappearance of the supposedly dead Chaereas into the king's courtroom in Babylon (trial 3). In Memphis (trial 9), Charicleia escapes the flames of her execution with the aid of a magical gemstone. In both of these instances, the magical illusion is laid bare for the readers. The ordeals of the cave of the syrinx and the water of the Styx (trial 6) that resolve the tangle of legal claims at the end of Achilles Tatius' novel remain semi-mysterious, even though the reader is given their respective aetiologies. The optics of the ordeals reestablish a sense of awe and majesty to the unfolding of justice after the gamesmanship of the courtroom fails to accomplish anything other than the perpetuation of conflict.

Most of the trials result in justice, at least as measured by Photius' criterion that the heroes are vindicated and the villains are punished. In four cases, the verdict affirms the narrative's construction of the just ending (trials 1, 2, 6, 11). In another four cases, three from Heliodorus' novel, the verdicts are clearly unjust (trials 5, 7, 8, 9). In the trials of Aristippus and Cnemon in democratic Athens, justice backfires in the trials. Athens represents a place where the legal processes run amok: as Theron points out to his fellow pirates, in Athens, even if the plaintiffs drop their suit, it is impossible to escape the magistrates and the demos (C 1,10,5). In Achilles Tatius, the justice of the trials is not by the civic culture of Ephesus, but by the participants' verbal jousting. Their gaming of the process itself presents to the reader many twists where the outcome is uncertain. In the end, the ordeals vindicate the novel's heroine, as well as her rival, Melite, who functions as a secondary heroine.

In a few instances, trials are derailed and end without a formal verdict (trials 4, 8, 11) and instead are settled by a *paterfamilias*: Hermocrates stops the trial of Chaereas for murder in order to give Callirhoe a funeral and Hydaspes, together with Charicles, exonerates Theagenes of the charge of bride theft and legitimizes his marriage to Charicleia. In contrast, the efforts of Cnemon's father to seek resolution to the crises in his oikos fail when he dutifully seeks justice from the Athenian courts. As just one member among the elite, he is disempowered by the democratic system of justice. Likewise, Dionysius, the leading citizen of Miletus as well as the ostensible father of Callirhoe's infant son, fails when he brings his suspicions about the integrity of his home and family to the attention of the Persian judicial system. Two of the trials—the most complex in terms of their circumstances and argumentation—have ambiguous endings. The trial of Mithridates (3) and the trial of Melite and Clitophon (5) are masterpieces of narrative ingenuity, yet result in verdicts contrary to the protagonists' interests.

Finally, we see characters falling victim to the law when they try to circumvent or resist the system. Chaereas is the best illustration of this attitude. Passively brought into the Babylonian court, he is disadvantaged by his lack of knowledge of the law; nevertheless, he fights for his rights. When the king proves to be dilatory in pronouncing the final verdict, Chaereas takes matters into his own hands and joins the Egyptian rebels in their war against the Persian king. Similarly, Cnemon (trial 7) becomes involved in a legal problem not of his own making. Even his father, Aristippus, a law-abiding citizen, is victimized by the legal process and loses everything (trial 8). Another father, Charicles, tries to use the law to win back his daughter and fails in his first attempt to lead a militia to rescue her from her abductor (trial 11). He finally is reunited with his daughter just in time for her to leave his control and marry the man who abducted her. The dilemma of the daughter with two fathers is moot as the couple is wed and elevated to the position of priesthood of the Sun and Moon in Meroe, thereby restoring the majesty of the law—that is, the law of an empire that is governed through virtue.

The Greek novels are part of a much larger discourse about the evolving relationship between Roman law and the cultural memory of the how legal institutions functioned in autonomous Greek poleis. We see trials set both in Greek cities and in imperial capitals, each having positive and negative traits. This mixed view of the merits of local versus imperial justice reflects a deliberately non-committal stance. The process whereby Roman law came to set the standards for litigation in the Roman Empire was slow. Individuals strategically adapted to the gaps created by a pluralistic legal environment. This understanding of law pervades the Greek novels. Outright critique of the Roman system is rare; when it appears, it is very carefully disguised in Persian dress or phrased in philosophical adages about tyranny and the necessity for the ruler to embody the virtues of self-control and willingness to heed the advice of the council and the people. Differentials in social class are relatively muted in the trials in the Greek novels. Most trials involve high-ranking, wealthy individuals—occasionally mistaken for slaves and beggars. The trials in the novels emphasize legal status and social identity, and restore the protagonists to their rightful, innate, superior social status.

We return again to the question of how the novels' authors and audiences understood the ongoing transformation of law in the eastern provinces of the Roman Empire. We have seen examples of the types of legal consciousness that

Ewick and Silbey identified in their sociological analysis of modern attitudes to the law. The law is presented as majestic, hierarchical and separate from 'normal' life in scenes where emphasis is placed on the arrangement of the courtroom, such as the court in Babylon (trial 3) and the pavilion outside the walls of Meroe (trials 10 and 11) where the grandeur of imperial power is evoked most distinctively. Chariton's depiction of the two trials in Syracuse magnifies the setting by emphasizing the inclusion of all the citizen body in the audience to the spectacle of Theron's execution. In the portrayal of the assembly of Athens (trial 7), Heliodorus seems to be following Chariton; however, in that case, the size of the audience yields a confusing and erroneous verdict. The novels present ample instances of the consciousness that the law is a game. This appears most clearly in Achilles Tatius' second trial (trial 6), where the brinksmanship between competing teams of advocates escalates to the point where it seems the game will never end. The ordeals thus serve a dual purpose: they function as the final die roll to settle a bet while at the same time reinforcing the boundary between the sacred and the profane by delegating the power to pronounce a verdict to the divine realm. Mithridates (trial 3) is the ultimate inside player: he knows the rules of Persian court etiquette, whereas Dionysius has the tables turned against him and is at the mercy of a foreign legal culture. In contrast, Charicleia, also a Greek in a foreign land (trial 10), quickly learns the rules of the game by enlisting the support of the native sages—and, more significantly, her mother, the queen. Against all odds, she skillfully checkmates the king and wins her prize: the acknowledgment of her true parents.

The novels present a panorama of impressions of how individuals might navigate the legal system. The study of imaginary trial scenes contributes to our picture of the life of the law, broadly defined. The perception of the law—law's imaginative context—influenced the attitudes and expectations of the people who used as well as avoided the procedures of the courtroom. There must have been some more or less stable reference point in reality or in the general legal consciousness that inspired these imaginary trials. The novels' readers, some of whom had an education that emphasized the importance of rhetoric and exposed them to the practicalities of law, had some preconception of what a trial entailed.

With the novels of Chariton, Achilles Tatius, and Heliodorus, we have three snapshots of the evolution of legal consciousness at three discrete points in time: a generation or two after the Augustan legislation in the first century C.E., a moment between Hadrian's promotion of Hellenism and Caracalla's extension of citizenship to all inhabitants of his empire, and a view from the aftermath of the Severan legal reforms and perhaps also Constantine's efforts to revise and revive the moral legislation of Augustus. In this light, the trials in the novels shed light on part of the complex evolution of perceptions, discourses, and realities of law, and enhance our understanding of the perception of justice in the legally pluralistic society of the Roman Empire.

Bibliography

Texts, Translations, and Commentaries

Chariton

Anonymous 1764. *Chariton: The Loves of Chaereas and Callirrhoe*, English translation, 2 vols., London: T. Becket & P. A. De Hondt.
Blake, W. E. 1938. *Charitonis Aphrodisiensis de Chaereas et Callirhoe Amatoriarum Narrationum Libri Octo*, Oxford: Clarendon Press.
Goold, G. P. (ed.), 1995. *Chariton: Callirhoe, Loeb Classical Library*, Cambridge, Mass.: Harvard University Press.
Lucke, C. and K.-H. Schäfer. 1985. *Chariton: Kallirhoe*, Leipzig: Reclam.
Molinié, G. 1979. *Chariton: Le roman de Chairéas et Callirhoé, Collection des universités de France,* Paris: Belles lettres.
Omitowoju, R. 2011. 'Chariton: *Callirhoe*', in: *Greek Fiction: Callirhoe, Daphnis and Chloe, Letters of Chion*, H. Morales (ed.), New York: Penguin, 3-134.
Plepelits, K. 1976. *Chariton von Aphrodisias: Kallirhoe.* Stuttgart: Anton Hiersemann.
Reardon, B. P. 1989. 'Chariton: *Chaereas and Callirhoe*', in: *Collected Ancient Greek Novels*, B. P. Reardon (ed.), Berkeley and Los Angeles: University of California Press, 17-124.
Trzaskoma, S. 2010. *Two Novels from Ancient Greece: Chariton's Callirhoe and Xenophon of Ephesos' An Ephesian Story: Anthia and Habrocomes*, Indianapolis: Hackett.

Achilles Tatius

Garnaud, J.-P. 1991. *Achille Tatius d'Alexandrie: Le Roman de Leucippé et Clitophon*, Paris: Les Belles Lettres.
Gaselee, S. and E. H. Warmington. 1969. *Achilles Tatius, Loeb Classical Library*, rev. ed., Cambridge, Mass.: Harvard University Press.
Plepelits, K. 1980. *Achilleus Tatios: Leukippe und Kleitophon*, Stuttgart: Anton Hiersemann.
Vilborg, E. (ed.), 1955. *Achilles Tatius: Leucippe and Clitophon, Vol. 1: Text*, Stockholm: Almqvist & Wiksell.
— (ed.), 1962. *Achilles Tatius, Leucippe and Clitophon, Vol 2: Commentary*, Stockholm: Almqvist & Wiksell.
Whitmarsh, T. 2001. *Achilles Tatius: Leucippe and Clitophon*, Oxford and New York: Oxford University Press.
Winkler, J. J. 1989. 'Achilles Tatius: *Leucippe and Clitophon*', in: *Collected Ancient Greek Novels*, B. P. Reardon (ed.), Berkeley and Los Angeles: University of California Press, 171-284.

Heliodorus

Bekkero, I. 1855. *Heliodori Aethiopicorum libri decem,* Leipzig: Teubner.

Colonna, A. 1938. *Heliodori Aethiopica, Scriptores graeci et latini*, Rome: Typis Regiae officinae polygraphicae.

Morgan, J. R. 1978. 'A Commentary on the Ninth and Tenth Books of Heliodoros' *Aithiopika*', Ph.D. dissertation, Oxford University.

— 1989. 'Heliodorus: *An Ethiopian Story*', in *Collected Ancient Greek Novels*, B. P. Reardon (ed.), Berkeley and Los Angeles: University of California Press, 349-588.

Rattenbury, R. M. and T. W. Lumb. 1935. *Héliodore: Les Éthiopiques (Théagène et Chariclée)*, 3 vols., Paris: Les Belles Lettres.

Works Cited

Aldrete, G. S. 1999. *Gestures and Acclamations in Ancient Rome*, Baltimore: The Johns Hopkins University Press.

Alföldy, G. 1974. 'The Crisis of the Third Century as Seen by Contemporaries', *GRBS* 15, 89-111.

Allen, D. S. 2000. *The World of Prometheus: The Politics of Punishing in Democratic Athens*, Princeton: Princeton University Press.

Altheim, F. 1948-1950. 'Helios und Heliodoros von Emesa', *Literatur und Gesellschaft im ausgehenden Altertum*, Halle/Saale: M. Niemeyer, 93-124.

Alvares, J. 1993. 'The Journey of Observation in Chariton's Chaereas and Callirhoe', Ph.D. dissertation, University of Texas at Austin.

— 2000. 'A Hidden *Magus* in Chariton's *Chaireas and Callirhoe*', *Hermes* 128, 383-384.

Anderson, G. 1982. *Eros Sophistes: Ancient Novelists at Play, American Classical Studies, 9,* Chico, Calif.: Scholars Press.

— 1984. *Ancient Fiction: The Novel in the Graeco-Roman World*, London: Croom Helm.

— 1994. *Sage, Saint, and Sophist: Holy Men and Their Associates in the Early Roman Empire*, London and New York: Routledge.

Anderson, J. G. C. 1927. 'Augustan Edicts from Cyrene', *JRS* 17, 33-48.

Anderson, M. J. 1997. 'The 'Sophrosyne' of Persinna and the Romantic Strategy of Heliodorus' *Aethiopica*', *CPh* 92, 303-322.

Ando, C. 2000. *Imperial Ideology and Provincial Loyalty in the Roman Empire*, Berkeley and Los Angeles: University of California Press.

— 2011a. 'Law and the Landscape of Empire', in: S. Benoist, A. Daguet-Gagey and C. Hoët-Van Cauwenberghe (eds.), *Figures d'empire, fragments de mémoire: pouvoirs et identités dans le monde romain impérial (IIe s. av. n. è.-VIe s. de n. è.)*, Villeneuve-d'Ascq: Presses universitaires du Septentrion, 25-47.

— 2011b. *Law, Language and Empire*, Philadelphia: University of Pennsylvania Press.

— 2012. *Imperial Rome AD 193 to 284: The Critical Century, The Edinburgh History of Ancient Rome*, Edinburgh: Edinburgh University Press.

Arjava, A. 1998. 'Paternal Power in Late Antiquity', *JRS* 88, 147-165.

Arnott, W. G. 1994. 'Longus, Natural History, and Realism', in: J. A. Tatum (ed.), *The Search for the Ancient Novel*, Baltimore: The Johns Hopkins University Press, 199-215.

Aubert, J.-J. 2010. 'The Setting and Staging of Christian Trials', in: F. de Angelis (ed.), *Spaces of Justice in the Roman World*, Leiden and Boston: Brill, 277-309.
Bablitz, L. E. 2007. *Actors and Audience in the Roman Courtroom*, London and New York: Routledge.
Baker, A. J. E. 2012. 'Doing Things with Words: The Force of Law and Magic in Apuleius' *Metamorphoses*', *Trends in Classics* 4, 352-362.
Bal, M. 1985. *Narratology: Introduction to the Theory of Narrative*. 2d ed., Toronto: University of Toronto Press. Original edition, *De theorie van vertellen en verhalen* 2d ed., Muiderberg: Coutinho 1980.
Balot, R. K. 1998. 'Foucault, Chariton, and the Masculine Self', *Helios* 25, 139-168.
Barkan, I. 1935. 'Capital Punishment in Ancient Athens', Ph.D. dissertation, University of Chicago.
Barker, E. T. E. 2009. *Entering the Agon: Dissent and Authority in Homer, Historiography and Tragedy*, Oxford and New York: Oxford University Press.
Barr, W. 1987. *The Satires of Persius*, Liverpool: Francis Cairns.
Bartlett, R. 1986. *Trial by Fire and Water: The Medieval Judicial Ordeal*, Oxford: Clarendon Press.
Bartsch, S. 1989. *Decoding the Ancient Novel: The Reader and the Role of Description in Heliodorus and Achilles Tatius*, Princeton: Princeton University Press.
Bartsch, W. 1934. *Der Charitonroman und die Historiographie*, Leipzig: C. & E. Vogel.
Barwick, K. 1928. 'Die Gliederung der Narratio in der rhetorischen Theorie und ihre Bedeutung für die Geschichte des antiken Romans', *Hermes* 63, 261-287.
Baslez, M.-F. 1992. 'De l'histoire au roman: la Perse de Chariton', in: M.-F. Baslez, P. Hoffmann and M. Trédé (eds.), *Le monde du roman grec*, Paris: Presses de l'École normale supérieure, 199-212.
Bauman, R. A. 1996. *Crime and Punishment in Ancient Rome*, London and New York: Routledge.
Beard, M. 1993. 'Looking (Harder) for Roman Myth: Dumézil, Declamation and the Problems of Definition', in: F. Graf (ed.), *Mythos in mythenloser Gesellschaft: Das Paradigme Roms*, Stuttgart: B.G. Teubner, 44-64.
Benton, L. 2002. *Law and Colonial Cultures: Legal Regimes in World History, 1400-1900*, Cambridge and New York: Cambridge University Press.
Bergman, P. and M. Asinow 1996. *Reel Justice: The Courtroom Goes to the Movies*, Kansas City: Andrews and McMeel.
Bers, V. 1985. 'Dikastic *Thorubos*', in: P. Cartledge and D. Harvey (eds.), *Crux: Essays in History Presented to G. E. M. de Ste. Croix*, London: Imprint Academic, 1-15.
— 2003. *Demosthenes, Speeches 50-59*, Austin: University of Texas Press.
Bertrand, J.-M. 1988. 'Les *boucôloi* ou le monde a l'envers', *REA* 110, 139-149.
Billault, A. 1979. 'Approche du problème de l' ἔκφρασις dans les romans grecs', *BAGB*, 109-204.
— 1989. 'De l'histoire au roman: Hermocrate de Syracuse', *REG* 102, 540-548.
— 1990. 'L'inspiration des ἐκφράσεις d'oeuvres d'art chez les romanciers grecs', *Rhetorica* 8, 153-160.
— 1991. *La création romanesque dans la littérature grecque à l'époque impériale*, Paris: Presses Universitaires de France.
Birchall, J. 1996. 'The Lament as a Rhetorical Feature in the Greek Novel', *Groningen Colloquia on the Novel* 7, 1-17.

Bloomer, W. M. 1997. 'Schooling in Persona: Imagination and Subordination in Roman Education', *ClAnt* 16, 57-78.

Boatwright, M. T. 2000. *Hadrian and the Cities of the Roman Empire*, Princeton: Princeton University Press.

Bodel, J. 2010. 'Kangaroo Courts: Displaced Justice in the Roman Novel', in: F. de Angelis (ed.), *Spaces of Justice in the Roman World*, Leiden and Boston: Brill, 311-329.

Bonner, S. F. 1949. *Roman Declamation in the Late Republic and Early Empire*, Liverpool: University Press of Liverpool.

Borgogno, A. 1971. 'Menandro in Caritone', *RFIC* 99, 257-263.

Bornecque, H. 1902. *Les Déclamations et les déclamateurs d'après Sénéque le Père*, Lille: Université de Lille.

Bourdieu, P. 1977. *Outline of a Theory of Practice,* translated by R. Nice, *Cambridge Studies in Social and Cultural Anthropology* 16, Cambridge and New York: Cambridge University Press. Original edition, *Esquisse d'une théorie de la pratique, précédé de trois études d'ethnologie kabyle*, Switzerland: Librairie Droz, 1972.

Boureau, A. 1989. 'Propositions pour une histoire restreinte des mentalités', *Annales: Histoires, Sciences Sociales* 44, 1491-1504.

Bowersock, G. W. 1994. *Fiction as History: Nero to Julian, Sather Classical Lectures 58*, Berkeley and Los Angeles: University of California Press.

— 1995. *Martyrdom and Rome*, Cambridge and New York: Cambridge University Press.

Bowie, E. L. 1977. 'The Novel and the Real World', in: B. P. Reardon (ed.), *Erotica Antiqua: Acta of the International Conference on the Ancient Novel Held in Bangor, Wales, 12th-17th July 1976,* Bangor, Wales: n.p., 91-96.

— 1982. 'The Importance of Sophists', *YClS* 27, 29-59.

— 1989. 'The Greek Novel', in: P. E. Easterling and B. M. W. Knox (eds.), *The Cambridge History of Classical Literature*, Cambridge and New York: Cambridge University Press, 123-149.

— 1994. 'The Readership of Greek Novels in the Ancient World', in: J. A. Tatum (ed.), *The Search for the Ancient Novel*, Baltimore: The Johns Hopkins University Press, 435-459.

— 1996. 'Heliodorus (4)', in: S. Hornblower and A. Spawforth (eds.), *Oxford Classical Dictionary*, Oxford and New York: Oxford University Press, 676.

— 2002. 'The Chronology of the Earlier Greek Novels since B. E. Perry: Revisions and Precisions', *AncNarr* 2, 47-63.

Bowie, E. L. and S. J. Harrison 1993. 'The Romance of the Novel', *JRS* 83, 159-178.

Bradley, K. R. 1994. *Slavery and Society at Rome*, Cambridge and New York: Cambridge University Press.

Bremmer, J. 2008. 'Priestly Personnel of the Ephesian Artemision: Anatolian, Persian, Greek, and Roman Aspects', in: B. Dignas and K. Trampedach (eds.), *Practitioners of the Divine: Greek Priests and Religious Officials from Homer to Heliodorus*, Washington, DC and Cambridge, Mass.: Center for Hellenic Studies and Harvard University Press, 37-53.

Brethes, R. 2006. 'Le discours du prêtre chez Achille Tatius, (VIII,9): une déconstruction de la *paideia*', in: B. Pouderon and J. Peigney (eds.), *Discours et débats dans l'ancien roman: actes du colloque de Tours, 21-23 octobre 2004*, Lyon: Maison de l'Orient et de la Méditerranée - Jean Pouilloux, 177-190.

— 2007. *De l'idéalisme au réalisme: une étude du comique dans le roman grec,* Cardo, Salerno: Helios.

Briant, P. 2002. *From Cyrus to Alexander: A History of the Persian Empire*, translated by P. T. Daniels, Winona Lake, Indiana: Eisenbrauns. Original edition, *Histoire de l'Empire Perse de Cyrus à Alexandre*, Paris: Fayard, 1996.

Brooks, P. 2000. *Troubling Confessions*, Chicago: University of Chicago Press.

Brulé, P. 1978. *La piraterie crétoise hellénistique*, Paris: Les Belles Lettres.

Brunt, P. 1961. 'Charges of Provincial Maladministration under the Early Principate', *Historia* 10, 189-229.

Bryen, A. Z. 2012. 'Judging Empire: Courts and Culture in Rome's Eastern Provinces', *Law and History Review* 30, 771-811.

Buckland, W. W. 1908. *The Roman Law of Slavery: The Condition of the Slave in Private Law from Augustus to Justinian*, Cambridge: Cambridge University Press.

Bund, E. 1964. 'Iustitium', in: K. Ziegler, W. Sontheimer and A. F. v. Pauly (eds.), *Der Kleine Pauly: Lexikon der Antike. Auf der Grundlage von Pauly's Realencyclopädie der classischen Altertumswissenschaft*, Stuttgart: A. Druckenmüller, 24.

Bushala, E. W. 1968. 'Torture of Non-Citizens in Homicide Investigations', *GRBS* 9, 61-68.

Calder, W. M., III and J. M. R. Cormack (eds.), 1962. *Monumenta Asiae Minoris antiqua. 8 vols, Publications of the American Society for Archaeological Research in Asia Minor,* Manchester: Manchester University Press.

Calderini, A. 1913. *Caritone di Afrodisia: le avventure di Chaerea e Calliroe*, Turin: Fratelli Bocca.

— 1959. 'La ἐγγύησις matrimoniale nei romanzieri greci e nei papiri', *Aegyptus* 39, 29-39.

Callu, J.-P. 1984. 'Le jardin des supplices au bas-empire', *Du châtiment dans la cité: Supplices corporels et peine de mort dans le monde antique (Rome 9-11 novembre 1982)*, Rome: L'École française de Rome, 313-359.

Cameron, A. 2011. *The Last Pagans of Rome*, Oxford and New York: Oxford University Press.

Cantarella, E. 1991a. *I supplizi capitali in Grecia e Roma*, Milan: Rizzoli.

— 1991b. '*Moicheia*. Reconsidering a Problem', in: M. Gagarin (ed.), *Symposion 1990: Vorträge zur griechischen und hellenistischen Rechtsgeschichte (Pacific Grove, California, 24-26, September 1990)*, Köln: Böhlau, 289-296.

Capponi, L. 2010. 'Spaces of Justice in Roman Egypt', in: F. de Angelis (ed.), *Spaces of Justice in the Roman World*, Leiden and Boston: Brill, 251-276.

Carey, C. 1988. 'A Note on Torture in Athenian Homicide Cases', *Historia* 39, 241-245.

— (ed.) 1989. *Lysias: Selected Speeches, Cambridge Greek and Latin Classics*, Cambridge and New York: Cambridge University Press.

Cave, T. 1988. *Recognitions. A Study in Poetics*, Oxford: Clarendon Press.

Chaniotis, A. 1996. 'Conflicting Authorities: *Asylia* between Secular and Divine Law in the Classical and Hellenistic Poleis', *Kernos* 9, 65-86.

Chew, K. 2003. 'The Representation of Violence in the Greek Novels and Martyr Accounts', in: S. Panayotakis, M. Zimmerman and W. Keulen (eds.), *The Ancient Novel and Beyond*, Leiden: Brill, 129-141.

Chuvin, P. 1991. 'La date des *Éthiopiques* d'Héliodore', *Chronique des derniers païens*, Paris: Fayard, 321-325.

Cohen, D. 1983. *Theft in Athenian Law*, Munich: Beck.

— 1991. *Law, Sexuality, and Society: The Enforcement of Morals in Classical Athens,* Cambridge and New York: Cambridge University Press.

Coleman, K. M. 1990. 'Fatal Charades: Roman Executions Staged as Mythological Enactments', *JRS* 80, 44-73.

Coles, R. A. 1966. *Reports of Proceedings in Papyri, Papyrologica Bruxellensia 4*, Bruxelles: Fondation Égyptologique Reine Elisabeth.

Colin, J. 1965a. 'Apulée en Thessalie: fiction ou vérité', *Latomus* 24, 330-345.

— 1965b. *Les villes libres de l'Orient gréco-romain et l'envoi au supplice par acclamations populaires, Collections Latomus 82*, Brussells-Berchem: Latomus.

Colonna, A. 1950. 'L'assedio di Nisibis del 350 d. C. e la cronologia di Eliodoro Emiseno', *Athenaeum* 28, 79-87.

Connolly, S. 2010. *Lives Behind the Laws: The World of the Codex Hermogenianus*, Bloomington: Indiana University Press.

Connors, C. 2002. 'Chariton's Syracuse and Its Histories of Empire', *Ancient Narrative Supplement* 1, 12-26.

Corcoran, S. 1996. *The Empire of the Tetrarchs: Imperial Pronouncements and Government, AD 284-324*, Oxford and New York: Oxford University Press.

— 2006. 'Before Constantine', in: N. Lenski (ed.), *The Cambirdge Companion to the Age of Constantine*, Cambridge and New York: Cambridge University Press, 35-58.

Cover, R. M. 1983. 'Nomos and Narrative', *Harvard Law Review* 97.1, 4-64.

Cresci, L. R. 1978. 'La figura di Melite in Achille Tazio', *A&R* 23, 74-82.

Cribiore, R. 2001. *Gymnastics of the Mind: Greek Education in Hellenistic and Roman Egypt,* Princeton: Princeton University Press.

Crook, J. A. 1955. *Consilium Principis: Imperial Councils and Counsellors from Augustus to Diocletian*, Cambridge and New York: Cambridge University Press.

— 1967a. *Law and Life of Rome, 90 B.C. - A. D. 212*, Ithaca: Cornell University Press.

— 1967b. 'Patria Potestas', *CQ* 17, 113-122.

— 1995. *Legal Advocacy in the Roman World*, Ithaca, New York: Cornell University Press.

Csapo, E. and W. J. Slater 1995. *The Context of Ancient Drama*, Ann Arbor: University of Michigan Press.

Daube, D. 1972. 'The *lex Julia* Concerning Adultery', *The Irish Jurist* 7, 373-380.

de Angelis, F. 2010. 'The Emperor's Justice and Its Spaces in Rome and Italy', in: F. de Angelis (ed.), *Spaces of Justice in the Roman World*, Leiden and Boston: Brill, 127-159.

De Temmerman, K. 2002. 'Institutional Realia in Chariton's *Callirhoe:* Historical and Contemporary Elements', *Humanitas* 54, 165-187.

— 2009. 'Chaereas Revisited: Rhetorical Control in Chariton's 'Ideal' Novel *Callirhoe', CQ* N. S. 59 (1), 247-262.

— 2014. *Crafting Characters: Heroes and Heroines in the Ancient Greek Novel*, Oxford and New York: Oxford University Press.

Denvir, J. (ed.), 1996. *Legal Reelism: Movies as Legal Texts*, Urbana: University of Illinois Press.

Dmitriev, S. 2005. *City Government in Hellenistic and Roman Asia Minor*, Oxford and New York: Oxford University Press.

Dolin, K. 2007. *A Critical Introduction to Law and Literature*, Cambridge and New York: Cambridge University Press.

Doniger, W. 2000. *The Bedtrick: Tales of Sex and Masquerade*, Chicago: University of Chicago Press.

Doulamis, K. 2001. 'Rhetoric and Irony in Chariton: A Case-Study from Callirhoe', *AncNarr* 1: 55-72.

— 2011. 'Forensic Oratory and Rhetorical Theory in Chariton Book 5', in: K. Doulamis (ed.), *Echoing Narratives: Studies of Intertextuality in Greek and Roman Prose Fiction,* Eelde and Groningen: Barkhuis and Groningen University Library, 21-48.

Dover, K. J. 1989. *Greek Homosexuality*, Cambridge, Mass.: Harvard University Press.
Dowden, K. 1996. 'Heliodoros: Serious Intentions', *CQ* 46, 267-285.
Dowling, M. B. 2006. *Clemency and Cruelty in the Roman World*, Ann Arbor: University of Michigan Press.
Dubischar, M. 2001. *Die Agonszenen bei Euripides: Untersuchungen zu ausgewählten Dramen*, Stuttgart and Weimar: J. B. Metzler Verlag.
DuBois, P. 1991. *Torture and Truth*, New York: Routledge.
Duchemin, J. 1968. *L'ΑΓΩΝ dans la tragédie grecque*, Paris: Les Belles Lettres.
Ducrey, P. 1968. *Le traitement des prisonniers de guerre dans la Grèce antique des origines à la conquête romaine*, Paris: de Boccard.
Duncan-Jones, R. P. 1974. 'The Use of Prices in the Latin Novel', *The Economy of the Roman Empire: Quantitative Studies*, Cambridge and New York: Cambridge University Press.
Durham, D. B. 1938. 'Parody in Achilles Tatius', *CPh* 33, 1-19.
Easterling, P. E. and B. M. W. Knox (eds.), 1989. *The Cambridge History of Classical Literature. Vol. I, pt. 4: The Hellenistic Period and the Empire,* Cambridge and New York: Cambridge University Press.
Eden, K. 1986. *Poetic and Legal Fiction in the Aristotelian Tradition*, Princeton: Princeton University Press.
Edsall, M. 1996. 'The Role and Characterization of the Priest in the Ancient Novel', Ph.D. dissertation, Columbia University.
Edwards, D. R. 1987. 'Acts of the Apostles and Chariton's Chaereas and Callirhoe: A Literary and Sociohistorical Study', Ph.D. dissertation, Boston University.
— 1991. 'Surviving the Web of Power: Religion and Politics in the Acts of the Apostles, Josephus, and Chariton's *Chaereas and Callirhoe*', in: L. Alexander (ed.), *Images of Empire*, Sheffield: Sheffield Academic Press, 179-201.
— 1994. 'Defining the Web of Power in Asia Minor', *Journal of the American Academy of Religion* 57, 699-718.
Egger, B. M. 1990. 'Women in the Greek Novel: Constructing the Feminine', Ph.D. dissertation, University of California, Irvine.
— 1994a. 'Looking at Chariton's Callirhoe', in: J. R. Morgan and R. Stoneman (eds.), *Greek Fiction: The Greek Novel in Context*, London and New York: Routledge, 31-48.
— 1994b. 'Women and Marriage in the Greek Novels: The Boundaries of Romance', in: J. A. Tatum (ed.), *The Search for the Ancient Novel*, Baltimore: The Johns Hopkins University Press, 260-280.
Elsom, H. E. 1992. 'Callirhoe: Displaying the Phallic Woman', in: A. Richlin (ed.), *Pornography and Representation in Greek and Rome*, Oxford and New York: Oxford University Press, 212-230.
Elster, M. 1991. 'Römisches Strafrecht in den *Metamorphosen* des Apuleius', *Groningen Colloquia on the Novel* 4, 135-154.
Evans Grubbs, J. 1989. 'Abduction Marriage in Antiquity: A Law of Constantine (*CTh* IX.24.1) and its Social Context', *JRS* 79, 59-83.
— 1993. 'Constantine and Imperial Legislation on the Family', in: J. Harries and I. Wood (eds.), *The Theodosian Code*, Ithaca: Cornell University Press, 120-142.
— 1995. *Law and Family in Late Antiquity: The Emperor Constantine's Marriage Legislation*, Oxford and New York: Oxford University Press.
— 2010. 'Hidden in Plain Sight: *Expositi* in the Community', in: V. Dasen and T. Späth (eds.), *Children, Memory, and Family Identity in Roman Culture*, Oxford and New York: Oxford University Press, 293-310.

Ewick, P. and S. S. Silbey 1998. *The Common Place of Law: Stories from Everyday Life, Language and Legal Discourse*, Chicago: University of Chicago Press.

Ferguson, R. A. 1990. 'The Judicial Opinion as Literary Genre', *Yale Journal of Law and Humanities* 2, 201-219.

Ferrini, M. F. 1987-88. 'Achille Tazio V 25-27: Analisi di un discorso diretto nel romanzo greco', *AION(filol)* 9-10, 151-171.

— 1991. 'Discorsi giudiziari e altro nel romanzo greco antico', *AFLM* 24, 31-60.

Feuillâtre, E. 1966. *Études sur les 'Éthiopiques' d'Héliodore: Contribution à la connaissance du roman grec,* Paris: Presses Universitaires de France.

Forsdyke, S. 2008. 'Street Theatre and Popular Justice in Ancient Greece: Shaming, Stoning and Starving Offenders Inside and Outside the Courts', *Past and Present* 201, 3-50.

Foucault, M. 1978. *The History of Sexuality*, translated by R. Hurley, New York: Vintage Books.

— 1979. *Discipline and Punish*, New York: Vintage. Original edition, *Surveiller et punir: naissance de la prison*, Paris: Gallimard, 1975.

— 1988. *The History of Sexuality, Vol. 3, The Care of the Self,* translated by R. Hurley, New York: Vintage Books.

Fournier, J. 2010. *Entre tutelle romaine et autonomie civique: l'administration judiciaire dans les provinces hellénophones de l'empire romain, 129 av. J.-C. - 235 ap. J. C., Bibliothèque des écoles françaises d'Athènes et de Rome, BEFAR*, Athènes: École française d'Athènes.

Freyburger, G. 1992. 'Le droit d'asile à Rome', *LEC* 60, 139-151.

Frier, B. W. 1985. *The Rise of the Roman Jurists*, Princeton: Princeton University Press.

Frye, R. N. 1983. *The History of Ancient Iran*, Munich: Beck.

Fusillo, M. 1991. *Naissance du roman*, translated by M. Abrioux, Paris: Seuil.

Futre Pinheiro, M. 1989. 'Aspects de la problématique sociale et économique dans le roman d'Héliodore', in: P. Liviabella Furiani and A. M. Scarcella (eds.), *Piccolo mondo antico: Le donne, gli amori, i costumi, il mondo reale nel romanzo antico*, Naples: Edizioni Scientifiche Italiane, 17-42.

Gabba, E. 1982. 'Political and Cultural Aspects of the Classicistic Revival in the Augustan Age', *ClAnt* 1, 43-65.

Gabelmann, H. 1984. *Antike Audienz- und Tribunalszenen*, Darmstadt: Wissenschaftliche Buchgesellschaft.

Gagarin, M. 1986. *Early Greek Law*, Berkeley and Los Angeles: University of California Press.

— 1988. *The Murder of Herodes: A Study of Antiphon 5*, Frankfurt and New York: Verlag Peter Lang.

— 1996. 'The Torture of Slaves in Athenian Law', *CPh* 91, 1-18.

Galsterer, H. 1986. 'Roman Law in the Provinces: Some Problems of Transmission', in: M. H. Crawford (ed.), *L'impero romano e le strutture economiche e sociale delle province*, Como: Edizioni New Press, 13-27.

Garnsey, P. 1967. 'Adultery Trials and the Survival of the *Quaestiones* in the Severan Age', *JRS* 57, 56-60.

— 1970. *Social Status and Legal Privilege in the Roman Empire*, Oxford: Clarendon Press.

Gaughan, J. E. 2010. *Murder Was Not a Crime: Homicide and Power in the Roman Republic*, Austin: University of Texas Press.

Gebhardt, U. C. J. 2009. *Sermo iuris: Rechtssprache und Recht in der augusteischen Dichtung, Mnemosyne Supplements 315*, Leiden and Boston: Brill.

Geertz, C. 1973. 'Thick Description: Toward an Interpretive Theory of Culture', *The Interpretation of Cultures: Selected Essays*, New York: Basic Books, 3-30.

Gernet, L. 1981. *The Anthropology of Ancient Greece*, translated by J. Hamilton and B. Nagy, Baltimore: The Johns Hopkins University Press. Original edition, *Anthropolgie de la grèce antique,* Paris: François Maspero, 1968.

Giovannini, A. and E. Grzybek 2008. *Der Prozess Jesu: Jüdische Justizautonomie und römische Strafgewalt. Eine philologisch-verfassungsgeschichtliche Studie*, München: Verlag Ernst Vögel.

Gleason, M. W. 1995. *Making Men: Sophists and Self-Presentation in Ancient Rome*, Princeton: Princeton University Press.

Glotz, G. 1904. *L'ordalie dans la Grèce primitive*, Paris: Albert Fontemoing.

Goldhill, S. 1995. *Foucault's Virginity: Ancient Erotic Fiction and the History of Sexuality*, Cambridge and New York: Cambridge University Press.

Gras, M. 1984. 'Cité grecque et lapidation', *Du châtiment dans la cité: supplices corporels et peine de mort dans le monde antique. (Rome 9-11 november 1982)*, Rome: L'École française de Rome, 75-89.

Grodzynski, D. 1984. 'Tortures mortelles et catégories sociales: Les *Summa Supplicia* dans le droit romain aux IIIe et IV siècles', *Du châtiment dans la cité: supplices corporels et peine de mort dans le monde antique (Rome 9-11 novembre 1982)*, Rome: L'École française de Rome, 361-403.

Guez, J.-P. 2009. 'Homme tyrannique, homme royal dans le roman de Chariton', in: C. Bost-Pouderon, S. Montanari and B. Pouderon (eds.), *Passions, vertus et vices dans l'ancien roman. Actes du colloque de Tours, 19-21 octobre 2006*, Paris: de Boccard, 23-38.

Gunderson, E. 2000. *Staging Masculinity: The Rhetoric of Performance in the Roman World*, Ann Arbor: University of Michigan Press.

— 2003. *Declamation, Paternity, and Roman Identity: Authority and the Rhetorical Self*, Cambridge and New York: Cambridge University Press.

Habicht, C. 1997. 'Roman Citizens in Athens (228-31 B.C.)', in: M. C. Hoff and S. I. Rotroff (eds.), *The Romanization of Athens. Proceedings of an International Conference Held at Lincoln, Nebraska (April 1996)*, Oxford: Oxbow Books, 9-17.

Hägg, T. 1966. 'Die *Ephesiaka* des Xenophon Ephesios—Original oder Epitome?', *C&M* 27, 118-161.

— 1971. *Narrative Technique in Ancient Greek Romances: Studies of Chariton, Xenophon Ephesius, and Achilles Tatius*, Uppsala: Almquist & Wiksells.

— 1983. *The Novel in Antiquity*, Berkeley and Los Angeles: University of California Press.

— 1987. '*Callirhoe* and *Parthenope*: The Beginnings of the Historical Novel', *ClAnt* 6, 184-204.

— 2004. 'The Black Land of the Sun: Meroe in Heliodoros' Romantic Fiction', in: T. Hägg, L. B. Mortensen and T. Eide (eds.), *Parthenope: Selected Studies in Ancient Greek Fiction (1969-2004)*, Copenhagen: Museum Tusculanum Press, 345-375.

Haight, E. H. 1945. *More Essays on Greek Romances*, New York: Longmans, Green & Co.

Hall, E. 1989. *Inventing the Barbarian: Greek Self-Definition through Tragedy*, Oxford: Clarendon Press.

Hallett, J. P. 1984. *Fathers and Daughters in Roman Society: Women and the Elite Family*, Princeton: Princeton University Press.

Halm-Tisserant, M. 2013. *Réalités et imaginaires des supplices en Grèce ancienne*. 2nd ed, *Études anciennes. Série grecque*, Paris: Les Belles Lettres. Original edition, 1998.

Hansen, M. H. 1975. *Eisangelia: The Sovereignty of the People's Court in Athens in the Fourth Century B.C. and the Impeachment of Generals and Politicians*, Odense: Odense University Press.

— 1976. *Apagoge, Endeixis and Ephegesis against Kakourgoi, Atimoi and Pheugontes: A Study in the Athenian Administration of Justice in the Fourth Century B.C., Odense University Classical Studies 8,* Odense: Odense University Press.
— 1977. 'How did the Athenian *Ekklesia* Vote?', *GRBS* 18, 123-137.
— 1978. '*Dēmos, Ecclesia* and *Dicasterion*', *GRBS* 19, 127-146.
— 1982. 'The Athenian *Heliaia*', *C&M* 33, 9-47.
— 1987. *The Athenian Assembly in the Age of Demosthenes*, Oxford: Blackwell.
— 1991. *The Athenian Democracy in the Age of Demosthenes*, Oxford: Blackwell.
Harker, A. 2008. *Loyalty and Dissidence in Roman Egypt: The Case of the Acta Alexandrinorum*, Cambridge and New York: Cambridge University Press.
Harris, E. M. 1990. 'Did the Athenians Regard Seduction as a Worse Crime than Rape?', *CQ* 40, 370-377.
— 1994. ''In the Act' or 'Red Handed'? *Apagoge* to the Eleven and the Furtum Manifestum', in: G. Thür (ed.), *Symposion 1993: Vorträge zur griechischen und hellenistischen Rechtegeschichte*, Köln: Böhlau Verlag, 169-184.
Harris, W. V. 1986. 'The Roman Father's Power of Life and Death', in: R. S. Bagnall and W. V. Harris (eds.), *Studies in Roman Law in Memory of A. Arthur Schiller*, Leiden: Brill, 81-95.
— 1989. *Ancient Literacy*, Cambridge, Mass.: Harvard University Press.
— 1994. 'Child-Exposure in the Roman Empire', *JRS* 84, 1-22.
— 2001. *Restraining Rage: The Ideology of Anger Control in Classical Antiquity*, Cambridge, Mass.: Harvard University Press.
Harrison, A. R. W. 1968. *The Law of Athens*. 2 vols. *Vol. 1. The Family and Property*, Oxford: Clarendon Press.
— 1971. *The Law of Athens*. 2 vols. *Vol. 2. Procedure*, Oxford: Clarendon Press.
Harriss, C. 2008. 'Policing Propp: Toward a Textualist Definition of the Procedural Drama', *Journal of Film and Video* 60, 43-59.
Hartog, F. 1988. *The Mirror of Herodotus*, Berkeley and Los Angeles: University of California Press.
Haynes, K. C. M. 2003. *Fashioning the Feminine in the Greek Novel*, London and New York: Routledge.
Headlam, J. W. 1893. 'On the πρόκλησις εἰς βάσανον', *CR* 7, 1-5.
— 1894. 'Response to 'Slave Torture in Athens,' by C. V. Thompson', *CR* 8, 136-137.
Heller, A. and A.-V. Pont (eds.), 2012. *Patrie d'origine et patries électives: les citoyennetés multiples dans le monde grec d'époque romaine. Actes du colloque internationale de Tours, 6-7 november 2009, Scripta Antiqua 40*, Paris: Ausonius.
Henderson, I. H. 2003. 'Speech Representation and Religious Rhetorics in Philostratus' *Vita Apollonii*', *SR* 32, 19-37.
Herman, D. 1997. 'Scripts, Sequences, and Stories: Elements of a Postclassical Narratology', *PMLA* 112, 1046-1059.
— 2009. 'Cognitive Narratology', in: P. Hühn, J. Pier, W. Schmid and J. Schönert (eds.), *Handbook of Narratology*, Berlin and New York: Walter de Gruyter, 30-43.
Hersch, K. K. 2010. *The Roman Wedding Ritual and Meaning in Antiquity*, Cambridge and New York: Cambridge University Press.
Highet, G. 1973. 'The Huntsman and the Castaway', *GRBS* 14, 35-40.
Hinard, F. 1987. 'Spectacle des exécutions et espace urbain', *L'urbs: espace urbaine et histoire (1e s. ap. J.-C.). Actes du colloque international organisé par le Centre nationale de la*

recherche scientifique et l'École française de Rome (Rome, 8-12 mai 1985), Rome: École française de Rome, 111-125.

Hirzel, R. 1909. 'Die Strafe der Steinung', *Abhandlungen der philologisch-historischen Klasse der Königlich sächsischen Gesellschaft der Wissenschaften* 27, 223-266.

Holloway, R. R. 2000. *The Archaeology of Ancient Sicily*, London: Routledge.

Honoré, T. 1994. *Emperors and Lawyers*, 2d ed, Oxford: Clarendon Press.

Hopkins, K. 1993. 'Novel Evidence for Roman Slavery', *Past and Present* 138, 3-27.

Hopwood, K. 1998. ''All That May Become a Man': The Bandit in the Ancient Novel', in: L. Foxhall and J. Salmon (eds.), *When Men Were Men: Masculinity, Power and Identity*, London and New York: Routledge, 195-204.

Hunter, R. L. 1994. 'History and Historicity in Chariton', *ANRW* II.34.2, 1056-1086.

— 2008. 'Ancient Readers', in: T. Whitmarsh (ed.), *The Cambridge Companion to the Greek and Roman Novel*, Cambridge and New York: Cambridge University Press, 261-271.

— 2009. 'The Curious Incident…: *Polypragmosyne* and the Ancient Novel', in: M. Paschalis, S. Panayotakis and G. Schmeling (eds.), *Readers and Writers in the Ancient Novel*, Groningen: Barkhuis Publishing & Groningen University Library.

Hunter, V. J. 1994. *Policing Athens: Social Control in the Attic Lawsuits, 420-320 B.C.*, Princeton: Princeton University Press.

Jauss, H. R. 1982. *Toward an Aesthetic of Reception*, Minneapolis: University of Minnesota Press.

Jolowicz, H. F. 1952. *Historical Introduction to the Study of Roman Law*. 2nd ed., Cambridge and New York: Cambridge University Press.

Jones, A. H. M. 1937. *Cities of the Eastern Roman Provinces*. Oxford: Clarendon Press.

— 1940. *The Greek City from Alexander to Justinian*, Oxford: Clarendon Press.

Jones, C. P. 1992. 'Hellenistic History in Chariton of Aphrodisias', *Chiron* 22, 91-102.

— 2007. 'Juristes romains dans l'orient grec', *CRAI*, 1333-1359.

Jones, M. 2012. *Playing the Man: Performing Masculinities in the Ancient Greek Novel*. Oxford and New York: Oxford University Press.

Kadri, S. 2005. *The Trial: A History, from Socrates to O.J. Simpson*, New York: Random House.

Kaimio, M. 1995. 'How to Manage in the Male World: the Strategies of the Heroine in Chariton's Novel', *AAntHung* 36, 119-132.

Kanavou, N. 2015. 'A Husband is More Important Than a Child', *Mnemosyne* 68, 937-955.

Kapparis, K. 1995. 'When Were the Athenian Adultery Laws Introduced?', *RIDA* 42, 97-122.

— 1999. 'Apollodoros 'Against Neaira' [D 59]', *Untersuchungen zur antiken Literatur und Geschichte* Bd. 53, Berlin and Hawthorne, N.Y.: Walter de Gruyter.

— 2000. 'Has Chariton Read Lysias 1 'On the Murder of Eratosthenes'?', *Hermes* 128, 380-383.

Karabélias, E. 1990. 'Le roman de Chariton d'Aphrodisias et le droit: Renversements de situation et exploitation des ambiguïtés juridiques', in: G. Nenci and G. Thür (eds.), *Symposion 1988: Vorträge zur griechischen und hellenistischen Rechtsgeschichte (Siena-Pisa, 6-8 Juni 1988)*, Cologne: Bohlau Verlag, 369-396.

Kelly, B. 2011. *Petitions, Litigation, and Social Control in Roman Egypt*, *Oxford Studies in Ancient Documents*, Oxford and New York: Oxford University Press.

Kensky, M. Z. 2010. *Trying Man, Trying God: The Divine Courtroom in Early Jewish and Christian Literature, Wissenschaftliche Untersuchungen zum Neuen Testament 2 Reihe*, Tübingen: Mohr Siebeck.

Kestner, J. 1973-1974. 'Ekphrasis as Frame in Longus' *Daphnis and Chloe*', *CW* 67, 166-171.

Keuls, E. 1985. *The Reign of the Phallus: Sexual Politics in Ancient Athens*, Berkeley and Los Angeles: University of California Press.

Keydell, R. 1966. 'Zur Datierung der *Aithiopika* Heliodors', in: P. Wirth (ed.), *Festschrift F. Dölger*, Heidelberg, 345-350.

Kloft, H. 1989. 'Imagination und Realität. Überlegungen zur Wirtschaftsstruktur des Romans *Daphnis und Chloe*', *Groningen Colloquia on the Novel* 2, 45-61.

Konstan, D. 1994a. 'Premarital Sex, Illegitimacy, and Male Anxiety in Menander and Athens', in: A. L. Boegehold and A. C. Scafuro (eds.), *Athenian Identity and Civic Ideology*, Baltimore: The Johns Hopkins University Press, 217-235.

— 1994b. *Sexual Symmetry: Love in the Ancient Greek Novel and Related Genres*, Princeton: Princeton University Press.

— 1998. 'Acts of Love: A Narrative Pattern in the Apocryphal Acts', *JECS* 6, 15-36.

— 2009. 'The Active Reader and the Ancient Novel', in: M. Paschalis, S. Panayotakis and G. Schmeling (eds.), *Readers and Writers in the Ancient Novel*, Groningen: Barkhuis Publishing & Groningen University Library, 1-17.

Kudlien, F. 1989. 'Kindesaussetzung im antiken Roman: Ein Thema zwischen Fiktionalität und Wirklichkeit', in: H. Hofmann (ed.), *Groningen Colloquia on the Novel*, Groningen: Egbert Forsten, 25-44.

Lacombrade, C. 1970. 'Sur l'auteur et la date des *Éthiopiques*', *REG* 83, 70-89.

Laffi, U. 2013. *In greco per i Greci: ricerche sul lessico greco del processo civile e criminale romano nelle attestazioni di fonti documentarie romane*, Pubblicazioni del Cedant, 12, Pavia: IUSS Press.

Lalanne, S. 2006. *Une éducation grecque: rites de passage et construction des genres dans le roman grec ancien, Textes à l'appui. Histoire classique*, Paris: Découverte.

Lane Fox, R. 1987. *Pagans and Christians*, New York: Knopf.

Lanfranchi, F. 1938. *Il diritto nei retori romani: contributo alla storia dello sviluppo del diritto romano*, Milan: Giuffrè.

Laplace, M. 1980. 'Les légendes troyennes dans le 'roman' de Chariton, *Chairéas et Callirhoé*', *REG* 93, 83-125.

— 1983. 'Légende et fiction chez Achilles Tatius: les personnages de Leucippé et de Iô', *BAGB*, 311-318.

— 1994. 'Récit d'une éducation amoureuse et discours panégyrique dans les *Éphésiaques* de Xénophon d'Éphèse: Le romanesque antitragique et l'art de l'amour', *REG* 107, 440-479.

Lassen, E. M. 1992. 'The Ultimate Crime: Parricidium and the Concept of Family in the Late Roman Republic and Early Empire', *C&M* 43, 147-161.

Lateiner, D. 1997. 'Abduction Marriage in Heliodorus' *Aethiopica*', *GRBS* 38, 409-439.

Lea, H. C. 1968. *Superstition and Force: Essays on the Wager of Law—The Wager of Battle—The Ordeal—Torture*. 2d ed, New York: Greenwood Press. Original edition, 1870.

Lenardon, R. J. 1978. *The Saga of Themistocles*, London: Thames and Hudson.

Lesky, A. 1959. 'Aithiopika', *Hermes* 87, 27-38.

— 1966. *A History of Greek Literature*, New York: Thomas Y. Crowell. Original edition, *Geschichte der griechischen Literatur,* 2d ed., Bern: Francke, 1963.

Létoublon, F. 2003. 'La lettre dans le roman grec, ou les liaisons dangereuses', in: S. Panayotakis, M. Zimmerman and W. Keulen (eds.), *The Ancient Novel and Beyond*, Leiden: Brill, 271-288.

Lightfoot, C. S. 1988. 'Facts and Fiction – the Third Siege of Nisibis (AD 350)', *Historia* 37, 106-125.

Lincoln, A. T. 2000. *Truth on Trial: The Lawsuit Motif in the Fourth Gospel*, Peabody, Mass.: Hendrickson Publishers.

Liviabella Furiani, P. 1985. 'Achille Tazio VIII 9.9 sgg. e Platone, *Leggi* XII 961 a-b: un esempio di imitazione e deformazione', *Prometheus* 11, 179-182.

— 1988. '*Gamos* e *kenogamion* nel romanzo di Achille Tazio', *Euphrosyne* n.s. 16, 271-280.

Lloyd, M. 1992. *The Agon in Euripides*, Oxford: Clarendon Press.

Long, J. 1996. *Claudian's In Eutropium, or How, When, and Why to Slander a Eunuch*, Chapel Hill and London: University of North Carolina Press.

Luginbill, R. D. 2000. 'Chariton's Use of Thucydides' *History* in Introducing the Egyptian Revolt (*Chaireas and Callirhoe* 6.8)', *Mnemosyne* 53, 1-11.

MacDowell, D. M. 1963. *Athenian Homicide Law in the Age of the Orators*, Manchester: Manchester University Press.

— 1978. *The Law in Classical Athens*, Ithaca: Cornell University Press.

— (ed.) 1988. *Aristophanes: Wasps*, Oxford: Clarendon Press.

MacMullen, R. 1966. *Enemies of the Roman Order: Treason, Unrest, and Alienation in the Empire*, Cambridge, Mass.: Harvard University Press.

— 1990. 'Judicial Savagery in the Roman Empire', *Changes in the Roman Empire: Essays in the Ordinary*, Princeton: Princeton University Press, 204-217.

Maffi, A. 1986. 'La confessione giudiziaria nel diritto greco', *L'aveu. Antiquité et Moyen Âge. Actes de la table ronde organisée par l'École française de Rome, avec le concours du CNRS et de l'Université de Trieste, Rome 28-30 mars 1984*, Paris: de Boccard, 7-26.

Manuwald, G. 2000. 'Zitate als Mittel des Erzählens – Zur Darstellungstechnik Charitons in seinem Roman *Kallirhoe*', *WJA* 24, 97-122.

Maróth, M. 1979. 'Le siège de Nisibe en 350 ap. J.-Ch. d'après des sources syriennes', *AAntHung* 27, 239-243.

Marrou, H. I. 1956. *A History of Education in Antiquity*, translated by G. Lamb, New York: Sheed and Ward. Original edition, *Histoire de l'education dans l'antiquité,* 3d ed., Paris: Seuil.

Mason, H. J. 1974. *Greek Terms for Roman Institutions*, Toronto: Hakkert.

May, J. M. 1988. *Trials of Character: The Eloquence of Ciceronian Ethos*, Chapel Hill: University of North Carolina Press.

McDonald, W. A. 1943. *The Political Meeting Places of the Greeks*, Baltimore: The Johns Hopkins University Press.

McGinn, T. A. J. 1998. *Prostitution, Sexuality and the Law in Ancient Rome*, Oxford and New York: Oxford University Press.

— 2002. 'The Augustan Marriage Legislation and Social Practice: Elite Endogamy versus Male 'Marrying Down'', in: J.-J. Aubert and B. Sirks (eds.), *Speculum Iuris: Roman Law as a Reflection of Social and Economic Life in Antiquity*, Ann Arbor: University of Michigan Press, 46-93.

— 2004. *The Economy of Prostitution in the Roman World: A Study of Social History and the Brothel*, Ann Arbor: University of Michigan Press.

Merry, S. E. 1988. 'Legal Pluralism', *Law and Society Review* 22, 869-896.

Meyer, E. A. 2004. *Legitimacy and the Law in the Roman World: Tabulae in Roman Belief and Practice*, Cambridge and New York: Cambridge University Press.

Millar, F. 1977. *The Emperor in the Roman World (31 BC - AD 337)*, Ithaca: Cornell University Press.

— 1981. 'The World of the Golden Ass', *JRS* 71, 63-75.

— 1993. 'The Greek City in the Roman Period', in: M. H. Hansen (ed.), *The Ancient Greek City-State: Symposium on the occasion of the 250th Anniversary of the Royal Danish Academy of Sciences and Letters July, 1-4 1992*, Copenhagen: Munksgaard, 232-260.
— 1996. 'Emperors, Kings, and Subjects: The Politics of Two Level Sovereignty', *SCI* 15, 159-173.
— 1999. 'The Greek East and Roman Law: The Dossier of M. Cn. Licinius Rufinus', *JRS* 89, 90-108.
Miller, S. G. 1978. *The Prytaneion: Its Function and Architectural Form*, Berkeley and Los Angeles: University of California Press.
Minchin, E. 2001. *Homer and the Resources of Memory*, Oxford and New York: Oxford University Press.
Mirhady, D. C. 1996. 'Torture and Rhetoric in Athens', *JHS* 116, 119-131.
Missiou, A. 1993. 'ΔΟΥΛΟΣ ΤΟΥ ΒΑΣΙΛΕΩΣ: The Politics of Translation', *CQ* 43, 377-391.
Mitteis, L. 1891. *Reichsrecht und Volksrecht in den östlichen Provinzen des römischen Kaiserreichs*, Leipzig: Teubner.
Modrzejewski, J. M. 1986. 'La loi des Égyptiens: le droit grec dans l'Égypte romaine', in: B. G. Mandilaras (ed.), *Proceedings of the XVIII International Congress of Papyrology (Athens, 25-31 May 1986)*, Athens: Greek Papyrological Society, 383-399.
Mommsen, T. 1899. *Römisches Strafrecht*, Leipzig: Duncker & Humblot.
Mommsen, T., P. Krueger, and A. Watson (eds.), 1985. *The Digest of Justinian*, 4 vols., Philadelphia: University of Pennsylvania Press.
Montiglio, S. 2013. *Love and Providence: Recognitions in the Ancient Novel*, Oxford and New York: Oxford University Press.
Moore, S. F. 1973. 'Law and Social Change: The Semi-Autonomous Social Field as an Appropriate Subject of Study', *Law and Society Review* 7, 719-746.
— 1978. *Law as Process: An Anthropological Approach*, London and Boston: Routledge & K. Paul.
Morales, H. 2004. *Vision and Narrative in Achilles Tatius' Leucippe and Clitophon*, Cambridge and New York: Cambridge University Press.
— 2008. 'The History of Sexuality', in: T. Whitmarsh (ed.), *The Cambridge Companion to the Greek and Roman Novel*, Cambridge and New York: Cambridge University Press, 39-55.
Morgan, J. R. 1978. 'A Commentary on the Ninth and Tenth Books of Heliodoros' *Aithiopika*', Ph.D. dissertation, Oxford University.
— 1982. 'History, Romance, and Realism in the *Aithiopika* of Heliodoros', *ClAnt* 1, 221-265.
— 1989a. 'Heliodorus: An Ethiopian Story', in: B. P. Reardon (ed.), *Collected Ancient Greek Novels*, Berkeley and Los Angeles: University of California Press, 349-588.
— 1989b. 'A Sense of the Ending: The Conclusion of Heliodoros' *Aithiopika*', *TAPhA* 119, 299-320.
— 1989c. 'The Story of Knemon in Heliodoros' *Aithiopika*', *JHS* 109, 99-113.
— 1993. 'Make-Believe and Make Believe: The Fictionality of the Greek Novels', in: C. Gill and T. P. Wiseman (eds.), *Lies and Fiction in the Ancient World*, Exeter: University of Exeter Press, 175-229.
— 1996. 'The Ancient Novel at the End of the Century: Scholarship Since the Dartmouth Conference', *CPh* 91, 63-73.
— 2009. 'The Emesan Connection: Philostratus and Heliodorus', in: K. Demoen and D. Praet (eds.), *Theios Sophistes: Essays on Flavius Philostratus' Vita Apollonii*, Boston: Brill, 263-281.

Musurillo, H. A. 1954. *The Acts of the Pagan Martyrs: Acta Alexandrinorum*, Oxford and New York: Oxford University Press.

— (ed.), 1972. *The Acts of the Christian Martyrs*, Oxford: Clarendon Press.

Nadeau, J. Y. 1970. 'Ethiopians', *CQ* 20, 339-349.

Nader, L. 1997. *Law in Culture and Society*, Berkeley and Los Angeles: University of California Press.

Nader, L. and H. F. Todd (eds.), 1978. *The Disputing Process: Law in Ten Societies*, New York: Columbia University Press.

Nicholas, B. 1962. *An Introduction to Roman Law*, Oxford: Clarendon Press.

Nimis, S. A. 1998. 'Memory and Description in the Ancient Novel', *Arethusa* 31, 99-122.

— 2003. '*In Mediis Rebus:* Beginning Again in the Middle of the Ancient Novel', in: S. Panayotakis, M. Zimmerman and W. Keulen (eds.), *The Ancient Novel and Beyond*, Leiden: Brill, 255-269.

Norden, F. 1912. *Apulejus von Madaura und das römische Privatrecht*, Leipzig: Teubner.

Nussbaum, M. C. 1995. *Poetic Justice: The Literary Imagination and Public Life*, Boston: Beacon Press.

O'Sullivan, J. N. 1986. 'Notes on Xenophon of Ephesus Books III and IV', *RhM* 129, 77-89.

— 1994. *Xenophon of Ephesus: His Compositional Technique and the Birth of the Novel, Untersuchungen zur antiken Literatur und Geschichte*, Berlin and New York: Walter de Gruyter.

Oakley, J. H. and R. H. Sinos 1993. *The Wedding in Ancient Athens*, Madison: The University of Wisconsin Press.

Ogden, D. 1997. 'Rape, Adultery, and the Protection of Bloodlines in Classical Athens', in: S. Deacy and K. F. Pierce (eds.), *Rape in Antiquity*, London: Duckworth, in association with the University of Wales, 25-41.

Oliver, J. H. 1953. *The Ruling Power: A Study of the Roman Empire in the Second Century After Christ through the Roman Oration of Aelius Aristides, Transactions of the American Philosophical Society 43*, Philadelphia: American Philosophical Society.

— 1980. 'From Gennêtai to Curiales', *Hesperia* 49, 30-56.

Olsen, S. 2012. 'Maculate Conception: Sexual Ideology and Creative Authority in Heliodorus' *Aethiopica*', *AJPh* 133, 301-322.

Omitowoju, R. 2002. *Rape and the Politics of Consent in Classical Athens*, Cambridge and New York: Cambridge University Press.

Ormand, K. 2010. 'Testing Virginity in Achilles Tatius and Heliodorus', *Ramus* 39, 160-197.

Oudot, E. 1992. 'Images d'Athènes dans les roman grecs', in: M.-F. Baslez, P. Hoffmann and M. Trédé (eds.), *Le monde du roman grec*, Paris: Presses de l'École normale supérieure, 101-111.

Oudshoorn, J. G. 2007. *The Relationship between Roman and Local Law in the Babatha and Salome Komaise Archives: General Analysis and Three Case Studies on Laws of Succession, Guardianship and Marriage, Studies on the Texts of the Desert of Judah*, Boston: Brill.

Papathomas, A. 2010. 'Heliodors *Aithiopika* 9.26.1 als Reminiszenz der kaiserzeitlichen Institution der Sklavenanakrisis', *Mnemosyne* ser. 4, 63, 625-634.

Parker, R. 1983. *Miasma: Pollution and Purification in Early Greek Religion*, Oxford and New York: Oxford University Press.

Parks, E. P. 1945. *The Roman Rhetorical Schools as Preparation for the Courts Under the Early Empire*, Baltimore: The Johns Hopkins Press.

Parsons, P. J. 2007. '4811. Novel (*'Panionis'*)', *The Oxyrhynchus Papyri*, London: Egypt Exploration Society in Graeco-Roman Memoirs, 47-53.

Paschalis, M., S. Panayotakis, and G. Schmeling (eds.), 2009. *Readers and Writers in the Ancient Novel, Ancient Narrative Supplementum* 12. Groningen: Barkhuis Publishing & Groningen University Library.

Peachin, M. 1996. *Iudex vice Caesaris: Deputy Emperors and the Administration of Justice During the Principate*, Stuttgart: Steiner.

Pease, A. S. 1907. 'Notes on Stoning among the Greeks and Romans', *TAPhA* 38, 5-18.

Penwill, J. 1978. 'The Letters of Themistocles: An Epistolary Novel?', *Antichthon* 12, 83-108.

Perkins, J. 2002. 'Social Geography in the Apocryphal Acts of the Apostles', in: M. Paschalis and S. Frangoulidis (eds.), *Space in the Ancient Novel*, Groningen: Barkhuis Publishing and the University Library Groningen, 118-131.

Perry, B. E. 1930. 'Chariton and His Romance from a Literary-Historical Point of View', *AJPh* 51, 93-134.

— 1967. *The Ancient Romances: A Literary-Historical Account of Their Origins*, Berkeley and Los Angeles: University of California Press.

Pervo, R. I. 1987. *Profit with Delight: The Literary Genre of the Acts of the Apostles*, Philadelphia: Fortress Press.

— 1994. 'Early Christian Fiction', in: J. R. Morgan and R. Stoneman (eds.), *Greek Fiction: The Greek Novel in Context*, London and New York: Routledge, 239-254.

Plescia, J. 1970. *The Oath and Perjury in Ancient Greece*, Tallahassee: Florida State University Press.

Pomeroy, S. B. 2007. *The Murder of Regilla: A Case of Domestic Violence in Antiquity*, Cambridge, Mass.: Harvard University Press.

Porter, J. R. 1997. 'Adultery by the Book: Lysias I (*On the Murder of Eratosthenes*) and Comic Diegesis', *EMC* 40, n.s. 16, 421-453.

— 2003. 'Chariton and Lysias 1: Further Considerations', *Hermes* 131, 433-440.

Posner, R. A. 1998. *Law and Literature: Revised and Enlarged Edition*. 2d ed., Cambridge, Mass.: Harvard University Press.

Pospíšil, L. 1958. *Kapauku Papuans and Their Law*, New Haven: Dept. of Anthropology, Yale University.

Potter, D. 1993. 'Martyrdom as Spectacle', in: R. Scodel (ed.), *Theater and Society in the Classical World*, Ann Arbor: University of Michigan Press, 53-88.

— 1996. 'Performance, Power, and Justice in the High Empire', in: W. J. Slater (ed.), *Roman Theater and Society: E. Togo Salmon Papers*, Ann Arbor: University of Michigan Press, 129-159.

Pouderon, B. and J. Peigney (eds.), 2006. *Discours et débats dans l'ancien roman: actes du colloque de Tours, 21-23 octobre 2004, Collection de la Maison de l'Orient et de la Méditerranée* 36, Lyon: Maison de l'Orient et de la Méditerranée - Jean Pouilloux.

Pouilloux, J. 1983. 'Delphes dans les *Éthiopiques* d'Héliodore: La réalité dans la fiction', *JS*, 259-286.

Price, S. R. F. 1984. *Rituals and Power: The Roman Imperial Cult in Asia Minor*, Cambridge and New York: Cambridge University Press.

Pringsheim, F. 1950. *The Greek Law of Sale*, Weimar: H. Bohlaus Nachfolger.

Raditsa, L. F. 1980. 'Augustus' Legislation Concerning Marriage, Procreation, Love Affairs and Adultery', *ANRW* II.13, 278-339.

Rattenbury, R. M. 1926. 'Chastity and Chastity Ordeals in Ancient Greek Romances', *Proceedings of the Leeds Philosophical and Literary Society, Literary and Historical Section*, 59-71.

Reardon, B. P. 1971. *Courants littéraires grecs des IIe et IIIe siècles après J.-C.*, Paris: Les Belles Lettres.

— 1982. 'Theme, Structure and Narrative in Chariton', in: J. J. Winkler and G. Williams (eds.), *Later Greek Literature*, Cambridge and New York: Cambridge University Press, 1-27.

— 1991. *The Form of Greek Romance*, Princeton: Princeton University Press.

— 1994. 'Achilles Tatius and Ego-Narrative', in: J. R. Morgan and R. Stoneman (eds.), *Greek Fiction: The Greek Novel in Context*, London and New York: Routledge, 80-96.

— 1996. 'Chariton', in: G. L. Schmeling (ed.), *The Novel in the Ancient World*, New York and Leiden: Brill, 309-335.

Reeve, M. D. 1989. 'Conceptions', *PCPhS* 35, 81-112.

Richlin, A. 1996. 'How Putting the Man in Roman Put the Roman in Romance', in: N. Hewitt, J. O'Barr and N. Rosebaugh (eds.), *Talking Gender: Public Images, Personal Journeys, and Political Critiques*, Chapel Hill: University of North Carolina Press, 14-35.

Richter, D. S. 2011. *Cosmopolis: Imagining Community in Late Classical Athens and the Early Roman Empire*, Oxford and New York: Oxford University Press.

Rickert, G. 1989. *EKΩN and AKΩN in Early Greek Thought*, Atlanta: Scholars Press.

Rife, J. L. 2002. 'Officials of the Roman Provinces in Xenophon's *Ephesiaca*', *ZPE* 138, 93-108.

Rigsby, K. J. 1996. *Asylia: Territorial Inviolability in the Hellenistic World, Hellenistic Culture and Society 22*, Berkeley and Los Angeles: University of California Press.

Rilinger, R. 1988. *Humiliores - Honestiores: Zu einer sozialen Dichotomie im Strafrecht der römischen Kaiserzeit*, Munich: R. Oldenbourg.

Robert, L. 1937. *Études anatoliennes*, Paris: de Boccard.

Robiano, P. 1992. 'Les gymnosophistes éthiopiens chez Philostrate et chez Héliodore', *REA* 94, 413-428.

Rocca, R. 1976. 'Eliodoro e i due Ippoliti Euripidei', *Materiali e contributi per la storia della narrativa greco-latina* 1, 25-31.

Rogers, G. M. 2012. *The Mysteries of Artemis of Ephesos: Cult, Polis, and Change in the Graeco-Roman World*, New Haven: Yale University Press.

Rohde, E. 1914. *Der griechische Roman und seine Vorläufer*. 3d ed., Wiesbaden: Breitkopf & Härtel.

Rougemont, G. 1992. 'Delphes chez Héliodore', in: M.-F. Baslez, P. Hoffmann and M. Trédé (eds.), *Le monde du roman grec*, Paris: Presses de l'École normale supérieure, 93-99.

Ruiz-Montero, C. 1989. 'Caritón de Afrodisias y el mundo real', in: P. Liviabella Furiani and A. M. Scarcella (eds.), *Piccolo mondo antico: Le donne, gli amori, i costumi, il mondo reale nel romanzo antico*, Naples: Edizioni Scientifiche Italiane, 109-149.

— 1991. 'Aspects of the Vocabulary of Chariton of Aphrodisias', *CQ* 41, 484-489.

— 1994. 'Chariton von Aphrodisias: Ein Überblick', *ANRW* II.34.2, 1006-1054.

— 1996. 'The Rise of the Greek Novel', in: G. L. Schmeling (ed.), *The Novel in the Ancient World*, New York and Leiden: Brill, 29-85.

Russell, D. A. 1983. *Greek Declamation*, Cambridge and New York: Cambridge University Press.

Saïd, S. 1994. 'The City in the Greek Novel', in: J. A. Tatum (ed.), *The Search for the Ancient Novel*, Baltimore: The Johns Hopkins University Press, 216-236.

— 1999. 'Rural Society in the Greek Novel, or The Country Seen from the Town', in: S. Swain (ed.), *Oxford Readings in the Greek Novel*, Oxford and New York: Oxford University Press, 83-107.
Saller, R. P. 1991. 'Corporal Punishment, Authority, and Obedience in the Roman Household', in: B. Rawson (ed.), *Marriage, Divorce and Children in Ancient Rome*, Oxford: Clarendon Press, 144-165.
— 1994. *Patriarchy, Property and Death in the Roman Family*, Cambridge: Cambridge University Press.
Sandy, G. N. 1989. 'Antonius Diogenes: The Wonders Beyond Thule', in: B. P. Reardon (ed.), *Collected Ancient Greek Novels*, Berkeley and Los Angeles: University of California Press, 775-782.
Saunders, T. J. 1991. *Plato's Penal Code: Tradition, Controversy, and Reform in Greek Penology*, Oxford and New York: Oxford University Press.
Scafuro, A. C. 1997. *The Forensic Stage: Settling Disputes in Graeco-Roman New Comedy*, Cambridge and New York: Cambridge University Press.
Scarcella, A. M. 1970. 'Realtà e letterature nel paessagio sociale ed economico del romanzo di Longo Sofista', *Maia* 22, 103-131.
— 1976. 'Aspetti de diritto e del costume matrimoniali nel romanzo di Eliodoro', *Materiali e contributi per la storia della narrativa greco-latina* 1, 57-95.
— 1977. 'Les structures socio-économiques du roman de Xénophon d'Éphèse', *REG* 110, 249-262.
— 1990. 'Nomos nel romanzo greco d'amore', *GIF* 42, 243-266.
Schank, R. C. and R. P. Abelson 1977. *Scripts, Plans, Goals, and Understanding: An Inquiry into Human Knowledge Structures, The Artificial Intelligence Series*, Hillsdale, N.J.: L. Erlbaum Associates; distributed by the Halsted Press Division of John Wiley and Sons.
Schiavone, A. 2012. *The Invention of Law in the West*, translated by J. Carden and A. Shugaar, Cambridge, Mass.: Harvard University Press.
Schmeling, G. 1974. *Chariton, Twayne's World Authors Series* 295, New York: Twayne.
Schmitz, T. 1997. *Bildung und Macht: Zur sozialen und politischen Funktion der zweiten Sophistik in der griechischen Welt der Kaiserzeit*, Munich: C. H. Beck.
— 2000. 'Plausibility in the Greek Orators', *AJPh* 121, 47-77.
Schwartz, J. 1967. 'Quelques observations sur des roman grecs', *AC* 36, 536-552.
Schwartz, S. 1999. 'Callirhoe's Choice: Biological *vs* Legal Paternity', *GRBS* 40, 23-52.
— 2000-2001. 'Clitophon the *Moichos*: Achilles Tatius and the Trial Scene in the Greek Novel', *AncNarr* 1, 93-113.
— 2003a. 'Rome in the Greek Novel? Images and Ideas of Empire in Chariton's Persia', *Arethusa* 36, 375-394.
— 2003b. 'The Trial Scene in the Greek Novels and in Acts', in: T. Penner and C. Vander Stichele (eds.), *Contextualizing Acts: Lukan Narrative and Greco-Roman Discourse*, Atlanta: Scholars Press, 103-135.
— 2005. 'The Delicts of the Countryside in Longus' *Daphnis and Chloe*', in: J.-J. Aubert and Z. Várhelyi (eds.), *A Tall Order: Writing the Social History of the Ancient World*, Munich: K. G. Saur, 263-283.
— 2007. 'From Bedroom to Courtroom: The Adultery Type-Scene and the Acts of Andrew', in: T. Penner and C. Vander Stichele (eds.), *Mapping Gender in Ancient Religious Discourses*, Leiden: Brill, 267-311.
— 2010. 'Chronotopes of Justice in the Greek Novel: Trials in Narrative Spaces', in: F. de Angelis (ed.), *Spaces of Justice in the Roman World*, Leiden and Boston: Brill, 331-356.

— 2012. 'The Κρίσις Inside: Heliodorus' Variations on the Bedtrick', in: M. Futre Pinheiro, M. B. Skinner and F. I. Zeitlin (eds.), *Narrating Desire: Eros, Sex, and Gender in the Ancient Novel*, Berlin: De Gruyter, 161-180.

Scourfield, J. H. D. 2003. 'Anger and Gender in Chariton's *Chaereas and Callirhoe*', in: S. M. Braund and G. W. Most (eds.), *Ancient Anger: Perspectives from Homer to Galen*, Cambridge and New York: Cambridge University Press, 163-184.

Segal, C. 1984. 'The Trials at the End of Achilles Tatius' *Clitophon and Leucippe*: Doublets and Complementaries', *SIFC* 3d ser. 2, 83-91.

Shackleton Bailey, D. R. (ed.), 2000. *Valerius Maximus: Memorable Doings and Sayings*, Cambridge, Mass.: Harvard University Press.

Shaw, B. D. 1984. 'Bandits in the Roman Empire', *Past and Present* 105, 3-52.

Sherwin-White, A. N. 1963. *Roman Society and Roman Law in the New Testament*, Oxford: Clarendon Press.

Sinko, T. 1940/46. 'De ordine quo erotici scriptores graeci sibi successisse videantur', *Eos* 41, 23-45.

Skinner, M. L. 2010. *The Trial Narratives: Conflict, Power, and Identity in the New Testament*, Louisville, Ky.: Westminster John Knox Press.

Slater, W. J. 1995. 'The Theatricality of Justice', *CB* 71, 143-157.

Smith, J. O. 1996. 'The High Priests of the Temple of Artemis at Ephesus', in: E. Lane (ed.), *Cybele, Attis, and Related Cults: Essays in Memory of M. J. Vermaseren*, New York: E.J. Brill, 323-335.

Smith, S. D. 2007. *Greek Identity and the Athenian Past in Chariton: The Romance of Empire*, *Ancient Narrative Supplementum* 9, Groningen: Barkhuis & Groningen University Library.

Sokolowski, F. 1955. *Lois sacrées de l'Asie Mineure*, Paris: de Boccard.

Southern, P. 2007. *The Roman Army: A Social and Institutional History*, Santa Barbara, Calif.: ABC-CLIO.

Spawforth, A. J. 2012. *Greece and the Augustan Cultural Revolution*, Cambridge and New York: Cambridge University Press.

Starr, R. J. 1990/1. 'Reading Aloud: *Lectores* and Roman Reading', *CJ* 86, 337-343.

Staveley, E. S. 1972. *Greek and Roman Voting and Elections*, Ithaca: Cornell University Press.

Stephens, S. A. 1994. 'Who Read Ancient Novels?', in: J. A. Tatum (ed.), *The Search for the Ancient Novel*, Baltimore: The Johns Hopkins University Press, 405-418.

Stephens, S. A. and J. J. Winkler (eds.), 1995. *Ancient Greek Novels: The Fragments*, Princeton: Princeton University Press.

Summers, R. G. 1967. 'A Legal Commentary on the *Metamorphoses* of Apuleius', Ph.D. dissertation, Princeton University.

— 1970. 'Roman Justice and Apuleius' *Metamorphoses*', *TAPhA* 101, 511-531.

— 1971. 'Apuleius' *Juridicus*', *Historia* 21, 120-126.

Swain, S. 1996. *Hellenism and Empire: Language, Classicism, and Power in the Greek World, AD 50-250*, Oxford: Clarendon Press.

Szepessy, T. 1957. 'Die *Aithiopika* des Heliodors und der griechische sophistische Liebesroman', *AAntHung* 5, 241-259.

— 1972. 'Die Neudatierung des Heliodorus und die Belagerung von Nisibis', *Actes de la XIIe conférence internationale d'études classiques: Eirene, Cluj-Napoca, 2-7 Oct. 1972*, Budapest and Amsterdam: Hakkert, 279-287.

— 1976. 'Le siège de Nisibe et la chronologie d'Héliodore', *AAntHung* 24, 247-276.

Talbert, R. J. A. 1984. *The Senate of Imperial Rome*, Princeton: Princeton University Press.

Tanner, T. 1979. *Adultery in the Novel: Contract and Transgression*, Baltimore: The Johns Hopkins University Press.

Teitler, H. C. 1985. *Notarii et Exceptores: An Inquiry into the Role and Significance of Shorthand Writers in the Imperial and Ecclesiastical Bureaucracy of the Roman Empire (from the Early Principate to c. 450 A.D.)*, Amsterdam: Gieben.

Thomas, C. M. 1995. 'At Home in the City of Artemis: Religion in Ephesos in the Literary Imagination of the Roman Period', in: H. Koester (ed.), *Ephesos Metropolis of Asia: An Interdisciplinary Approach to its Archaeology, Religion, and Culture*, Valley Forge, Pa.: Trinity Press International, 81-117.

— 1998. 'Stories Without Texts and Without Authors: The Problem of Fluidity in Ancient Novelistic Texts and Early Christian Literature', in: R. F. Hock, J. B. Chance and J. Perkins (eds.), *Ancient Fiction and Early Christian Narrative*, Atlanta: Scholars Press, 273-291.

— 2003. *The Acts of Peter, Gospel Literature, and the Ancient Novel: Rewriting the Past*, Oxford and New York: Oxford University Press.

Thomas, Y. 1984. 'Vitae necisque potestas. Le père, la cité, la mort', *Du châtiment dans la cité: supplices corporels et peine de mort dans le monde antique (Rome 9-11 november 1982)*, Rome: L'École française de Rome, 499-548.

— 1986. 'Confessus pro iudicato. L'aveu civil et l'aveu pénal à Rome', *L'aveu. Antiquité et Moyen Âge. Actes de la table ronde organisée par l'École française de Rome, avec le concours du CNRS et de l'Université de Trieste, Rome 28-30 mars 1984*, Paris: de Boccard, 89-117.

Thür, G. 1977. *Beweisführung vor den Schwurgerichtshöfen Athens: Die Proklesis zur Basanos*, Vienna: Verlag der österreichische Akademie des Wissenschaften.

— 1996. 'Reply to D. C. Mirhady: Torture and Rhetoric in Athens', *JHS* 116, 132-134.

Tilg, S. 2010. *Chariton of Aphrodisias and the Invention of the Greek Love Novel*, Oxford and New York: Oxford University Press.

Todd, S. C. 1993. *The Shape of Athenian Law*, Oxford: Clarendon Press.

Treggiari, S. M. 1981. '*Contubernales* in *CIL* 6', *Phoenix* 35, 42-69.

— 1991. *Roman Marriage: Iusti Coniuges From the Time of Cicero to the Time of Ulpian*, Oxford and New York: Oxford University Press.

Treloar, A. 1972. 'Aethiopians', *Prudentia* 4, 42-50.

Treston, H. J. 1923. *Poine: A Study of Ancient Greek Blood-Vengeance*, New York: Longmans, Green & Co.

Trzaskoma, S. M. 2010. 'Chariton and Tragedy: Reconsiderations and New Evidence', *AJPh* 131, 219-231.

— 2011. 'The Anabasis of Chaereas and Callirhoe', *AncNarr* 9, 1-35.

Turpin, W. 1991. 'Imperial Subscriptions and the Administration of Justice', *JRS* 81, 101-118.

Usener, H. and L. Radermacher (eds.), 1904-1929. *Dionysius Halicarnaseus Quae Exstant*. Stuttgart: Teubner.

van Bremen, R. 1996. *The Limits of Participation: Women and Civic Life in the Greek East in the Hellenistic and Roman Periods*, Amsterdam: J. C. Gieben.

Van der Valk, M. H. A. L. H. 1941. 'Remarques sur la date des *Éthiopiques* d'Héliodore', *Mnemosyne* 9, 97-100.

van Mal-Maeder, D. 2001. 'Déclamations et romans: La double vie des personnages romanesques', in: B. Pouderon, C. Hunzinger and D. Kasprzyk (eds.), *Les personnages du roman grec: actes du colloque de Tours, 18-20 novembre 1999*, Lyon: Maison de l'Orient Mediterraneen-Jean Pouilloux, 29-58.

— 2003. 'La mise en scène déclamatoire chez les romanciers latins', in: S. Panayotakis, M. Zimmerman and W. Keulen (eds.), *The Ancient Novel and Beyond*, Leiden: Brill, 345-355.
— 2007. *La fiction des déclamations*, Leiden and Boston: Brill.
Vérilhac, A.-M. and C. Vial 1998. *Le mariage grec: du VIe siècle av. J.-C. à l'époque d'Auguste*, Paris: de Boccard.
Vidén, G. 1993. *Women in Roman Literature, Studia Graeca et Latin Gothoburgensia 57*, Göteborg: University on Göteborg, Department of Classical Studies.
Vismara, C. 1994. 'Domitien, spectacles, supplices et cruauté', *Pallas* 40, 413-420.
Walbank, F. W. 1984. 'Monarchies and Monarchic Ideas', in: F. W. Walbank, A. E. Astin, M. W. Frederiksen and R. M. Ogilvie (eds.), *The Cambridge Ancient History*, Cambridge and New York: Cambridge University Press.
Watson, A. 1987. *Roman Slave Law*, Baltimore: The Johns Hopkins University Press.
Watson, P. A. 1995. *Ancient Stepmothers: Myth, Misogyny and Reality*, New York: Brill.
Watts, E. J. 2006. *City and School in Late Antique Athens and Alexandria*, Berkeley and Los Angeles: University of California Press.
Webb, R. 2001. 'Progymnasmata as Practice', in: Y. L. Too (ed.), *Education in Greek and Roman Antiquity*, Leiden and Boston: Brill, 289-317.
Weinreich, O. 1962. *Der griechische Liebesroman*, Zürich: Artemis.
Weisberg, R. 1992. *Poethics and Other Strategies of Law and Literature*, New York: Columbia University Press.
White, J. L. 1972. *The Form and Structure of the Official Petition, Society of Biblical Literature Dissertation Series* 5, Missoula, Montana: Society of Biblical Literature.
Whitmarsh, T. 1998. 'The Birth of a Prodigy: Heliodorus and the Genealogy of Hellenism', in: R. Hunter (ed.), *Studies in Heliodorus*, Cambridge: Cambridge Philological Society, 93-124.
— 2003. 'Reading for Pleasure: Narrative, Irony, and Erotics in Achilles Tatius', in: S. Panayotakis, M. Zimmerman and W. Keulen (eds.), *The Ancient Novel and Beyond*, Leiden: Brill, 191-205.
— 2005. 'The Greek Novel: Titles and Genre', *AJPh* 126 (4), 587-611.
— 2011. *Narrative and Identity in the Ancient Greek Novel: Returning Romance*, Cambridge and New York: Cambridge University Press.
— (ed.), 2008. *The Cambridge Companion to the Greek and Roman Novel.* Cambridge and New York: Cambridge University Press.
Wiedemann, T. 1981. *Greek and Roman Slavery*, New York: Routledge.
Williams, W. 1974. 'The *Libellus* Procedure and the Severan Papyri', *JRS* 64, 86-103.
Wills, L. M. 1990. *The Jew in the Court of the Foreign King*, Minneapolis: Fortress Press.
— 1994. 'The Jewish Novellas', in: J. R. Morgan and R. Stoneman (eds.), *Greek Fiction: The Greek Novel in Context*, London and New York: Routledge, 223-238.
— 1995. *The Jewish Novel in the Ancient World*, Ithaca: Cornell University Press.
Winkler, J. J. 1999. 'The Mendacity of Kalasiris and the Narrative Strategy of Heliodoros' *Aithiopika*', in: S. Swain (ed.), *Oxford Readings in the Greek Novel*, Oxford and New York: Oxford University Press, 286-350.
Winterbottom, M. 1982. 'Schoolroom and Courtroom', in: B. Vickers (ed.), *Rhetoric Revalued: Papers from the International Society for the History of Rhetoric*, Binghamton, New York: Center for Medieval and Early Renaissance Studies.
Wolff, H. J. 1939. *Written and Unwritten Marriages in Hellenistic and Postclassical Roman Law*, Haverford: American Philological Association.

— 1951. *Roman Law: An Historical Introduction*, Norman, Okla.: University of Oklahoma Press.

Wycherley, R. E. 1978. *The Stones of Athens*, Princeton: Princeton University Press.

Youtie, H. C. 1975. 'ΥΠΟΓΡΑΦΕΥΣ: The Social Impact of Illiteracy in Greco-Roman Egypt', *ZPE* 17, 201-221.

Zeitlin, F. I. 2003. 'Living Portraits and Sculpted Bodies in Chariton's Theater of Romance', in: S. Panayotakis, M. Zimmerman and W. Keulen (eds.), *The Ancient Novel and Beyond*, Leiden: Brill, 71-83.

Zimmermann, F. 1957. 'Kallirhoes Verkauf durch Theron: eine juristisch-philologische Betrachtung zu Chariton', *Aus der byzantinischen Arbeit der Deutschen Demokratische Republik*, Berlin, 72-81.

Ziolkowski, T. 1997. *The Mirror of Justice: Literary Reflections of Legal Crises*, Princeton: Princeton University Press.

Zuiderhoek, A. 2008. 'On the Political Sociology of the Imperial Greek City', *GRBS* 48, 417-445.

— 2009. *The Politics of Munificence in the Roman Empire: Citizens, Elites and Benefactors in Asia Minor*, Cambridge and New York: Cambridge University Press.

Indices

Index locorum

General index